Reforming Arbitration Reform

Reforming Arbitration Reform

Emerging Voices, New Strategies and Evolving Values

Edited by

Crina Baltag
Mark Feldman

Wolters Kluwer

Published by:
Kluwer Law International B.V.
PO Box 316
2400 AH Alphen aan den Rijn
The Netherlands
E-mail: lrs-sales@wolterskluwer.com
Website: www.wolterskluwer.com/en/solutions/kluwerlawinternational

Sold and distributed by:
Wolters Kluwer Legal & Regulatory U.S.
920 Links Avenue
Landisville, PA 17538
United States of America
E-mail: customer.service@wolterskluwer.com

ISBN 978-94-035-4327-7

e-Book: ISBN 978-94-035-4337-6
web-PDF: ISBN 978-94-035-4347-5

Editors

Crina Baltag, FCIArb, is Professor Assoc. in International Arbitration at Stockholm University and a qualified attorney-at-law, with over twenty years of extensive practice in various aspects of international dispute resolution, private and public international law. Professor Baltag is the academic director of the LLM in International Commercial Arbitration Law at Stockholm University and member of the Board of the SCC Arbitration Institute. Professor Baltag has been appointed as arbitrator in numerous arbitrations under the rules of the ICC, LCIA, SIAC, SCC, FAI, VIAC, CAM-CCBC, etc., and has acted as expert and counsel in various international commercial and investment arbitrations. Professor Baltag conducts arbitrations in English, Portuguese and Romanian. Professor Baltag's academic work includes published volumes *Construction Arbitration in Central and Eastern Europe: Contemporary Issues* [co-author, Wolters Kluwer, 2019]; *Investors, States, and Arbitrators in the Crosshairs of International Investment Law and Environmental Protection* [co-author, BRILL, 2020]; *The Energy Charter Treaty: The Notion of Investor* [author, Wolters Kluwer, 2012] etc., and numerous publications in leading legal journals and reviews, including 'Recent Trends in Investment Arbitration on the Right to Regulate, Environment, Health and Corporate Social Responsibility: Too Much or Too Little?' [*ICSID Review: Foreign Investment Law Journal*, Oxford University Press, 2023], etc. Professor Baltag is the managing editor of Kluwer Arbitration Blog and member of editorial boards of prestigious journals and book series in the field, including of the *Journal of International Arbitration*. Professor Baltag is the chair of the Academic Council of the Institute for Transnational Arbitration of the Center for American and International Law, and the Director of the Global Diploma Course in International Arbitration of the Chartered Institute of Arbitrators.

Mark Feldman is Interim Dean and Professor of Law at Peking University School of Transnational Law. Professor Feldman also serves as Vice Chair of the Academic Council of the Institute for Transnational Arbitration of the Center for American and International Law.

He previously served as a member of the T20 Saudi Arabia Task Force on Trade, Investment and Growth, as a member of the E15 Initiative Task Force on Investment

Policy (World Economic Forum/ICTSD), and as Chief of NAFTA/CAFTA-DR Arbitration in the Office of the Legal Adviser at the U.S. Department of State. As Chief, he represented the United States as a respondent or non-disputing party in more than a dozen investor-State disputes and provided legal counsel supporting the negotiation of US bilateral investment treaties and investment chapters of free trade agreements (including TPP and US-China BIT negotiations). His government experience also includes service as a law clerk to Judge Eric L. Clay on the U.S. Court of Appeals for the Sixth Circuit and as a Peace Corps volunteer in Lesotho during South Africa's transition to democracy. In the private sector, he practised law for several years at Covington & Burling.

Contributors

Daniel Ávila II' is a senior associate in Reed Smith's International Arbitration Group practising in the areas of international arbitration, complex commercial litigation, and transnational investment law. As part of the firm's Latin American Business Team, Daniel assists clients on dispute resolution matters across the region in both English and Spanish. Daniel has extensive experience in international and domestic arbitration, handling disputes under various international and domestic arbitral institutions and rules, including under ICSID, ICC, Cámara de Comercio de Bogotá, ICDR, LCIA, UNCITRAL, and AAA Rules. Prior to joining Reed Smith, Daniel worked at a renowned law firm in Bogotá, Colombia.

Daniel recently co-authored The Guide to Arbitration in Latin America's chapter on The Growing Appeal of Regional Arbitral Centres in Latin America and the Caribbean published by the Global Arbitration Review/Latin Lawyer. As the Communications Officer for the Institute for Transnational Arbitration (ITA), Daniel led the publishing of the ITA Guide to Latin American Arbitral Institutions, covering thirty institutions based out of twenty countries in Latin America and the Caribbean. Daniel is currently the Chair of the International Law Section of the Houston Bar Association, the Pro Bono Head for the Houston office of Reed Smith, and the Global Associate Chair of UNIDOS, Reed Smith's Latinx/Hispanic Business Affinity Group.

Chiann Bao is Chartered Arbitrator and CEDR-Accredited Mediator. She has been appointed in almost hundred ad hoc and institutional arbitrations totalling several billion USD in dispute. She is a co-chair of the IBA Arbitration Committee. From 2018 to 2024, she served as a Vice President of the ICC Court of Arbitration and from 2010 to 2018, she served as the Secretary General of the HKIAC and was subsequently appointed as a Council Member of the HKIAC. Tri-qualified in New York, England and Wales and Hong Kong, Chiann previously practised in international law firms in New York and Hong Kong. Chiann is ranked as a Global Elite Thought Leader by Who's Who Legal Arbitration and has been designated as one of the most in-demand arbitrators globally by Chambers & Partners. In 2022, Chiann was awarded the Global Arbitration

Review 'best lecture' for her Proskauer Rose Lecture. Chiann is a member of ASIL's Asia-Pacific Interest Group.

Andrea K. Bjorklund is a full professor and the L. Yves Fortier Chair in International Arbitration and International Commercial Law at McGill University Faculty of Law in Montreal, Canada. She acts as arbitrator and expert in both investment and commercial arbitrations. She has been appointed to the ICSID roster of arbitrators by the Government of Canada and is on the panel of arbitrators of several leading institutions, including the Beijing Arbitration Commission/Beijing International Arbitration Center and the Shenzhen Court of International Arbitration. From 2012 to 2015 she was the Chair of the ITA's Academic Council. In 2022, she gave lectures at the Hague Academy of International Law. Before entering the academy, she was an attorney-adviser on the NAFTA arbitration team in the Office of the Legal Adviser of the U.S. Department of State. She also worked at the U.S. International Trade Commission and in private practice at Miller & Chevalier in Washington, D.C. She is President of the Council for International Dispute Settlement (CIDS) and a member of the Institute of International Law.

Petra Butler is the Executive Dean of and a professor at the Faculty of Law, University of Canterbury. Petra specializes in domestic and international human rights and international commercial law with an emphasis on international commercial contracts and international dispute resolution. Petra has particular expertise in law reform, including leading the Commonwealth Secretariat studies into judicial diversity in small Commonwealth states and into international commercial arbitration in the Commonwealth. Petra is a fully qualified German and New Zealand lawyer and admitted as a barrister to the High Court of New Zealand. Petra is also the Director of the Institute of Small and Micro States (ISMS). Petra is a senior research fellow at the British Institute of International and Comparative Law, a fellow of the Arbitrators' and Mediators' Institute of New Zealand, a member of the ITA Academic Council and a consultant to UNCITRAL and UNIDROIT.

Laurence Boisson de Chazournes is a professor at the University of Geneva and has been a visiting professor in numerous universities. She is the Director of the Geneva LLM in International Dispute Settlement (MIDS).

She is an experienced arbitrator who regularly sits for various international arbitration bodies, such as the International Centre for Settlement of Investment Disputes (ICSID), the International Chamber of Commerce (ICC), the Permanent Court of Arbitration (PCA), the Arbitration Institute of the Stockholm Chamber of Commerce (SCC), and the Court of Arbitration for Sport (CAS). In addition, she was a member of the CAS ad hoc Division during the PyeongChang Olympic Games. Moreover, she served as a chairperson for WTO arbitration panels on pre-shipment inspections.

Laurence Boisson de Chazournes frequently acts as Advocate and Counsel before the International Court of Justice (ICJ), the International Tribunal for the Law of the Sea (ITLOS) and other dispute settlement fora. She has authored and edited thirty-four books and has written over 270 articles and contributions to collective books.

Manjiao Chi is Full Professor and Founding Director, Center for International Economic Law and Policy, School of Law, University of International Business and Economics (UIBE), Beijing. His research area covers international economic law and policy, dispute settlement and sustainable development. Manjiao is or was, among others, Deputy Chair, Academic Forum on ISDS; Deputy Chair, China International Investment Arbitration Forum; Executive Council Member, American Society of International Law; Standing Committee Member, Chinese Society of International Law; visiting professor of several law faculties of leading universities; visiting scholar of the Max-Planck Institute (Heidelberg), UNIDROIT and Columbia Law School; consultant for several international organizations; founding editor of the Asian Yearbook of International Economic Law; and lecturer at the Hague Academy of International Law (2021) and the UN Audiovisual Library of International Law (2023). Manjiao has rich experience in international commercial arbitration, WTO and investment arbitration and is Chairperson Candidate of EU Trade and Sustainable Development (TSD) expert panel proceedings. He was also a member of the Chinese delegation in investment treaty negotiations. He holds BA, LLM and PhD in Law.

Kabir Duggal is Senior Fellow and Advisor at the Center for International Commercial and Investment Arbitration at Columbia Law School (CICIA) and an attorney in Arnold and Porter's New York office, focusing on international arbitration and public international law matters, serving as both arbitrator and mediator. He is recognized as a 'Chartered Arbitrator' (the highest ranking for arbitrators) by both the Chartered Institute of Arbitrators and the Asian Institute of Alternative Dispute Resolution. He also frequently serves as an expert on international arbitration and public international law matters. Dr Duggal is also a Lecturer-in-Law at Columbia Law School, an adjunct Professor at Fordham Law School, and a Course Director and a Faculty Member for the Columbia Law School-Chartered Institute of Arbitrators Comprehensive Course on International Arbitration. He also acts as a Consultant for the United Nations Office of the High Representative for Least Developed Countries (UN-OHRLLS) on the creation of a novel 'Investment Support Program'. Dr Duggal works closely with the U.S. Department of Commerce's Commercial Law Development Program (CLDP) as an expert. He has also conducted training and capacity-building sessions for several governments on public international law and dispute resolution matters. He has published over sixty articles and has spoken at over three hundred arbitration events all over the world. He is also a passionate advocate for diversity, equity, and inclusion issues and frequently writes and speaks on these issues. He is the Co-Founder of REAL (Racial Equality for Arbitration Lawyers), a non-profit seeking to create greater representation in international arbitration. He is a graduate of the University of Mumbai, University of Oxford (DHL-Times of India Scholar), NYU School of Law (Hauser Global Scholar), Leiden Law School (2019 CEPANI Academic Prize), and is currently pursuing an SJD from Harvard Law School. Dr Duggal is admitted to practise law in New York, District of Columbia, England & Wales (as a Barrister), and in India.

Alice Fremuth-Wolf is the Market Head for Austria & CEE region at Nivalion in Vienna. Before joining Nivalion, Alice was Secretary General of the Vienna International

Arbitral Centre (VIAC) for ten years. She is a lecturer for arbitration at the Institute of Civil Procedure Law at the Law Faculty of Vienna University and frequently acts as a guest lecturer. She has authored numerous articles and books on arbitration and ADR. In addition to her academic career, she worked as an associate for the leading law firms Wolf Theiss and Baker McKenzie in Vienna where she passed the Austrian bar exam, acting as counsel and arbitrator in international arbitration and mediation cases. Alice graduated in Law from Vienna University (Mag. iur.), holds a PhD in Law (Dr iur.) and an LLM (London School of Economics). She is also a trained mediator and mediation advocate.

Maria Fernanda Garza is the former Chair of the International Chamber of Commerce (ICC), having completed her chairmanship in June 2024. She was the first woman to hold that position in the organization's hundred-year history. She is the CEO of Orestia, a manufacturer of home improvements and water solutions products, operating USMCA region, Latin America and Asia. Ms Garza is a strong advocate of business ethics and corporate governance and is a board member of the Corporate Responsibility Alliance AliaRSE and other business organizations. She has also served on the group of advisors and leaders of the B20 and the United Nations Internet Governance Forum.

Kevin W. Gray is a Canadian barrister, specializing in complex transnational litigation and arbitration. He is also Assistant Professor of Law at Peking University School of Transnational Law, where he teaches courses in Transnational and Constitutional Law and Legal Theory.

Eduardo Grebler is a partner of Grebler Mohallem Greco, a fellow of the Chartered Institute of Arbitrators and a member of the list of arbitrators of the Mercosur Protocol of Olivos. He has published extensively on arbitration, international contracts and private international law, as Professor of International Law at the Pontifical Catholic University of Minas Gerais. Eduardo has been recognized by *Chambers Latin America, Who's Who Legal, Leaders League* and *The Legal 500* on his work in arbitration and corporate law. Eduardo holds a Bachelor's in Law from the Federal University of Minas Gerais and a Master of Law (LLM) from the Columbia University School of Law. He is fluent in Portuguese, English, Spanish and French.

Filipe Greco is a partner at Grebler Mohallem Greco. He represents clients in arbitrations before the International Chamber of Commerce (ICC) and several Brazilian arbitration chambers, in addition to having experience as secretary and assistant to arbitral tribunals in commercial and investment matters. Filipe is the author of the book *Past, Present and Perspectives for the Future of Investment Protection by International Law*, as well as the author of several articles in the fields of arbitration, international law, international trade, and international contracts. Filipe is Professor of Private International Law and Constitutional Law at private universities in Brazil. He holds a Bachelor's in Law from the Federal University of Minas Gerais, having completed undergraduate studies at the *Università Degli Studi di Bologna* and also holds a Master of Laws in International Law from the Federal University of Minas Gerais. He is fluent in Portuguese, English, Italian and French.

Guillaume Guez Maillard is a PhD candidate at the University of Geneva and the University of Paris 1 Panthéon-Sorbonne. His research focuses on the different facets of the international jurisdictional function, with a particular emphasis on inherent powers. He is currently a Research Associate on a Swiss National Science Foundation project and a non-tenured teaching associate at the University Savoie Mont Blanc and the Catholic University of Lille. He was a research and teaching assistant at the Faculty of Law of the University of Geneva. He is involved in several international proceedings before the International Court of Justice, the International Tribunal for the Law of the Sea and other tribunals. He previously worked as Judge Mohamed Bennouna's Judicial Fellow at the International Court of Justice.

Pasha L. Hsieh is Jean Monnet Chair Professor and Lee Kong Chian Fellow at the Singapore Management University Yong Pung How School of Law. Prior to academia, he served as a Legal Affairs Officer at the WTO Appellate Body Secretariat and as an associate at Shearman & Sterling LLP. His monograph, *New Asian Regionalism in International Economic Law*, was published by Cambridge University Press and has been translated into Chinese and Japanese. He is a member of the editorial boards of the *Journal of International Economic Law* and the *Journal of World Investment & Trade*.

Jennifer A. Ivers was Counsel at White & Case LLP at the time of writing and practised with the International Arbitration Group in Washington, D.C., where she specialized in international arbitration and litigation. Jennifer advised foreign sovereigns and private corporations in high-stakes international disputes, acting as counsel in US litigation and in arbitrations before numerous arbitral fora, including ICSID and the ICC, as well as in ad hoc arbitrations under the UNCITRAL Arbitration Rules. Jennifer has been recognized as a Rising Star in the United States and in Commercial Arbitration by the *International Financial Law Review* and served as a member of the ICCA Cross-Institutional Task Force on Gender Diversity in International Arbitral Appointments and Proceedings. She previously worked at the Office of the Chief Counsel for International Commerce at the U.S. Department of Commerce and is a graduate of the Georgetown University Law Center and Georgetown University. The views expressed herein are her own and are not representative of any employer.

Margie-Lys Jaime, PhD., FCIArb, is Professor of Law at the University of Panama and Chief of the Office of Investment Arbitration at the Ministry of Economy and Finances of the Republic of Panama. She represents Panama at UNCITRAL Working Group III on ISDS reform and acts as a consultant and expert in commercial, trade and investment matters. Her practice includes international litigation, maritime disputes, commercial arbitration, investor-state dispute settlement, and international trade.

Dr Jaime has been appointed to the list of Conciliators and Arbitrators of ICSID by the Republic of Panama (2022-2028) and as a Member of the Permanent Court of Arbitration (2024-2030). She received her PhD in Law and LLM in International Economic Affairs Law from the University of Paris II (Pantheon-Assas), an LLM in Arbitration and International Business Law from the University of Versailles (France), and an LLM in International Business and Economic Law with a Certificate in WTO Studies from Georgetown University Law Center.

Meg Kinnear is an independent arbitrator and founder of LKDR LLC, an international dispute resolution firm. She was Vice President of the World Bank and Secretary General of ICSID from 2009 to 2024. Prior to that, she led the Trade Law Bureau of Canada (1999-2009), was Executive Assistant to the Deputy Minister of Justice Canada (2006-2009) and counsel in the Civil Litigation Section of Justice Canada (1984-2006). She is a member of the Bars of Ontario and the District of Colombia. She is a frequent speaker and author on topics related to arbitration and investment law.

Aditya Laddha is an international disputes lawyer and a doctoral candidate and research assistant at the University of Geneva. His research focuses on the limits of jurisdiction *ratione materiae* of international courts and tribunals and international judicial function. He is involved in various international proceedings before the International Court of Justice and other tribunals. After completing his LLM from the Geneva International Dispute Settlement (MIDS) programme, he served as a Judicial Fellow at the International Court of Justice (2020-2021) in the Hague. He has also worked at the Centre for Trade and Investment Law, New Delhi, where he assisted the Government of India in legal disputes, international negotiations and policy relating to international trade and investment law.

Carolyn B. Lamm is a partner at White & Case LLP; Chair of International Arbitration of the Americas; Lead Counsel in international arbitrations in ICSID, ICC and other fora and related litigation in US Courts for foreign states, foreign state-owned companies, and foreign corporate entities; arbitrator on the ICSID List, first nominated by the United States and then by the Government of Uzbekistan. She served as arbitrator in proceedings under the ICSID, ICC, SAIC, ICDR, AAA, UNCITRAL (ad hoc and administered by LCIA) rules, etc. She was Distinguished Faculty Co-Chair, White & Case LLM International Arbitration at the University of Miami School of Law; Immediate Past President, American Bar Endowment; Member, Advisory Council and previously Governing Board of ICCA; Council of the American Law Institute (elected 1999): Counsellor for the Restatement 4th of Foreign Relations; Advisory Committee for the Restatement of International Commercial and Investment Arbitration. She was Past President of the District of Columbia Bar and American Bar Association. She is a frequent lecturer and author in the field of international arbitration and Chairman of the Board of the American-Uzbekistan Chamber of Commerce. She is Member of the Board of Trustees, University of Miami (2020-2023) and honorary professor at Tashkent State University, School of Law.

Zongyao Li, based in Singapore, is a senior associate in the international arbitration practice of Allen Overy Shearman Sterling LLP. He has advised clients in arbitrations conducted under the auspices of the International Chamber of Commerce (ICC), Singapore International Arbitration Centre (SIAC), Hong Kong International Arbitration Centre (HKIAC), International Centre for Settlement of Investment Disputes (ICSID), China International Economic and Trade Arbitration Commission (CIETAC), as well as ad hoc proceedings. He has also advised clients in litigation before Chinese courts and acted as Tribunal Secretary in arbitration proceedings. His industrial experience includes construction, infrastructure, energy, joint ventures, real estate, private equity, and technology. Additionally, Zongyao is an Associate Research Fellow at the Center for International Economic Law and Policy, University of International Business and Economics in Beijing. He has published several articles on international arbitration and investment and has also been invited to speak on matters involving international arbitration.

Jeffrey (Chieh) Lo, MCIArb, LLM (Stanford), is a PhD Candidate at the Dickson Poon School of Law, King's College London. Before pursuing his doctoral degree, he served as the Legal Counsel at the Chinese Arbitration Association International (CAAI) and as the Head of the International Arbitration, Promotion and Research Division at the Chinese Arbitration Association, Taipei (CAA). He specializes in international economic law, including international trade law, investment law, arbitration, and international dispute settlement.

Lucas Macedo is a senior investment manager at Nivalion in Zug, Switzerland. He was an in-house attorney for several years with multinational groups (AES and ENEL) in the Latin American energy sector, handling complex litigation and arbitration, and regulatory affairs. Previously, Lucas acted in law firms in Brazil (BNI Advogados) and Germany (Orrick, Herrington & Sutcliffe). Lucas is admitted to the Brazilian and Portuguese Bar, holds a law degree from the State University of Londrina, a specialization in Civil Procedure from Fundação Getúlio Vargas, and an LLM in Transnational Arbitration and Dispute Settlement from SciencesPo Paris. Lucas is a faculty member of the post-graduation course on International Arbitration at the University of Lisbon, a guest lecturer at international arbitration courses and sits as a volunteer on the Board of Directors of the NGO Liter of Light Brazil.

Anamaria Marin is a senior associate at SLCG, part of the international arbitration team based in Milan. She is qualified in England & Wales and was awarded an LLM in International Dispute Resolution from QMUL. She acts as counsel in international commercial arbitrations, representing parties in construction and energy disputes, seated across different jurisdictions. Anamaria is a member of the Steering Committee of Young ArbitralWomen Practitioners (YAWP) and a coach of the University of Florence Vis Moot team.

Michael Mcilwrath served as Chair of the ICC's Governing Body for Dispute Resolution Services from 2019 to 2024. He is the CEO of MDisputes (www.mdisputes.com), a company that provides in-house counsel support for international commercial disputes. He is also an adjunct professor at Bocconi Law School and an officer of the IBA's Mediation Committee. Mr Mcilwrath previously spent twenty-two years as the head of litigation of multinational companies, most recently as Vice President of Baker Hughes Company and before that with General Electric Oil & Gas. In 2017, Arbitral Women recognized him as a Champion of Change.

Mark McLaughlin is Assistant Professor of Law at Singapore Management University and the Singapore International Dispute Resolution Academy. His research focuses on the reform of arbitration and mediation, international economic law, and the intersection of law and technology.

Mark has been a trainer for government officials around the world in managing their investment treaty commitments and navigating investor-state disputes. In 2022, he became a member of the ISDS Academic Forum. He has published in leading international journals on novel areas of law, such as investor-state mediation, state-owned enterprises, and artificial intelligence. He holds an LLB from the University of Glasgow and a PhD from the China University of Political Science and Law, where he was a lecturer in international investment law.

Loukas Mistelis is the Clive Schmitthoff Professor of Transnational Commercial Law and Arbitration at the Centre for Commercial Law Studies, Queen Mary University of London and a Partner with Clyde & Co LLP, based in London. He is an acknowledged authority on international dispute resolution and investment treaty law. In 2006, he was listed as one of the 'leading lights in international arbitration' and since 2007 he is listed on the Who's Who Commercial Arbitration and since 2017 as Global Thought Leaders in International Arbitration. He has been listed in the Legal500 International Arbitration Powerlist since its inaugural year (2019). He also regularly sits as an arbitrator and acts as counsel and expert in arbitration proceedings. His substantial arbitration experience covers ad hoc and ICC, ICSID, LCIA, UNCITRAL, GCC, SCC, Swiss Chambers, DIAC, VIAC and Moscow cases.

He is a widely published author with more than fifteen books (including *Comparative International Commercial Arbitration*, *Arbitrability*, and *Mandatory Rules in International Arbitration*) and hundred articles and is also the editor of the *World Arbitration Reporter*, the Oxford Monograph Series in International Arbitration, Co-editor in Chief of the *European Investment Law and Arbitration Review* and the *Jus Mundi International Arbitration Review*, and editor of many other journals including *Arbitration International*.

Amr Omran is a counsel at Freshfields Bruckhaus Deringer based in Dubai. He is a member of the firm's International Arbitration Group and heads the Dubai office's Middle East Law Practice. Amr represents clients in construction, commercial and investor-state proceedings under all major arbitration rules and different systems of law. He also sits as an arbitrator and is a judge on the Appeals Panel of the International Basketball Federation. He is the ICC YAAF Representative for the Middle East Chapter, a Delegate to the ICC Commission on Arbitration and ADR, an officer of the International Bar Association and a member of the Equal Representation for Expert Witnesses Pledge Young Practitioners Sub-committee. He has been ranked in legal directories and recognized as one of Africa's thirty Most Prominent Young Arbitration Practitioners. Amr holds a licence en droit from Cairo University, an LLM in Comparative Law from McGill University, an LLM in International and Comparative Law from the American University in Cairo, and an LLM from Harvard Law School. Before joining Freshfields, Amr worked at the World Bank in Washington, DC, and the Public Prosecution Office in Cairo. Amr is a native Arabic speaker and fluent in English. He is admitted to the Egyptian Bar Association and the New York Bar. He is also registered as a legal consultant with the Dubai Legal Affairs Department.

Federico Ortino is Professor of International Economic Law and Co-Director of the Centre for International Governance and Dispute Resolution (CIGAD) at the Dickson Poon School of Law, King's College London. He is a member of the ILA Committee on the Rule of Law and International Investment Law; consultative member of the Investment Treaty Forum; one of the general editors of the International Trade and Investment Law Series with Hart Publishing; editorial/advisory board member of the *Journal of International Economic Law*, *Journal of International Dispute Settlement* and *Journal of World Investment and Trade*. He has written on both world trade law and international investment law. *The Origin and Evolution of Investment Treaty Standards: Stability, Value and Reasonableness* (OUP, 2019) and *The Oxford Handbook on International Arbitration* (OUP, 2020, co-edited with Thomas Schultz) are among his recent books. He has been involved as an expert in projects with UNCTAD, ITC, OECD, IISD and WEF. He is a consultant to Clifford Chance, advising governments and private companies on international trade law matters.

Previously, he was Founding Committee Member (and former co-Treasurer) of the Society of International Economic Law; co-rapporteur to the ILA Committee on the Law of Foreign Investment; Director, Investment Treaty Forum, British Institute of International and Comparative Law in London; Legal Officer at the United Nations Conference on Trade and Development, Division on Investment and Enterprises. He is a qualified attorney in Italy and in the state of New York. He holds LLB, University of Florence; LLM, Georgetown University Law Center; PhD, European University Institute.

Lorenzo Palestini is a lecturer at the Geneva LLM in International Dispute Settlement (MIDS), a joint programme of the Graduate Institute of International and Development Studies and the University of Geneva. His doctoral thesis, *La protection des intérêts juridiques de l'Etat tiers dans le procès de délimitation maritime* (*The Protection of the Legal Interests of Third States in Maritime Delimitation Proceedings*) (Bruxelles: Bruylant, 2020), was awarded the 2021 Paul Guggenheim Prize. As a consultant in public international law disputes, he also co-leads a project on the *International Judicial Function under Pressure* financed by the Swiss National Science Foundation. He has acted as Counsel and Advocate for the Republic of Colombia before the International Court of Justice.

Dilini Pathirana holds a Bachelor of Laws and a Master of Laws from the University of Colombo, Sri Lanka. She received a PhD in International Law from the China University of Political Science and Law, Beijing, China. Since 2009, Dilini has worked as a faculty member in the Faculty of Law at the University of Colombo where she teaches International Investment Law for undergraduate law students and International Economic Law for postgraduate students. Since 2021, Dilini has served as the Director of the Legal Research Unit of the Faculty of Law, University of Colombo.

Facundo Pérez-Aznar is a senior researcher at the Geneva Centre of International Dispute Settlement (CIDS) and an adjunct professor of International Economic Law at the University of Buenos Aires (UBA). He worked for several years as a legal counsel in the Department of International Affairs of the General Attorney's Office of Argentina, which represents Argentina's interests in international investment disputes (mostly in ICSID and UNCITRAL arbitrations). He previously worked as a legal officer in the Latin American Economic Integration Directorate at Argentina's Ministry of Foreign Affairs. Facundo has advised different governments and international organizations on international investment and trade law matters as an independent expert and consultant. He also acts as a member of different international dispute settlement boards. His areas of research and publications include international dispute settlement, substantive standards in international investment agreements and regulatory matters. Facundo holds a law degree from the National University of La Plata, Argentina, as well as a Master's and a PhD in International Law from the Geneva Graduate Institute of International and Development Studies, Switzerland.

Hélène Ruiz Fabri is a professor at the Sorbonne Law School (University of Paris 1 Panthéon-Sorbonne), back after nine years of secondment to be the Director of the Max Planck Institute Luxembourg for Procedural Law, where she headed the Department of International Law and Dispute Resolution. She is an associate member of the Institute of International Law, a former President of the European Society of International Law and a holder of the CNRS Silver Medal for the excellence of her scientific research. She has published extensively on international law and dispute settlement and was the editor-in-chief of the *Max Planck Encyclopedia of International Procedural Law* (OUP) and the *Journal of World Investment and Trade* (Brill). She teaches International Economic Law, General International Law, Investment and Environment. She also has experience in legal practice, especially advising various organizations on human rights or cultural diversity and acting as a judge or an arbitrator (ICSID, UNCITRAL, regional agreements).

Victoria Shannon Sahani is the Associate Provost for Community and Inclusion at Boston University and Professor of Law at Boston University School of Law. She is an internationally recognized legal scholar in domestic and international arbitration law and third-party litigation funding law. She is an award-winning teacher and serves as an independent arbitrator, consultant, and expert witness. In addition to publishing numerous book chapters, law review articles and essays, she co-authored the book *Third-Party Funding in International Arbitration* (Wolters Kluwer, 1st and 2d ed.) (with Lisa Bench Nieuwveld), the first book in the world on this topic. She is the immediate past Chair of the Academic Council for the Institute for Transnational Arbitration (ITA), Chair-Elect of the Association of American Law Schools (AALS) Section on International Law, a Counsellor of the American Society of International Law (ASIL), an Elected Member of the American Law Institute (ALI), and an American Bar Foundation (ABF) Fellow. Before joining academia, she worked at the International Chamber of Commerce (ICC)'s International Court of Arbitration and practised law at

Pillsbury. She graduated from Harvard Law School and Harvard College and is licensed to practise law in New York and the District of Columbia.

Edoardo Stoppioni is Professor of Public Law at the University of Strasbourg, where he teaches and conducts research in the fields of public international law, philosophy of law and human rights. He holds Master's in Comparative Law and International Law from Sorbonne Law School, along with a PhD in International Law from the same university. Additionally, he is a member of the Commission consultative des droits de l'homme of the Grand-Duchy of Luxembourg.

Filippo Zuti Giachetti is Counsel at MDisputes practising international arbitration and a qualified Italian lawyer and Solicitor of England and Wales. He holds an LLM from the University of Cambridge and successfully completed the Blockchain Regulator Certification Program at UNIC. Filippo is also an assistant editor to the Managing Editor for the Kluwer Arbitration Blog, a coach of the University of Florence Vis Moot team and a visiting lecturer at the University of Florence.

Summary of Contents

Table of Contents

Introduction: Reforming Arbitration Reform: The Need for Addressing the Legitimacy of International Arbitration Through the Lenses of Emerging Voices, New Strategies, and Evolving Values

Crina Baltag & Mark Feldman

This book marks the 20th anniversary of the Institute for Transnational Arbitration (ITA) and the American Society of International Law (ASIL) Conference, and it is based on the 20th ITA-ASIL Conference which took place on 29 March 2023 in Washington DC.

The editors of this book co-chaired the 20th ITA-ASIL Conference and developed the core theme of the conference, which examined the reform of international arbitration reform. The thought behind this topic rests first on a reflective assessment of the prior ITA-ASIL Conferences in an evolutionary manner. Second, the topic captures the imperative need to critically consider the legitimacy of international arbitration in the context of how new strategies and voices, evolving values, emerging rule-makers and the need for genuine inclusion (which requires awareness of intersectional identities) can lead to a new age of international arbitration. Such evaluation of legitimacy concerns can extend to consideration of existential challenges to the very nature of international arbitration.

New voices are reshaping international arbitration practice by adopting innovative reform strategies and upholding evolving values. International, supranational and domestic actors are each playing significant roles as rule-makers, with varying degrees of transparency. Forces driving those developments include sustainability, inclusiveness and regionalism. Sustainability and inclusiveness, including the rebalancing of a range of social and environmental interests, will most likely affect international arbitration on many levels. One key challenge for the future will certainly be determining how to apply emerging standards in concrete ways and in particular disputes.

On regionalism, rulemaking affecting international arbitration practice today, in significant part, is regional rulemaking by international and supranational actors.

In addressing these issues, the book diverges from existing publications by endeavouring to cover both commercial and investment arbitration and by focusing on international, supranational and domestic actors, each playing significant roles as rule-makers in international arbitration. The past years have highlighted internal and external concerns for international commercial and investment arbitration. To name a few, the COVID pandemic fast-tracked the reconsideration of efficiency and appropriateness of arbitration by focusing attention on remote hearings, virtual deliberations of arbitral tribunals, and increased use of technology, among others; questions of proper conduct of arbitration translated into reconsidering conflicts in the 2024 International Bar Association (IBA) Guidelines on Conflict of Interest in International Arbitration, and in the enactment of additional soft law tools, such as the International Council for Commercial Arbitration (ICCA) Standards of Practice in International Arbitration. Existential concerns regarding the future of investment arbitration were reflected in particular in the United Nations Commission on International Trade Law (UNCITRAL) Working Group III: Investor-State Dispute Settlement Reform, which currently addresses, among other policy options, the possibility of creating a multilateral investment court, i.e., an adjudicatory mechanism as an alternative to arbitration. Existential concerns in an investment arbitration context also have been reflected in the prohibition by the Court of Justice of the European Union (CJEU) in the *Achmea* judgment, and later in *Komstroy*, of investment arbitration where European Union (EU) Member States are involved. Such regional concerns have extended to the international sphere, with now US, Swiss, and Australian courts, to name a few, assessing their attitude towards the recognition and enforcement of arbitral awards broadly.[1]

The introductory chapters in this book set certain general themes which are picked up in the subsequent chapters. Professor Loukas Mistelis starts from the nature of international arbitration as a sui generis and transnational process, which has visibly generated a tension between the increased regulatory activity of arbitration and its stakeholders, on the one side, and the core interest of arbitration users and the arbitration community, on the other. With this in mind, the author suggests the imperative need of a dialogue between regulators and users of international arbitration, essential to ensure that any arbitration reforms are meaningful and successful. Professors Hélène Ruiz Fabri and Edoardo Stoppioni address the reform of arbitration reform through the lens of intersectionality. At the outset, the authors clarify that the theory of intersectionality, originally pioneered by feminist theory and critical race theory, can provide arbitration practitioners with a language for addressing the complex challenges underpinning international investment law and its reform today. In doing so, the authors take three case studies focusing on the intersections between investment law and, successively, race, environmental protection and indigenous

1. *See*, for example, *9Ren, NextEra, PV Investors v. Spain*, US Court of Appeals for the District of Columbia Circuit, available at https://jusmundi.com/en/document/other/en-9ren-holding-s-a-r-l-v-kingdom-of-spain-final-brief-for-nextera-energy-global-holdings-b-v-et-al-and-9ren-holding-s-a-r-l-thursday-10th-august-2023, accessed 16 Dec. 2024.

peoples. Rightfully, the authors urge us to use the idea of intersectionality to help us think about discrimination from new perspectives, with particular attention accorded to interactions between different forms of discrimination. Professor Laurence Boisson de Chazournes, together with Lorenzo Palestini, Guillaume Guez Maillard and Aditya Laddha, take a broad look at the international judicial function which, in past years, has received particular scrutiny in the context of World Trade Organization (WTO) Appellate Body practice; the backlash in that context, in certain instances, has been well deserved. The chapter considers whether adjudicators of universal State-to-State mechanisms share part of the blame. The authors, by looking at alleged instances of judicial overreach and proposed corrective mechanisms, examine whether there is a correlation between backlash and the way the judicial function is exercised. They reach the conclusion that there is an intricate balance required between judicial autonomy and the constraints imposed by state sovereignty and that maintaining an equilibrium between the two is essential for the survival of international dispute resolution mechanisms.

The second part of the book is prompted by the need to explore the impact of new voices and evolving values in international arbitration and the reform triggered or at least influenced by the emerging set of high-profile and behind-the-scenes stakeholders. The authors of the chapters in this part of the book infer that stakeholders are influencing the practice area by adopting innovative reform strategies (including energized, targeted campaigns) and upholding evolving values (including heightened environmental and social interests, as well as diversity in all its forms). Dr Alice Fremuth-Wolf and Lucas Macedo examine the role of third-party funders in arbitration, now a well-established stakeholder in international dispute resolution, by approaching the potential conflicts of interest between funders and arbitrators, as well as potential ethical dilemmas between funders, funded parties and their lawyers, with a focus on Environmental, Social, and Governance (ESG) factors. Professor Margie-Lys Jaime approaches the role of developing states in international investment arbitration by examining the roles these States played as early as the New York Convention on the Recognition and Enforcement of Foreign Arbitral Awards (1958) and more recently and actively in the UNCITRAL Working Group III discussions and other international investment arbitration policy reform efforts. Professor Jaime indicates that many developing States have built their contributions on their first-hand knowledge of arbitration in both commercial and investment disputes. In her chapter on small (Island) States and international dispute resolution, Professor Petra Butler addresses the small States' power of collaboration on the international law plane, referring to two examples, one where small States affected considerable change by working together, namely climate change, and one, where small States could revolutionize international commercial access to justice if they would work together. Two further chapters in the second part of the book reflect upon the impact of diversity as a value to be upheld, even more so in international arbitration. In the first one, Carolyn Lamm and Jennifer Ivers address the key issues in promoting, as well as advancing, gender diversity in international arbitration. Useful for the readers, Carolyn Lamm was the chair of the groundbreaking ICCA Cross-Institutional Task Force on Gender Diversity in Arbitral Appointments and Proceedings, with an update launched in 2022. In their chapter,

Carolyn Lamm and Jennifer Ivers acknowledge the tremendous progress that has been made in advancing the role of women as counsel and as arbitrators in international arbitration, but that significant work remains to further promote the role of women in arbitration. The conclusions of the chapter urge arbitration practitioners, including those in law firms, arbitral institutions, public and private entities, litigation funders, and other organizations, to continue to highlight and undertake efforts on gender diversity to maintain speed in efforts to advance women in arbitration going forward. In the second chapter on the topic, Professor Kabir Duggal and Kevin Gray consider the recent developments in scholarship on diversity, inclusion, equity, and belonging in international arbitration. The chapter concludes that international arbitration may be facing a legitimacy crisis but that this crisis may be resolved by providing for legitimacy in the selection of participants in the process. As such, explain the authors, achieving diversity and inclusion in the field is not only an ethical matter and an improver of decision-making quality but also a key to arbitration's future. The next two chapters in the second part of the book focus on institutional stakeholders in international arbitration. Chiann Bao and Amr Omran discuss the role of professional organizations, in particular of the IBA, in shaping legal values, developing arbitral best practice, and providing platforms for cross-fertilization among diverse legal systems. The authors emphasize that IBA, through its Arbitration Committee, has provided robust frameworks to evaluate impartiality and independence in arbitral proceedings, streamlining the taking of evidence, etc., all these duly acknowledged and often observed by arbitral tribunals, arbitration institutions and national courts. Maria Fernanda Garza, former Chair of the International Chamber of Commerce (ICC), and Michael McIlwrath, Past Chair of the ICC's Governing Body for Dispute Resolution Services, address the nature of institutions that offer dispute resolution services. Within this framework, they pose the obvious – but legitimate – questions in the context of a book on arbitration reform: What is the purpose that dispute resolution institutions serve, and to whom is an institution accountable with respect to whether and how it accomplishes its purpose in a world experiencing rapid changes? The authors build their critical analysis on their personal experience with the ICC and its International Court of Arbitration, in particular from the perspective of the role governance plays in global dispute resolution services. The last chapter in the second part of the book looks at the role of the diversity of arbitration institutions, as relevant stakeholders in international arbitration, as well as the activities these institutions undertake and which go to the core values of the arbitration process. Daniel Ávila II reflects upon the outcomes of the ITA's Guide to Latin American Arbitral Institutions of 2023, the second survey of this type, after the one conducted in 2011. The author acknowledges the proliferation of regional arbitral institutions and their role in handling disputes arising from the increased trade with the LATAM region and focuses on the emergence of new voices in arbitration, particularly in the Caribbean, where multiple new centres have opened their doors and have integrated new aspects into their arbitration rules to meet the growing demand for diversity in arbitration.

The third part of the book addresses another emerging force driving international arbitration reform: regionalism. In this section, the authors discuss the increasing importance of regionalism with respect to rulemaking that impacts international arbitration practice, with a particular focus on Asia (the Association of Southeast Asian Nations (ASEAN) and China), Europe (EU) and South America (Mercado Común del Sur (Southern Common Market) (MERCOSUR) and Brazil). Professor Pasha Hsieh and Jeffrey Lo examine how ASEAN-led rulemaking efforts in the area of international investment law – driven in significant part by the principle of ASEAN centrality – have contributed to a new Asian regionalism that reflects an Asia-wide consensus on investment law reforms. Professor Federico Ortino argues that the EU's complex supranational structure has made the implementation of its novel international investment law reform agenda considerably more challenging, while investment facilitation may provide the EU with an important opportunity to advance an investment law strategy that aligns effectively with core EU values. Professor Facundo Pérez Aznar identifies several challenges associated with the regionalization of Brazil's Agreements on Cooperation and Facilitation of Investments (ACFI) within MERCOSUR and the region, including the coexistence, in the region, of two distinct investment law regimes (an ACFI-based regime and an investor-state dispute settlement regime). Professors Mark McLaughlin and Dilini Pathirana discuss ASEAN's role in the development of a 'Legal Silk Road' in an international arbitration context, in which a commitment to harmonizing and refining international dispute resolution mechanisms can support the emergence of a stable legal infrastructure in the region. Professor Manjiao Chi and Zongyao Li analyse the significant and rapid updating, in an international arbitration context, of laws, institutions and practices in China, most notably through the ongoing development of an amended Arbitration Law. Eduardo Grebler and Felipe Greco argue that foreign investment protection within MERCOSUR, from the perspective of foreign investors, is more rhetorical than substantive, given the current content of Brazil's ACFI and the related MERCOSUR Protocol for Investment Cooperation and Facilitation (PCFI).

The final part of the book explores the future of international arbitration in light of the existing reforms. One of the chapters of this final part is a transcript of the interview of Meg Kinnear, former Secretary General of the International Centre for Settlement of Investment Disputes, World Bank, by Professor Andrea Bjorklund. The interview is part of the ITA Academic Council's Preserving Perspectives: International Arbitrators in Their Own Words series, a set of recorded interviews with key figures of international arbitration aimed at memorializing the evolution of modern international arbitration in the words of those who have led it. Meg Kinnear's interview by Andrea Bjorklund is presented in this book in co-authorship with Anamaria Marin and Filippo Zuti Giachetti. Reflecting on the reform of investor-State dispute settlement, Meg Kinnear suggests that investment arbitration, as a dispute resolution mechanism, works well in 99.9% of the cases, in particular if viewed in comparison with the domestic courts system. This, perhaps, is a suggestion to reflect upon the value arbitration brings, with reference to the original scope of arbitration as an alternative to litigation, with the main advantage of offering efficiency in the resolution of disputes. The last chapter of the book, authored by Professor Victoria Sahani, immediate Past Chair of the Academic Council of the ITA, addresses the evolving values of international arbitration. Professor Sahani first refers to the most fundamental of the classical values of international arbitration, which is non-violent dispute settlement, followed by other fundamental values, such as customizability and autonomy, all tempered by a third fundamental, classical value of international arbitration: fairness. Professor Sahani reminds readers that international arbitration faces a legitimacy crisis which goes to the core of these fundamental and evolving values, ultimately forcing stakeholders to seriously reassess the practice area.

We hope that readers will find value in this book, as we are all responsible for upholding the legitimacy of international arbitration.

CHAPTER 1

Arbitration Reforms for What Reason? Some Fundamental Introductory Remarks

Loukas Mistelis

Arbitration reform projects have become a regular occurrence. International (commercial or investment) arbitration continues to grow, notwithstanding debates about the legitimacy of arbitration as a private process. Arbitration is now subject to a multitude of regulatory sources, and several new regulators have emerged. In addition to international treaties and national laws, arbitration rules and other soft law instruments proposed by several formulating agencies have taken centre stage. Given the nature of international arbitration as a sui generis and transnational process, there is a tension between the increased regulatory activity and the core interest of arbitration users and the arbitration community. This chapter provides a classification of various reform projects and suggests a dialogue between regulators and users of international arbitration. Such dialogue and the active engagement of key stakeholders of the arbitration process in reform projects are essential in order to ensure that reforms are meaningful and successful.

I INTRODUCTION AND BACKGROUND

In the last forty years, there has been an unprecedented wave, if not frenzy, of reforms (different forms and shapes) in international arbitration. Why is this the case, and how do drafters of rules of law approach this process? It seems that these are two questions which have received little or no attention so far.

Four decades back, the adoption of the 1985 United Nations Commission on International Trade Law (UNCITRAL) Model Law of International Commercial Arbitration[1] prompted the reform or enactment of many national arbitration laws, some of which covered both international and domestic arbitration. Interestingly enough, the most popular (traditional) arbitration seats have enacted different laws which often may have been inspired or made an attempt to follow the principles of the Model Law but remain distinct and as such are not considered Model Law jurisdictions.[2] Other arbitral seats and, in particular, all most major emerging arbitral seats, such as Singapore, Hong Kong and many jurisdictions in the Middle East, have adopted the Model Law either without changes (the so-called vanilla adoption) or with some additions.[3]

In fact, the Model Law was developed as a legislative model which states could adopt as is or with additions and modifications, and hence its enactment or adoption by national legislatures is no surprise. What is critical is that states adopting the Model Law fully subscribe to nine key principles.[4] A jurisdiction would qualify as a Model Law one when adopting legislation similar to the Model Law when primarily: (a) the legislation critically regulates the relationship between arbitral tribunals and national courts to the effect that national courts only have a reduced and largely anticipated role in connection to arbitration proceedings and (b) the legislation ensures that party autonomy is respected.

Until the Model Law (1985), the main forms of regulation of arbitration proceedings were: (a) international treaties;[5] (b) national legislation, either in the form of a dedicated arbitration statute[6] or a specific section of the Code of Civil Procedure;[7] and (c) arbitration rules[8] which are soft law. Since 1985, however, there has been a

1. UNCITRAL Model Law on International Commercial Arbitration was adopted in 1985, and several amendments were adopted in 2006. It is now enacted (either in the 1985 or in the 2006 version) in 93 states in 126 jurisdictions. *See* https://uncitral.un.org/en/texts/arbitration/modellaw/commercial_arbitration/status, accessed 16 Dec. 2024.
2. In England, the main arbitration statute is the 1996 English Arbitration Act, and it applies to both domestic and international arbitrations; in France, the 2011 French Decree which is incorporated in the French Code of Civil Procedure as Book IV has distinct parts for domestic and international arbitration; and in Switzerland, the 1987 Private International Law Act (as amended) focuses on international arbitration only.
3. Some jurisdictions have also introduced additional provisions about arbitrability (e.g., Germany, Spain), enforcement of provisional measures rendered by tribunals (e.g., Germany), law applicable to the validity of the arbitration agreement (e.g., Spain).
4. *See* Gerold Herrmann, Introductory Note on the UNCITRAL Model Law on International Commercial Arbitration, *Uniform Law Review*, Volume 13, Issue 1, January 1985, pp. 285-296 https://doi.org/10.1093/ulr/os-13.1.285.
5. *See*, for example, the Convention on the Recognition and Enforcement of Foreign Arbitral Awards, adopted on 10 Jun. 1958, and entered into force on 7 Jun. 1959 ('New York Convention'); European Convention on International Commercial Arbitration, adopted on 21 Apr. 1961 in Geneva.
6. *See*, for example, the 1925 United States Federal Arbitration Act of the various English Arbitration Statutes from 1698, 1950, 1979 and most recently in 1996.
7. *See*, for example, the 10th Book of the German Code of Civil Procedure or Book IV the French Code of Civil Procedure.
8. *See*, for example, the Arbitration Rules of the ICC, LCIA, and the UNCITRAL Arbitration Rules.

proliferation of legal instruments, including Guidelines,[9] various sets of rules,[10] codes of conduct,[11] protocols,[12] guides,[13] notes[14] and others.[15]

Arbitration rules and laws have evolved significantly, and the plethora of sources manifests a desire by various groups at national or international levels to regulate international arbitration, while some resistance to such overregulation takes the form of self-regulation. The question of whether arbitration is overregulated has already been posed[16] but remains answered. The question remains because arbitration is an unconventional area of law (and it is largely a process rather than a law) so that its regulation is challenging. This becomes more acute when one approaches the issue of reform from a more legislative or theoretical perspective. In the following two sections, we will look at the question of why regulation of arbitration is distinct and unconventional (section II) before classifying the various reform models and attempts (section III) and finally offering some conclusions (section IV).

II WHY REGULATION OF ARBITRATION IS DISTINCT?

International arbitration has witnessed a steady growth in the last thirty-thirty-five years during which period on the one hand there is an increase in arbitration regulation, and on the other hand regular reporting on the number of cases has been reasonably consistent. Each arbitral institution has its own way of reporting cases, and

9. *See*, for example, IBA Guidelines on Conflicts of Interest in International Arbitration 2004, and amended in 2024.
10. *See*, for example, IBA Rules on Taking of Evidence in International Arbitration 1999, 2010 and 2021 or its more inquisitorial counterpart, the Rules on Conduct of the Taking of Evidence in International Arbitration (The Prague Rules).
11. *See*, for example, ICSID and UNCITRAL Code of Conduct for Arbitrators in International Investment Disputes (2024).
12. *See*, for example, various protocols developed by the CPR at https://drs.cpradr.org/rules/protocols-guidelines, accessed 16 Dec. 2024.
13. *See*, for example, the various IBA Guides and Reports.
14. *See*, for example, the UNCITRAL Notes on Organising Arbitration Proceedings or the LCIA Guidance Note at https://www.lcia.org/adr-services/guidance-note.aspx, accessed 16 Dec. 2024.
15. *See*, for example, practice guidelines for international arbitration by the Chartered Institute of Arbitrators at https://www.ciarb.org/resources/professional-practice-guidelines/international-arbitration/, accessed 16 Dec. 2024.
16. *See* Ugo Draetta, The Transnational Procedural Rules for Arbitration and the Risks of Overregulation and Bureaucratization, *ASA Bulletin*, Volume 33, Issue 2, 2015, pp. 327-342 https://doi.org/10.54648/asab2015025; Catherine A. Rogers, Arbitrators, Barbers & Taxidermists, *Ethics in International Arbitration* (Oxford, 2014; online edition at Oxford Academic), https://doi.org/10.1093/law/9780198713203.003.0003, accessed 16 Dec. 2024; Dalma Demeter, *Dalma, Freedom versus Security in Regulating ADR and International Arbitration* (2015). Trade Development through the Harmonization of Commercial Law (Muruga Perumal Ramaswamy & Joao Ribeiro, eds, *Comparative Law Journal of the Pacific (CLJP) in Association with UNCITRAL RCAP and the New Zealand Association of Comparative Law*, 2015), Available at SSRN: https://ssrn.com/abstract=2825059 or http://dx.doi.org/10.2139/ssrn.2825059, accessed 16 Dec. 2024; and U. Liukkunen, Lex Mercatoria in International Arbitration, in: J Klabbers & T Piiparinen, eds, *Normative Pluralism and International Law: Exploring Global Governance*. ASIL Studies in International Legal Theory. Cambridge University Press, 2013, pp. 201-228.

hence reports do not fully capture the real numbers, more or on case ad hoc cases.[17] Still, the numbers have been growing and it is often posited that arbitration is the preferred method for the resolution of cross-border disputes. The importance of arbitration as the primary private dispute resolution of commercial disputes is evidenced by a series of surveys ever since 2006[18] and is generally undisputed. Arbitration is a neutral and flexible process and therefore particularly suitable for cross-border disputes where no party wishes to submit to the courts of the other party.

While arbitration has been in operation in various formal or less formal iterations for several centuries, if not millennia,[19] modern arbitration is linked to the creation of international arbitral institutions such as the London Court of International Arbitration (LCIA), Permanent Court of Arbitration (PCA) in the late nineteenth century and the International Chamber of Commerce (ICC) in the early twentieth century and the adoption of the New York Convention on the Recognition of Foreign Arbitral Awards in 1958.[20]

Arbitration is in its primary and main form the expression of the will of contracting or disputing parties to have their disputes resolved outside the jurisdiction of national courts and instead use this prominent and now well-established form of private justice.[21]

A The Sui Generis Transnational Nature of Arbitration

Arbitration is the result of party autonomy, and such autonomy is now confirmed by most national arbitration laws and the New York Convention. International arbitration is defined as:

> ... a specially established mechanism for the final and binding determination of disputes, concerning a contractual or other relationship with an international element, by independent arbitrators, in accordance with procedures, structures and substantive legal or non-legal standards chosen directly or indirectly by the parties.[22]

---

17. *See* the regular reports by James Clanchy at https://www.jamesclanchy.com/knowhow/arbitration-statistics, accessed 16 Dec. 2024 which include ad hoc arbitration.
18. *See* https://www.qmul.ac.uk/arbitration/research/, accessed 16 Dec. 2024 and the analysis by Loukas Mistelis, International Arbitration: Corporate Attitudes and Practices, *American Review of International Arbitration*, Volume 15, 2004, pp. 525-593.
19. Paschalis Paschalidis, Note: The Heirs of Pausimachus v City of Kalymnos Arbitration, *Arbitration International*, Volume 39, Issue 4, 2023, pp. 571-580 https://doi.org/10.1093/arbint/aiad043. *See also* Mikaël Schinazi, *The Three Ages of International Commercial Arbitration* (Cambridge, 2022); Derek Roebuck, Sources for the History of Arbitration: A Bibliographical Introduction, *Arbitration International* Volume 14, Issue 3, 1998, pp. 237-344 https://doi.org/10.1093/arbitration/14.3.237 and F. Grisel, Arbitration as a Dispute Resolution Process: Historical Developments, in: Stefan Kröll, Andrea Bjorklund & Franco Ferrari, eds, *Cambridge Compendium of International Commercial and Investment Arbitration*. Cambridge University Press, 2023, pp. 3-26.
20. *Supra* n. 5.
21. Stephen J. Ware, Private Ordering and Commercial Arbitration: Lasting Lessons from Mentschikoff, *J. Disp. Resol.*, 2019, 1, at 3.
22. Julian D.M. Lew, Loukas A. Mistelis & Stefan M. Kröll, *Comparative International Commercial Arbitration* (Kluwer, 2004), at para 1-1, p. 1.

It is often said that arbitration is a creature of a contract, and its main consequence is that disputes covered by an arbitration agreement are effectively removed from the jurisdiction of national courts. It is also often suggested that the vast majority of arbitration cases do not interact with the national courts. At the same time, the contract between the parties is one key regulatory source of each arbitration. This would suggest that arbitration has a certain autonomy from national legal systems. The autonomous nature of the arbitration as a jurisdiction or even legal order is not only attractive to arbitrators, who arguably enjoy a wide discretion in organising and conducting arbitral proceedings, but also particularly supported by sociologists[23] and legal scholars focusing on international business transactions (*droit des affaires internationales*) transnational law and *lex mercatoria*[24] or arbitration theorists[25] who some[26] have described as 'dreamers'.

Autonomous arbitration has received less support in recent years as most modern arbitration laws, in particular, those based on the UNCITRAL Model Law on International Commercial Arbitration,[27] rely primarily on territoriality and the seat of arbitration: the perceived wisdom is that arbitration is regulated by the law of the seat.[28] At the same time, it is uncontroversial that arbitration law has all the key features of transnational law,[29] which do not fit into narrow traditional categories: arbitration is regulated by national laws,[30] international law,[31] soft law, codified or uncodified.[32] In that sense, arbitration law is transnational law.[33] Hence, even if arbitration is deemed

23. *See* generally the seminal study by Yves Dezalay & Bryant Garth, *International Commercial Arbitration and the Construction of a Transnational Legal Order* (University of Chicago Press, 1996).
24. *See*, for example, Chia-Jui Cheng, ed., *Clive M. Schmitthoff's Select Essays on International Trade Law* (Nijhoff, 1988); C. Schmitthoff, Finality of Arbitral Awards and Judicial Review, in J. Lew, ed., *Contemporary Problems in International Arbitration*, 1987, pp. 230-240.
25. Julian Lew, Achieving the Dream: Autonomous Arbitration, *Arbitration International*, Volume 22, 2014, pp. 179-204 https://doi.org/10.1093/arbitration/22.2.179.
26. Ralf Michaels, Dreaming Law Without a State: Scholarship on Autonomous International Arbitration as Utopian Literature, *London Review of International Law*, Volume 1(1), 2013, pp. 35-62 https://doi.org/10.1093/lril/lrt008.
27. *See* https://uncitral.un.org/en/texts/arbitration/modellaw/commercial_arbitration, accessed 16 Dec. 2024.
28. *See* Loukas Mistelis, Delocalization and Its Relevance in Post-Award Review, in: Fabien Gelinas & Frederic Bachand, eds, *25 Years of the UNCITRAL Model Law*. Juris 2013, pp. 165-179 and Loukas Mistelis, Reality Test: Current State of Affairs in Theory and Practice Relating to 'Lex Arbitri', *The American Review of International Arbitration*, Volume 17(2), 2006, pp. 156-180 https://doi.org/10.1515/9783110915648.1005.
29. Philip Jessup, *Transnational Law* (Yale University Press, 1956).
30. E.g., English Arbitration Act, US Federal Arbitration Act, Swiss Private International Law Act.
31. E.g., 1958 New York Convention on the Recognition and Enforcement of Foreign Arbitral Awards.
32. E.g., Arbitration Rules, such as those issued by ICC, LCIA, UNCITRAL as well as instruments promulgated under the auspices of IBA (Rules om Taking of Evidence, or Guidelines on Conflict of Interests), the Chartered Institute of Arbitrators, ICCA and others.
33. *See* Dezalay & Garth, *supra* n. 23.

not autonomous, it is a process with multiple dimensions[34] and hence sui generis. As a result, its legal nature is a matter of scholarly attention.[35]

Notwithstanding academic debates as to the nature of arbitration, its significance is not debated by its users (commercial parties and lawyers alike) save perhaps the quest for further efficiency;[36] in the last fifteen-twenty years, there have been occasional intense debates as to the legitimacy of arbitration.[37] This is not the place to discuss the various approaches to legitimacy nor the essence and justification (or not) of such critiques. Suffice to state that all these debates, often relating to investment arbitration, have now also impacted commercial arbitration and have prompted several reforms. At the same time, the key question posed at the outset remains: How are reforms approached in arbitration, and who drives them?

B Arbitration and Law Reform

If the premise is correct that arbitration is the creature of a contract, then any attempt to legislate arbitration or to reform existing arbitration law is a trigger of an inevitable tension. Parties wish to design their arbitration and set the parameters of the jurisdiction of the arbitral tribunal, while national legislators and other regulators set their own objectives, such as supervising the arbitral process and promoting efficiency.

We have already indicated that arbitration law has multiple regulatory sources: party autonomy, national law (statutory law or case law), international law (treaties and custom), soft law (informal and formal codifications) such as arbitral rules

---

34. *See* Jan Paulsson, Arbitration in Three Dimensions, *International and Comparative Law Quarterly*, Volume 60(2), 2011, pp. 291-323 https://doi.org/10.1017/S0020589311000054.
35. *See* Asaf Siniver, Territorial Disputes and International Law: Reclaiming the Sui Generis Nature of Arbitration, *Int Polit*, 2024, https://doi.org/10.1057/s41311-024-00585-6; Jan Paulsson, *The Idea of Arbitration* (Oxford 2013); Emmanuel Gaillard, *Legal Theory of International Arbitration* (Brill 2010). On the juridical nature of arbitration *see* Lew Mistelis & Kröll, *supra* n. 22, at Chapter 5.
36. Loukas Mistelis, Efficiency: What Else? Efficiency as the Emerging Defining Value of International Arbitration: Between Systems Theories and Party Autonomy, in: Thomas Schultz & Frederico Ortino, eds, *The Oxford Handbook of International Arbitration.* Oxford Handbooks, 2020, pp. 349-376. *See also* Loukas Mistelis, International Arbitration: Corporate Attitudes and Practices, *American Review of International Arbitration,* Volume 15, 2004, pp. 525-593.
37. *See,* for example, Susan D. Franck, The Legitimacy Crisis in Investment Treaty Arbitration: Privatizing Public International Law Through Inconsistent Decisions, *Fordham Law Review,* Volume 73, 2005, p. 1521, also available at: https://ir.lawnet.fordham.edu/flr/vol73/iss4/10, accessed 16 Dec. 2024; Charles N. Brower & Stephan W. Schill, Is Arbitration a Threat or a Boon to the Legitimacy of International Investment Law?, *Chicago Journal of International Law,* Volume 9(2), 2009, Art. 5, available at https://chicagounbound.uchicago.edu/cjil/vol9/iss2/5, accessed 16 Dec. 2024; S. Schill, Conceptions of Legitimacy of International Arbitration, in: D. Caron, S. Schill, A.C. Smutny & E. Triantafilou, eds, *Practising Virtue: Inside International Arbitration.* Oxford, Oxford University Press 2015, pp. 106-124; T. Schultz, Legitimacy Pragmatism in International Arbitration: A Framework for Analysis, in: J. Kalicki & M.A. Raouf, eds, *Evolution and Adaptation: The Future of International Arbitration.* ICCA Congress Series No. 20, Wolters Kluwer, 2019, available at SSRN: https://ssrn.com/abstract=3175905, accessed 16 Dec. 2024; S. Schill, Legitimacy of Investment Arbitration, in: Kröll, Bjorklund & Ferrari, eds, *Cambridge Compendium of International Commercial and Investment Arbitration.* Cambridge University Press, 2022, pp. 1825-1852.

elaborated by arbitral institutions or other formulating agencies[38] such as the International Bar Association (IBA)[39] or the Chartered Institute of Arbitrators.[40]

Law reform is typically associated with the modernisation of the law: it is the process of moving a regulatory framework forward and is often inspired by other models. For example, the adoption of the UNCITRAL Model Law on International Commercial Arbitration prompted a wave of reforms in arbitral legislation in many jurisdictions, especially those which had no regulation of international arbitration or those which were deemed to have a rather antiquated law. Occasionally, law reform takes the form of legal transplants.[41] For example, certain national legislation of arbitration has inspired or been used as a blueprint for other national legislators.

In this respect, law reform happens,[42] for example, to: (a) provide a regulatory framework where none previously existed (lawmaking); (b) correct errors in legislation; (c) respond or address court decisions which may have applied the (previous) law correctly but produced undesired or absurd results; (d) modernise law by making changes which are the result of a shift in social or public policy. In this respect, law reform embodies and promotes the objectives of the state (in the case of national legislation) or policy objectives of an institution (in the case of arbitral institutions). These may be aligned with the objectives of disputing parties, but this is not always the case. This is, in particular, not the case when there is an ideological motive around law reform. In this respect, the challenge, as the source of tension, is to ensure that state interests are coordinated with the needs of parties and their desire for party autonomy. To give a few examples:

- Would law reform enhance or restrict party autonomy?
- Do we trust arbitrators in terms of disclosure of potential conflicts of interest or do we want to have prescriptive regulation on the topic?
- Would the power of the arbitrators to determine their own jurisdiction remain a key part of the process?
- What is the appropriate level of standard setting in terms of procedural due process?

---

38. Ian F. Fletcher, Loukas A. Mistelis & Marise Cremona, *Foundations and Perspectives of International Trade Law* (Sweet & Maxwell, 2001), in particular Chapter 1 by Mistelis (Is Harmonisation a Necessary Evil? Use and Abuse of Comparative Law and the Future of Harmonisation, pp. 1-27).
39. https://www.ibanet.org/resources, accessed 16 Dec. 2024.
40. https://www.ciarb.org/resources/professional-practice-guidelines/international-arbitration/, accessed 16 Dec. 2024.
41. *See*, for example, Alan Watson, *Legal Transplants: An Approach to Comparative Law* (University of Georgia Press, 1993); Pierre Legrand, The Impossibility of 'Legal Transplants'. *Maastricht Journal of European and Comparative Law*, Volume 4(2), 1997, pp. 111-124 https://doi.org/10.1177/1023263X9700400202; Loukas A. Mistelis, Regulatory Aspects: Globalization, Harmonization, Legal Transplants, and Law Reform: Some Fundamental Observations, *Int'l L.*, Volume 34, 2000, p. 1055.
42. *See*, for example, James Lee, Not Time to Make a Change? Reviewing the Rhetoric of Law Reform, *Current Legal Problems*, Volume 76(1), 2023, pp. 129-172 https://doi.org/10.1093/clp/cuad004.

- Would review of the arbitral awards remain restricted to instances where the tribunal did not exercise its jurisdiction properly and where there has been a serious procedural irregularity?

All these questions also apply *mutatis mutandis* in respect of reform of investment treaty arbitration where the main sources or regulation are international treaties[43] (such as the International Centre for Settlement of Investment Disputes (ICSID) Convention,[44] the Energy Charter Treaty[45] and bilateral investment treaties (BITs), free trade agreements and treaties with investment protection standards) and arbitration rules.[46] In most instances, the role of national law in regulating investment arbitration is quite limited, save for jurisdictions which have a threshold regulation of investment treaty arbitration in their constitution.[47] Recent law reform of investment treaty arbitration took the form of abrupt and wholesale termination of many bilateral treaties[48] notwithstanding the existence of sunset clauses which would normally apply to the effect that the treaty retains some validity over a period after the termination date.[49]

Broadly speaking, law reform should make law better and more efficient.

---

43. As of August 2024, there are 2,834 Bilateral Investment Treaties of which 2,222 are in force; and 467 (multilateral) Treaties with investment protection provisions of which 390 are in force. *See* for more details: https://investmentpolicy.unctad.org/international-investment-agreements, accessed 16 Dec. 2024.
44. 1965 Convention on the Settlement of Investment Disputes Between States and Nationals of Other States (International Centre for Settlement of Investment Disputes [ICSID]) 575 UNTS 159.
45. 1994 Energy Charter Treaty [ECT] 2080 UNTS 100.
46. *See*, for example, ICSID Arbitration Rules as amended in 2022.
47. *See*, for example, the 1999 Turkish Constitution Reform which was introduced in part to allow the state to enter into arbitration agreements or various attempts in Ecuador to reform the constitution with view of restricting arbitration related to petrochemical resources. *See also* Laurence Boisson de Chazournes & Brian McGarry, What Roles Can Constitutional Law Play in Investment Arbitration?, *Journal of World Investment & Trade*, Volume 15(5-6), 2014, pp. 862-888 https://doi.org/10.1163/22119000-01506005, Available at SSRN: https://ssrn.com/abstract=2808253, accessed 16 Dec. 2024.
48. *See* Agreement for the termination of Bilateral Investment Treaties between the Member States of the European Union, SN/4656/2019/INIT, *OJ L* 169, 29.5.2020, pp. 1-41; Matteo Fermeglia & Alessandra Mistura, Killing All Birds with One Stone: Is This the End of Intra-EU BITs (as we know them), https://www.ejiltalk.org/killing-all-birds-with-one-stone-is-this-the-end-of-intra-eu-bits-as-we-know-them/ (May 2020); Charbel Moarbes, Agreement for the Termination of Bilateral Investment Treaties Between the Member States of the European Union, *International Legal Materials*, Volume 60(1), 2021, pp. 99-137 https://doi.org/10.1017/ilm.2020.65; Andrea Carska-Sheppard, Issues Relevant to the Termination of Bilateral Investment Treaties, *Journal of International Arbitration*, Volume 26(6), 2009, pp. 755-771 https://doi.org/10.54648/joia2009041.
49. *See* August Reinisch & Sara Mansour Fallah, Post-Termination Responsibility of States?: The Impact of Amendment/Modification, Suspension and Termination of Investment Treaties on (Vested) Rights of Investors, *ICSID Review – Foreign Investment Law Journal*, Volume 37 (1-2), 2022, pp. 101-120 https://doi.org/10.1093/icsidreview/siab023; Arthur Lauvaux, Towards a Bumpy Ride into the Sunset: On the Mutual Termination of IIAs and Their Sunset Clauses, *Arbitration International*, Volume 38(3), 2022, pp. 203-212 https://doi.org/10.1093/arbint/aiac010; Johannes Tropper, 'The Treaty to End All Investment Treaties. The Termination Agreement of Intra-EU BITs and Its Effect on Sunset Clauses', *Völkerrechtsblog*, 12 May 2020, https://doi.org/10.17176/20200513-013127-0.

III DIFFERENT TYPES OF ARBITRAL REFORMS: A CLASSIFICATION

Recent experiences suggest that (rules of) law reform initiatives and projects may take different forms and shapes and may be initiated and supported by different groups. We attempt to tentatively classify such modern reform projects in international (commercial and investment) arbitration and provide some examples for each of the three main trends/categories.

A Corrective, Modernisation and Fine-Tuning Reforms

It is inevitable that laws and rules cannot address every single issue and sometimes need to address provisions which although well intended may not be applied by courts in a way that drafters anticipated. There may also be matters which were not considered at the time of drafting. Hence, corrections, gap-filling, modernisations and fine-tuning should be and are the bulk of law reforms. The consequences of such reforms are the reassurance of their users' community and also a marketing function: the law or rules of law have been modernised and are state-of-the-art; we have a competitive edge, so come to us, use our laws and rules.

The best example for this category would be the Modernisation of ICSID Rules in 2022.[50] ICSID, with a unique and vast experience in administering investment disputes, embarked on a modernisation of its 2006 Rules with a view of addressing concerns about the efficiency and legitimacy of the process, including transparency, ethics and third-party funding. Overall, this carefully crafted reform received very positive feedback.[51] All major arbitral institutions are updating their rules from time to time with a view of addressing concerns and correcting smaller or bigger matters that must be addressed.

A similar approach is taken by national legislators. The French law reform in 2011 is such an effective example.[52] The French law which has different regimes for domestic and international arbitration had to address how the systems interrelate, give more power to French courts to support arbitration, where requested or required, and fine-tune other provisions.

In England, there is also currently a project to fine-tune and modernise the 1996 English Arbitration Act, a project which has been prepared by the Law Commission[53] as a result of a very broad public consultation which is continuing in the UK Parliament.[54] Some of the changes are fundamental, such as the law governing the arbitration agreement, while others are more in the category of fine-tuning. The current draft bill treads very carefully, given the popularity of London as an arbitral seat.

50. https://icsid.worldbank.org/resources/rules-amendments.
51. Ignacio Torterola & Farhod Sharipov, The 2022 ICSID Arbitration Rules: Modernizing International Investment Dispute Resolution, *ICSID Rev Foreign Investment L J* 2024 https://doi.org/10.1093/icsidreview/siae010.
52. https://iai-site.cdn.prismic.io/iai-site/35f2f1df-54a6-4ea2-8dba-0701886b45aa_FRENCH_LAW_ON_ARBITRATION.pdf, accessed 16 Dec. 2024.
53. https://lawcom.gov.uk/project/review-of-the-arbitration-act-1996/, accessed 16 Dec. 2024.
54. https://lawcom.gov.uk/arbitration-bill-re-introduced-to-parliament/, accessed 16 Dec. 2024.

Another example is the modernisation of the Greek International Arbitration Law which, however, has not also addressed the need for reform of the domestic arbitration law.[55]

In this category, one would also cover pure lawmaking, the adoption of legislation where no such legislation existed in the past; such an example is the introduction of an arbitration law in Cambodia in 2006.[56]

B Following Trends and Innovation

In addition to core arbitral regulation which would cover, for instance, the procedural and jurisdictional powers of the tribunal, broad guidelines about arbitration procedure, the relation of national courts to arbitration tribunals, there are occasional innovations adopted by arbitration laws and more typically by rules of arbitral institutions.

The best 'recent' example is the adoption of emergency arbitrator proceedings by many arbitral institutions.[57] The first institution to adopt emergency arbitration in some form[58] was the American Arbitration Association which adopted the first set of rules in 1999 and an opt-out system for international cases with the 2006 International Centre for Dispute Resolution (ICDR) Rules. Stockholm Chamber of Commerce (SCC), Singapore International Arbitration Centre (SIAC) and others followed, including the ICC Rules (2017 and 2021), the LCIA Rules (2014 and 2020), and the Hong Kong International Arbitration Centre (HKIAC) Rules (2018) and now virtually all new sets of rules.

There are several other examples, such as the adoption of rules regarding disclosures about third-party funding and the forms adopted for arbitrators to make disclosures about their independence, impartiality and availability. Similarly, the adoption of rules about the timeframes within which arbitrators should produce an award or the introduction of expedited or simplified procedures.

C Deconstructive or Recalibration Reforms

Last but not least, some reforms aim at overhauling or recalibrating arbitration. Such reforms are typical in investment arbitration: an example is the effort to substantially change investment arbitration (or Investor-State Dispute Settlement (ISDS) as it often wrongly is referred to)[59] with a view of moving from private arbitration (with the

55. https://arbitrationblog.kluwerarbitration.com/2023/06/04/greeces-new-law-on-international-commercial-arbitration/ and https://aria.law.columbia.edu/unpacking-the-new-greek-law-on-international-commercial-arbitration/, accessed 16 Dec. 2024.
56. https://cdc.gov.kh/wp-content/uploads/2022/04/Law-on-Commercial-Arbitration_full-text_060306.pdf, accessed 16 Dec. 2024.
57. Cameron Sim, *Emergency Arbitration* (Oxford University Press, 2021).
58. The ICC has had for many years the pre-arbitral referee system.
59. The acronym 'ISDS' stands for Investor-State Dispute Settlement (and not arbitration) and as such would encapsulate litigation and mediation. However, critics of 'ISDS' particularly, if not exclusively, direct their critique to investment treaty arbitration, while they often embrace investor state mediation as well as reasserting the role of the state by insisting on litigation.

consent of a state to arbitrate expressed in a treaty or a contract or a national law) to a multilateral investment court system.[60] A great deal of these efforts are framed *inaccurately* as procedural reforms and are the focus of UNCITRAL's Working Group III, which covers not only procedural matters but also some jurisdictional and substantive law reforms.[61]

Many of these reform proposals are the results of intense criticism to investment treaty arbitration by non-governmental organisations (NGOs)[62] and academics[63] and some states which have been on the responding end of claims. As a matter of fairness, several states (such as Argentina and Egypt, to name but two) with a very large number of cases initiated against them are not in any way protagonists of these reform initiatives.

As a result, discussions are not only led by states but also largely influenced and driven by regional economic integration organisations (notably, the European Union (EU)), academics[64] and NGOs and with only limited input from users of the process, such as claimants (whether national persons or legal entities).

An empirical survey in 2020-21 tried to capture claimant views.[65] It is a matter of debate whether investors are sufficiently consulted in the current reform proposals, although they do initiate such cases.

In some respects, investment law and arbitration should have first focused on substantive reforms (investment treaties) and then moved to procedural and jurisdictional reforms.[66] Systemically, if these reform proposals are adopted, they would substantially change the fabric of investment treaty arbitration from a restorative justice system to a more distributive justice system.[67]

Undoubtedly, every now and then, such major changes can occur and, if adopted, would be qualified as deconstructive of recalibrating reforms. These are one-in-a-generation changes and often would reflect policies and prevailing ideology at the time. The current process of reform of investment arbitration would go on for a few more years, and its eventual acceptance is, at present, a matter of mere speculation. What is critical is the engagement of all relevant constituencies in such reform projects.

---

60. *See* https://policy.trade.ec.europa.eu/enforcement-and-protection/multilateral-investment-court-project_en, accessed 16 Dec. 2024.
61. *See* https://uncitral.un.org/en/working_groups/3/investor-state, accessed 16 Dec. 2024.
62. *See*, for example, CEO and TNI's report: https://www.tni.org/files/download/profitingfrominjustice.pdf, accessed 16 Dec. 2024.
63. *See*, for example, Gus Van Harten, *Gus, Investment Treaty Arbitration and Public Law* (Oxford, 2008).
64. *See* the Academic Forum for ISDS: https://www.jus.uio.no/ior/english/research/projects/copiid/academic-forum/, accessed 16 Dec. 2024.
65. *See* https://www.qmul.ac.uk/arbitration/media/arbitration/docs/QM-CCIAG-Survey-ISDS-2020.pdf, accessed 16 Dec. 2024, a survey conducted by QMUL with the support of CCIAG.
66. *See* https://www.global-solutions-initiative.org/policy_brief/reforming-investor-state-dispute-settlement-and-promotion-of-trade-and-investment-cooperation/, accessed 16 Dec. 2024 the report prepared at the request of T20 and endorsed from the G20 meeting in Saudi Arabia.
67. *See* https://globalarbitrationreview.com/mistelis-calls-aristotelean-approach-isds-reform, accessed 16 Dec. 2024 (behind a paywall).

IV CONCLUDING REMARKS

As it emerges from the above-proposed classification of reform projects, it is paramount that one embarks on reform projects with full awareness of the objectives and reasons for such reform.

Several pieces of legislation, such as major conventions (e.g., New York Convention and major Human Rights Conventions), constitutions and national codifications (such as the French Civil Code), have stood the challenges of time simply because they have codified principles which are (now) widely accepted and have also included a level of flexibility for adjudicators to apply the rules.

It has occasionally been stated that arbitration is chameleon-like or, more eloquently, has a Protean nature.[68] Arbitration thrives when key rules and principles are codified and when legislation and regulation are enabling rather than prescriptive. It is part of the arbitration's fabric that parties and arbitrators can adapt rules to their needs.

The current 'needs' of arbitration users focus on issues of efficiency (can arbitration be quick when the parties so wish without compromising due process and increasing costs?); managing costs and duration of proceedings (is arbitration a viable option financially for the case at hand, and does it represent value for money? Is the duration of the process quicker than similar processes in national courts which the parties may use?); addressing issues of diversity as a way of legitimacy of the process (do arbitrators reside or are trained locally or do they come from the big arbitration seats? Is there sufficient social mobility or are arbitrators coming from big law firms and barrister chambers and are trained in the big international universities? Can they relate to the disputing parties?); and aspects of ethics (is the process fair? Are arbitrators and experts independent and impartial, and are all requisite disclosures made?).

International Arbitration remains very strong in the traditional seats (London, Paris, the US and other European seats) and is now very well established in Southeast Asia and the Middle East. It is also growing very fast in Latin America, Africa and Central and South Asia. One would hope that such growth would not be the victim of ill-conceived reforms.

Law reform should aim at enhancing the legitimacy of international (investment or commercial) arbitration as an institution and a process. In this respect, the legitimacy of any law reform project itself is to be assessed against the engagement of all relevant interest groups or constituencies, including the users, and the acceptance of such reform. Such acceptance may take the form of ratification by a legislature, the popularity of an arbitral seat following reforms and inclusion or preclusion of such new rules in arbitration agreements. In other words, for the reform of arbitration to be successful, it must be pragmatic rather than ideological and reduce the codification to key enabling principles.

---

68. William W. Park, The 2002 Freshfields Lecture: Arbitration's Protean Nature: The Value of Rules and the Risks of Discretion, *Arbitration International*, Volume 19, Issue 3, 1 Sep. 2003, pp. 279-301 https://doi.org/10.1093/arbitration/19.3.279.

CHAPTER 2

Reforming the Reform? Taking Intersectionality Seriously

Hélène Ruiz Fabri & Edoardo Stoppioni

Given that demands for arbitration reform come from very different perspectives that need to be reconciled, this chapter proposes to use the theory of intersectionality, originally pioneered by feminist theory and critical race theory and their thinking on reforming structures of domination, to think about how to reform international investment arbitration reform. After defining intersectionality as a tool, the chapter argues that it can provide us with a language for addressing the complex challenges underpinning international investment law and its reform today. To demonstrate this, it takes three case studies focusing on the intersections between investment law and, successively, race, environmental protection and indigenous peoples.

I INTRODUCTION

The debates on the legitimacy of International Investment Law and Investor-State Dispute Settlement (ISDS) began almost twenty years ago. Today, they resemble a discussion on the existential crisis of the field. This evolution triggered a move towards reform through very active processes at both International Centre for Settlement of Investment Disputes (ICSID) and United Nations Commission on International Trade Law (UNCITRAL), along with a substantial amount of literature.[1]

In such a context, a focus on the 'reform of the reform', as proposed by the book editors, incites a meta-theoretical approach to the debates on the reform. Indeed, a

1. Van Harten, Gus & Anil Yilmaz Vastardis, 'Critiques of Investment Arbitration Reform: An Introduction', *The Journal of World Investment & Trade*, 24(3), 363-371 (2023) https://doi.org/10.1163/22119000-12340290.

review of these debates reveals that they are very intense and polarized. On the one hand, there is a 'reformist' stance. Based on the assumption that the system of international rights of foreign investors is necessary, or at least is worth it, this first approach seeks to salvage, rather than challenge, the legitimacy of international investment law and dispute settlement by primarily trying to improve the latter. The works of the UNCITRAL Working Group III or the recently revised ICSID rules are a good testimony of this trend, which seems at first glance dominant. On the other hand, an 'anti-reformist' stance denounces a merely procedural reform of the system, asserting that the central problem of investment law lies in the scheme of special legal rights it grants to foreign investors.[2] Accordingly, reforms – as approached so far – are considered as best futile since major reform efforts do not challenge (or even address) this system of special rights. These reform efforts seem procedural, whereas the changes needed would be substantive. Thus, the debate looks like a simple alternative between homeostasis and revolution: either we reform the system to keep it (somehow, an approach close to Tomasi di Lampedusa's formula in *The Leopard*: 'If we want everything to stay as it is, everything has to change') or we reject it as profoundly flawed, to change it in its basic conception.

Because of this configuration of the discourses on the reform, a question immediately comes to mind. Do we place the idea of 'reforming the reform' towards the reformist pole or rather towards the anti-reformist pole? Both options can be envisaged. At the same time, a more profound question arises: is such a binary alternative satisfactory, considering all the complexity of modern international law challenges?

We live in a complex time, which we have become accustomed to calling the Anthropocene.[3] It is a time when the Intergovernmental Panel on Climate Change (IPCC) is telling us that we no longer have time to ignore the threat of climate change.[4] It is a time when what we are used to call 'populisms' are challenging the discourse of human rights and liberal democracies.[5] It is a time when demands for social justice are multiplying and clashing.[6] Younger generations are urging us to act, without further delay, to protect the planet for future generations, and their demands are not only environmental. They could not be, as we already knew through the rise of the concept of sustainable development. The aforementioned issues obviously intersect. But what are our tools to consider these intersections and verify whether international law instruments can take these intersections seriously? Our proposition is precisely to give a go at intersectionality.

2. Heath, J. Benton, 'The Anti-Reformist Stance in Investment Law', *The Journal of World Investment & Trade*, 24(4-5), 564-600 (2023) https://doi.org/10.1163/22119000-12340303.
3. Maljean-Dubois, Sandrine (ed.), *Anthropocene, White Paper 02* (ILA Paris, 2023), https://www.ilaparis2023.org/wp-content/uploads/2022/08/ADI-ILA-anthropocene-EN-PLANCHES.pdf (Accessed 16 Dec. 2024).
4. IPCC (Intergovernmental Panel on Climate Change), *AR6 Synthesis Report: Climate Change 2023*, https://www.ipcc.ch/report/ar6/syr/ (Accessed 16 Dec. 2024).
5. Alston, Philip, 'The Populist Challenge to Human Rights', *Journal of Human Rights Practice*, 9(1), 1-15 (2017) https://doi.org/10.1093/jhuman/hux007.
6. Fraser, Nancy, 'Social Justice in the Age of Identity Politics: Redistribution, Recognition, and Participation', *Geographic Thought* (Routledge, 2008), 72-89.

II INTERSECTIONALITY AS A TOOL

Intersectionality is a fascinating tool for legal theory. While it can be understood as a metaphor, it is important to be aware of its intellectual history to understand its functioning as a critical tool.

Intersectionality as a Metaphor

The idea of intersectionality is commonly traced back to 1988 when Kimberlé Crenshaw wrote a seminal article titled 'Demarginalizing the Intersection of Race and Sex'.[7] There, Crenshaw used the metaphor of intersecting streets to give an account of the complexity of discrimination: looking at the recruitment experiences of Black women, she realized that these individuals were facing discrimination not solely based on their race or gender but rather jointly as Black women. Studying cases like the one of Emma DeGraffenreid,[8] Kimberlé Crenshaw realized that these people were standing at the intersection of two grounds of discrimination: racial discrimination was coming from one direction and gender discrimination was coming from another. This sort of convergence impacted these women's lives in ways that the law was not equipped to address.

In this sense, intersectionality raises awareness of the complexity of social justice claims. As Kimberlé Crenshaw said, intersectionality 'is just a metaphor for understanding the way that multiple forms of inequality or disadvantage sometimes compound themselves'.[9] Intersectionality was conceived as a tool to unveil this complexity: as intersectional discrimination experiences are 'greater than the sum of racism and sexism (...) any analysis that does not take intersectionality into account cannot sufficiently address the particular manner in which Black women are subordinated'.[10] Much to the contrary, the established legal tools considering a 'single-axis framework'

7. Crenshaw, Kimberlé, *Demarginalizing the Intersection of Race and Sex: A Black Feminist Critique of Antidiscrimination Doctrine, Feminist Theory and Antiracist Politics,* Feminist legal theories (Routledge, 2013) 23-51.
8. Emma DeGraffenreid, along with other black women, sued General Motors in 1976 for discrimination, claiming the company did not hire them because of their race and gender. The judge dismissed the lawsuit because General Motors had black and women employees. However, Emma was raising the issue that black workers at the company, who usually performed industrial jobs, were men. Equally, women employees at General Motors, who generally did secretarial work, were white. The judge refused to allow Emma to combine her race and gender claims because he believed that would give her preferential treatment. However, neither black men nor white women experienced simultaneous oppression from both frontlines. *See* Rivera, Sara, 'Emma DeGraffenreid and the Intersectionality Metaphor', *Medium* (13 Oct. 2020), https://ferauoft.medium.com/emma-degraffenreid-and-the-intersectionality-metaphor-39d1abb77fec (Accessed 16 Dec. 2024).
9. Crenshaw, Kimberlé, 'What is Intersectionality', NAIS People of Color Conference 2017, https://www.youtube.com/watch?v=ViDtnfQ9FHc (Accessed 16 Dec. 2024).
10. Crenshaw, Kimberlé Williams, 'Demarginalizing the Intersection of Race and Sex: A Black Feminist Critique of Antidiscrimination Doctrine, Feminist Theory, and Antiracist Politics', *University of Chicago Legal Forum* (1989), 140.

and ignoring the complexity of reality were erasing 'Black women in the conceptualization, identification and remediation of race and sex discrimination by limiting inquiry to the experiences of otherwise-privileged members of the group.'[11]

Thus understood, the idea of intersectionality can be used beyond the issue of discrimination to help us think about a phenomenon in its different facets, not one after the other but together, with their interactions. It encourages us to look at the way power functions against subjects that it sets at the margins and how the law can operate to effectively tackle the functioning of this marginalization. As a legal theory tool, it stresses the fundamental idea that we need to have a language to address the complex functioning of power. As it was recalled, intersectionality represents 'the predominant way of conceptualizing the relation between systems of oppression which construct our multiple identities and our social locations in hierarchies of power and privilege'.[12] In this sense, intersectionality is a critical theory tool.

Intersectionality as a Tool of Critical Theory

Intersectionality is not any kind of metaphor. It is important to recall that it is a theoretical tool that was crafted within a clear philosophical context, embedded in critical theory and Black feminism. As Vivian May stressed, intersectionality 'does have a historical trajectory that needs to be accounted for meaningfully and a set of commitments that, likewise, need to be engaged substantively (not nominally or via empty gestures)'.[13]

Anne-Marie Hancock reconstructed an intellectual history of the concept: this history explains why intersectionality must be understood as a critical theory tool to avoid its 'cooptation as a tool for reform at the margins, rather than its being a framework with the potential to radically reform our structures of government and public policies, as well as to make other changes'.[14] Within this mindset, she reconstructed the 'visibility project'[15] of intersectionality: Black feminists had understood that power was operating in a way both to render invisible to the naked eyes of their subaltern communities and to mainstream the 'social location, the margins'[16] into society, an operation that had legal implications.[17]

Changing this approach entails an epistemological shift: 'intersectionality conceptualizes power relationally, but not in a binary fashion'.[18] 'Conceptualizing reality in a way that takes the politics of subaltern communities as seriously as the politics of mainstream society means that one can no longer self-locate as either on a margin or

11. *Ibid.*
12. Carastathis, Anna, 'The Concept of Intersectionality in Feminist Theory', *Philosophy Compass*, 9(5), 304 (2014) https://doi.org/10.1111/phc3.12129.
13. May, Vivian, *Pursuing Intersectionality, Unsettling Dominant Imaginaries* (Routledge, 2015), 12.
14. Hancock, Anne-Marie, *Intersectionality – An Intellectual History* (OUP, 2016), 13.
15. *Ibid.*, 12.
16. *Ibid.*, 81.
17. Crenshaw, Kimberlé Williams, 'Mapping the Margins: Intersectionality, Identity Politics, and Violence against Women of Color', *Stanford Law Review*, 43(6), 1241-1299 (1991) https://doi.org/10.2307/1229039.
18. Hancock, Anne-Marie, *Intersectionality – An Intellectual History* (OUP, 2016), 118.

in a center.'[19] As a critical tool, intersectionality encourages us to look at how the law has an impact at the margins and at how power operates in constructing complex relations that the law can tend to ignore. Whenever the law operates in a way to reduce these complex relations into a bilateral, simplified fashion, it tends to ignore and exclude the problems of those who are set at the margins.

Intersectionality as a Field

Because of this impressive potential of intersectionality to become a viewpoint to explore the functioning of power in complex configurations, this critical tool has progressively grown to become much more than simply a metaphor. For this reason, scholarship has progressively described it as a 'field of study',[20] a paradigm[21] or a social literacy.[22]

Beyond the linguistic aspect, intersectionality has become the fundamental tool to reconsider the very philosophical ground of feminism. Many scholars have started talking about an intersectional feminist philosophy based on a particular agenda concerning power's subjugation. In this sense, 'taken together, Crenshaw's essays catalyzed a tectonic shift in the nature of feminist theorizing by suggesting that black women's experiences demanded new paradigms in feminist theorizing, creating an analytic framework that exposed through use of a powerful metaphor exactly what it meant for systems of power to be interactive, and explicitly tying the political aims of an inclusive democracy to a theory and account of power'.[23]

Nevertheless, this success of intersectionality has also caused its expansion and burgeoning in legal literature, sometimes at the expense of the integrity of its social project background. This 'citational ubiquity'[24] has '[given] the sense that "everyone" does intersectional work, there seems to be less agreement about what exactly intersectionality is'.[25] Being conscious of this problem entails not using intersectionality as a cosmetic jargon but taking into account its project as a tool of social justice, coming from Black feminism and pursuing a deeply critical and radical aim.

Intersectionality and International Investment Law?

Different calls for reform have stressed the limits of the tools of liberal international law to articulate contemporary demands for social justice. In this sense, our fundamental

19. *Ibid.*, 82.
20. Cho, Sumi K., Kimberlé Williams Crenshaw & Leslie McCall, 'Toward a Field of Intersectionality Studies: Theory, Applications, and Praxis', *Signs: Journal of Women in Culture and Society*, 38(4), 785-803 (2013) https://doi.org/10.1086/66960.
21. Hancock, Anne-Marie, 'When Multiplication Doesn't Equal Quick Addition: Examining Intersectionality as a Research Paradigm', *Perspectives on Politics*, 5(1), 63-79 (2007) https://doi.org/10.1017/s1537592707070065.
22. Berger, Michele Tracy & Kathleen Guidroz (eds), *The Intersectional Approach: Transforming the Academy through Race, Class, and Gender* (University of North Carolina Press, 2009).
23. Cooper, Brittney, 'Intersectionality', in Lisa Disch & Mary Hawkesworth (eds), *The Oxford Handbook of Feminist Theory* (2015), 386.
24. Wiegman, Robyn, *Object Lessons* (Duke University Press, 2012).
25. Cooper, Brittney, 'Intersectionality', in Lisa Disch & Mary Hawkesworth (eds), *The Oxford Handbook of Feminist Theory* (2015), 385.

proposition is that intersectionality can provide us with a language for addressing the complex challenges underlying international investment law and its reform today.

To reflect on this question, we will take three examples, i.e., three case studies. Each of them contemplated a diversity of scenarios of contestation, articulating multiple challenges for ISDS and international investment law. In each case, the tribunal approached this complexity in bilateral terms, breaking down the issues into a bilateral relationship between investment protection and a so-called non-investment value. By reducing the complexity to a simple alternative, tribunals have provided answers that some have found satisfactory and others unacceptable.

Our aim here is instead to take a step back and ask whether, as things stand, ISDS and international investment law can grasp complexity and whether they can take intersectionality seriously. These case studies are meant to test whether international investment law structures are unable to pursue the project of intersectionality, to deal with complex power relations of different social groups. We aim to understand how international investment law left those groups who are at the margins in a situation of invisibility. However, we also selected these cases because they were an opportunity to hear new voices, often young authors who propose new ways of talking about the issues involved, as this is also an important path to pursue inclusion and diversity.

III FIRST INTERSECTION: RACE

The first intersection to be explored here is that between investment protection and race. This issue holds significant importance from an intersectional perspective. Due to intersectionality's genealogy being linked to black feminism and CRT, race plays a fundamental role in reflecting how power intersects with various situations. At first glance, one might wonder what there is to say about the relationship between international investment law and race. Yet, the fact that the issue is underexplored is in itself a significant problem. Recent scholarship has shown that the debate on the colonial origins can shed essential light on how international investment law deals with racial issues.[26]

An ICSID case, *Bernhard von Pezold v. Zimbabwe*, which resulted in a much-criticized award in 2015, is emblematic of this issue.[27] The investment case is interesting because it is a snapshot of a broader phenomenon directly related to Zimbabwe's complex history, namely land reform issues.[28] The reforms have their roots in the highly problematic land distribution system inherited from the colonial era, which was based on legislation that facilitated and consolidated the forced eviction of black people from their ancestral lands without compensation or due process and that

26. Gathii, James Thuo & Ntina Tzouvala, 'Racial Capitalism and International Economic Law: Introduction', *Journal of International Economic Law,* 25(2), 199-206 (2022) https://doi.org/10.1093/jiel/jgac025.
27. *Bernhard von Pezold v. Zimbabwe* (Award), ICSID Arbitral Tribunal, Case No. ARB/10/15, 28 Jul. 2015.
28. On the broader economic history of Zimbabwe, *see* Muzondidya, James, 'From Buoyancy to Crisis, 1980-1997', in Brian Raftopoulos & Alois Mlambo (eds), *Becoming Zimbabwe: A History from the Pre-Colonial Period to 2008* (Harare: Weaver Press, 2009), 167-200.

was qualified as an 'odious inheritance'.[29] In particular, two Acts in 1930 and 1969 had allocated the most fertile lands to the white minority while leaving the black majority with barren land, structuring a legal system that – in the words of the International Committee of Jurists – functioned to 'strengthen white dominion over the most fertile and economically important land and maintain the African population as a labouring class'.[30]

The colonial system of land distribution established a lasting extreme inequality, laying the groundwork for a liberation struggle that culminated in the country gaining independence in 1980. Following Zimbabwe's independence, the matter of land reform persisted as an existential concern, prompting landless black Zimbabweans to occupy both private and public land while advocating for change. In 2000, Robert Mugabe's government sought to conclusively address the issue. Two constitutional amendments (Amendments 16 and 17) were enacted, limiting compensation for the compulsory acquisition of farmland and stripping away the right to challenge such acquisitions by divesting national courts of jurisdiction. Numerous foreign investors engaged in large-scale agricultural ventures in Zimbabwe subsequently lodged multiple claims, including those before ICSID tribunals under bilateral investment treaties (BITs), marking the backdrop of the *von Pezold* case.[31]

The potential for intersectionality, in this case, is clear: the investment framework is connected here to many different situations, such as the history of colonialism as a complex historical background, a democratic challenge to the *status quo*, human rights concerns in terms of discrimination, and racial justice issues.

Scholars have criticized the highly problematic nature of the approach of the tribunal while trying to articulate these different factors. In this regard, some have highlighted the linguistic and cultural bias entrenched in the award, calling white farmers' land occupations 'invasions' (thus borrowing the language of the claimants).[32] They have also emphasized significant structural biases, noting that the tribunal's awarding of remedies, such as an uncommon instance of restitution and an unusually high amount of moral damages, prioritized the individual property rights of white commercial farmers over those of historically disadvantaged populations, thus perpetuating historical injustices, according to critics.

We will focus here on the legal reasoning of the tribunal. It can be stated that, in this case, the tribunal took investment protection as an exclusive prism, finding essentially a violation of the expropriation and the full protection and security clauses. On both legal grounds, the reasoning was harshly criticized.

29. Openshaw, Karen S. & Patrick C.R. Terry, 'Zimbabwe's Odious Inheritance: Debt and Unequal Land Distribution', *McGill International Journal of Sustainable Development Law and Policy*, 11(1), 39 (2015).
30. On the unjust land distribution system of the colonial era, *see* International Committee of Jurists, 'Racial Discrimination and Repression in Southern Rhodesia' (1976) ICJ Report, p. 11.
31. Asmelash, Henok, 'The Legacy of the SADC Tribunal in International Investment Law', in Helene Ruiz Fabri & Edoardo Stoppioni (eds), *International Investment Law: An Analysis of Major Decisions* (Hart Publishing, 2022).
32. Tzouvala, Ntina, 'Invested in Whiteness: Zimbabwe, the von Pezold Arbitration, and the Question of Race in International Law', *Journal of Law and Political Economy*, 2(2), 2022 https://doi.org/10.5070/lp62258226.

As Asmelash noted concerning expropriation, the tribunal dealt very rapidly with issues that were extremely complex in terms of racial discrimination and interaction with colonial history. It was quick to characterize the expropriation as illegal, as no 'prompt adequate and effective compensation' had been paid to the investor. This allowed the tribunal not to dig too much into the public purpose of the measure. Only because 'the parties pleaded so extensively on these matters'[33] did the tribunal briefly consider whether the land reform programme met the requirement of a lawful expropriation. And, although it acknowledged that a small number of black-owned farms had also been expropriated, 'it took only a single paragraph for the tribunal to conclude that the land reform program was racially discriminatory' and, 'in another single paragraph, it dismissed Zimbabwe's argument that the land reform program was necessary to right historical wrongs'.[34]

Asmelash stressed how the discourse of the tribunal rapidly found that the expropriation measures were discriminatory against white investors, failing to ponder deeply racial discrimination issues that were nevertheless fundamental for the constitutional history of the country. The tribunal recognized that racial discrimination could possibly be justified in certain cases, for example, in the context of affirmative action aimed at redressing historical inequalities, but it 'was at pains to stress'[35] that it was 'not unsympathetic to national aspirations to correct colonial wrongs' and observed that 'the discrimination in favour of indigenous Zimbabweans was necessary in order to remedy the unconscionable anti-aboriginal policies implemented throughout the Rhodesian era'.[36] Nevertheless, the constitutional amendment (Amendment 17) was not one of the 'legitimate policies that justifiably discriminate by race in order to address historical wrongs'.[37] The tribunal distinguished between pre- and post-2000 land reform programmes to justify its finding that the former was 'adequately founded and justifiable', while the latter were 'enacted in response to political pressure',[38] instead of addressing the fundamental necessity to rectify historical land disparities.

Ntina Tzouvala exerted a similar critique, most notably concerning the arguments on exceptions. The tribunal swiftly rejected the respondent's assertion according to which forcibly removing landless protesters occupying the lands of white investors would have resulted in widespread bloodshed and further heightened social and political tensions, notably stating that 'the purpose of any State, and particularly its police force, is to maintain order in spite of such instabilities rather than stepping back and allowing the citizenry to devolve into anarchy'.[39] In this context, Tzouvala showed how problematic the 'rhetoric of the award' is: 'the line of argument followed by the arbitrators equated whiteness with productivity, prudence, and also vulnerability while conceptualizing blackness as inherently violent, chaotic, and destructive. In this argumentative universe, only the state's repressive capabilities can prevent the sliding

33. *Bernhard von Pezold v. Zimbabwe*, para. 499.
34. Asmelash, *supra* n. 31, 538-539 pointing at award's paras 501 and 502.
35. Asmelash, *supra* n. 31, 539.
36. *Bernhard von Pezold v. Zimbabwe*, para. 652.
37. *Bernhard von Pezold v. Zimbabwe*, para. 653.
38. *Bernhard von Pezold v. Zimbabwe*, para. 656.
39. *Bernhard von Pezold v. Zimbabwe*, para. 642.

of black-majority polities into total chaos, which is understood as being their default state'.[40] Deconstructing the discourse of the tribunal, she considered that 'the presumption inherent in this passage appears to be that the natural state of Zimbabwe's black citizenry is one of chaos and violence and it can only be tamed through the use of extensive violence'.[41]

Looking at the intersection between investment protection and race, we can conclude that investment arbitration fails to grasp the full spectrum of complex legal relations that cannot be reduced and simplified to a bilateral 'investor rights vs State obligations' paradigm. Tzouvala pointed this out indirectly linking the idea to neoliberal legality. In a neoliberal mindset, 'bilateral relations between individuals are understood to be voluntary and premised on juridical (if not factual) equality, while bilateral relations between individuals and the state are thought to be hierarchical and coercive. This typology is also at the very heart of international investment law and reflected in its dispute settlement structure: what is of legal interest is the relationship between the state on the one hand and the investor on the other'. Nevertheless, 'as US legal realists observed over one hundred years ago, property rights involve bundles of rights, obligations, privileges, immunities, etc. that implicate more than two parties'.[42]

Comparing this approach with the decisions rendered in other fora, we can also consider that this type of approach strongly undermines the legitimacy of the tribunal itself. Similar cases were presented to the Southern African Development Community Tribunal (SADC Tribunal), which employed a parallel line of reasoning, for example, in the *Campbell* case. Following the expropriation by the Zimbabwean government of a series of white-owned commercial and agricultural lands, seventy-nine applicants filed a consolidated application with the SADC Tribunal challenging the legality of the expropriations.[43] The tribunal ruled that the expropriation of farmland was unlawful because it was based on racial discrimination, and the applicants had not been compensated. Thus, the tribunal acknowledged the significance of addressing discriminatory expropriation to confront the enduring consequences of colonial land dispossession. However, akin to the ICSID tribunal, it provided Zimbabwe with no flexibility to address challenges in implementation. The perceived incapacity of the SADC Tribunal to dispense justice led to its demise.[44] This instance underscores the importance of comprehensively addressing the diversity of challenges to ensure the legitimacy of adjudication.

---

40. Tzouvala, Ntina, 'Full Protection and Security (for Racial Capitalism)', *Journal of International Economic Law* 25(2), 224-241 notably 225 (2022) https://doi.org/10.1093/jiel/jgac019.
41. *Ibid.*, 231.
42. *Ibid.*, 232.
43. *Mike Campbell (Pvt) Ltd. and Others v. The Republic of Zimbabwe*, SADC Tribunal Case No. 2/2007.
44. Asmelash, Henok, 'Southern African Development Community Tribunal', in Helene Ruiz Fabri (ed.), *Max Planck Encyclopedia of International Procedural Law* (OUP, 2016), https://opil.ouplaw.com/display/10.1093/law-mpeipro/e2496.013.2496/law-mpeipro-e2496?rskey = aQy7JP&result = 2&prd = MPIL (Accessed 16 Dec. 2024); Asmelash, Henok, 'The Legacy of the SADC Tribunal in International Investment Law', in Helene Ruiz Fabri & Edoardo Stoppioni (eds), *International Investment Law: An Analysis of Major Decisions* (Hart Publishing, 2022). *See also* Konstantinos D. Magliveras and Gino J. Naldi, 'When Politics Prevail Over the Rule of Law: The Demise of the SADC Tribunal', *International Human Rights Law Review*, 10(1), 124-154 (2021)

IV SECOND INTERSECTION: PROTECTING THE ENVIRONMENT

'Trade and the environment' and 'investment and the environment' have been among the core debates in international economic law for a quarter of a century. Do international economic obligations curtail the policy space of states to the extent that they cannot take action to protect the environment?

From its first report, the World Trade Organization (WTO) Appellate Body has attempted to frame the issue in terms of prohibiting 'clinical isolation',[45] especially when dealing with exceptions: international economic law must breathe the rest of international law to communicate with non-trade values. This balancing would be the key to resolving the conflict or articulating trade commitments and non-trade requirements related to health or the environment. This approach of 'weighing and balancing'[46] has not overcome the difficulties, and the feasibility of such a balancing exercise in ISDS has been strongly criticized as the *EcoOro v. Colombia* case, for example, shows.[47]

More recently, the environmental challenge has acquired even stronger characteristics by incorporating the challenge of climate change. The much-criticized recent *Rockhopper v. Italy* case is a prime example,[48] and a particularly interesting one for our intersectionality inquiry.[49]

Rockhopper obtained an exploration licence for the Ombrina Mare field in 2005. The exploration having confirmed the presence of oil in 2008, Rockhopper applied for

https://doi.org/10.1163/22131035-01001001; Zongwe, Dunia, 'The Contribution of Campbell v. Zimbabwe to the Foreign Investment Law on Expropriations', *Comparative Research in Law & Political Economy. Research Paper No. 50/2009* (2009), https://digitalcommons.osgoode.yorku.ca/clpe/158.

45. *United States – Standards for Reformulated and Conventional Gasoline*, Panel and Appellate Body Report adopted on 20 May 1996, WT/DS2/9.
46. *European Communities – Measures Affecting Asbestos and Asbestos-Containing Products*, Appellate Body Report adopted on 5 Apr. 2001, WT/DS/135/ABR, para. 172.
47. *Eco Oro Minerals Corp. v. Republic of Colombia*, ICSID Case No. ARB/16/41, Decision on Jurisdiction, Liability and Directions on Quantum, 9 Sep. 2021. Colombia had argued that Art. 2201 of the Canada-Colombia FTA, which contains a general exception for measures 'necessary [t]o protect human, animal or plant life or health' and 'the conservation of living or non-living exhaustible natural resources', applied so as to exclude its liability to pay compensation. The majority held that Art. 2201(3) was 'permissive', in that it allowed Colombia to adopt or apply measures for the purpose of environmental conservation, provided that such measures were not arbitrary, unjustifiably discriminatory, or a disguised restriction on international investment. However, the arbitrators considered that, had the parties wished this provision to exclude the obligation to pay compensation, they would have drafted the provision in terms similar to those used in Annex 811 on decision-making powers. In the arbitrators' view, the contrary interpretation would contradict the provisions of Annex 811, 'which expressly acknowledges that in certain circumstances a measure taken for the protection of the environment may constitute indirect expropriation' (para. 831).
48. *Rockhopper Exploration Plc, Rockhopper Italia S.p.A. and Rockhopper Mediterranean Ltd v. Italian Republic*, ICSID Case No. ARB/17/14, Final Award, 23 Aug. 2022 (available at: https://jusmundi.com/en/document/decision/en-rockhopper-exploration-plc-rockhopper-italia-s-p-a-and-rockhopper-mediterranean-ltd-v-italian-republic-final-award-wednesday-24th-august-2022 (Accessed 16 Dec. 2024)) and Dissent by Pierre-Marie Dupuy.
49. Arcuri, A., 'On How the ECT Fuels the Fossil Fuel Economy: Rockhopper v Italy as a Case Study', *Europe and the World: A Law Review*, 7(1): 3, 20, (2023) https://doi.org/10.14324/111.444.ewlj.2023.03.

a production concession. This application sparked such strong protests from the local community that the national government proposed in 2010 the adoption of Law No. 128, which prohibited any new offshore drilling projects, thus potentially compromising the project's viability insofar as it was silent on its applicability to current projects. This was clarified in 2012 when an exception to the 2010 law was made for drilling projects in progress before its entry into force, with the explicit aim of avoiding potential future disputes from permit holders. The amendment could therefore have allowed the granting of the production concession to Rockhopper. However, this exemption triggered new popular protests and political tensions between the central and regional authorities, culminating in ten Italian regional councils proposing a referendum on repealing the exemption. To avoid this referendum, Law No. 208 passed in December 2015 removed the exception and therefore subjected Ombrina Mare to the ban. In the meantime, the Ministry in charge found in August 2015 that the environmental impact assessment conducted and provided by Rockhopper showed the relevant environmental provisions had been complied with. Rockhopper then applied for the final exploitation authorization which was legally supposed to be delivered within a fortnight. The Ministry kept silent until January 2016, when it found the exploitation of the site to be prohibited, in light of Law No. 208. This led directly to the rejection of Rockhopper's application.

As a result, Rockhopper started ICSID proceedings based on the Energy Charter Treaty (ECT), claiming that the denial of a licence to exploit the offshore oil field resulted in an expropriation. This case is almost a stereotype of the criticisms levelled at ISDS: on the one hand, local people are opposing fossil fuel policy, expressing environmental and climate change concerns, and democratic support to policies addressing these concerns. On the other hand, an investor claims rights under the treaty regime. Finally, a tribunal takes a very narrow view of its role.

Indeed, the tribunal took the view that Rockhopper had acquired 'the right that it would be awarded the production concession to exploit the field in Ombrina Mare'.[50] The rejection of Rockhopper's application was, therefore, an expropriatory measure. The tribunal was not convinced by Italy's police powers argument based on the use of the precautionary principle and environmental concerns. The tribunal found that the issue of a positive opinion on the environmental compatibility assessment of 7 August 2015 had ended any permissible use of the precautionary principle. The granting of the environmental compatibility decree showed that the environmental issues had already been considered and decided and that it was no longer possible to invoke environmental reasons to justify a lawful expropriation under Article 13(1)(a) to (d) of the ECT (i.e., the requirements that a sovereign must fulfil to avoid the consequences of an abusive expropriation). Moreover, the tribunal considered that 'the more likely reason for the position taken by the Respondent culminating in the letter of 29 January 2016 is the political and civic engagements as discussed earlier in this Award'.[51] In fact, the

50. *Rockhopper Exploration Plc, Rockhopper Italia S.p.A. and Rockhopper Mediterranean Ltd v. Italian Republic,* Final Award, para. 196.
51. *Rockhopper Exploration Plc, Rockhopper Italia S.p.A. and Rockhopper Mediterranean Ltd v. Italian Republic,* Final Award, para. 198.

tribunal looks like it used political tensions to disqualify environmental concerns as if these political tensions were not precisely due to environmental and climate concerns. As a result, the award held Italy internationally liable for expropriation and EUR 185 million in compensation, over EUR 240 million with interest.

How was such an outcome possible? As Antonio Marzal has insightfully deconstructed, the explanation lies in the tribunal's lack of consideration for the environmental concerns and claims of the local population, whereas we are at the heart of intersectionality. According to him, the way the tribunal conducted its reasoning shows that it considered environmental norms and concerns irrelevant to determine, from a strictly 'legal' point of view, first, whether an expropriation had occurred and, second, the amount of compensation due to the investor. Indeed, the tribunal treated these two issues as objective questions of fact, independent of any environmental considerations. It is in this regard that the decision appears, despite the efforts of the arbitrators to argue otherwise, to be deeply troubling. Turning a blind eye to the environmental dimension of the case can only lead to one result: as Marzal summarized, 'the way in which the reasoning of the Rockhopper award expels any environmental considerations has the effect of making climate change interventions considerably more costly – by increasing the scope of regulations considered to be expropriatory, and by inflating the amounts that will need to be paid in compensation'.[52]

The problematic issue of an ISDS that is deaf to environmental concerns is also reflected in the calculation of compensation, for which the tribunal opted for DCF, although the exploitation had never begun. Many authors have criticized the DCF method, which allows for what Ignaz Seidl-Hohenveldern called 'Nostradamus prophecies'[53] that do not consider values other than investment, including those concerning the future. Here, we face an interesting question for reform: it is possible to change the procedure, question the appropriateness of the DCF and strengthen the text of expropriation clauses in BITs. Would this be enough?

V THIRD INTERSECTION: INDIGENOUS POPULATIONS

Our final example concerns the role of local populations. One of the most classic criticisms of International Investment Law and ISDS is their asymmetric nature: the treaties provide special rights for investors but obligations only for the state and none for the investor. In many ways, the fact that arbitral tribunals barely listen to the actors most affected by the impact of the investment, especially in extractive activities, namely local populations, reinforces this asymmetry.

52. Marzal, Toni, 'Polluter Doesn't Pay: The Rockhopper v Italy Award', *EJIL:Talk!* (19 Jan. 2023), https://www.ejiltalk.org/polluter-doesnt-pay-the-rockhopper-v-italy-award/ (Accessed 16 Dec. 2024).

53. Seidl-Hohenveldern, Ignaz, 'L'évaluation des dommages dans les arbitrages transnationaux', *Annuaire français de droit international,* 24 (1987).

Many cases could be relevant, but we will focus on the particularly telling *Bear Creek v. Peru* case.[54] This case embodies another aspect of the encounter between international investment law and social justice: the so-called social licence. This is not a strictly legal concept. Still, it expresses the acceptance of an economic project by a local population that will bear its positive or negative impact.[55]

Bear Creek Mining Corporation, a Canadian investor, sought to invest in Peru to develop the Santa Ana silver mine near the border with Bolivia. In 2007, Bear Creek was granted authorization to acquire, own and operate the relevant mining concessions. However, local communities strongly opposed the development of the Santa Ana mine, including through violent protests.[56] Opposition to the mining project from some of the neighbouring indigenous communities arose throughout 2008-2011 due to concerns about the unequal distribution of the benefits of the project between them and the environmental effects of the project. The local population feared that the Bear Creek mining activity would negatively affect their land and, consequently, their cultural identity. While Bear Creek Mining had consulted with local communities during this period, the sufficiency of these consultations was questioned and with them whether the applicant had obtained a social licence. To deal with the social unrest, the newly elected government revoked the supreme decree granting permission for the operation, which halted the mining project.

The tribunal, established based on the Canada-Peru Free Trade Agreement in force since 1 August 2009, recognized that there had been an indirect expropriation.[57] According to the majority, 'there has been a clear economic impact', depriving the investor of all the critical rights obtained through the decree. In other words, because Bear Creek could legally do nothing with the Santa Ana project, the value of the investment had been substantially impaired,[58] and the Claimant should receive almost USD 19 million as damages.

When dealing with the social licence, the majority of the tribunal noted that 'even though the concept of "social license" is not clearly defined in international law, all relevant international instruments are clear that consultations with indigenous communities are to be made with the purpose of obtaining consent from all the relevant communities'.[59] The same majority considered that it was primarily the responsibility of host states to establish a legal framework for effective consultation processes with the local population and that 'Respondent, after its continuous approval and support of

54. *Bear Creek Mining Corporation v. Republic of Peru*, ICSID Case No. ARB/14/21, Award, 30 Nov. 2017.
55. Perrone, Nicolás M., 'The International Investment Regime and Local Populations: Are the Weakest Voices Unheard?', *TLT* 7, 383 (2016) https://doi.org/10.1080/20414005.2016.1242249; Anaya, S. James & Sergio Puig, 'Mitigating State Sovereignty: The Duty to Consult with Indigenous Peoples', *U. Toronto L.J.*, 67, 435 (2017) https://doi.org/10.3138/utlj.67.1.
56. *Bear Creek Mining Corporation v. Republic of Peru*, ICSID Case No. ARB/14/21, Award, 30 Nov. 2017, paras 190 et seq.
57. *Bear Creek Mining Corporation v. Republic of Peru*, ICSID Case No. ARB/14/21, Award, 30 Nov. 2017 (available at: https://www.italaw.com/sites/default/files/case-documents/italaw9381.pdf (Accessed 16 Dec. 2024)) and Dissent Philippe Sands (available at: https://www.italaw.com/sites/default/files/case-documents/italaw10107.pdf).
58. *Bear Creek* Award, para. 375.
59. *Bear Creek* Award, para. 406 (emphasis in the original).

Claimant's conduct, cannot in hindsight claim that this conduct was contrary to the ILO Convention 169 or was insufficient, and caused or contributed to the social unrest in the region.'[60]

In contrast, Philippe Sands, the dissenting arbitrator, argued that foreign investors also play an essential role in building the local population's trust. He contended that International Labour Organization (ILO) Convention 169, which requires states to obtain the free, prior and informed consent of indigenous peoples, also imposes an obligation on foreign investors not to engage in actions that may affect human rights and the fact that ILO Convention 169 imposes direct obligations only on states and not on foreign companies would not mean that the convention was 'without significance or legal effects' for private companies.[61] Crucially, he stressed that both foreign investors and local communities have rights under international law.

Sands concluded that a possible explanation for the adverse responses of certain communities to the investor's project could be that the investor did not engage the trust of *all* potentially affected communities. 'Different communities were treated in a different way, and ... all groups within Claimant's own identified area of influence – whether direct or indirect – were not treated in the same manner.'[62] Even if the investor was on notice of those numerous communities, it failed to take the appropriate steps to address the concerns of those communities, as not all of them were consulted, as required by ILO Convention 169.[63] However, the majority rejected this position, noting that ILO Convention 169 only imposes an obligation on states and that the local community was not a party to the investment arbitration.[64]

As Nicolas Perrone has noted, 'the international investment regime treats local communities as an absent actor. Foreign investment relations involve more than a foreign investor who wants to extract gold and a state that needs to decide whether this is environmentally acceptable. Very often, a local community is also interested in the same resources – often indigenous peoples. Locals may want to continue their current economic activities, such as agriculture or small-scale mining, and may have legal entitlements over the land. What the international investment regime does in a quiet – but effective – manner is to render invisible these local entitlements and community values'.[65]

60. Paine, Joshua, 'Bear Creek Mining Corporation v Republic of Peru, Judging the Social License of Foreign Investments and Applying New Style Investment Treaties', *ICSID Review*, 33(2), 340-348 (2018) https://doi.org/10.1093/icsidreview/siy014; Marcoux, Jean-Michel & Andrew Newcombe, 'Bear Creek Mining Corporation v Republic of Peru: Two Sides of a "Social License" to Operate', *ICSID Review*, 33(3), 653-659 (2018) https://doi.org/10.1093/icsidreview/siy020. The authors note that 'With the exception of a brief reference to the concept in *Copper Mesa v Ecuador*, the idea of a social license to operate had not appeared in any publicly available IIA arbitral decisions until Bear Creek v Peru' (p. 653). *See Copper Mesa Mining Corporation v. Republic of Ecuador*, PCA Case No. 2012-2, Award 15 Mar. 2016, para. 6.28.
61. Dissent Philippe Sands, para. 10.
62. Dissent Philippe Sands, para. 18.
63. Dissent Philippe Sands, para. 19.
64. *Bear Creek* Award, para. 666.
65. Perrone, Nicolás M., 'The "Invisible" Local Communities: Foreign Investor Obligations, Inclusiveness, and the International Investment Regime', *AJIL Unbound*, 113, 16 (2019) https://doi.org/10.1017/aju.2018.92.

The intersectional aspect is prominent, but are the paths shown by Philipp Sands sufficient to change the posture of ISDS? Tribunals have started changing their attitude towards third parties and opening to *amici curiae*.[66] More rarely, some states have brought counterclaims,[67] and some tribunals have started recognizing investors' obligations[68] or working on due diligence duties. Policymakers are introducing investors' obligations in BITs.[69]

Is this enough to tackle all these problems holistically? In a context where the traditional architecture of the system already makes it complicated to conceptualize the (bilateral) relationship between investment and human rights or other so-called non-investment values, how to deal with the more complex human rights scenarios of indigenous peoples whose ancestral worldview is axiologically diametrically different? More generally, and here, we circle back to our starting point, how to legally think of nature as not only a reservoir of available resources that can be appropriated. Who bears the duty of care?

VI CONCLUSION

The discourses on reform show that considering criticisms of international investment law and ISDS is variable. Some issues are taken more seriously than others. Procedural changes are perceived as generally more accessible, as it is easier to change a seemingly technical framework than to address problems holistically.

Intersectionality has shown all the limits of a law that functions based on a 'single-axis framework', as it ignores the complexity of reality by limiting enquiry to the experiences of otherwise privileged members of the group. Therefore, an intersectional approach calls for deconstructing and critiquing the methods ISDS has built to

66. Think of *Methanex Corporation v. United States of America, UNCITRAL,* (Decision on Authority to Accept Amicus Submissions, 25 Jan. 2001, https://www.italaw.com/sites/default/files/case-documents/italaw9106.pdf (Accessed 16 Dec. 2024)) and the following case law on the topic. Bernasconi-Osterwalder, Nathalie & Lise Johnson, *International Investment Law and Sustainable Development: Key Cases from 2000-2010,* IISD ebook, 2011, 83-84 (available at: https://www.iisd.org/system/files/publications/investment-law-sustainable-development-ten-cases-2010s.pdf (Accessed 16 Dec. 2024)).
67. Think of *Burlington Resources Inc. v. Republic of Ecuador*, ICSID Case No. ARB/08/5, Decision on Ecuador's Counterclaims, 7 Feb. 2017, https://www.italaw.com/sites/default/files/case-documents/italaw8206.pdf (Accessed 16 Dec. 2024).
68. Think, for example, of *Urbaser S.A. and Consorcio de Aguas Bilbao Bizkaia, Bilbao Biskaia Ur Partzuergoa v. The Argentine Republic*, ICSID Case No. ARB/07/26 (http://www.italaw.com/cases/1144 (Accessed 16 Dec. 2024)). As noted by Stefanie Schacherer, the award 'points to the distinction between negative and positive obligations investors. Negative obligations require the investor not to violate human rights, whereas positive obligations require a positive (proactive) action by the investor to ensure that the local population enjoys its human rights. The *Urbaser* case moves in the direction of a positive obligation for investors to ensure an effective right to water, although in the specific case, the tribunal found that there was no international law basis for the investor's positive obligation on the right to water'. In Bernasconi-Osterwalder, Nathalie, Martin Dietrich Brauch & Stefanie Schacherer, *International Investment Law and Sustainable Development: Key Cases from the 2010s,* IISD ebook, 2018, 26.
69. Thus, the Protocol to the Agreement Establishing the African Continental Free Trade Area on Investment includes Chapter 5 on Investor Obligations. *See* at: https://edit.wti.org/document/show/e5d51824-c467-4e24-922b-3fb376d89550 (Accessed 16 Dec. 2024).

reconstruct its own idiom of complex social realities. Indeed, the single-axis framework entails a precise vehiculation of power within the legal system and the silencing of those voices set at the margins.

However, a growing number of new voices argue that the perspective needs to be reversed. In a 2017 report, the ILO already highlighted that indigenous peoples[70] are strongly affected by climate change and the policies that address it.[71] But it also suggested that indigenous peoples should be seen not only as victims but also as agents of change.[72] From victims to change agents: this should not only be a slogan. However, are we ready to listen seriously to all voices calling for reform to achieve real change?

70. Puig, Sergio, *At the Margins of Globalization* (CUP, 2021).
71. Maestrini, Eugenia, 'Kiruna, Mining and Reindeer: How Sami Communities Are Paying the Price for the Green Transition', 7 Mar. 2023, at: https://www.theperspective.se (Accessed 16 Dec. 2024).
72. ILO (International Labour Organization), *Indigenous Peoples and Climate Change: From Victims to Change Agents through Decent Work* (2017), ix: 'In order for climate action to be successful, indigenous peoples must be seen as powerful agents of change, accorded access to decent work opportunities and the ability to participate in the development, implementation and evaluation of sustainable policies and measures aimed at combating climate change.'

CHAPTER 3

The International Judicial Function: Criticisms and Corrective Mechanisms

Laurence Boisson de Chazournes, Lorenzo Palestini, Guillaume Guez Maillard & Aditya Laddha[*]

Having reached its zenith at the beginning of the twenty-first century, the international judicial function is now confronted with the swing of the pendulum, evidenced by various manoeuvres that hinder international dispute settlement mechanisms, such as the World Trade Organization (WTO) Appellate Body. While contemporary research has addressed 'backlash' from a multidisciplinary perspective, this chapter considers whether adjudicators of universal State-to-State mechanisms share part of the blame. By looking at alleged instances of judicial overreach and proposed corrective mechanisms, it examines whether there is a correlation between backlash and the way the judicial function is exercised. The chapter also explores the role of increased dialogue between actors and beneficiaries in informal processes, such as the 'Walker' process. The purpose is to provide insights into the boundaries of the international judicial function and what constitutes interference in the exercise of that function.

I INTRODUCTION

To investigate the international judicial function is to study the heart of dispute settlement mechanisms. If one takes a down-to-earth approach centred on the separation of

* This chapter has been prepared in the framework of the research project – '*The International Judicial Function under Pressure: Do Courts and Tribunals Go Off the Rails?*' – financed by the Swiss National Science Foundation (https://data.snf.ch/grants/grant/204724) (accessed 16 Dec. 2024). The authors would like to express their gratitude to the research assistants, Ms Aparna Nagabhushana and Mr Eduardo Cavalcanti de Mello Filho, for their valuable contribution to the Project.

powers, adjudicators are here to interpret and apply the law mechanically. They are essentially *dispute-settlers*, relieved from broader responsibilities vis-à-vis the parties and non-parties to the procedure.[1] While this view accounts for an important aspect of the international judicial function, a more nuanced approach suggests that adjudicators are also community servants.[2] For Sir Gerald Fitzmaurice, adjudicators should notably 'make general pronouncements of law and principle that might enrich and develop the law'.[3] However, as stated by Sir Robert Jennings, 'development' should only be 'incidental' to the disposal of the case since the 'strength' of jurisprudence precisely rests in that 'it arises from actual situations'.[4] In fact, the further adjudicators move away from concrete disputes to hypothetical scenarios, the closer they inevitably get to the legislative function rather than the judicial one. The further they move away from the facts of a given case, the greater they run the risk of being perceived as having exceeded their mandate, especially if they strayed into non-essential reasoning.

Today, the judicialisation of international relations is sometimes met with reluctance. The international judicial function is under attack from its makers, the sovereigns that now question the work of various dispute settlement mechanisms. While contemporary multidisciplinary projects aim to address backlash against international courts and tribunals through the lenses of legitimacy and effectiveness, they have analysed neither the concrete criticisms raised against the exercise of the judicial function nor whether the corrective devices go too far and end up affecting essential features of that function. Against this background, the research project on which this chapter is based conducted a comprehensive study of the criticisms and corrective mechanisms involved. In doing so, it sought to answer two questions. What are the boundaries of the international judicial function and what constitutes interference in the exercise of that function? In exploring these questions, the research project relied on qualitative mixed methods and, in particular, comparative approaches. The project looked at the international judicial function in a *horizontal* manner, focussing on universal state-to-state dispute settlement mechanisms, such as the International Court of Justice (ICJ) and the World Trade Organization (WTO) dispute settlement system. The project also considered regional or private-to-state mechanisms when they provided insights into specific criticisms and corrective mechanisms relevant to universal state-to-state mechanisms.

Section II delves into specific criticisms, selected from a wide range of criticisms gathered through the research project, which relate to the *non ultra* and *non infra petita* principles, the importance of reasoning in decision-making and matters of jurisdiction in cases involving incidental issues. Section III takes stock of corrective devices such as authentic interpretation and interim reviews in the decision-making

1. Speech of H.E. Judge Donoghue, *The Roles of International Judge and Foreign Ministry Lawyer*, 29 Oct. 2021, https://www.icj-cij.org/sites/default/files/press-releases/0/000-20211029-PRE-01-00-EN.pdf (accessed 16 Dec. 2024).
2. F. Zarbiyev, *Judicial Activism in International Law: A Conceptual Framework for Analysis*, 3(2) JIDS 247, 254 (2012) https://doi.org/10.1093/jnlids/ids005.
3. G. Fitzmaurice, *Hersch Lauterpacht: The Scholar as Judge*, 37 BYIL 1, 14-15 (1961).
4. R. Jennings, *The Role of the International Court of Justice*, 68(1) BYIL 1, 41(1997) https://doi.org/10.1093/bybil/68.1.1.

process. Section IV provides concluding remarks on the delicate balance of international judicial function, emphasising the need for ongoing dialogue in the reform process. The chapter seeks to contribute to a more nuanced understanding of the delicate balance that international adjudicators must maintain. An examination of the international judicial function, which stands as an equal counterpart of the international arbitral function, could offer valuable ideas for the reform process within international arbitration.

II PROPER EXERCISE OF AND OVERREACHING IN THE JUDICIAL FUNCTION

This section examines three controversial questions in international litigation that either constitute instances of judicial overreach or amount to exercising the judicial function on the verge of overreach. To locate the edge separating the proper from the improper is essentially to find the right balance between the autonomy vested in judicial function and the countervailing constraints exerted on that function.

A Looking Past the Submissions of the Parties: Reshaping the Dispute

Aside from the matter of jurisdiction, which in the international field depends on the willingness of sovereigns to consent to adjudication, one should not forget that, in theory, international courts and tribunals must reply to the submissions raised by the parties, as well as abstain from deciding issues that were not referred to in those submissions.[5] According to Hugh Thirlway, adjudicators are not so much seised of disputes as they are seised of formal submissions relating to specific aspects of what are often much wider disputes.[6] This brings into focus a crucial aspect of adjudication: whether courts and tribunals can ignore, modify and eventually add to the submissions raised by the parties.

Two procedural principles, derived from Roman law, appear to restrain the freedom of adjudicators. The principles of *non ultra* and *non infra petita* underscore the confined mandate of courts and tribunals. These principles reflect the constraint that the parties to the proceedings exert on the judicial function.[7] Yet, there is another principle, likewise derived from Roman law, which counteracts the two. By relying on the maxim of *jura novit curia*, international courts and tribunals have asserted their

5. *Request for interpretation of the Judgment of November 20th, 1950, in the asylum case, Judgment of November 27th, 1950: I.C.J. Reports 1950, p. 395*, 402; *Compañía de Aguas del Aconquija and Vivendi Universal v. Argentina*, ICSID Case No. ARB/97/3, Decision on Annulment of 3 Jul. 2002, § 86.
6. H. Thirlway, *The Law and Procedure of the International Court of Justice: Fifty Years of Jurisprudence*, 776 (OUP 2013).
7. A. Tanzi, *On Judicial Autonomy and the Autonomy of the Parties in International Adjudication, with Special Regard to Investment Arbitration and ICSID Annulment Proceedings*, 33(1) LJIL 57, 60 (2020) https://doi.org/10.1017/s0922156519000554.

autonomy by addressing legal questions not presented by the parties to the proceedings.[8] The interplay between, on the one hand, the *non ultra* and *non infra petita* principles and, on the other hand, the *jura novit curia* principle is fundamental for the purpose of identifying the boundaries of the judicial function. Whenever a court or tribunal has failed to live by the instructions given by the parties, whenever it has departed from their submissions or terms of reference, the presumption to be eventually rebutted is that of overreach.[9] The jurisprudence, however, is far from consistent.

The ICJ has on occasions shown restraint and at times displayed significant autonomy. In the *Arrest Warrant of 11 April 2000* case, the ICJ ultimately accepted the Democratic Republic of Congo's (DRC's) decision to withdraw its submission concerning the alleged unlawful exercise of universal jurisdiction by Belgium. This display of self-restraint is rendered conspicuous by the fact that the remaining submission related to the immunity of the DRC's foreign minister could not arise 'as a matter of logic', absent the previous establishment of Belgium's criminal jurisdiction.[10] By not addressing the logically anterior question that could have rendered the immunity debate moot, the ICJ chose to base its decision on a mere assumption, thus sacrificing legal rigour to satisfy the will of the parties. Yet the ICJ took an altogether different approach in the *Nuclear Tests* cases brought against France. Although New Zealand and Australia had explicitly requested a finding that the nuclear tests were unlawful, the ICJ instead chose to substitute the applicants' determination of what they wanted to achieve with its own appreciation of their 'ultimate objective'.[11] By reshaping the dispute into one exclusively aimed at obtaining the cessation of the nuclear tests, the ICJ dodged the controversial matter of the legality of the tests that had already occurred. While in the first case the ICJ relied on *non ultra petita* to justify its perhaps overly cautious attitude,[12] its display of judicial autonomy in the latter cases verges on judicial overreach since the ICJ arguably departed from the *non infra petita* principle.

Arbitration also attests to different approaches. The *case concerning the location of boundary markers in Taba between Egypt and Israel* exemplifies judicial restraint. Here, the Arbitral Tribunal was faced with a *compromis* that prevented it from selecting locations for the disputed markers other than those advanced by the parties to the proceedings.[13] When it became clear that the location of the final pillar did not coincide

8. *See* criticism made by South Korea on ruling on matters not requested in *WTO DSB Minutes of Meeting*, WT/DSB/M/428, 26 Apr. 2019, para. 9.2.
9. The WTO Panel and Appellate Body reports have been criticised, during the Dispute Settlement Body meetings wherein the reports were put to adoption, for having made observations on points not raised during hearings nor argued by the parties. *See*, for instance, New Zealand's statement in *Canada – Measures affecting the importation of milk and the exportation of dairy products: Recourse to Article 21.5 of the DSU by New Zealand and the United States, Appellate Body Report, WT/DS103/AB/RW – WT/DS113/AB/RW and Panel Report, WT/DS103/RW – WT/DS113/AB/RW*, in *WTO DSB Minutes of Meeting*, WT/DSB/M/116, 18 Dec. 2001, para. 40.
10. *Arrest Warrant of 11 April 2000 (Democratic Republic of the Congo v. Belgium), Judgment, I.C.J. Reports 2002, p. 3*, 19, § 46.
11. *Nuclear Tests (Australia v. France), Judgment, I.C.J. Reports 1974, p. 253*, 263, § 30; *Nuclear Tests (New Zealand v. France), Judgment, I.C.J Reports 1974, p. 457*, 467, § 31.
12. *Arrest Warrant of 11 April 2000, supra* n. 10, 18, § 43.
13. *Case concerning the location of boundary markers in Taba between Egypt and Israel, Decision of 29 September 1988*, XX (Part I) R.I.A.A 3, 45-46, § 176.

with the points advanced by either party,[14] the Tribunal considered that it was nevertheless unable to retain the correct position. It thus sided with Egypt, that is, the less mistaken of the two parties. This raises the question of whether there should be limits to *non ultra petita*. For, as rightly observed by Sir Gerald Fitzmaurice, the rule may indeed 'hamper the tribunal in coming to a correct decision, and might even cause it to arrive at a legally incorrect one'.[15] This precedent should be compared to the award rendered in the *British and American Northeastern territories* case in which the Arbitrator chose a line different from those put forward by the parties to the proceedings.[16] This award shows a measure of activism in so far as the adjudicator appears to have gone beyond its mandate.[17]

In the field of investor-state arbitration, having specific regard to International Centre for Settlement of Investment Disputes (ICSID), the principles of *non infra* and *non ultra petita* are under scrutiny due to the existence of an annulment procedure for invalidating awards. While manifest excess of power is often invoked before annulment committees, the principle of *jura novit arbiter* is well established in jurisprudence.[18] However, the question arises as to whether the principle is overtaken by the right of the parties to be heard on every matter that is raised *proprio motu* from the bench.

B Poor and Non-essential Reasoning: Straddling Between Too Little and Too Much

Reasoning is another aspect of decision-making that requires further scrutiny when investigating the scope of the international judicial function. Failure to state reasons is one of the recognised grounds for challenging the validity of judgments and awards.[19]

14. *Ibid.*, 58-67, §§ 214-245.
15. G. Fitzmaurice, *The Law and Procedure of the International Court of Justice, 1951-4: Questions of Jurisdiction, Competence and Procedure*, 34 BYIL 1, 103-104 (1958). *See also*, A. Orakhelashvili, *The International Court and Its Freedom to Select the Ground upon Which It Will Base Its Judgment*, 56(1) ICLQ 171, 177 (2007) https://doi.org/10.1093/iclq/lei155; P. Weil, *Some Observations on the Arbitral Award in the Taba Case*, 23(1) Isr. Law Rev 1, 23 (1989) https://doi.org/10.1017/s0021223700009523.
16. *Arbitral award relating to the boundaries of British and American Northeastern territories, Decision of 10 January 1831*, XXVIII (Part V) R.I.A.A 33, 37-44. *See also*, *Dispute between Argentina and Chile concerning the Beagle Channel (18.02.1977)*, exchange of diplomatic notes concerning the awards, XX1 (Part II) R.I.A.A 53, 232.
17. *See* K.H. Kaikobad, *The Quality of Justice: 'Excès de Pouvoir' in the Adjudication and Arbitration of Territorial and Boundary Disputes*, 296-297 and 299-302 in G.S. Goodwin-Gill & S. Talmon (eds), *The Reality of International Law: Essays in Honour of Ian Brownlie* (OUP 1999).
18. Tanzi, *supra* n. 7; C. Schreuer, *Three Generations of Annulment Procedures*, 30 in E. Gaillard & Y. Banifatemi (eds), *Annulment of ICSID Awards* (Stämpfli 2004); J. Paulsson, *International Arbitration and the Generation of Legal Norms: Treaty Arbitration and International Law*, 879 in A. Jan van den Berg (ed.), *International Arbitration 2006: Back to the Basics?* (Wolters Kluwer 2007).
19. *See*, Art. 35(c) of the '*Model Rules on Arbitral Procedure with a General Commentary*', II ILC Ybk 83,86 (1958); *See*, criticisms made by European Union (EU) on poor reasoning in *WTO DSB Minutes of Meeting*, WT/DSB/M/257, 21 Oct. 2008, para. 55; Turkey on insufficient legal analysis in *WTO DSB Minutes of Meeting*, WT/DSB/M/465, 31 May 2022, para. 3.2; EC on failure to address arguments in *WTO DSB Minutes of Meeting*, WT/DSB/M 189, 19 May 2005, para. 69.

Yet, what is often criticised today is the prolixity of courts and tribunals or, in other words, their propensity to address legal issues that are not indispensable for the settling of disputes. The concern is not so much with overly elliptical reasoning but rather with *excessive reasoning* and the judge-made law aftertaste that comes with it. Unlike those who trust courts to be agents for the development of international law,[20] many believe today that obiter dicta are symptoms of bad decision-making, while judicial economy is always to be praised. The principle of *judicial economy* requires adjudicators to address only those issues that are of more direct and conclusive relevance for the resolution of a case. The problem is that when parties have included multiple submissions in their pleadings, the principle frequently appears to collide with that of *non infra petita*. International courts and tribunals are indeed faced with what appears to be an intractable problem. Failure to address certain submissions might constitute an excess of power. Yet to embark on submissions that have become superfluous may entail straying into non-essentials, another alleged symptom of judicial overreach.[21]

Article 17(12) of the WTO Dispute Settlement Understanding highlights the tension between these two constraints. This provision requires the Appellate Body to address 'each' of the legal issues covered in a Panel's report. Until recently, the provision was supposedly interpreted in a strict manner that did away with judicial economy. The Appellate Body often addressed every legal issue including those that had become irrelevant.[22] Today, departure from the principle of *non infra petita* is sometimes perceived positively, especially when the dispute has been resolved based on distinct legal arguments.[23] The question that arises is whether departure from *non infra petita* can be justified by reasons of judicial economy. In other words, when a submission has truly become irrelevant, is adherence to *non infra petita* more problematic than departure from that principle?

The ICJ took no shortcuts in the *Oil Platforms* case but instead did something rather uneconomical and extraordinary. Relying on its alleged 'freedom to select the ground upon which it (can) base its judgment',[24] it decided to begin its examination with the USA's defence based on essential security interests. In other words, it ruled on self-defence without previously having checked whether that state had committed a wrongful act in the first place. According to former Judge Kooijmans, we are faced with 'an upsurge of misplaced activism' and the first ever '*obiter dictum*' to have 'found a

20. *See*, for instance, remarks made by States in relation to the role of ICJ in the development of law before the United Nations General Assembly: Singapore and Senegal, A/65/PV.38 (UNGA), 28 Oct. 2010; India, A/77/PV.27 (UNGA), 2 Nov. 2022, 5; Chile, A/72/PV.34 (UNGA), 26 Oct. 2017, 19-20; USA, A/68/PV.41 (UNGA), 31 Oct. 2013, 16.
21. F.M. Palombino, *Judicial Economy and Limitation of the Scope of the Decision in International Adjudication*, 23(4) LJIL 909, 926 (2010) https://doi.org/10.1017/s0922156510000476.
22. A. Alvarez-Jiménez, *The WTO Appellate Body's Exercise of Judicial Economy*, 12(2) JIEL 393 (2009) https://doi.org/10.1093/jiel/jgp010; *see* remarks made by USA in *WTO DSB Minutes of Meeting*, WT/DSB/M 379, 23 May 2016, paras 6.4-6.6.
23. *United States – Subsidies on Upland Cotton (US – Upland Cotton)*, Appellate Body Report, WT/DS267/AB/R, 3 Mar. 2005, §§ 510-511.
24. *Oil Platforms (Islamic Republic of Iran v. United States of America), Judgment, I.C.J. Reports 2003*, p. 161, 180, § 37.

place in the operative part of a judgment'.[25] What is striking is that had the ICJ followed the logical order, there would have been no need to assess self-defence since the court later found that the respondent had not breached the rights of Iran under the Treaty of Amity. Could it be that the ICJ chose to go beyond the dispute-settler model to expose its view regarding the prohibition of the use of force in international relations? Whether such displays of autonomy are compatible with the judicial function is a controversial question.

C Indispensable Issues and Applicable Law: Broadening the Scope of Subject Matter Jurisdiction

Most international courts and tribunals are entrusted with specific subject matter jurisdiction, i.e., jurisdiction limited to a single treaty or set of interrelated instruments. In fact, even courts that have been assigned with general jurisdiction encompassing a wide array of subject matters are often faced with reservations and other limitations that significantly reduce the set of issues that can be brought to litigation. Thus, jurisdiction is not all encompassing but usually limited to definite matters. Yet, disputes rarely fit into neatly assorted compartments. Confronted with instances of so-called mixed disputes,[26] adjudicators have drawn different lines for judicial over-reach. While some have tried to evaluate 'where... the weight of the dispute lies',[27] others have verified whether ruling on a submission would first entail addressing an indispensable incidental issue located beyond the scope of their jurisdiction.[28] Which of the two ways is the appropriate approach and, ultimately, can adjudicators hide behind the proper exercise of the judicial function to justify the expansion of their jurisdiction? The reaction of China following the *South China Sea Arbitration* serves as a notable example illustrating the potential for strong responses when States consider that jurisdiction is expanded beyond its perceived limit.[29]

The debate is particularly relevant before the dispute settlement mechanisms referred to in the United Nations Convention on the Law of the Sea (UNCLOS). In recent years, the International Tribunal for the Law of the Sea (ITLOS) and several arbitral tribunals established in accordance with this convention have been seised of

25. P. Kooijmans, *The ICJ in the 21st Century: Judicial Restraint, Judicial Activism, or Proactive Judicial Policy*, 56(4) ICLQ 741, 752 (2007) https://doi.org/10.1093/iclq/lei223. *See also, Oil Platforms (Islamic Republic of Iran v. United States of America), Judgment, I.C.J. Reports 2003*, p. 161, *Separate Opinion of Judge Higgins*, 225.
26. W. Qu, *The Issue of Jurisdiction over Mixed Disputes in The Chagos Marine Protection Area Arbitration and Beyond*, 47(1) ODIL 40 (2016) https://doi.org/10.1080/00908320.2016.1124484; Stefan Talmon, *The Chagos Marine Protected Area Arbitration: Expansion of the Jurisdiction of UNCLOS Part XV Courts and Tribunals*, 65(4) ICLQ 927, 946 (2016) https://doi.org/10.1017/s0020589316000403.
27. *The Chagos Marine Protected Area Arbitration (Republic of Mauritius v. United Kingdom of Great Britain and Northern Ireland)*, PCA 2011-03, Award of 18 Mar. 2015, §§ 211 and 229.
28. *The South China Sea Arbitration (Republic of the Philippines v. People's Republic of China)*, PCA 2013-19, Award of 29 Oct. 2015, § 153.
29. *See* China's statement before the United Nations General Assembly, A/75/PV.39 (UNGA), 8 Dec. 2020.

disputes that spilled over into fields other than the law of sea, such as human rights,[30] use of force[31] and land territorial disputes.[32] In the *Dispute Concerning Coastal State Rights in the Black Sea, Sea of Azov, and Kerch Strait,* in addition to UNCLOS rights, questions of sovereignty over Crimea were also at stake.[33] The tribunal adopted a strict test, looking at whether the 'implicated issue' constituted an *indispensable prerequisite* for addressing the law of the sea-related aspects of the case.[34] The Appellate Body of the WTO has also shown restraint in similar circumstances. In *Tax Measures on Soft Drinks and Other Beverages*, Mexico argued that its breach of WTO obligations was justified since the USA had previously breached its obligations under North American Free Trade Agreement (NAFTA). The Appellate Body refused to consider Mexico's argument, explaining that to do so it would have had to look beyond the covered agreements, thus becoming an adjudicator of non-WTO disputes.[35]

In contrast, the *'Enrica Lexie' Incident* case favoured a more lenient approach. In this case, an arbitral tribunal was again faced with a claim located on the brink of UNCLOS, namely the Italian submission, according to which India had violated the immunity of its marines by asserting criminal jurisdiction over them. In addressing this issue, the tribunal considered whether 'the issue of the entitlement to exercise jurisdiction over the incident', which divided Italy and India, could 'be satisfactorily answered without addressing the question of the immunity of the Marines'.[36] It then explained that, in order to provide a 'complete answer' to the question posed by the parties, the Tribunal had to examine incidentally whether the marines enjoyed immunity.[37] While the first decision shows signs of restraint from the tribunal, the latter might well constitute an instance of judicial overreach, a precedent in which adjudicators relied on considerations about the judicial function to broaden the extent of their material jurisdiction. It is however interesting to note that Italy and India did not consider these observations as judicial overreach. They both welcomed and accepted the decision.[38]

30. *Arctic Sunrise Arbitration (The Netherlands v. Russian Federation)*, PCA 2014-02, Award of 15 Aug. 2015.
31. *M/V 'Saiga' (No. 2) (Saint Vincent and the Grenadines v. Guinea)*, Judgment, ITLOS Reports 1999, 10; *M/V 'Virginia G' (Panama/Guinea-Bissau)*, Judgment, ITLOS Reports 2014, 4; *Guyana v. Suriname*, PCA 2004-04, Award of 17 Sep. 2007.
32. *The Chagos Marine Protected Area Arbitration, supra* n. 27; *The South China Sea Arbitration, supra* n. 28; *Dispute Concerning Coastal State Rights in the Black Sea, Sea of Azov, and Kerch Strait (Ukraine v. Russian Federation)*, Award of 21 Feb. 2020.
33. *Dispute Concerning Coastal State Rights in the Black Sea, Sea of Azov, and Kerch Strait*, Award of 21 Feb. 2020, §§ 43-198 and 492(a).
34. *Ibid.*, §154. This strict test was appreciated by Russia as the Tribunal considered its main argument that the dispute was in fact around Ukraine's sovereign claim over Crimea. *See Press release on the decision of The Hague Arbitration Court concerning coastal state rights in the case of Ukraine v. the Russian Federation,* Russian Ministry of Foreign Affairs, 22 Feb. 2020, https://mid.ru/en/foreign_policy/international_safety/1427934/ (accessed 16 Dec. 2024).
35. *Mexico-Tax Measures on Soft Drinks and Other Beverages,* Appellate Body Report, WT/DS308/AB/R, § 78.
36. *The 'Enrica Lexie' Incident (Italian Republic v. Republic of India)*, PCA 2015-28, Award of 21 May 2020, § 805.
37. *Ibid.*, § 808.
38. *Will accept tribunal ruling in marines case, Centre tells SC*, 4 Jul. 2020, https://www.thehindu.com/news/national/will-accept-tribunal-ruling-in-marines-case-centre-tells-sc/article31984

The extent of subject matter jurisdiction becomes more ambiguous when relevant treaties include broad references to international law in the provisions relating to the law to be applied by the settlement mechanisms.[39] Articles such as 293(1) of UNCLOS, which states that judges and arbitrators must apply this treaty and 'other rules of international law not incompatible with this convention', raise a question that begs to be answered: can adjudicators rely on applicable law to expand their jurisdiction? To answer negatively is to favour self-restraint. Considering that the case law is rather inconsistent,[40] it is not clear whether positive answers may be regarded necessarily as indicators of judicial overreach.

III CORRECTIVE MECHANISMS AND INTERFERENCE IN THE JUDICIAL FUNCTION

Having addressed three potential instances of judicial overreach, this section turns to examine two corrective mechanisms that either constitute apposite instruments of state control or interferences in the exercise of the judicial function by adjudicators. The case law referred to in these sub-sections is merely illustrative of the many legal issues involved.

A Authentic Interpretations: Confining the Judicial Interpretative Freedom

Through authentic interpretations, State parties to international agreements attempt to maintain or reassert control over nothing less than the content of relevant rules of international law. In practice, authentic interpretative notes or declarations are often used to remind adjudicators that theirs, unlike the authority withheld by treaty-makers, is merely a *delegated* form of interpretative authority. The main difficulties arise when authentic interpretations are used alongside judicial or arbitral proceedings, either to pre-emptively forestall undesirable judicial outcomes or to 'counteract unwelcome interpretative developments'.[41] As such, authentic interpretations raise difficult questions concerning the interplay between the rights of State parties to the treaty and the exercise of judicial function, and in particular, about the limits separating this corrective mechanism from interference with that function.

922.ece (accessed 16 Dec. 2024); *Enrica Lexie*, Italian Ministry of Foreign Affairs, 2 Jul. 2020 https://www.esteri.it/en/sala_stampa/archivionotizie/comunicati/2020/07/caso-enrica-lexie/ (accessed 16 Dec. 2024).

39. P. Tzeng, *Jurisdiction and Applicable Law under UNCLOS*, 126(1) YLJ 242 (2016); M. Forteau, *Regulating the Competition Between International Courts and Tribunals: The Role of Ratione Materiae Jurisdiction under Part XV of UNCLOS*, LPICT 190 (2016); M. Wood, *The International Tribunal for the Law of the Sea and General International Law*, 22(3) Int J Mar Coast Law 351 (2007) https://doi.org/10.1163/157180807781870345.
40. *Guyana v. Suriname*, *supra* n. 31, §§ 402-452 and 488(2); *Arctic Sunrise Arbitration*, *supra* n. 30, §§ 187-198 and 192.
41. K. Berner, *Authentic Interpretation in International Law*, 76 ZaöRV 845, 877 (2016); G. Zarra, *Uses and Abused of Authentic Interpretations of International Investment Agreements: Reflections on the Role of Arbitral Tribunals as Masters of the Judicial Function*, EJIL: Talk!, 28 Aug.

Under Article 31.3(a) of the Vienna Convention on the Law of Treaties, the interpreter must 'take into account … any subsequent agreement between the parties regarding the interpretation of the treaty or the application of its provisions'. The question then arises as to whether adjudicators are bound by authentic interpretations. For instance, in the *Dispute between Argentina and Chile concerning the Beagle Channel*, Argentina's main contention was that the arbitrators did not consider the 1893 Protocol, accepted by both Argentina and Chile, to have 'supplemented and clarified the 1881 Treaty' and as an 'authentic interpretation' of the said treaty in determining the territorial and maritime boundaries.[42] Interestingly, the International Law Commission explained that subsequent agreements do not 'necessarily possess a conclusive effect'.[43] Yet, if the purpose of interpretation is to discover the intention of the parties, it may be difficult to accept that arbitrators can substitute their own assessment of that intention for that expressly stated by the parties in their interpretative notes. This is especially so if the treaty to be interpreted expressly provides that the authentic interpretation 'shall be binding'.[44]

Another closely related issue is that of time.[45] If authentic interpretations are considered to bind the courts and tribunals not only for the future but also upon their issuance and, therefore, to already pending proceedings, there is a risk of interference with the exercise of the judicial function. Thus, States could impose an interpretation favourable to them to change the fate of a case. To prevent this, some instruments, such as the 2019 Netherlands Model bilateral investment treaty (BIT), suggest that authentic interpretations shall only bind arbitral tribunals that are established after the issuance of such interpretations. In this way, these instruments effectively shield tribunals from outside interference.

In some cases, authentic interpretations may conceal treaty amendments. Concealed amendments mark the dividing line between genuine corrective mechanisms and unacceptable interferences in the exercise of the judicial function. Yet, the dividing line is often blurred, as stressed by Article IX(2) of the Agreement establishing the WTO, which states that the interpretation procedure 'shall not be used in a manner that would undermine the amendment provisions'. Can adjudicators sanction such violations of amendment procedures, or must they accept these changes of rules as if they were authentic interpretations? In particular, where such concealed amendments occur

2020, https://www.ejiltalk.org/uses-and-abuses-of-authentic-interpretations-of-international-investment-agreements-reflections-on-the-role-of-arbitral-tribunals-as-masters-of-the-judicial-function/ (accessed 16 Dec. 2024); A. Roberts, *Power and Persuasion in Investment Treaty Interpretation: The Dual Role of States*, 104 AJIL 179 (2010) https://doi.org/10.5305/amerjintelaw.104.2.0179.

42. *Dispute Between Argentina and Chile concerning the Beagle Channel (18.02.1977)*, *supra* n. 16, 233.
43. United Nations, *Report of the International Law Commission*, 70th session (2018), UN Doc. A/73/10, 24, § 4, https://legal.un.org/ilc/reports/2018/english/a_73_10_advance.pdf (accessed 16 Dec. 2024).
44. *See, e.g.*, Art. 14.D.9 of the United States-Mexico-Canada Agreement (30 Sep. 2018).
45. C. Titi, *The Timing of Treaty Party Interpretation*, EJIL: Talk!, 18 Aug. 2020, https://www.ejiltalk.org/the-timing-of-treaty-party-interpretations/ (accessed 16 Dec. 2024).

in the course of judicial or arbitral proceedings, how should international courts and tribunals react to such interferences?

These issues take on even greater importance in the field of investor-state arbitration, where the parties to the dispute do not coincide with the parties to the bilateral or multilateral investment treaty to be interpreted. The NAFTA Free Trade Commission's interpretative note of 20 April 2001 is a case in point. This note was intended, *inter alia*, to correct the finding of an award that the fair and equitable treatment standard enshrined in Article 1105 NAFTA required treatment in addition to or beyond the minimum standard of treatment of aliens provided under customary international law. Its reception by the arbitral tribunals was the subject of opposed reactions. In *Pope & Talbot Incorporated v. Canada*, the tribunal strongly criticised the Commission's note. It asserted that the Commission had in fact acted *ultra vires* and that its note was not an authentic interpretation but rather a disguised amendment that could not retroactively affect its previous decision.[46] In contrast, the tribunal in *ADF Group Incorporated v. USA* explained that a NAFTA Chapter 11 tribunal cannot determine for itself whether a 'document submitted to it as an interpretation by the parties ... is an "amendment"'.[47] In essence, these two cases reveal different conceptions of the autonomy of adjudicators confronted with authentic interpretations.

B Interim Reviews: Supervising the Decision-Making Process

In the field of international dispute settlement and, in particular, international trade dispute settlement, interim reviews provide State parties to a dispute with a last opportunity to influence the outcome of the proceedings. Confronted with interim reports that explicitly divulge the content of the decisions, parties are given a final occasion to comment upon the findings reached by the adjudicators. The process is ordinarily innocuous for the dispute settlement mechanism tasked with resolving the dispute. Indeed, when comments to interim reports aim only at rectifying the factual record, the procedure promotes the sound administration of justice while posing little threat to the independence of the dispute settlement mechanism. The situation, however, becomes thorny when, this close to the finish line, parties introduce new evidence and arguments or otherwise challenge the conclusions of the adjudicators.[48]

Before the WTO dispute settlement mechanism, the terms of the debate have suddenly changed since the beginning of the Appellate Body's crisis. Previously, some wished to remove interim reviews altogether, while others, including the USA and Chile,[49] suggested that these reviews should also be provided at the appeal stage. This

46. *Pope & Talbot Incorporated v. Canada*, Ad Hoc Tribunal (UNCITRAL), Award on Damages of 31 May 2002, § 47.
47. *ADF Group Incorporated v. United States*, ICSID Case No. ARB(AF)/00/1, Award of 9 Jan. 2003, § 177.
48. A. Steinbach, *The DSU Interim Review: Need for Its Elimination or Extension to the Appellate Body Stage?*, 12(2) JIEL 417 (2009) https://doi.org/10.2139/ssrn.2544577.
49. Dispute Settlement Body Special Session, *Negotiations on Improvements and Clarifications of the Dispute Settlement Understanding on Improving Flexibility and Member Control in WTO Dispute Settlement: Textual Contribution by Chile and the United States*, WTO Doc. TN/DS/W/52, 14

proposal raised more concerns since, at the level of appeal, comments to interim reviews would necessarily target the Appellate Body's legal reasoning, the factual record being already conclusively set at the previous panel stage.[50] Those who, on the contrary, recommended that interim reviews be removed completely stressed that this stage lengthened the proceedings, threatened the exercise of the judicial function and overall added little value considering the possibility to appeal.[51] Yet today, the Appellate Body can no longer hear appeals.

Under these circumstances, the question that arises is whether interim review at the WTO Panel stage will acquire new meaning for the parties involved in trade disputes. Like in the context of dispute settlement under regional trade agreements that provide for interim reports but no appeal procedures,[52] the interim review stage before WTO panels might indeed gain in significance. Will this increase in importance come at the expense of the proper exercise of the judicial function? The risk is rendered all the greater by the fact that dissatisfied parties can prevent the adoption of panel reports by appealing in the void. Under the current day situation, panels might be tempted to resolve disputes in a mutually acceptable way, rather than in a legally correct manner.[53] The proceedings might thus tilt in the direction of diplomatic negotiations rather than adjudication. One would expect that parties will increasingly remind the panellists of their terms of reference, what they must address and, in particular, what they must not enter into. Yet the concern is that parties will use the interim review phase in even more disruptive manners, thus questioning, for example, the interpretations of WTO rules advanced by panels.

Whether there is room for interim reviews in other fields of international dispute settlement, apart from international trade dispute settlement, is likewise a matter that ought to be carefully considered.

IV DISCOVERING THE INTERNATIONAL JUDICIAL FUNCTION THROUGH DIALOGUE

The examination of the international judicial function highlights the intricate balance required between judicial autonomy and the constraints imposed by state sovereignty. The various criticisms and corrective mechanisms discussed in this chapter underscore

Mar. 2003, https://docs.wto.org/dol2fe/Pages/FE_Search/FE_S_S009-DP.aspx?language=E&CatalogueIdList=63478,67682,51129,106302,70544,15104,46381&CurrentCatalogueIdIndex=5&FullTextHash=&HasEnglishRecord=True&HasFrenchRecord=True&HasSpanishRecord=True (accessed 16 Dec. 2024).

50. C.D. Ehlermann, *Reflections on the Appellate Body of the World Trade Organization (WTO)*, 97 Proceedings of the ASIL Annual Meeting 77, 86 (2003).
51. Steinbach, *supra* n. 48. *See also*, J. Baachus & S. Lester, *Trade Justice Delayed Is Trade Justice Denied: How to Make WTO Dispute Settlement Faster and More Effective*, Free Trade Bulletin, 20 Nov. 2019, https://www.cato.org/free-trade-bulletin/trade-justice-delayed-trade-justice-denied-how-make-wto-dispute-settlement (accessed 16 Dec. 2024).
52. *See, e.g.*, Art. 20.13(7) of The Dominican Republic, Central America and United States Free Trade Agreement (5 Aug. 2004).
53. W. Weiss, *Guest Post on the Appellate Body*, International Economic Law and Policy Blog, 13 Dec. 2019, https://ielp.worldtradelaw.net/2019/12/guest-post-on-the-appellate-body.html (accessed 16 Dec. 2024).

the complexity and significance of maintaining this equilibrium. In the context of increasing scrutiny and the potential for judicial overreach, it is essential to foster a deeper understanding and ongoing dialogue about the role and boundaries of international adjudicators.

Despite the challenges, initiatives like the informal process led by Facilitator David Walker demonstrate the potential for positive outcomes. This process, while unable to prevent the WTO Appellate Body's demise, stirred the debate concerning the proper exercise of the judicial function.[54] The Facilitator met with the WTO Members to constructively review the criticisms and, more importantly, the suggested solutions to the crisis in small group-format meetings, as well as larger open-ended meetings to ensure transparency and inclusiveness in the process. Within the Facilitator's reports to the General Council of the WTO, one can find converging points, that is, common criticisms and solutions raised by the WTO Members. Similarly, since the 2022 WTO Ministerial Conference, another Facilitator, Marco Molina, has held informal meetings with the WTO Members on the issue of dispute settlement reform to uncover their interests and concerns behind their reform proposals. The objective of these meetings was to find practical solutions to the concerns identified by Members,[55] and eventually, a draft Ministerial Decision on the Dispute Settlement was released.

In addition to stimulating the discussions among the WTO Members, the 'Walker process' also sought to promote regular dialogue between the General Council and the Appellate Body as such. The idea was to establish a mechanism whereby the WTO Members, once a year, would informally express their views on certain issues, including on the proper functioning of the Appellate Body. The idea is enticing but perilous in so far as discussions might potentially intrude into delicate matters relating to ongoing proceedings. However, clear ground rules aimed at preserving the independence of adjudicators might render the proposal interesting not only in the context of the WTO but also before other mechanisms and tribunals. The importance of such dialogues cannot be understated. Through continuous and structured dialogue between adjudicators, users and beneficiaries, it is possible to ensure that the judicial function remains balanced, transparent, and effective.

54. G. Marceau, *Never Waste a Good Crisis: The End of the WTO Dream, or the Beginning of Something Greater?*, 17(2) IOLR 345, 348 (2020).
55. P. Ølberg, *Special Meeting of the General Council*, 14 Feb. 2024, https://docs.wto.org/dol2fe/Pages/SS/directdoc.aspx?filename=q:/Jobs/GC/385.pdf&Open=True (accessed 16 Dec. 2024).

CHAPTER 4

Third-Party Funding in the Era of Arbitration Reform and ESG: What Lies Ahead?

Lucas Macedo & Alice Fremuth-Wolf[*]

This chapter examines the role of third-party funders in arbitration, a now well-known stakeholder in international dispute resolution. It discusses how funding addresses concerns regarding the legitimacy of arbitration and access to justice by providing meritorious cases with the funding necessary to pursue substantive justice. The chapter approaches the potential conflicts of interest between funders and arbitrators, as well as potential ethical dilemmas between funders, funded parties and their lawyers. The chapter then explores the impact of Environmental, Social, and Governance (ESG) factors on third-party funding in arbitration, especially on climate change-related disputes. It then debates the evolving definition of a 'fundable' case, emphasizing funders' increasing attention to climate-aligned cases. The role of funders as gatekeepers in filtering out meritless legal claims, non-governmental organizations (NGOs), and other stakeholders in supporting ESG-related disputes is highlighted, along with the complex dynamics of balancing financial returns and social responsibility as well as the challenges in proving causation and the duration of such claims, both fundamental investment criteria for commercial funders. The chapter concludes that arbitration and commercial litigation funding plays an increasingly important role in an interdependent justice system, with forthcoming case law

* The authors especially thank Kirstin Dodge (Head of North America, Southern Europe & Latin America and ISDS expert at Nivalion AG) for her invaluable support and input in drafting this chapter.

paving the way for the growth of funding availability for meritorious ESG-aligned cases.

I THIRD-PARTY FUNDERS IN ARBITRATION: TROUBLEMAKERS OR GATEKEEPERS?

While arbitration is the preferred method of dispute resolution in international trade within the globalized economy, it has not been spared from criticism over the years. That has resulted in many recent reforms, from national laws to institutional rules, from international investment treaties to soft law guidelines. In parallel, third-party funding has grown[1] to become a fundamental stakeholder in the dispute resolution environment and is also the subject of significant debate and is frequently addressed in arbitration reform.

While proponents argue that funding facilitates access to justice by enabling parties with limited financial resources to pursue meritorious claims, critics express concerns about potential conflicts of interest and the alleged commercialization of disputes.

In fact, third-party funders play a pivotal role in enhancing access to justice by enabling parties, particularly smaller entities or individuals for whom legal costs are often prohibitive, to have their day in court. This aligns with broader legal principles emphasizing the rule of law as well as fairness and equity in dispute resolution by helping to level the playing field.

For parties with the financial means to pursue a dispute, transferring the associated costs allows them to make a different, often more efficient, use of their capital, e.g., investing in the company's core business, while at the same time limiting their downside risk due to the inherent non-recourse nature of litigation funding.

Critics allege that third-party funding leads to a commodification of legal claims whereby funding is no longer seen as a means of ensuring justice for litigants but is said to have transformed into a tool for the profit maximization of investors. In addition, it is claimed that third-party funding results in an increase in vexatious and meritless claims, also referred to as the 'moral hazard' problem, whereby an actor (in this case, the claimant) is incentivized to take bigger risks than it normally would because it does not bear the full costs of that risk, thereby clogging courts with 'frivolous litigation'.[2] Further, critics argue that third-party funding may lead to an increase in the total costs of proceedings as claimants might be inclined to accept higher fees by their lawyers

1. The global litigation funding market was estimated at USD 15.8 billion in 2022 and is expected to grow at an annual rate of 9% from 2023 to 2028. Globe Newswire, *Global Litigation Funding Investment Market Is Poised to Touch US$ 24.3 Billion by the End 2028, Driven by Increasing Awareness About Litigation Financing*, https://www.globenewswire.com/en/news-release/2023/08/09/2721731/0/en/Global-Litigation-Funding-Investment-Market-is-poised-to-touch-US-24-3-billion-by-the-end-2028-driven-by-increasing-awareness-about-litigation-financing.html (accessed 16 Dec. 2024).
2. Swiss Re, *US Litigation Funding and Social Inflation: The Rising Costs of Legal Liability*, https://www.swissre.com/institute/research/topics-and-risk-dialogues/casualty-risk/us-litigation-funding-social-inflation.html (accessed 16 Dec. 2024).

knowing that the funder pays the bill. Another source of concern are so-called hit-and-run claims by impecunious claimants that would 'blackmail' the respondents into settlement due to their fear that even if the respondent wins the case and is awarded its attorneys' fees and costs, the claimant would not be able to pay the award.

Yet, there have only been a few isolated cases in which claimants appear to have engaged in such abusive tactics,[3] and there is no evidence that funders are supporting frivolous claims with the intention of defying adverse cost awards.[4] Indeed, empirical studies show that using litigation funding often speeds up the resolution of cases, lowers overall legal costs, and helps weed out weak/meritless claims. This is because the nature of litigation funding, where funders only get paid if the case is successful (no win, no fee), naturally deters support for unlikely-to-succeed claims.[5] This gatekeeping or 'quality control' role is reinforced by industry practice that less than 10% of the applications end up in a funding agreement.[6]

Despite the lack of evidence supporting the concerns above, they still have led to a call for prohibition or regulation of certain aspects of third-party funding, as discussed later in this chapter.

II ETHICAL CONSIDERATIONS IN THIRD-PARTY FUNDING

Critics of third-party funding also often raise ethical concerns, in particular regarding potential conflicts of interest which can materialize in two different ways: First, the presence of a funder could compromise the actual or apparent independence or impartiality of the arbitral tribunal, thereby compromising any resulting award. The second concern is a potential conflict of interest between the funder, the funded party and the funded party's lawyer, whose interests may not always align perfectly. These two issues are addressed below.

3. A well-known example of a situation where '*exceptional circumstances*' led to the imposition of a security for costs order to the claimant was *RSM Production Corporation v. Saint Lucia*, ICSID Case No. ARB/12/10.
4. For a more in-depth discussion of Security for Costs in ISDS proceedings, *see* Kirstin Dodge, Jonathan Barnett, Lucas Macedo & Patryk Kulig, *Third-Party Funding and Reform of the ICSID Arbitration Rules*, Romanian Arbitration Journal (Wolters Kluwer, Year 15, Vol. 55, 2021), pp. 26-29.
5. Suneal Bedi & William C. Marra, *What If Litigation Funding Reduces Litigation?* https://thehill.com/opinion/congress-blog/4222882-what-if-litigation-funding-reduces-litigation/ (26 Sep. 2023). *See also* Samuel Antill & Steven R. Grenadier, *Financing the Litigation Arms Race*, Journal of Financial Economics, Volume 149, Issue 2, 2023, pp. 218-234, https://www.sciencedirect.com/science/article/pii/S0304405X23000995 (accessed 16 Dec. 2024).
6. International Council For Commercial Arbitration (ICCA), *Report of The ICCA-Queen Mary Task Force on Third-Party Funding In International Arbitration*, p. 242, https://cdn.arbitration-icca.org/s3fs-public/document/media_document/Third-Party-Funding-Report%20.pdf (accessed 16 Dec. 2024). Others report that '*fewer than 5% of litigation funding applicants ever walk away with a finalized agreement*', *see* Matthew Oxman & Allen Yancy, *The Entrepreneurial Attorney: Insider Tactics for Obtaining Litigation Funding*, https://www.reuters.com/legal/legalindustry/entrepreneurial-attorney-insider-tactics-obtaining-litigation-funding-2022-12-13/ (accessed 16 Dec. 2024).

A Potential Conflicts of Interest Between Funder and Arbitrator

It is a fundamental principle in arbitration that the decision-making authority, i.e., the arbitrator, must be and remain impartial and independent of the parties and their counsel, with the consequence that an undisclosed conflict of interest may become a cause for an eventual annulment or denial of enforcement of the award by the competent State court(s). Thus, arbitrators are required to investigate and disclose any possible facts or circumstances that may give rise to doubts as to their independence and impartiality vis-à-vis the parties throughout the proceedings. The involvement of funders has added another layer to this because of the funder's interest in the outcome of the proceedings. Thus, any financial, business, professional or personal relationship between the funder and the arbitrator may call into question the arbitrator's impartiality and independence.

Reasoning that an arbitrator cannot investigate or disclose their past or present business, financial, professional, or other material relationship with a funder without being aware of the fact that the case is being funded by a third party to the dispute, many arbitration institution rules (for commercial[7] and also investment[8] arbitration) have recently added the requirement that a party must disclose such circumstance, together with the identity of the funder.[9]

Some have argued that a funded party should also be required to disclose the funding agreement. But while the disclosure of the existence and identity of the funder protects the integrity of the arbitral process as such, an additional disclosure of the terms of the third-party funding agreement itself is not required for arbitrators to identify and disclose potential conflicts of interest. Further, such disclosure may give an unfair advantage to an opposing party by revealing strategic and commercially sensitive information, including the strengths and weaknesses of a case (from a funder's view) or the amount of funds that have been made available to the funded party. Unless specifically justified in the context of a particular case, e.g., when the

7. Recent examples from commercial arbitration rules are: Arts 7.1, 8.1, 9.5 and 9.6 CAM-CCBC Rules 2022; Art. 22 DIAC Rules 2022; Art. 21 bis BCDR Arbitration Rules 2022; Art. 6 para. 1.11 and Art. 13a VIAC Rules 2021; Art. 11(7) ICC Rules 2021; Art. 54 ACICA Arbitration Rules 2021 (Art. 41 ACICA Expedited Arbitration Rules 2021); Art. 14 AAA-ICDR Arbitration Rules 2021; Art. 5 BVI IAC Arbitration Rules 2021; Art. 30 TIAC Arbitration Rules 2021; Art. 43 CAM Rules 2020; Art. 44 HKIAC Administered Arbitration Rules 2018 (section 98U of the Arbitration Ordinance in Hong Kong).
8. Recent examples from investment arbitration rules are: Rule 14 and Rule 53 ICSID Arbitration Rules 2022; Rule 23 ICSID Additional Facility Arbitration Rules 2022; Art. 6 para. 1.11 and Art. 13a VIAC Investment Rules 2021; Art. 24(l) SIAC Investment Rules 2017; Art. 27 CIETAC Investment Rules 2017; Art. 8.26 CETA; Proposal on the Modernization of the Treaty – Energy Charter Treaty; ISDS Reform – UNCITRAL WG III and the latest version on TPF provisions – Procedural Rules Reform and Cross-Cutting Issues | United Nations Commission On International Trade Law).
9. These disclosure requirements exist despite the fact that prospective and current arbitrators will certainly know whether they have any such connections to a funder, and alternatively could identify the funder(s) with which they have connections in their standard statements of independence and disclosure.

circumstances determine that the funded party should disclose whether the funding agreement covers a potential adverse costs award, there is no reason why any disclosure regarding the terms of the funding should be required. And even in such rare cases, there is no support for requiring disclosure of more than the specific clauses at issue.[10]

The 2024 revised International Bar Association (IBA) Guidelines on Conflict of Interest,[11] which serve as a benchmark for disclosure requirements, sensibly deal with this issue, limiting disclosure to the identity of the party's funder or insurer and not extending it to the funding agreement itself.

General Standard 6 on 'Relationships' first provides in para b that: *'(a)ny legal entity or natural person having a controlling influence on a party, or a direct economic interest in, or a duty to indemnify a party for the award to be rendered in the arbitration, may be considered to bear the identity of such party'*, explaining that *'(t)hird-party funders and insurers may have a direct economic interest in the prosecution or defence of the case in dispute, a controlling influence on a party to the arbitration, or influence over the conduct of proceedings, including the selection of arbitrators. These distinctions may be relevant when considering whether such entities should be considered to bear the identity of a party'*.

Consequently, General Standard 7 a) obliges parties to inform the tribunal, the other parties and institution of *'any relationship, direct or indirect, between the arbitrator and any person or entity with a direct economic interest in, or a duty to indemnify a party for, the award to be rendered in the arbitration'*. The rationale behind this disclosure requirement is to *'(...) reduce the risk of an unmeritorious challenge of an arbitrator's impartiality or independence based on information learned after the appointment. The parties' duty of disclosure of any relationship, direct or indirect, between the arbitrator and the party (and/or another company of the same group of companies, and/or an individual having a controlling influence on the party in the arbitration and/or any legal or natural person over which a party has a controlling influence), extends to relationships with a legal entity or natural person having a direct economic interest in, or a duty to indemnify a party for, the award to be rendered in the arbitration, such as an entity providing funding for the arbitration'*.

The revised IBA Guidelines thereby balance the need of the arbitrator to be made aware of the existence of a funder for conflict of interest purposes while protecting the

10. For a more extensive discussion of the issue of disclosure of funding in arbitration, *see* Jonathan Barnett, Lucas Macedo & Jacob Henze, *Third-Party Funding Finds Its Place in the New ICC Rules*, https://arbitrationblog.kluwerarbitration.com/2021/01/05/third-party-funding-finds-its-place-in-the-new-icc-rules/ (accessed 16 Dec. 2024) and Kirstin Dodge et al., *Can Third-Party Funding Find the Right Place in Investment Arbitration Rules?*, https://arbitrationblog.kluwerarbitration.com/2022/01/31/can-third-party-funding-find-the-right-place-in-investment-arbitration-rules/ (accessed 16 Dec. 2024).
11. *See* International Bar Association, *IBA Guidelines on Conflicts of Interest in International Arbitration*, https://www.ibanet.org/document?id=Guidelines-on-Conflicts-of-Interest-in-International-Arbitration-2024 (accessed 16 Dec. 2024) and https://www.ibanet.org/document?id=Guidelines-on-Conflicts-of-Interest-in-International-Arbitration-comparison-2014-2024 (accessed 16 Dec. 2024) for the comparison between the 2014 and 2024 versions (5 Apr. 2024).

confidential nature of the underlying funding relationship between the funder and the funded party.

B Potential Conflicts of Interest Between Funder and Funded Party

The involvement of a third-party funder bears the potential for another 'conflict of interest' dilemma due to the tripartite relationship created between the funder, the funded party, and the funded party's lawyer.[12]

Commercial funders have a predominantly economic interest in the outcome of the dispute, and thus, its perspectives and desired outcome of the funded case, i.e., to protect its investment and secure a reasonable return, may not always be aligned with the funded party's interests. These situations can occur when the funded party may have other elements in sight aside from the disputes' direct financial proceeds. In such cases, the party receiving funding may have additional goals beyond just resolving the dispute, such as preserving a business relationship with the other party or seeking non-monetary solutions. In addition, disagreements about settlement offers might arise due to differing expectations between the funder and the funded party.[13] When such disagreements appear, the lawyers representing the funded party, to whom they owe their full professional fiduciary duties, should advise their clients on when and for what amount it would be prudent to settle.

Considering potential settlement scenarios and their impact on the litigation funding agreement, in particular, the proceeds remaining for the funded party after the deduction of the funder's compensation are part of the thorough due diligence that the funder performs before making its investment decision. The joint engagement of the funded party, its lawyer and the funder during this due diligence phase guarantees that all parties are 'on the same page' as to the strengths and weaknesses of the funded case and the consequences of potential outcomes. After having performed such thorough analysis and reached a funding decision, funders can resort to passively monitoring the case, leaving strategy decisions including settlements entirely to the funded party and its lawyers.

It is noteworthy that the rare instances in which disputes between the funder and the funded party arise tend to happen after the successful completion of a case, where the funded party seeks to escape its obligations vis-à-vis the funder after having received the benefit of the funding deal.[14]

12. For a discussion of the tensions arising out of funding relationships, *see* Jonathan Barnett & Stephanie Feldman, *Lines in the Sand: Funder, Funded, Lawyer*, https://arbitrationblog.kluwerarbitration.com/2023/05/23/lines-in-the-sand-funder-funded-lawyer/ (accessed 16 Dec. 2024).
13. Waine Attrill, *Ethical Issues in Litigation Funding*, https://portal.omnibridgeway.com/docs/default-source/site-documents/ethical-issues-paper-imf09---globalaw-conference.pdf (accessed 16 Dec. 2024). *See also* Vicki Waye, *Conflicts of Interests Between Claimholders, Lawyers and Litigation Entrepreneurs*, Bond Law Review Volume 19, Issue 1, 2008, Art. 9, http://www.austlii.edu.au/au/journals/BondLRev/2007/9.pdf (accessed 16 Dec. 2024).
14. This was the case in the recent dispute between Therium Litigation Funding A IC and Bugsby Property LLC regarding the enforceability of their funding agreement challenged by Bugsby following the UK Supreme Court's decision in *PACCAR v. Competition Appeal Tribunal* [2023]

The recent *Burford v. Sysco* saga[15] case is a good example. The dispute concerned whether Burford, as the funder of Sysco's court litigation, which related to an alleged price-fixing arrangement against poultry, beef and pork producers, was entitled to veto Sysco's proposed settlements with the defendants. According to Burford, a limited right to withhold settlement approval in Sysco's cases was granted to it as part of a renegotiation of its original funding agreement with Sysco that settled Burford's claims against Sysco for breach of the original litigation funding agreement. Sysco allegedly violated an anti-assignment prohibition by entering into side deals and assigning away some of its claims. To compensate Burford for the resulting loss of anticipated proceeds, the revised terms of the funding agreement granted Burford a higher economic stake in the unassigned claims as well as the power to veto future settlement proposals to ensure that Sysco (which then had less interest in pursuing the claims) would not settle for amounts that would deprive Burford of its return.

When Sysco negotiated settlements with several food suppliers, Burford objected to these settlements, arguing that they undervalued Sysco's claims and commenced London Court of International Arbitration (LCIA) arbitration under the funding agreement to enjoin Sysco from executing these settlements. Sysco responded by filing a lawsuit seeking to block the LCIA proceedings, asserting in a related public relations campaign that Burford was abusively forcing the company to continue litigating claims against its will. Burford emphasized throughout the dispute that the original funding agreement, like its other funding agreements, did not grant it the power to veto settlements and that the dispute with Sysco arose only because of Sysco's breach of the original funding agreement after receiving millions of dollars to support its litigation. The cases ended with a settlement, under which Sysco assigned its claims to a Burford entity.

The potential 'abuse of powers' by funders nevertheless led the European Union (EU) Committee on Legal Affairs, based on the so-called Voss Report,[16] to recommend that the EU Commission issue a Directive to prevent improper control by funders over legal proceedings, to prevent funders from charging 'excessive' fees, and to require disclosure of funding to courts, administrative authorities and defendants.[17] This

UKSC 28; cf. *Therium v. Bugsby*, Judgment of the High Court of Justice of England and Wales [2023] EWHC 2755, https://jusmundi.com/en/document/decision/en-therium-litigation-funding-a-ic-v-bugsby-property-llc-judgment-of-the-high-court-of-justice-of-england-and-wales-2023-ewhc-2755-friday-3rd-november-2023 (accessed 16 Dec. 2024).

15. Dai Wai Chin Feman, *Breaching a Litigation Funding Agreement: The Sysco/Burford Story*, https://news.bloomberglaw.com/us-law-week/breaching-a-litigation-funding-agreement-the-sysco-burford-story (accessed 16 Dec. 2024); Litigation Finance Journal, *Legal Battle Between Burford and Sysco Ends as Both Parties Dismiss All Claims*, https://litigationfinancejournal.com/legal-battle-between-burford-and-sysco-ends-as-both-parties-dismiss-all-claims/#more-11564 (accessed 16 Dec. 2024).
16. European Parliament – Committee on Legal Affairs, Rapporteur: Axel Voss, *Draft Report With Recommendations to the Commission On Responsible Private Funding of Litigation*, https://www.europarl.europa.eu/doceo/document/JURI-PR-680934_EN.pdf (accessed 16 Dec. 2024).
17. European Parliament, *Resolution of 13 September 2022 with Recommendations to the Commission on Responsible Private Funding of Litigation*, https://www.europarl.europa.eu/doceo/document/TA-9-2022-0308_EN.html (accessed 16 Dec. 2024).

proposal and the Voss Report have been heavily criticized by the International Legal Finance Association (ILFA), which rebutted the accusations against the funding industry and pointed out that the Voss proposal is based on several false premises, misinformation and lack of empirical data. Further, the ILFA argued that the imposition of burdensome regulations on the funding industry, such as forcing disclosure of sensitive information, including the funding agreement to the opposing party and capping the success fee of the funder without taking into consideration the inherent risks associated with funding, would decrease available funding, ultimately harming small and medium-sized enterprises (SMEs) and consumers who are the main beneficiaries of funding.[18] In response, the Commission has decided to first conduct a mapping study of the existing European litigation funding landscape before issuing any new regulations.[19]

The litigation funding industry has also recently come under scrutiny in the United States. In addition to pointing to the potential conflicts of interest and alleged need to protect funded parties discussed above, critics of litigation funding in the US argue that it is being abused by '*left-wing activists aiming to hijack the US legal system*', including the '*funding of lawsuits to combat climate change*' that '*impede oil and mining projects*'.[20] More recently, the U.S. Chamber of Commerce – a 'pro-business' political lobbying organization[21] – has alleged that litigation funding could '*enable foreign adversaries to undermine US national and economic security*',[22] a claim that the ILFA has also thoroughly discredited.[23]

The above examples show that limited regulation of litigation funding may be appropriate to address specific, concrete issues, such as disclosure of the existence and identity of funders to ensure the independence and impartiality of arbitral tribunals. However, proposals to regulate litigation funding may be motivated by interests that have little to do with the realities of funding, including debates regarding environmental, social and governance (ESG) issues that are addressed in the following section.

18. International Legal Finance Association, *Resourcing the Rule of Law in Europe*, https://uploads-ssl.webflow.com/5ef44d9ad0e366e4767c9f0c/6498d39ac7b645dcdc5b9a4d_Resourcing%20the%20Rule%20of%20Law%20in%20Europe_Full%20report.pdf (accessed 16 Dec. 2024).
19. Marialuisa Taddia, *EU Commission Plans Litigation Funding Study Before Any Regs*, https://www.law360.com/articles/1693732 (accessed 16 Dec. 2024).
20. Emily Siegel, *Litigation Finance Has Become 'Money Play', House Lawmakers Told*, https://news.bloomberglaw.com/business-and-practice/litigation-finance-has-become-money-play-house-lawmakers-told (accessed 16 Dec. 2024).
21. *See, e.g.*, https://www.uschamber.com/program/policy/government-affairs#:~:text=The%20Chamber%20is%20an%20effective,%2Dstanding%20pro%2Dbusiness%20reputation (accessed 16 Dec. 2024).
22. U.S. Chamber of Commerce, *Statement for the Record for the House Oversight Hearing, 'Unsuitable Litigation: Oversight of Third-Party Litigation Funding'*, https://www.uschamber.com/lawsuits/statement-for-the-record-for-the-house-oversight-hearing-unsuitable-litigation-oversight-of-third-party-litigation-funding (accessed 16 Dec. 2024).
23. International Legal Finance Association (ILFA), *Statement for the Record International Legal Finance Association United States House of Representatives Committee on Oversight and Accountability*, https://docs.house.gov/meetings/GO/GO00/20230913/116346/HHRG-118-GO00-20230913-SD016.pdf (accessed 16 Dec. 2024).

III THE IMPACT OF ESG ON THIRD-PARTY FUNDING

A What Used to Be a 'Fundable' Case?

Now, let us turn to the cases to be funded. The intrinsic nature of legal claims presupposes that a claimant has an arguable case that their rights have been violated and that legal counsel is willing to, and may ethically, assert those rights on behalf of the claimant.[24]

The fundamental bargain in litigation finance arrangements is that the funder assumes the risk of losing all invested funds if the case is lost in return for a success fee if the case is won. Because of the risk-taking, funders go through a series of additional criteria, including the legal merits of the claim, the necessary budget to pursue the claim, the amounts being (realistically) claimed, the defendant's solvency and collection risk, and the expected duration of the case until receipt of proceeds, whether through settlement or final award and enforcement. In this context, strong financial and legal basis together with good enforcement prospects were the main drivers for a case to be considered 'fundable'. This is now changing.

B What Has Changed?

The year 2024 marks the 20th anniversary of the ESG acronym's first appearance in the United Nations Global Compact report 'Who Cares Wins', along with financial industry recommendations on how to take ESG factors into account in capital allocation and portfolio management.[25] Since then, the ESG movement has become a global phenomenon expected to reach over USD 33 trillion in assets under management by 2026.[26] The movement has gained significant traction in light of climate change concerns (and manifestations), most notably since the 2015 Paris Agreement and the following UN Climate Change Conferences (COPs), which have made clear the role of fossil fuel emissions in increasing global temperatures and the measures necessary to phase them out. Most recently, COP 28 resulted in a commitment by 110 nations to triple renewable energy capacity by 2030.[27]

24. A 'claimant' may also be a defendant asserting a counterclaim. There are also circumstances in which a defendant without a counterclaim may obtain litigation funding. *See, e.g.*, Emily Samra, *The Business of Defense: Defense-Side Litigation Financing*, University of Chicago Law Review, Volume 83, Issue 4, 2016, Art. 20, https://chicagounbound.uchicago.edu/uclrev/vol83/iss4/20 (accessed 16 Dec. 2024).
25. The Global Compact, United Nations, *Who Cares Wins: Connecting Financial Markets to a Changing World*, https://documents1.worldbank.org/curated/en/280911488968799581/pdf/113237-WP-WhoCaresWins-2004.pdf (accessed 16 Dec. 2024).
26. PWC, *ESG-focused Institutional Investment Seen Soaring 84% to US$33.9 Trillion in 2026, Making Up 21.5% of Assets under Management: PwC Report*, https://www.pwc.com/gx/en/news-room/press-releases/2022/awm-revolution-2022-report.html (accessed 16 Dec. 2024).
27. France 24, *COP28: More Than 110 Nations Commit to Tripling Renewable Energy Capacity by 2030*, https://www.france24.com/en/environment/20231202-more-than-110-countries-join-cop28-deal-to-triple-renewable-energy-by-2030 (accessed 16 Dec. 2024).

This framework impacts all sectors of the economy and society, prompting litigation funders – positioned at the crossroads of the legal and financial industries – to adapt as the concept of what constitutes a 'fundable' case continues to evolve. Traditionally, and like other business ventures, third-party funders would primarily focus on the commercial elements of their activities, in other words, whether their investments would yield the expected returns to their shareholders/investors. The traditional concept of corporate social responsibility was not considered to be particularly relevant to the litigation funding industry. This has changed as ESG considerations have become a high-priority item in the agenda of most stakeholders.

The increased importance of ESG elements has significantly changed the criteria of a 'fundable' case for many funders. In the arbitration sphere, the impacts were first seen in investor-state disputes, a field that was already facing criticism for lack of transparency and other alleged defects. Climate change concerns further fuelled the reproach, based on the argument that the Investor-State Dispute Settlement (ISDS) system has resulted in regulatory chill preventing States from taking action to combat climate change, with investors having allegedly '*weaponized*' an '*unjust, undemocratic and dysfunctional*' system.[28]

The ISDS system is undergoing reform to address these criticisms. For example, in 2022, the International Centre for Settlement of Investment Disputes (ICSID) revised its Arbitration Rules, and the United Nations Commission on International Trade Law (UNCITRAL) Working Group III's efforts led to the adoption of a Code of Conduct for Adjudicators in July 2023 by UNCITRAL.[29] Another United Nations body, the Conference on Trade and Development (UNCTAD), has also advocated for the reform of the international investment treaties regime in light of the urgency of the need to take climate action, pointing out that ISDS may be used to challenge climate policies.[30] ESG concerns and notably climate change policies have thus entered the ISDS equation.

In support of their criticism, the UNCTAD cites *Eco Oro v. Colombia* and *RWE v. Netherlands* as recent examples '*directly impacting countries' efforts to combat climate*

28. *See* United Nations Secretary-General Note to the General Assembly by David R. Boyd, *Paying Polluters: The Catastrophic Consequences of Investor-State Dispute Settlement for Climate and Environment Action and Human Rights*, https://files.lbr.cloud/public/2023-11/Paying%20polluters%2C%20the%20catastrophic%20consequences%20of%20ISDS%20for%20climate%20and%20environment%20action%20and%20human%20rights_1.pdf?VersionId=o7acnXU2vI4FDuSy2fXsdwbjFyavkr3t (accessed 16 Dec. 2024).
29. United Nations Commission on International Trade Law (UNCITRAL) Working Group III, *Investor-State Dispute Settlement Reform Efforts*, https://uncitral.un.org/en/working_groups/3/investor-state (accessed 16 Dec. 2024). *See*, in particular, United Nations Commission on International Trade Law (UNCITRAL), Code of Conduct for Arbitrators in International Investment Dispute Resolution, https://uncitral.un.org/sites/uncitral.un.org/files/media-documents/uncitral/en/2318944_coc_arbitrators_e-book_eng.pdf (accessed 16 Dec. 2024), adopted on 7 Dec 2023.
30. In that sense, *see* United Nations Conference on Trade and Development (UNCTAD), *International Investment Agreements Issues* Notes, in particular, Issue 4 (September 2022) '*Treaty-Based Investor–State Dispute Settlement Cases And Climate Action*', Issue 2 (August 2023) '*Trends In The Investment Treaty Regime And A Reform Toolbox For The Energy Transition*', and Issue 3 (September 2023) '*Investment Facilitation in International Investment Agreements: Trends and Policy Options*', https://investmentpolicy.unctad.org/publications/series/2/international-investment-agreements (accessed 16 Dec. 2024).

change'.[31] In the first case, environmental measures aimed at protecting the Páramo Andean ecosystem by the Colombian government imposed a 50% reduction in the claimant mining company's licences. The arbitral tribunal majority held that the measures violated the minimum standard of treatment required by the applicable Colombia-Canada bilateral investment treaty (BIT), frustrating the investor's legitimate expectations.[32] In the second case, an investor challenged the Dutch government's plans to phase out coal power plants by 2030, alleging a violation of the Netherlands' obligations under the Energy Charter Treaty. The effort announced by the Dutch government to seek compliance with its commitments under the Paris Agreement was deemed by the investor to be tantamount to an expropriation of its investments, as the government would not have granted enough time or resources for the company's adaptation without severe financial loss.[33]

According to UNCTAD, such cases demonstrate that measures taken by States for the protection of the environment can be found by arbitral tribunals to constitute violations of international investment treaties, casting doubt on the countries' efforts to regulate the protection of the environment and climate adaptation.[34] Others have a different view, arguing that the ISDS system provides the stability and legal certainty required to foster cross-border investment, which will ultimately be necessary to fund the energy transition agenda.[35]

This is not to say that the tension between the protection of investors' rights and the ability of governments to regulate environmental, natural resources, and public health concerns is a new issue, as illustrated by the anti-smoking initiatives by States that Philip Morris challenged as early as 2010.[36] It is just that the scrutiny of such issues has intensified, and, as a result, the application of international law concepts by arbitral tribunals is also changing. As summarized in Prof. Philippe Sands' dissenting opinion in *Eco Oro* in 2021:

> In the age of climate change and significant loss of biological diversity, it is clear that society finds itself in a state of transition. The law – including international

31. United Nations Conference on Trade and Development (UNCTAD), *International Investment Agreements Issues Notes*, Issue 4, https://unctad.org/system/files/official-document/diaepcbinf 2022d7_en.pdf (September 2022).
32. *Eco Oro v. Colombia*, ICSID Case No. ARB/16/41 https://www.italaw.com/sites/default/files/case-documents/italaw16212.pdf (accessed 16 Dec. 2024), para. 821.
33. The procedure was withdrawn after German Courts granted the Netherlands request to issue an anti-arbitration declaration in light of the intra-EU nature of the dispute, considered to be incompatible with EU law. *See* Lisa Bohmer, *Rwe Requests Discontinuance of Coal Phase-Out Ect Claim Against the Netherlands, in View of German Supreme Court's Ruling On Anti-Intra-EU-Arbitration Declarations*, https://www.iareporter.com/articles/rwe-requests-discontinuance-of-coal-phase-out-ect-claim-against-the-netherlands-in-view-of-german-supreme-courts-ruling-on-anti-intra-eu-arbitration-declarations/ (accessed 16 Dec. 2024).
34. United Nations Conference on Trade and Development (UNCTAD), *International Investment Agreements Issues Notes*, Issue 4, https://unctad.org/system/files/official-document/diaepcbinf 2022d7_en.pdf (accessed 16 Dec. 2024).
35. Steven Burkill & Aaron Murhpy, *ISDS and Climate Change: What Happens Next?*, https://www.wfw.com/articles/isds-and-climate-change-what-happens-next/ (accessed 16 Dec. 2024).
36. *Philip Morris v. Uruguay*, ICSID Case No. ARB/10/7, https://investmentpolicy.unctad.org/investment-dispute-settlement/cases/368/philip-morris-v-uruguay (accessed 16 Dec. 2024).

> law – must take account of that state of transition, which gives rise to numerous uncertainties. Adjudicators – judges and arbitrators – recognise the need to proceed with caution at a time of transition and uncertainty.[37]

Then, in February 2024, an ICSID tribunal in *Red Eagle v. Colombia* again addressed the measures by the Colombian State to protect the Páramo ecosystem, rejecting all the claims on the merits. Prof. Philippe Sands formed the majority this time, deciding that the State's conduct was not arbitrary, unreasonable or disproportionate. Further, the tribunal ruled that the claimant did not have any legitimate expectation as the protection of water and the Páramo were lawful public policy objectives long known by the claimant.[38]

The juxtaposition of these cases exemplifies that what may have been once seen as a straightforward and uncontroversial exercise of a right to claim compensation under an international investment treaty may no longer be the case. This will inevitably impact the chances of success of claimants in ISDS disputes and be reflected in litigation funders' appetite to back such claims. Although investors have succeeded in past cases (and some still might), the availability of third-party funding for cases that challenge State's efforts to address climate change is likely to shrink due to the perceived legal and reputational risks associated with such cases or the funders' own ESG policies.

Let us thus discuss what can *now* be considered to be a fundable case.

C What Is a 'Fundable' Case Now?

The increased importance of fulfilling ESG goals, including addressing climate change, prompts litigation funders to have a very low or no appetite to support so-called non-climate-aligned claims, where litigants challenge or seek damages caused by the introduction of regulations or policies intended to achieve a reduction of greenhouse gas emissions or other environmental protection initiatives. For instance, cases in which investors seek to reverse or suspend legal measures phasing out coal-fired electricity generation or that suspend or ban natural gas extraction through fracking can be seen as non-climate-aligned.[39] Conversely, climate-aligned cases,[40] i.e., those tending to further the climate change agenda, are increasingly obtaining more support

37. *Eco Oro v. Colombia*, ICSID Case No. ARB/16/41 dissenting opinion by Professor Philippe Sands KC, para. 33, https://www.italaw.com/sites/default/files/case-documents/italaw16212.pdf (accessed 16 Dec. 2024).
38. *Red Eagle v. Colombia*, ICSID Case No. ARB/18/12, Award of 28 Feb. 2024, https://www.italaw.com/sites/default/files/case-documents/180718.pdf (accessed 16 Dec. 2024).
39. United Nations Secretary-General Note to the General Assembly by Boyd, *supra* n. 28.
40. Joana Setzer & Catherine Higham, *2023 Global Trends In Climate Change Litigation Report*, Grantham Research Institute on Climate Change and the Environment and Centre for Climate Change Economics and Policy, London School of Economics and Political Science, https://www.lse.ac.uk/granthaminstitute/wp-content/uploads/2023/06/Global_trends_in_climate_change_litigation_2023_snapshot.pdf (accessed 16 Dec. 2024).

from various stakeholders, from non-governmental organizations (NGOs) and regulators to shareholders.[41] Funders and their investors are no exception.

While the ISDS claims referred to above would be considered non-climate aligned, there are climate-aligned cases in which investors challenge state measures potentially hindering international climate change commitments or national regulations that should implement such undertakings. For example, when States take measures disfavouring renewable energy production and/or providing incentives to conventional, more polluting sources. In those circumstances, climate-aligned cases help promote the energy transition agenda.

This may become the case with Mexico's 2021 amendment to the electric power Industry Law prioritizing the dispatch of (State-owned) fossil fuel power plants, potentially negatively impacting renewable energy investors and affecting Mexico's energy transition commitment. The amendments are currently the subject of State-to-State consultations under the United States-Mexico-Canada Agreement (USMCA).[42]

Another interesting example is *Allard v. Barbados*, where the investor, an eco-tourism operator, alleged that the State's poor management of a sluice gate resulted in environmental damages, destroying the value of his investment.[43] While the tribunal rejected the claims, finding that the claimant failed to establish a causal link between the biome degradation and the State's conduct, it did recognize that the Full Protection and Security Standard in the applicable Canada-Barbados BIT included '*an obligation of the host State to protect foreign investments against environmental damage*'.[44]

Such cases will remain rather the exception than the rule, as the ISDS system is traditionally designed to protect the commercial interests of individual investors, not obligations that a State may have to its citizens or the broader public.[45] However, they represent an opportunity for litigation funders to invest in cases that are supportive of climate-friendly goals.

Regarding the 'Governance' element of ESG, one interesting area comprises derivative shareholder disputes, specifically cases such as those filed by minority shareholders to hold directors or controlling shareholders liable for mismanagement, greenwashing, and corrupt acts leading to company value depreciation. These disputes

---

41. *See* the four-part webinar series organized by Nivalion and Wöss & Partners, *Where the Rubber Meets the Road: The Reality of ESG Claims*, https://www.youtube.com/watch?v=DHrsS8PNqsY&list=PLnxf5_JG9O1LnRVtDYKD6spJ_u3l7bOxs (accessed 16 Dec. 2024).
42. David Bond & Francisco de Rosenzweig, *United States and Canada Request Consultations Over Mexico's Energy Policies Under USMCA*, https://www.whitecase.com/insight-alert/united-states-and-canada-request-consultations-over-mexicos-energy-policies-under (accessed 16 Dec. 2024).
43. Jarrod Hepburn, *Factual Findings Sink Merits Claims in Allard v. Barbados, as Tribunal Examines Investment-Environment Legal Interactions and Proportionality of Defence costs*, https://www.iareporter.com/articles/factual-findings-sink-merits-claims-in-allard-v-barbados-as-tribunal-examines-investment-environment-legal-interactions-and-proportionality-of-defence-costs/ (accessed 16 Dec. 2024).
44. *Allard v. Barbados*, PCA Case No. 2012-06, Award, p. 75, para. 252, https://www.italaw.com/sites/default/files/case-documents/italaw7594.pdf (accessed 16 Dec. 2024).
45. Joshua Paine, *Failure to Take Reasonable Environmental Measures as a Breach of Investment Treaty?*, Journal of World Investment & Trade, Volume 18, 2017, paras 745-754, https://doi.org/10.1163/22119000-12340058; https://core.ac.uk/download/pdf/224973308.pdf (accessed 16 Dec. 2024).

are frequently taken to arbitration due to arbitration clauses in the companies' bylaws.[46]

The compensation that is available to claimants in such cases plays a key role in determining whether the claimants can obtain funding to support the case. For example, Brazilian derivative suits offer the possibility that the (minority) shareholders will be awarded a 5% premium on top of the amount of damages awarded as an incentive and compensation for taking on the risk and costs of the dispute on behalf of all shareholders.[47] Such a premium can be used as a revenue source to cover litigation funders' fees in the case of success. External funding is a fundamental tool to level the playing field in these frequently 'David v. Goliath' situations, where shareholders have significantly less financial capacity than the sued corporations. The same imbalanced power dynamics exist in the antitrust private enforcement sphere, where Brazil has recently reformed its legislation to, *inter alia,* allow courts to advance financial compensation as provisional relief in follow-on claims. The earlier returns will likely increase the funding availability for these Governance-related claims.[48]

Another fertile ground for funding ESG disputes relates to supply chains. The growing regulatory trend requiring companies to identify, document, report and ultimately be liable for violations of human rights, forced labour, and greenhouse gas emissions with instruments such as the EU Corporate Sustainability Due Diligence Directive (CSDDD),[49] the German Supply Chain Act[50] and France's Corporate Duty of

---

46. In that sense, *see* the cases brought against JBS and Petrobras, although as of January 2024, Brazilian Courts have not yet finally concluded whether the Brazilian Government is or not bound by the arbitration clause included in Petrobras' bylaws. In Jack Ballantyne, *Brazilian Beef Company Faces Corruption Claim,* https://globalarbitrationreview.com/brazilian-beef-company-faces-corruption-claim (accessed 16 Dec. 2024) and Toby Fisher, *Petrobras Shareholders Fail to Revive Mega-Claim Against Brazil,* https://globalarbitrationreview.com/article/petrobras-shareholders-fail-revive-mega-claim-against-brazil (accessed 16 Dec. 2024).
47. Guilherme Pereira et al., *A Ação de Responsabilidade de Acionista Controlador e o Financiamento de Litígios* (Revista dos Tribunais, São Paulo, 2023), https://www.jusbrasil.com.br/doutrina/secao/1-delimitacao-do-objeto-do-artigo-6-a-acao-de-responsabilidade-de-acionista-controlador-e-o-financiamento-de-litigios-litigation-finance-e-special-situations-ed-2023/1865872901#a-307462539 (accessed 16 Dec. 2024).
48. Lucas Macedo & Eduardo Silva de Freitas, *A Silent Revolution? The Revamped Brazilian Private Enforcement System and Third-Party Funding,* https://www.lexology.com/library/detail.aspx?g=f13fa643-dfc6-48cf-9bc9-fee60343e23e (accessed 16 Dec. 2024).
49. On 14 Dec. 2023, the Council and the European Parliament reached a provisional deal on the CSDDD, aiming to enhance the protection of the environment and human rights in the EU and globally. The directive will set obligations for large companies regarding actual and potential adverse impacts on human rights and the environment, with respect to their own operations, those of their subsidiaries, and those carried out by their business partners. The provisional agreement reached with the European Parliament yet needs to be endorsed and formally adopted by both institutions. European Commission, *Proposal for a Directive of the European Parliament and of the Council on Corporate Sustainability Due Diligence and amending Directive (EU) 2019/1937,* https://eur-lex.europa.eu/legal-content/EN/TXT/?uri=CELEX%3A52022PC0071 (accessed 16 Dec. 2024).
50. The German Act on Corporate Due Diligence Obligations in Supply Chains came into force on 1 Jan. 2023. The law regulates the responsibility of German enterprises to respect human rights in global supply chains, including protection against child labour, the right to fair wages, as well as environmental protection. The respective obligations apply to their own business area, the actions of their contracting partners and the actions of other (indirect) suppliers. *See Act on Corporate Due Diligence Obligations in Supply Chains (Gesetz über die unternehmerischen*

Vigilance law imposes a set of duties and obligations throughout corporate supply chains.[51]

The cross-border and specific nature of these obligations is likely to make arbitration the preferred intra-supply-chain dispute resolution method to give contractual teeth to enforce this new class of corporate duties.[52] While commercial arbitration cases are frequently confidential, the most prominent publicly known example of supply-chain arbitration are the Bangladesh Accord on Fire and Building Safety arbitrations brought by workers' unions against global fashion brands in the aftermath of the Rana Plaza building collapse.[53] The supply-chain risk management trend is also observed in post-M&A disputes, as companies now frequently include ESG risk allocation clauses, including via representations and warranties, to mitigate said risks.[54]

D Current Challenges and Outlook

Navigating the changing tides in ESG and sustainability efforts is a complex task, especially considering that some elements can become a 'shield' for defendants as well as being a 'sword' for claimants. For example, in *Cortec Mining v. Kenya*, the arbitral tribunal dismissed the claims due to the investor's lack of compliance with the State's domestic environmental regulation.[55]

Sorgfaltspflichten in Lieferketten), https://www.csr-in-deutschland.de/SharedDocs/Downloads/EN/act-corporate-due-diligence-obligations-supply-chains.pdf?__blob=publicationFile (accessed 16 Dec. 2024).

51. For a very good overview, cf. the report of the webinar organized by Nivalion and Wöss & Partners on 17 and 24 Feb. 2023, Jonathan Barnett, *The Answer My Friend … Is Blowing in the Wind: ESG in EU-Related Supply Chains*, https://arbitrationblog.kluwerarbitration.com/2023/03/21/the-answer-my-friend-is-blowing-in-the-wind-esg-in-eu-related-supply-chains/ (accessed 16 Dec. 2024). *See also*, the key-note speech by Annette Magnusson, *The Expanding Universe of Climate Change Disputes* as well as all other contributions, in *ESG Webinar: ESG in EU Related Supply Chains*, https://www.youtube.com/playlist?list=PLnxf5_JG9O1KDhCJkyMYPxlf1zxg6lORf (accessed 16 Dec. 2024).
52. Ari Mackinnon, *The Rise of ESG Disputes and the Role of Arbitration in Resolving Them*, https://www.financierworldwide.com/the-rise-of-esg-disputes-and-the-role-of-arbitration-in-resolving-them (accessed 16 Dec. 2024).
53. The Accord on Fire and Building Safety in Bangladesh was signed between over 220 global fashion brands and retailers and trade unions in the aftermath of the Rana Plaza building collapse, containing an arbitration clause. The ensuing Rana Plaza arbitrations are considered a pioneer for business and human rights arbitration PCA cases 2016-36; 2016-37, https://pca-cpa.org/en/cases/152/ (accessed 16 Dec. 2024). Also in that sense, the 2019 Hague Rules on Business and Human Rights Arbitration provide for a promising consent-based avenue to resolve human rights violations related to business activities. For a discussion on how to integrate said rules with the investment arbitration system, *see* Anne van Aaken, Diane A. Desierto et al., *The Human Rights Remedy Gap in ISDS: The Potential of the Hague Rules on Business and Human Rights Arbitration*, https://uncitral.un.org/sites/uncitral.un.org/files/media-documents/uncitral/en/academic_forum_hague_rules_business_and_human_rights_arbitration_-_paper_and_ppt_at_46th_session.pdf (accessed 16 Dec. 2024).
54. Mackinnon, *supra* n. 52.
55. Damien Charlotin, *Analysis: in Kenya Award, Tribunal Reads Legality Requirement Into Investment Treaty and ICSID Convention, and Dismisses Claims Based on Mining License That Was Issued at Eleventh Hour Before Change in Government*, https://www.iareporter.com/ar

Particularly in climate change-related disputes, the challenge is to determine the causal link between actions such as greenhouse gas emissions and the damages suffered or anticipated by claimants. *Saul v. RWE* is the first case where an individual seeks to hold a large greenhouse gas emitter liable for losses and damages caused by climate change. The claimant, a mountain guide and farmer, has requested that RWE be required to pay a proportional contribution to safety measures that are required to avoid the outburst of the Palcacocha glacial lake near his home and accompanying flooding risk fuelled by glacial retreat attributed to anthropogenic climate change.[56]

The first instance German court summarily dismissed the case, finding that there was no legally relevant causation between RWE's CO_2 emissions and the endangerment of Saul's property. This was reversed by the Higher Regional Court of Hamm, which admitted the case on the grounds that companies can indeed be responsible for their share of climate change-related damages. The case now moves to the evidentiary stage, where further enquiry will be done on RWE's emissions since the beginning of industrialization and whether they contributed to accelerate glacier melting and the risk of flooding in the area where the claimant resides.[57] The so-called attribution science, an evolving field of research into the extent to which climate change makes natural disasters more or less likely, is fundamental to proving liability in these cases.[58]

Another challenge for Saul's case to be attractive to commercial litigation funders is that only a '*very small, symbolic amount*' is being claimed as actual damages.[59] This means that the potential proceeds are likely not going to be enough to adequately compensate for the necessary investment in this complex dispute. In addition, funders may be reluctant to support novel legal theories where the likely success of the claims cannot be supported by reference to precedent or established legal doctrine.

As we have mentioned above, duration is a critical issue for commercial litigation funders, and this is frequently a crucial issue in these novel types of disputes. Take Saul's case again. The matter was filed in November 2015, and as of the writing of this chapter in May 2024, over eight years have passed without resolution of the case or any reasonable expectation that the case will be resolved soon.

A funders' compensation is typically measured by its Internal Rate of Return (IRR), in which time has an exponential erosive effect. For instance, a 3x return of the invested capital for a funder over five years yields a 31.9% IRR. The same return over ten years is equivalent to 14.9% IRR.[60] In other words, a dispute likely to run for a

ticles/analysis-in-kenya-award-tribunal-reads-legality-requirement-into-investment-treaty-and-icsid-convention-and-dismisses-claims-based-on-mining-license-that-was-issued-at-eleventh-hour-before-change-i (accessed 16 Dec. 2024).

56. Will Frank et al., *The Case of Huaraz: First Climate Lawsuit on Loss and Damage Against an Energy Company Before German Courts*, https://link.springer.com/chapter/10.1007/978-3-319-72026-5_20 (accessed 16 Dec. 2024).
57. Frank et al., *supra* n. 56.
58. Camilla Hodgson, *Who Pays for Climate Change? The Peruvian Suing a German Utility*, https://www.ft.com/content/e26c5813-354b-4b6b-8bc1-70b39ef9837c (accessed 16 Dec. 2024).
59. Hodgson, *supra* n. 58.
60. Tets Ishikawa, *Funders' Pricing and the Real Value of Litigation Risks*, http://disputeresolutionblog.practicallaw.com/funders-pricing-and-the-real-value-of-litigation-risks/ (accessed 16 Dec. 2024).

decade would have to deliver a much higher relative return to meet a funder's IRR target. Other practical aspects may make long-duration disputes unappealing for litigation funders, such as limits on the lifetime of a funding vehicle.

However, those circumstances have not precluded the *Saul v. RWE* case from being financially supported by the Foundation for Sustainability (*Stiftung Zukunftsfähigkeit*) as part of a comprehensive strategy to pressure States and companies to act on climate change.[61] This has been the case in several other disputes where NGOs, pro bono legal support, philanthropies,[62] charities, crowdfunding initiatives and even State endowments – such as the New Zealand Environmental Legal Assistance Fund,[63] the Public Interest Law Participation Fund in British Columbia, Canada[64] and other public legal aid programmes – have played an important role.[65]

Thus, commercial litigation funding is merely one tool among many in the toolbox of ESG-related disputes. Commercial litigation funding is not the sole alternative to obtaining financial resources for resolving disputes with a favourable, ESG-aligned profile. This is especially true for non-monetary claims before State courts seeking purely injunctive relief,[66] which may result mainly in 'good karma'[67] for their supporters.

However, there is a universe of commercial litigation and arbitration ESG-related claims that involve a direct or indirect financial component to the claims sufficient to be attractive to both the funded party and commercial litigation funders. Arbitration cases are particularly good candidates for consideration, as they often have a shorter duration than state court litigations while frequently requiring investment of significant

61. *See* Stiftung Zukunftsfähigkeit, https://stiftungzukunft.org/unsere-aktivitaeten/der-fall-huaraz/ (accessed 16 Dec. 2024).
62. Notably, Uruguay received financial support from Bloomberg Philanthropies and Campaign for Tobacco Free Kids in *Philip Morris v. Uruguay*. *See supra* n. 36 and Cision, PR Newswire, *In Historic Win for Global Health, Uruguay Defeats Philip Morris Challenge to Its Strong Tobacco Control Laws*, https://www.prnewswire.com/in/news-releases/in-historic-win-for-global-health-uruguay-defeats-philip-morris-challenge-to-its-strong-tobacco-control-laws-586071611.html (accessed 16 Dec. 2024).
63. *See* New Zealand Environmental Legal Assistance Fund, https://environment.govt.nz/what-you-can-do/funding/environmental-legal-assistance-fund/?ref=the-wave.net (accessed 16 Dec. 2024).
64. *See* The Law Foundation of British Columbia, https://www.lawfoundationbc.org/project-funding/publicinterestlawparticipationfund/ (accessed 16 Dec. 2024).
65. Isabella Kaminski, *An Ocean of Opportunities? Climate Litigation is Doing so Well It's Now Being Eyed by Investors*, https://www.the-wave.net/climate-litigation-as-investment/ (accessed 16 Dec. 2024).
66. *See* such as *Urgenda Foundation v. State of the Netherlands*, where the claimants obtained a declaratory judgment and injunction to compel the Dutch government to reduce greenhouse gas emissions. Sabin Center for Climate Change Law, *Climate Change Litigation Databases*, https://climatecasechart.com/non-us-case/urgenda-foundation-v-kingdom-of-the-netherlands/ (accessed 16 Dec. 2024).
67. As stated by Anja Ipp (Climate Change Counsel) during the II Nivalion Legal Finance Summit on 27 Sep. 2023 in Frankfurt. *See in* Lucas Macedo, Anton Burri & Johannes Nickl, *Through the Looking Glass: The Rise of ESG Risks – II Nivalion Legal Finance Summit Report*, https://www.lexology.com/library/detail.aspx?g=56d50cd6-59ab-4aee-ad7a-4feb90b00051 (accessed 16 Dec. 2024).

upfront costs. Such cases are likely to increase in the future, with the implementation and enforcement of ESG-related obligations also impacting on the arbitration reform.[68]

IV CONCLUDING REMARKS

Third-party funders are no longer 'new kids' in the dispute resolution arena but well-established stakeholders, playing a pivotal role in enhancing access to justice by providing parties, for whom costs are a huge burden, the necessary funding to pursue their claims, thereby promoting the rule of law as well as fairness and equity in dispute resolution. Concerns have been voiced with respect to potential conflicts of interest issues, alleged 'abuse of powers', and cost escalation, which have, in turn, led to a call for regulation of the third-party funding market. Arbitration rules have tackled these issues and now increasingly provide for the disclosure of the existence and identity of funders to ensure the independence and impartiality of arbitrators. Empirical studies show that using litigation funding often speeds up the resolution of cases, lowers overall legal costs, and helps weed out weak/meritless claims. Thus, any proposals to further regulate litigation funding thereby hampering access to justice should be rejected.

Litigation funders act as gatekeepers in filtering out meritless legal claims.[69] The ESG panorama may take this notion one step further: In the future, funders may increasingly decline to support non-climate-aligned cases and, at the same time, help promote access to justice and the rule of law in climate-aligned disputes beyond the traditional commercial and legal criteria of what made a case fundable.

Research confirms investors' preference to have ESG goals embedded into companies' strategies and, increasingly, are requiring that companies in which they invest abide by ESG policies and standards.[70] The commercial litigation industry is not immune from this trend. Investors entrusting their capital to commercial litigation funders seek a financial return, but many want their capital to be invested in a sustainable manner that promotes responsible business practices.

It is true that the ESG movement has been the subject of criticism and political polarization,[71] something the litigation funding industry and arbitration itself have been through, as we have discussed. While in the past it was generally believed that

68. *See*, for example, the potential benefits of arbitration for resolution of climate change-related disputes listed in International Chamber of Commerce, *ICC Arbitration and ADR Commission Report on Resolving Climate Change Related Disputes through Arbitration and ADR*, https://iccwbo.org/news-publications/arbitration-adr-rules-and-tools/icc-arbitration-and-adr-commission-report-on-resolving-climate-change-related-disputes-through-arbitration-and-adr/ (accessed 16 Dec. 2024).
69. Caroline Dos Santos, *Third-party Funding in International Commercial Arbitration: A Wolf in Sheep's Clothing?* (ASA Bulletin December 2017 No. 4), p. 925, https://www.bakermckenzie.com/-/media/files/people/caroline-dos-santos/third-party-funding-in-ia--a-wolf-in-sheeps-clothing-asa-vol-35-issue-4.pdf (accessed 16 Dec. 2024).
70. PwC's Global Investor Survey 2023, https://www.pwc.com/gx/en/issues/c-suite-insights/global-investor-survey.html (accessed 16 Dec. 2024).
71. Andrew Winston, ESG Is under Attack. How Should Your Company Respond?, https://hbr.org/2023/12/esg-is-under-attack-how-should-your-company-respond (accessed 16 Dec. 2024).

such investors paid for their ideology with poor returns, ESG-focused strategies reportedly deliver market-equivalent returns to investors.[72] Conversely, ESG non-compliant investments may suffer as a result of reputational and, ultimately, financial harm. Market regulators are already imposing fines on companies that do not comply with ESG standards,[73] and global banks such as BNP Paribas have announced that they will no longer finance new oil and gas projects.[74]

Neither arbitration nor commercial litigation funding will be enough to ensure that companies and States adhere to their ESG commitments, but they both play a role in a complementary and interdependent enforcement system. It is not possible that commercial funders will support every ESG-aligned case, whether due to the nature or extent of the relief sought, the novelty of the legal theory and strategies, or other considerations within the funders' portfolio. However, this should not bar claims with legal and ethical merit from seeing the light of day. Successful cases pave the way for stronger and more predictable claims, which may attract more legal funding in the future.

In the meantime, litigation funders are showing an increased interest in investing in ESG-aligned cases, adding to the industry's contribution to access to justice and enforcement of the rule of law. Advocates of arbitration reform should, therefore, reject misguided efforts to regulate commercial litigation funders in ways that will reduce their ability or willingness to fund meritorious ESG-aligned cases.

72. Sally Hickey, '*The Impact of ESG on Performance Is Non-existent*', https://www.ftadviser.com/investments/2023/04/19/the-impact-of-esg-on-performance-is-non-existent/?page=1 (accessed 16 Dec. 2024).
73. Kanishka Singh, *SEC Charges Goldman Sachs Asset Management with Not Following ESG Investments Policies*, https://www.reuters.com/world/us/sec-charges-goldman-sachs-asset-management-not-following-esg-investments-2022-11-22/ (accessed 16 Dec. 2024).
74. Mark Segal, *BNP Paribas Ends Financing for New Oil and Gas Projects*, https://www.esgtoday.com/bnp-paribas-ends-financing-for-new-oil-and-gas-projects/ (accessed 16 Dec. 2024).

CHAPTER 5

The Role of Developing States in International Investment Arbitration

Margie-Lys Jaime

In 2020-2022, the New York Convention welcomed Ethiopia, Palau, Tonga, Seychelles, Belize, Malawi, Sierra Leone and Suriname as new Contracting States. During the same period, Djibouti, Kyrgyz, and Angola joined the International Centre for Settlement of Investment Disputes (ICSID) Convention. In addition, after denouncing the ICSID Convention, Ecuador re-joined the system in 2021. This shows a willingness from these States, Low- and Middle-Income economies, to be part of the system, but, at the same time, some of these countries, as well as other developing countries, are actively participating in the Working Group III discussions and other policy reforms of international investment arbitration. Indeed, many developing countries have numerous arbitrations and, hence, have gained first-hand knowledge. This chapter addresses the role of developing states in the reform process of Investor-State Dispute Settlement (ISDS) Reform.

I INTRODUCTION

On the one hand, the World Bank classifies countries, for analytical purposes, into four income groups: low, lower-middle, upper-middle, and high income.[1] On the other

1. The World Bank uses gross national income (GNI) per capita data in US dollars, converted from local currency using the World Bank Atlas method. Countries are classified each year on 1 July, based on the estimate of their GNI per capita for the previous calendar year. Before 1983, there was no distinction between lower-middle and upper-middle income. The World by Income and Region, https://datatopics.worldbank.org/world-development-indicators/the-world-by-income-and-region.html#: ~ :text = The%20World%20Bank%20classifies%20economies,%2Dmiddle%2C%20and%20high%20income (accessed 16 Dec. 2024).

hand, the United Nations maintains an official list of Least Developed Countries (LDCs) but not an official list of developing and developed countries.[2] Recently, the terms 'least developed countries' and 'developing countries' have been used in the context of the establishment of an Advisory Centre on international investment dispute resolution.[3] Although it is recognised that one of the main objectives of this Advisory Centre is to enhance the capacity of LDCs and developing countries, the categorisation into these two groups, if retained, would be for purposes of the draft statute only and without prejudice to any other classifications.[4] Moreover, there is no established international treaty for the designation of developed and developing regions, and, to some extent, the distinction could be problematic because it might not reflect reality.[5]

This chapter will maintain the distinction to highlight the contribution of developing states in the international investment arbitration arena, in particular those categorised as low- and medium-income States.

According to a study, in nearly 90% of investment treaty arbitration cases, the home state of the investors was a high-income country.[6] Under another study, investment arbitration was mainly between 'developed versus developing' countries until the mid-to-late 1990s, while since the mid-to-late 1990s, it has been a mixed 'developed versus developed' and 'developed versus developing' countries.[7] In other words, investors from developed countries might file claims against developing countries as well as against developed countries. This can be explained by the fact that investors from developed countries may have a higher level of investment abroad. Additionally, bilateral investment treaties ('BITs') have traditionally been signed by developing countries to promote and protect foreign investment (sometimes imposed by their developed commercial partners).

United Nations Conference on Trade and Development ('UNCTAD') data shows that since the 2000s, there has been an increase in South-South investment cooperation, which can be perceived by the rise of investment treaties signed among developing countries, particularly through free trade agreements (FTAs) and other preferential

2. United Nations, List of LDCs, https://www.un.org/ohrlls/content/list-ldcs (accessed 16 Dec. 2024).
3. UNCITRAL, Draft statute of an advisory centre on international investment dispute resolution (17 Feb. 2024), A/CN.9/WG.III/WP.238.
4. *Ibid.*, para. 6. *See also* Report of Working Group III (Investor-State Dispute Settlement Reform) on the work of its forty-seventh session (12 Feb. 2024), A/CN.9/1161, paras 39-40.
5. Since 2017, the Sustainable Development Goals (SDGs) report use geographic regions instead of the distinction of developed and developing regions. The distinction was removed from the standard country or area codes for statistical use (M49) in December 2021. However, users expressed the need to maintain the distinction based on the understanding that being part of either group is a sovereign decision. *See* United Nations, Historical and Updated Classification of Developed and Developing Regions (May 2022), https://unstats.un.org/unsd/methodology/m49/historical-classification-of-developed-and-developing-regions.xlsx (accessed 16 Dec. 2024).
6. Susan Franck, Empirically Evaluating Claims about Investment Treaty Arbitration, *North Carolina Law Review* (2008), Vol. 86, at 29.
7. Thomas Schultz & Cédric Dupont, Investment Arbitration: Promoting the Rule of Law or Over-empowering investors? A Quantitative Empirical Study, *EJIL* (2014), Vol. 25 No. 4, 1147-1168, 1154 https://doi.org/10.1093/ejil/chu075.

trade and investment agreements.[8] Over time, it has become evident that the more investment treaties a country has signed, the greater the risk of being sued by foreign investors.

By 2010, the total number of known treaty-based cases was 390, and the top five respondent States since 1987 were Argentina, Mexico, the Czech Republic, Ecuador, and Venezuela.[9] Ten years later, the cumulative known treaty-based investment arbitration reached 1,104 cases. The frequent respondent States, between 2011 and 2020, were Spain, Venezuela, Egypt, Czechia, and Peru.[10] Indeed, the spectrum of countries being sued has amplified and evolved over time. Still, investors from developed countries have brought most – about 70% – of the known cases in 2020.[11]

This chapter shall cover different aspects where low- and medium-income States have had a leading role in the development of Investor-State Dispute Settlement ('ISDS') and in particular with respect to: the termination and replacement of the old BITs (A); the growth of other forms of dispute resolution (B); the development of new procedural rules (C).

A The Termination and Replacement of the Old BITs

Low- and medium-income States have had a fundamental role in the renewal of the stock of International Investment Agreements ('IIAs'). When the ISDS system was established in 1965, with the creation of the International Centre for Settlement of Investment Disputes ('ICSID'), it was done especially to protect investors with contractual relationships with the host State and not for treaty-based arbitrations.[12] The drafters of the Convention could have never imagined the exponential growth of IIAs in the past thirty-plus years.

Latin American countries, in particular, were very sceptical about the establishment of ICSID as a Centre for resolving investment disputes, and, in any case, it was very unlikely that countries in Latin America would be willing to give a general waiver to submit their disputes to arbitration.[13] As it is commonly understood, Latin America has been for years influenced by the Calvo doctrine which was based on the assumption that: (1) equality, sovereignty, and independence are paramount rights of the States; (2) States, being equal, sovereign, and independent, have the right to expect non-interference from other States, and finally; (3) aliens have to abide by the local law of the State wherein they reside without invoking diplomatic protection of their governments in the prosecution of claims arising out of contracts, insurrection, civil

8. UNCTAD, South-South Cooperation in International Investment Agreements, U.N. Doc. UNCTAD/ITE/IIT/2005/3 (2005), 5.
9. UNCTAD, IIA issues Note (March 2011) issue 1, https://investmentpolicy.unctad.org/publications/series/2/international-investment-agreements (accessed 16 Dec. 2024).
10. UNCTAD, IIA issues Note (September 2021) issue 4, https://investmentpolicy.unctad.org/publications/series/2/international-investment-agreements (accessed 16 Dec. 2024).
11. *Ibid.*
12. W. Michael Reisman, Reflections on the Control Mechanism of the ICSID System, in *The Review of International Arbitral Awards*, 250-251 (Emmanuel Gaillard ed. 2008).
13. ICSID, *History of the ICSID Convention*, Vol. II-1, 61 (2009).

war or mob violence.[14] This explains why it was not until the mid-late 1990s that countries in the region started signing BITs and ratifying the ICSID Convention. The 1990s were also categorised by a wave of privatisation for many developing countries, seeking to attract foreign direct investment. Still, many unanticipated and undesired side effects of ICSID treaty-based arbitration started to come to light, such as the lack of consistency and predictability of the arbitral awards, which have in turn challenged ISDS legitimacy.[15]

The lack of consistency in arbitral decisions is by far one of the major concerns for developing countries, and Latin American countries in particular. This is more evident when arbitrators are called to interpret and apply IIAs from the twentieth century (i.e., old generation of investment treaties), which are written more broadly and, thus, make the arbitrators' task more complex. Indeed, because the myriad of IIAs might respond to different models adopted by countries, arbitrators may adopt different interpretations regarding the same legal issue. Furthermore, many of these treaties have no choice of law. As a result, the applicable law will depend on the rules of arbitration. For instance, in the case of ICSID Arbitration, Article 42(1) of the ICSID Convention states that in the absence of the agreement of the parties, 'the Tribunal shall apply the law of the Contracting state party to the dispute (including its rules on conflicts of laws) and such rules of international law as may be applicable'. This provides arbitrators with a broad power for interpreting IIAs. Hence, when interpreting an IIA, arbitral tribunals are confronted not only with the lack of clarity of the text but also with the lack of guidelines on how to interpret and fill the gaps of the applicable text while looking to other sources of international law.[16]

Perhaps, the most emblematic example of the lack of consistency in the ISDS system is represented by the claims brought by foreign investors against Argentina, after the sovereign debt restructuring that followed its financial crisis in the early 2000s.[17] As highlighted in *CMS v. Argentina* annulment, the ad hoc Committee cannot simply substitute its view of the law and its appreciation of the facts for those of the tribunal, notwithstanding the identified errors and lacunas in the award.[18] A similar scenario to the interpretation of the state of necessity exception can be found in the

14. Manuel R. Garcia-Mora, The Calvo Clause in Latin American Constitutions and International Law, *Marq.L. Rev.* (1950), Vol. 33, 205.
15. Margie-Lys Jaime, A New Legal Framework for Improving Investor-State Dispute Settlement (ISDS), in *Privatizing Dispute Resolution* 487 (Löic Cadiet, Burkhard Hess, Marta Requejo Isidro eds 2019).
16. Margie-Lys Jaime, Relying Upon Parties' Interpretation in Treaty-Based Investor-State Dispute Settlement: Filling the Gaps in International Investment Agreements, *Georgetown J. Int'l Law* (2014), Vol. 46, 261, 277.
17. William W. Burke-White, The Argentine Financial Crisis: State Liability under BITs and the Legitimacy of the ICSID System, *TDM* (2009), 6; Luis Castillo Argañarás, The State of Necessity as International Defense Raised by a State Undergoing a Financial Crisis. A Case Study, *TDM* (2007), 4; Alejandro Escobar, Argentina's Multiplication of Investor-State Arbitration Proceedings, in *Le Contentieux Arbitral Transnational Relatif à L'investissement: Nouveaux Développements* 219 (Charles Leben ed. 2006).
18. *CMS Gas Transmission Company v. Republic of Argentina* (25 Sep. 2007) Decision on the Application for Annulment, ICSID Case No. ARB/01/8, para. 136.

arena of contract claims versus treaty claims and the interpretation of the umbrella clause included in several IIAs.[19]

Furthermore, in *Chevron*, the Republic of Ecuador put forward the misinterpretation of Article II(7) of the investment treaty.[20] According to Ecuador, there was no indication 'that the parties to the Treaty contemplated lowering the standard for establishing a denial of justice through the Treaty provisions'.[21] However, in the words of the arbitral tribunal, 'Article II(7) was [] created as an independent treaty standard to address a lack of clarity in the customary international law regarding denial of justice.'[22] In other words, the fact that Article II(7) does not make any reference to denial of justice or to customary international law would open the door for looking beyond the denial of justice. Consequently, the arbitral tribunal held for the claimants holding that Ecuador breached Article II(7) of the BIT through the undue delay of the Ecuadorian courts in deciding the claimants' seven judicial court cases.[23] Misinterpretation of investment treaties, contrary to the willingness of the Parties to the treaty, was also evident in *Pope & Talbot*, where the arbitral tribunal was confronted with an interpretation given by the Parties that contradicted a previous decision made by the same arbitral tribunal.[24]

As a result of these contradictions and the lack of predictability and consistency in the system, several countries in Latin America started to withdraw from ICSID (Bolivia, Ecuador, Venezuela),[25] while others decided to terminate several of their BITs

19. Umbrella clauses, also called the 'respect clause', are those provisions included in several BITs concerning the host state commitment to observe 'any other obligation' it may have entered into with regard to investments by investors of the other parties. *See* Anthony C. Sinclair, The Origins of the Umbrella Clause in the International Law of Investment Protection, *Arbitration International* (2004), Vol. 20, 411 https://doi.org/10.1093/arbitration/20.4.411.
20. *Chevron Corp. and Texaco Petroleum Co. v. Ecuador*, UNCITRAL Arbitration Rules, Partial Award on the Merits, 53 (30 Mar. 2010). Pursuant to Art. II(7) of the Ecuador-United States BIT, 1997, '[e]ach Party shall provide effective means of asserting claims and enforcing rights with respect to investment, investment agreements, and investment authorizations'. Treaty between the United States of America and the Republic of Ecuador concerning the Encouragement and Reciprocal Protection of Investment, U.S.-Ecuador, Aug. 1993, S. Treaty Doc. No. 103-115 (1993).
21. *Ibid.*, para. 219.
22. *Ibid.*, para. 243.
23. *Ibid.*, para. 249.
24. The Free Trade Commission (FTC) under NAFTA interpreted Art. 1105 as a minimum standard pursuant to customary international law, while the arbitral tribunal affirmed that the concepts of 'fair and equitable treatment' and 'full protection and security' could not require treatment in addition to or beyond that which is required by that standard, and do not create additional substantive rights. Furthermore, the award on damages stated that irrespective of the interpretation given by the FTC, the arbitral tribunal must decide on the interpretation issue. *Pope & Talbot Inc. v. Government of Canada*, Award on the Merits of Phase II (10 Apr. 2001).
25. UNCTAD, Denunciation of the ICSID Convention and BITS: Impact on Investor-State Claims (December 2010). IIA Issues Note No. 2, UNCTAD/WEB/DIAE/IA/2010/6. *See also* Alejandro Escobar, Bolivia Exposes 'Critical' Date Ambiguity. The ICSID Convention is Ambiguous on when Obligations Survive Exit from the Treaty, *Global Arb Rev* (2017), Vol. 2, 3, 17; Emmanuel Gaillard, The Denunciation of the ICSID Convention *NYLJ* (26 Jun. 2007), 3, 6; David Samuels, Bolivia's Withdrawal from ICSID Happened So Fast, Few Had Time to React. Fortunately, for Investors That Won't Make a Difference, *Global Arb Rev* (2007), Vol. 2, 11, 12.

(Ecuador, Venezuela, South Africa, among others).[26] Beyond these unilateral reactions, Latin America was the source of a more radical response in the late 2000s: the creation of the Union of South American Nations (UNASUR) Arbitration Centre to 'compete' with ICSID. At first, the initiative was supported by Argentina, Bolivia, Brazil, Chile, Colombia, Ecuador, Guyana, Paraguay, Peru, Suriname, Uruguay, and Venezuela.[27] However, the Centre never took off. On the contrary, at least Ecuador has decided to rejoin ICSID.

It is, however, noted that the withdrawal of consent to ISDS is not an anti-foreign investment or anti-international law policy but rather a way to address State concerns with existing treaties and to enable countries to focus on developing new approaches to ISDS.[28] Similarly, it has been argued that termination of IIAs, either unilaterally or multilaterally, could 'give host states greater certainty regarding their potential exposure to claims or liability and could establish a clean slate on which host and home states could develop and implement policies that take into account evidence on attracting and governing investments in a manner consistent with the SDGs'.[29] Nonetheless, the International Institute for Sustainable Development (IISD) has attempted to develop a model of IIA to be used as a handbook for negotiators. According to IISD, the failure to negotiate binding multilateral rules for investment should not be a reason for abandoning the search for multilateral rules, but rather, 'it is an indication of their importance and of the fact that governments have not yet identified an appropriate negotiating agenda'.[30]

In recent years, UNCTAD's IIAs reform accelerator has highlighted the need to accelerate the reform of existing and ageing networks of IIAs to better respond to today's challenges while maintaining investment protection.[31] Here again, low- and middle-income States have played a significant role in pushing for the reform of IIAs. Indeed, these countries are the ones with more experience of how IIA provisions work in the real world. In other words, they are more likely to know what works in the

26. In 2021, twelve years after it denounced the agreement, Ecuador ratified the ICSID Convention. In 2009, the Ecuadorian government argued that the ICSID Convention violated Art. 422 of the Ecuadorian constitution, which prohibits international treaties in which the State cedes sovereign jurisdiction to international arbitration bodies. The argument is still valid for the denunciation of IIAs. *See* IISD, Investment Treaty New (7 Oct. 2021), https://www.iisd.org/itn/en/2021/10/07/ecuador-rejoins-the-icsid-convention/ (accessed 16 Dec. 2024).
27. Silvia Karina Fiezzoni, The Challenge of UNASUR Member Countries to Replace ICSID Arbitration, *Beijing Law Review* (2011) 134-144 https://doi.org/10.4236/blr.2011.23014.
28. Lise Johnson, Lisa Sachs, Brooke Guven & Jesse Coleman, Clearing the Path: Withdrawal of Consent and Termination as Next Steps for Reforming International Investment Law (April 2018) 8-9, https://ccsi.columbia.edu/files/2018/04/IIA-CCSI-Policy%EF%BF%BEPaper-FINAL-April-2018.pdf (accessed 16 Dec. 2024).
29. *Ibid.*, 9.
30. Aaron Cosbey, Howard Mann, Konrad von Moltke & Luke Eric Peterson, *IISD Model International Agreement on Investment for Sustainable Development* (2nd ed. 2006), https://www.iisd.org/system/files/publications/investment_model_int_handbook.pdf (accessed 16 Dec. 2024).
31. UNCTAD, Reforming Investment Dispute Settlement: A Stocktaking (IIA Issues Note, No. 1, March 2019). *See also*, UNCTAD, Recent Developments in the IIA Regime: Accelerating IIA Reform (IIA Issues Note, No. 3, August 2021).

system and what does not. In practice, countries may adopt a holistic approach, combining substantive and procedural reform options during the development of future treaties as well as the modernisation of existing ones.[32]

It shall be noted, however, that among the key reform proposals affecting developing and emerging economies, the adoption of a minimum tax for the largest MNEs could expose States to tax-related claims brought under their ISDS mechanisms, as tax measures are traditionally part of the investment promotion toolkit of these countries.[33] Therefore, there is a need for assessing potential impacts on the local economy as well as achieving greater coordination and cooperation between tax and investment policymakers.

In the African continent, the Protocol to the Agreement establishing the African Continental Free Trade Area on Investment (AfCFTA) is a good example of the incorporation of investors' obligations, including compliance with national and international law, as well as high standards of business ethics, investment-related human rights, and labour standards.[34] The Protocol also includes principles like the right to regulate and the respect of public policies and minimum standards concerning environment, labour, and consumer protection.

Other countries like Ecuador, even if they are part of ICSID, have decided to no longer negotiate or renegotiate investment treaties; instead, they are part of investment contracts where the investors have the choice of submitting their claims to international arbitration. This might explain the current work engaged by the International Chamber of Commerce (ICC) Institute of World Business Law and UNIDROIT on international investment contracts.[35] The project aims at developing guidance to foster the modernisation and standardisation of international investment contracts. In this sense, it will explore the interaction between the UNIDROIT Principles and common provisions in international investment contracts, and it will seek to address several recent developments in the area of international investment law, such as the increasing focus on corporate social responsibility and sustainability.[36]

32. *See* UNCTAD, Review of ISDS Decisions in 2019: Selected IIA Reform Issues (IIA Issues Note, No. 1, January 2021).
33. Among the key implications, an international minimum tax is expected to: (i) discourage MNEs from shifting profits and tax revenues to low-tax countries and also lead to less conduit investment through tax havens; (ii) reduce tax competition and the race to the bottom that has lowered tax revenues in many countries over the past three decades, particularly in developing and transition economies; and (iii) necessitate reviews of tax incentive regimes adopted by countries to attract investment. UNCTAD (August 2021) *supra* n. 31, p. 10.
34. AfCFTA, Protocol to the Agreement establishing the African Continental Free Trade Area on Investment (January 2023), https://edit.wti.org/document/show/e5d51824-c467-4e24-922b-3fb376d89550 (accessed 16 Dec. 2024).
35. IISD, *UNIDROIT and ICC Are Working on Investment Contract Harmonization*, Investment Treaty News, https://www.iisd.org/itn/en/2024/04/02/unidroit-and-icc-are-working-on-investment-contract-harmonisation/ (accessed 16 Dec. 2024).
36. UNIDROIT, https://www.unidroit.org/work-in-progress/investment-contracts-upicc/ (accessed 16 Dec. 2024).

B The Growth of Other Forms of Dispute Resolution

While the 'cooling off period' is a common tool in IIAs, the use of methods other than direct amicable dispute resolution was unusual until very recently. Indeed, it was not until the past ten or fifteen years that other methods of dispute resolution, such as conciliation and mediation, started to be fostered in the international arena.[37] This section will explore other forms of dispute resolution that have been put in place mainly by developing countries.

1 *Amicable Dispute Resolution Alternatives*

Mediation could be particularly useful for developing countries in the sense that it provides a space for attempting to resolve disputes at a minimum cost. According to a commentator, a rule-oriented international investment regime is important to developing countries – especially the smaller ones – because international law may provide developing countries an opportunity to lock in the effects of IIAs in domestic reform and enhance the coordination of policy implementation.[38] In other words, mediation could be particularly suitable to resolve investment disputes when one or both of the parties is a developing country.

Recent investment treaties contain a State's standing offer to mediate, which is subsequently accepted by an investor.[39] There are different types of mediation clauses: (i) clauses with an amicable settlement period and, potentially, a bare direction to seek 'amicable settlement' before arbitration; (ii) clauses explicitly permitting mediation or other specified amicable dispute resolution methods before arbitration; (iii) clauses affirmatively encouraging mediation or other amicable dispute resolution mechanisms during the amicable settlement period; (iv) clauses mandating mediation or other amicable dispute resolution procedures before arbitration; and (v) clauses permitting mediation at any point in time (stand-alone mechanism for mediation).[40]

United Nations Commission on International Trade Law (UNCITRAL) Working Group III has discussed different alternatives for providing mediation as an alternative dispute resolution in investment treaties, domestic legislation, and investment contracts, establishing favourable conditions for its use.[41] Generally, the Working Group III felt that mediation should be voluntary and flexible. In this sense, it was said during the discussions that mandatory commencement of mediation could delay the resolution of

37. *See* UNCTAD, Investor–State Disputes: Prevention and Alternatives to Arbitration (2010).
38. Roberto Echandi, What Do Developing Countries Expect from the International Investment Regime?, in *The Evolving International Investment Regime: Expectations, Realities, Options* 3-21 (J.E. Alvarez & K.P. Sauvant eds Oxford Academic, 2021).
39. ICSID, *Overview of Investment Treaty Clauses on Mediation* (2021), chrome-extension://efaidnbmnnnibpcajpcglclefindmkaj/https://icsid.worldbank.org/sites/default/files/publications/Overview_Mediation_in_Treaties.pdf (accessed 16 Dec. 2024).
40. *Ibid.*
41. UNCITRAL, Possible Reform of Investor-State Dispute Settlement (ISDS). Draft provisions on Mediation. A/CN.9/1150 (25 Apr. 2023). The Model Provisions allow parties to exercise control over the mediation process to reach a self-tailored outcome.

the dispute adding to costs.[42] Furthermore, the purpose of the Guidelines on Investment Mediation is to explain how mediation can be utilised to resolve investment parties from a practical perspective.[43] In July 2023, the Commission adopted both the UNCITRAL Model Provisions on Mediation and the UNCITRAL Guidelines on Mediation for International Investment Disputes.[44] In any event, it should be kept in mind that parties are the ones in control of the process and are expected to be actively engaged in the negotiations.

Another instrument under discussion within Working Group III is the Draft guidelines on the prevention of international investment disputes.[45] The guidelines do not contain specific recommendations; however, they are intended to guide States in the implementation of a coherent and effective dispute prevention and mitigation system. At the 47th session held in Vienna on 22-26 January 2024, Working Group III decided to instruct the Secretariat with the task of updating the draft guidelines on the prevention and mitigation of international investment disputes based on written comments received from delegations and inputs received during the intersessional meeting.

2 *State-State Cooperation and Facilitation of Foreign Investments*

State-to-state cooperation is another form of amicable dispute resolution that has been proposed as an alternative to ISDS. As it is well known, Brazil has not ratified any of the traditional BITs it has negotiated; instead, it has successfully executed 'Cooperation and Facilitation Investment Agreements'[46] (CFIA), with countries like Angola and Mexico, and agreed on similar investment provisions in FTAs with Chile and Egypt, in addition to the Intra-Mercosur Investment Facilitation Protocol.[47] Besides, Brazil is one of the largest economies that has never been part of ICSID.

The CFIA focuses on promoting cooperation between States to facilitate and encourage mutual investment, as well as the establishment of mechanisms for risk mitigation and prevention of disputes. Thus, it does not include ISDS as an option to resolve disputes. As a substitute, the CFIA creates two institutional arrangements: the Joint Committee and the Focal Point, which are intended to address the controversies and avoid litigation. The Joint Committee is composed of government representatives of the parties to the treaty and has the following functions and responsibilities: (a)

42. Report of Working Group III (Investor-State Dispute Settlement Reform) on the work of its forty-fifth session (New York, 27-31 Mar. 2023). A/CN.9/1131.
43. UNCITRAL, Possible Reform of Investor-State Dispute Settlement (ISDS). Draft guidelines on investment mediation, A/CN.9/1151 (25 Apr. 2023).
44. United Nations, https://unis.unvienna.org/unis/en/pressrels/2023/unisl344.html (accessed 16 Dec. 2024).
45. UNCITRAL, Possible Reform of Investor-State Dispute Settlement (ISDS). Draft guidelines on prevention and mitigation of international investment disputes. A/CN.9/WG.III/WP.235 (20 Nov. 2023).
46. A model of the agreement can be available at: https://investmentpolicy.unctad.org/international-investment-agreements/treaty-files/4786/download (accessed 16 Dec. 2024).
47. UNCTAD, Investment Policy Hub, https://investmentpolicy.unctad.org/international-investment-agreements/countries/27/brazil (accessed 16 Dec. 2024).

supervise the implementation and execution of this Agreement; (b) discuss and divulge opportunities for the expansion of mutual investment; (c) coordinate the implementation of the mutually agreed cooperation and facilitation agendas; (d) consult with the private sector and civil society, when applicable, on their views on specific issues related to the work of the Joint Committee; (e) seek to resolve any issues or disputes concerning investments of investors of a Party in an amicable manner; and (f) supplement the rules for arbitral dispute settlement between the Parties.[48] The Focal Point, also called the *Ombudsman*, works as a single window for investors where they can address their enquiries about investments in Brazil.[49] The responsibilities of the Focal Point include: (a) endeavour to follow the recommendations of the Joint Committee and interact with the National Focal Point of the other Party, by this Agreement; (b) follow up on requests and inquiries of the other Party or of investors of the other Party with the competent authorities and inform the stakeholders on the results of its actions; (c) assess, in consultation with relevant government authorities, suggestions and complaints received from the other Party or investors of the other Party and recommend, as appropriate, actions to improve the investment environment; (d) seek to prevent differences in investment matters, in collaboration with government authorities and relevant private entities; (e) provide timely and useful information on regulatory issues on general investment or on specific projects; and (f) report its activities and actions to the Joint Committee, when appropriate.[50]

Furthermore, any dispute shall be the object of consultations and negotiations and be previously examined by the Joint Committee, before initiating a State-to-State arbitration. In other words, only when an amicable solution is not reached and the parties decide not to follow the Joint Committee's report may an arbitration State-to-State be initiated. Although the affected investors are not part of the dispute resolution proceedings, they may participate in the bilateral meetings. The purpose of the arbitration is to determine the conformity (or nonconformity) of a State measure with the Agreement (Article 24.2). Still, if the arbitration award provides monetary compensation, the Party receiving such compensation shall transfer to the holders of the rights of the investment in question, after deducting the costs of the dispute (Article 24.13). The CFIA also includes provisions related to corporate social responsibility,

48. Article 17 of the CFIA model agreement.
49. Korea was the first country to introduce an Ombudsman option in 1999, providing tailored post-investment and grievance-settlement services for foreign investors and enterprises doing business in the country. The idea of the Ombudsman was to collect the grievances and complaints from foreign companies and analyse the nature and cause of these complaints, to be used as input to propose regulatory reforms. Based on the Ombudsman's examination of complaints, it can recommend policy improvements to the government and request policy reviews from relevant government bodies. Korea is an example of how a country can pass from a low-income economy to an important partner contributor to the World Bank's fund. Korea's experience is certainly a model role for developing countries. Amber van der Graaf, *Future of Manufacturing Foreign Investment Ombudsman: Internationalisation Policy Measure* (2018). The Republic of Korea has taken recent action to be considered part of developed regions. *See* United Nations, Historical and Updated Classification of Developed and Developing Regions, *supra* n. 5.
50. Article 18 of the CFIA model agreement.

corruption, and illegality, as well as provisions on investment and environment, labour, and health.[51] However, these provisions may not be subject to arbitration.

The African Protocol is another example of an agreement including investment promotion and facilitation provisions and establishing national focal points to provide support to investors.[52] It foresees the right for a State Party to submit a claim on behalf of its nationals through the exercise of diplomatic protection and the recourse to dispute prevention and management;[53] however, it does not exclude the possibility of ISDS.[54]

Beyond the Brazilian initiative and the protection of investments through international investment contracts, several countries have chosen to limit or not include ISDS in their investment agreement. That is the case of the United States-Mexico-Canada Agreement (USMCA), where ISDS is only available between the United States and Mexico. Because there are no other investment agreements with ISDS provisions in force between the United States and Canada, investors from Canada or the United States will not have access to ISDS.[55] ISDS between Canada and Mexico may be available under the CPTPP but not under the USMCA.

However, the ISDS mechanism between Mexico and the United States has two modalities: (i) Violation of the obligations of National Treatment, Most-Favoured Nation Treatment, and Direct Expropriation; and (ii) Violation of any [breach of the] Investment Chapter [obligation]. Furthermore, Annex 14-D requires that local remedies be exhausted for at least thirty months, subject to an open-ended futility exception. Investors are also required to submit waivers of the right to initiate or continue litigation along with their notice of arbitration (Annex 14.D.5.1(e)). Likewise, Appendix 3 prohibits US investors from submitting claims based on the USMCA if they have already been submitted to Mexican courts. Thus, even if the USMCA does not completely exclude ISDS, it is more limited and targeted than its predecessor North American Free Trade Agreement (NAFTA). Indeed, NAFTA marked the dawn of an era of investment treaties in the 1990s. Thirty years later, the USMCA seems to be indicating the beginning of a new age.

These unique initiatives show States' willingness to limit ISDS by using other forms of dispute resolution or by limiting the scope of ISDS. This could certainly have a practical impact in the way investors and host Sates address international investment disputes, as well as in the number of treaty-based investment arbitrations. Nevertheless, one can predict a progressive increase of contract-based arbitration.

51. Articles 14, 15, and 16 of the CFIA model agreement.
52. Protocol on Investment to the Agreement Establishing the African Continental Free Trade Area, Art. 8.
53. *See* Arts 1 and 2 of Annex 1 Rules and procedures governing the management and settlement of disputes under the protocol on investment to the agreement establishing the AfCFTA.
54. *Ibid.*, Arts 5 et seq.
55. The United States-Mexico-Canada Agreement (USMCA), https://investmentpolicy.unctad.org/international-investment-agreements/treaties/bit/3841/usmca-2018-/ (accessed 16 Dec. 2024). Still, established investors can only bring claims about expropriation and non-discrimination. They can no longer base allegations on the most controversial and unsettled concepts like fair and equitable treatment. *See* Annex 14-D.

3 *The Establishment of a Multilateral Investment Court*

Recently, several countries in Asia, such as Singapore and Vietnam, as well as emerging countries in Latin America, including Chile, have accepted the European Union's (EU's) new investment policy approach consisting of the establishment of a permanent investment court (first-instance tribunal and appeal tribunal), where investors would not be involved in the appointment of the decision-makers.

For instance, according to the Singapore-EU FTA, both the tribunal of first instance and the appeal tribunal are composed of six members appointed for an initial eight-year period, two appointed by the EU, two by Singapore, and the other two who shall not be nationals of any EU Member State or of Singapore, jointly nominated by both parties.[56] Likewise, the Vietnam-EU FTA creates an investment tribunal system by the establishment of a nine-member tribunal composed of three nationals of an EU Member State, three nationals of Vietnam, and three nationals of third countries, who are appointed for a four-year renewable term; however, as is the general rule, the tribunal shall hear cases in divisions consisting of three members, of whom one shall be a national of each of the parties and the third a national of a third country.[57] Regarding the appeal tribunal, this is reduced to six members appointed for a four-year renewable term.

The EU-Chile Association Agreement also provides for an Investment Court System, consisting of a tribunal of first instance initially composed of nine Judges and an appeal tribunal established to hear appeals initially composed of six members.[58] Before submission of a claim, the claimant shall: (a) withdraw any pending claim or proceeding before any domestic or international court or tribunal; (b) provide a written waiver that it will not initiate any claim or proceedings before any domestic or international court or tribunal under domestic or international law; (c) a declaration that it will not enforce any award rendered under this section before such award has become final (Article 10.28). Furthermore, a dispute may be settled amicably through negotiations, good offices, or mediation, where possible, and a claimant shall wait at least six months from the submission of the request for consultations and, where applicable, at least three months from the submission of the notice requesting a determination of the Respondent to be able to submit a claim to the Tribunal of First

56. Singapore-European Union, Investment Protection Agreement, Chapter 3 (Dispute Settlement), https://investmentpolicy.unctad.org/international-investment-agreements/treaties/treaties-with-investment-provisions/3545/eu---singapore-investment-protection-agreement-2018- (accessed 16 Dec. 2024).
57. European Union-Vietnam FTA, Chapter 8 (Trade in Services, Investment and E-Commerce, Chapter II (Investment) section 3 (Resolution of investment disputes), subsection 4 (Investment Tribunal System) Art. 12 (Tribunal), https://investmentpolicy.unctad.org/international-investment-agreements/treaties/treaties-with-investment-provisions/3616/eu---viet-nam-investment-protection-agreement-2019- (accessed 16 Dec. 2024).
58. EU-Chile Advanced Framework Agreement, https://policy.trade.ec.europa.eu/eu-trade-relationships-country-and-region/countries-and-regions/chile/eu-chile-agreement_en (accessed 16 Dec. 2024).

Instance (Article 10.28).[59] Certainly, this is an initiative by the EU and not an initiative led by developing countries; however, it shows a discomfort with the current ISDS system.

One of the main reasons for establishing a permanent court is to fight against the lack of predictability and inconsistency of the ISDS system. However, a permanent investment court could only avoid inconsistencies if it has jurisdiction concerning not only a specific IIA but also the existing myriad of IIAs. This is perhaps one of the reasons why the European Commission has decided to pursue the negotiation of a MIC in the framework of the UNCITRAL Working Group III.[60] This view, however, is far from being accepted by a plurality of developing countries. Many concerns surround the possibility of the establishment of such a structure, including the costs of such a structure as well as the compatibility with the current system (mainly ICSID and UNCITRAL). For these reasons, one could think of establishing an appellate mechanism without the creation of a MIC.[61] Indeed, the establishment of an appeal mechanism does not raise the same concerns than a permanent investment court would regarding the selection and appointment of the first-instance tribunal while addressing the concern of lack of predictability and consistency of the system.

C The Development of New Procedural Rules

Since 2017 Working Group III received the mission to: '(i) identify and consider concerns regarding ISDS; (ii) consider whether reform was desirable in the light of any identified concerns; and (iii) if so, develop any relevant solutions to be recommended to the Commission'.[62] Specifically, the UNCITRAL Working Group III on ISDS reform has decided to focus on the procedural aspects of ISDS rather than on the underlying investment protection standards. Therefore, many aspects have been developed over the past six years. In October 2023, Working Group III was able to start discussions on the draft provisions and cross-cutting issues.[63] Specifically, the UNCITRAL Secretariat presented twenty-five provisions for discussion divided into three sections.

Section A on conditions and limitations for submissions of claims includes provisions such as denial of benefits, counterclaims, and the right to regulate. Section B concerns the conduct of the proceedings, which are provisions that are likely to be

59. The determination of the Respondent is another policy improvement adopted by the Parties to promote an amicable settlement. In this sense, the claimant shall deliver a notice to the EU requesting a determination of the Respondent.
60. Council of the European Union, 'Multilateral Investment Court: Council Gives Mandate to the Commission to Open Negotiations' (20 Mar. 2018) EU News 5 5/2018, https://www.consilium.europa.eu/en/press/press-releases/2018/03/20/multilateral-investment-court-council-gives-mandate-to-the-commission-to-open-negotiations/ (accessed 16 Dec. 2024).
61. Margie-Lys Jaime, Reshaping Investor-State Dispute Settlement Through an Appellate Review Mechanism, in *The Investor-State Dispute Settlement System. Reform, Replace or Status Quo?* 137-156 (Alan M. Anderson & Ben Beaumont eds 2021).
62. *See* Working Group III (Investor-State Dispute Settlement Reform) on the work of its thirty-fifth session A/CN.9/935 (14 May 2018).
63. *See* UNCITRAL, Note by the Secretariat, Draft provisions on procedural and cross-cutting issues. A/CN.9/WG.III/WP.231; UNCITRAL, Note by the Secretariat, Annotations to the draft provisions on procedural and cross-cutting issues. A/CN.9/WG.III/WP.232.

accepted as procedural rules that might be adopted as an amendment or supplement to the UNCITRAL Arbitration Rules. In this sense, an investor willing to submit a claim under UNCITRAL Arbitration Rules would accept these rules tailored for ISDS. For most of the provisions, they mirror the status quo of arbitration practice; yet, for some of them, it might serve as the starting point for advancing a rule that reflects the concerns of States and other stakeholders. For example, the provision on Third-party funding might cover a greater disclosure than what is required by current arbitration rules, including the ICSID Arbitration Rules. Finally, section C on the decisions of the Tribunal includes a provision regarding the assessment of damages and compensation, as well as rules on the allocation of costs and the time for making a final decision. It was clear from the Working Group III discussions that except for the damages provision, the content of section C could be part of some kind of amendment of UNCITRAL Arbitration Rules, just as section B. On the other hand, some of the provisions could be part of treaty provisions, including in the Multilateral Investment Instrument, and, finally, some could be formulated as guidelines for States to adopt.

For some, part of these issues, in particular those of section A, might be outside of the Working Group III mandate; however, a group of developing countries noted that the mandate as it was set in 2017 said nothing specifically about 'procedural' matters.[64] In other words, it was a comprehensive mandate about ISDS, and the discretion belonged to the Working Group III to address the reform as it deemed fit. In particular, some developing States expressed their willingness to prioritise critical issues such as damages.[65] On the last day of the 47th session, the Working Group continued to discuss procedural and cross-cutting issues. After discussion, the Secretariat was requested to classify the draft provisions largely into three categories: (i) those that aimed to achieve harmonisation with existing procedural rules (including the 2022 ICSID Arbitration Rules) and could form a supplement to the UNCITRAL Arbitration Rules; (ii) those that would build on existing procedural rules and provisions found in recent investment treaties, which could be drafted as treaty provisions for adoption by States; and (iii) those that were not found in procedural rules addressing the so-called cross-cutting issues.[66] The outcome is still to be seen. At this point, it is clear that developing countries will have a word to say on these matters.

II CONCLUDING REMARKS

Low- and middle-income States play an increasing role in the international fora, actively participating in the reform of international arbitration, as well as being at the forefront of pushing evolving values. Furthermore, these States tend to have numerous

64. Report of Working Group III (Investor-State Dispute Settlement Reform) on the work of its forty-sixth session (Vienna, 9-13 Oct. 2023), A/CN.9/1160.
65. Güneş Ünüvar, *The Mandate Conundrum: Reflections on the 46th Session of the UNCITRAL Working Group III on ISDS Reform* (21 Nov. 2023), https://www.ejiltalk.org/the-mandate-conundrum-reflections-on-the-46th-session-of-the-uncitral-working-group-iii-on-isds-reform/ (accessed 16 Dec. 2024).
66. Report of Working Group III (Investor-State Dispute Settlement Reform) on the work of its forty-seventh session (12 Feb. 2024), A/CN.9/1161, p. 20.

arbitrations, and, thus, they come across these issues firsthand. For instance, Panama has been subject to twenty arbitrations, most of them under the ICSID Convention. Yet, 90% of these cases were filed in the last ten years and under the basis of treaties that date back to the twentieth century or the first part of the twenty-first century. The scenario of other Latin American countries is not much different. Colombia, for example, had its first ICSID case in 2016; however, since then, it has been subject to twenty cases under the ICSID Convention. Mexico has been a respondent in forty-seven cases, twenty-four of which were filed in the past five years.[67] Honduras, for its part, has had nine cases in 2023, which has motivated its recent withdrawal from the ICSID Convention.[68]

Indeed, different approaches have been taken, from terminating and renovating the stock of treaties to the full exclusion of ISDS, as well as active participation in different forums, including UNCITRAL Working Group III.

Admittedly, the new generation of international investment treaties goes far beyond the traditional IIAs focused on the protection of direct foreign investments. In this sense, the new generation of IIAs includes a series of obligations regarding not only investors' compliance with the host State legislation but also specific commitments related to policy issues such as corporate social responsibility, environment, labour, and health. In this sense, Latin America and the Caribbean have engaged in an active participation towards a comprehensive investment agenda to embark on a stronger and more sustainable development path.[69] Likewise, governments in Central Asia have sought to take the necessary steps to achieve sustainable development by shifting to a new generation of BITs with elements that change the focus from economic development to a wider development implication of investment protection.[70] In South Africa, ISDS decisions rendered based on the old generation of IIAs have also widespread concerns regarding the ISDS, fostering a new generation of IIAs. To this end, the Southern African Development Community Model Bilateral Investment Treaty (the SA Model BIT) was materialised in 2012.[71] In this same vein, the Pan-African Investment Code (PAIC) emerged in 2016 as a response to the old generation of treaties, which are indeed in favour of investors.[72] As a corollary, in 2019, the AfCFTA entered into force.[73]

However, procedural reform is a crucial pillar of the ISDS reform to tackle the concerns identified by Working Group III. Therefore, no doubt that developing

67. ICSID, https://icsid.worldbank.org/cases/case-database (accessed 16 Dec. 2024).
68. On 24 Feb. 2024, the World Bank received a written notice of denunciation from the Republic of Honduras, https://icsid.worldbank.org/news-and-events/communiques/honduras-denounces-icsid-convention#: ~ :text = On%20February%2024%2C%202024%2C%20the,from%20the%20Republic%20of%20Honduras (accessed 16 Dec. 2024).
69. *See* OECD et al., *Latin American Economic Outlook* (2023), https://repositorio.cepal.org/server/api/core/bitstreams/50120204-0eb0-46fd-af2b-99e3de70f5e7/content (accessed 16 Dec. 2024).
70. IISD, *Unlocking Sustainable Development in Central Asian Bilateral Investment Treaties*, Investment Treaty News (13 Jan. 2024), https://www.iisd.org/itn/en/2024/01/13/unlocking-sustainable-development-in-central-asian-bilateral-investment-treaties/ (accessed 16 Dec. 2024).
71. Lexology, *Investor-State Arbitration and the 'Next Generation' of Investment Treaties*, https://www.lexology.com/library/detail.aspx?g=f41db66d-a54d-4d23-b411-4835062f6b22 (accessed 16 Dec. 2024).
72. *Ibid.*
73. AfCFTA, https://au-afcfta.org/.

countries will continue to foster new developments in ISDS, including cross-cutting issues, such as the right to regulate and principles regarding damages and compensation. In this regard, it is critical for developing States, which are implicated in the vast majority of ISDS claims, to make clear that the most critical provisions such as the right to regulate and the assessment of damages and compensation should be prioritised over other provisions that can be found in existing rules.[74]

74. At the 47th Session in October, the Secretariat was requested to classify the draft provisions on procedural and cross-cutting issues (WP231) largely into three categories: (i) those that aimed to achieve harmonisation with existing procedural rules (including the 2022 ICSID Arbitration Rules) and could form a supplement to the UNCITRAL Arbitration Rules; (ii) those that would build on existing procedural rules and provisions found in recent investment treaties, which could be drafted as treaty provisions for adoption by States; and (iii) those that were not found in procedural rules addressing the so-called cross-cutting issues. UNCITRAL, Report of Working Group III (Investor-State Dispute Settlement Reform) on the work of its forty-seventh session (Vienna, 22-26 Jan. 2024) A/CN.9/1161 (12 Feb. 2024). To assist the Secretariat in this exercise, delegations were invited to submit written comments, possibly indicating the priority to be given and how they wished to make progress on the draft provisions.

CHAPTER 6

Small (Island) States and International Dispute Resolution

Petra Butler

The think piece canvasses small states' power of collaboration on the international law plane. It discusses two examples, one where small states affected considerable change by working together, namely climate change, and one where small states could revolutionise international commercial access to justice if they would work together. Small states, despite being often the most disadvantaged members of the global community, have the advantage of being more agile and better able to collaborate than their larger siblings. Their pioneering collaboration contributed to holding the causers of climate change accountable and has been direction-setting regarding measures to combat climate change and the climate change discourse. The example, discussed in the think piece, is the impact the collaboration among small states, in particular, the Pacific Island countries, could have regarding the business-to-business (B2B) access to commercial justice. The adaptation, the chapter argues, of a default B2B dispute resolution framework that would mitigate the current pitfalls of cross-border litigation by harnessing the advantages of international commercial arbitration and, depending on the region, mediation would allow small states to grow their economies and to take part more easily in global trade.

I INTRODUCTION

The climate change emergency has shone a spotlight on small states and their ability to use international dispute resolution mechanisms to facilitate change. This chapter will give a snapshot of the power small states have in using and creating international dispute mechanisms to affect change globally and for themselves.

There is no consensus what criteria should be used to classify a state as a small state. Hence, there is no agreed definition of a small state. There are many conceivable considerations that could be used to determine what is a small state, such as population, territorial size, gross domestic product, or military expenditure.[1] The United Nations, the World Bank, and the Commonwealth use 'population' as the defining characteristic of a small state.[2] Population speaks to and is often correlated with geographical size, GDP, and limited resources and capacity. However, even when population is used as the definitional basis, there is no agreement regarding the size of the population. The author based on the view of the majority of small states' stakeholders, i.e., international organisations, such as the World Bank and the Commonwealth, the Institute of Small and Micro States as well as academics, will use a 'population of 1.5 million people or less' to define small states.[3] The majority often extends the discussion of small states issues to slightly larger states that are part of the small state cluster and demonstrate the same characteristics as the neighbouring small states.[4]

Small states are located all over the world but predominantly are in Africa, the Caribbean, and the Pacific.[5] The majority of small states are small island developing states (SIDS). While sharing common challenges associated with the small size of their economies, significant migration, capacity constraints, and vulnerability to global crises, disasters, and climate change, small states are very diverse.[6] There is high variation among them in terms of, for example, population size,[7] income levels,[8] geography[9] and remoteness[10] that result in a wide spectrum of development outcomes. Politically, as a membership block, they have more power in the UN General Assembly

1. Steven Finizio, 'Small States and Integration: An Introduction' in Petra Butler et al. (eds) *Integration and International Dispute Resolution in Small States* (Springer, 2018) 3; *see also* critical discussion, Carina Alcoberro Llivina, 'Small States and Regional Dispute Resolution Mechanisms: The Caribbean and Pacific Experiences' in Petra Butler et al. (eds) *Integration and International Dispute Resolution in Small States* (Springer, 2018) 27, Chapter 2.
2. The World Bank in Small States (accessed 20 Jun. 2024); Andrea Ó Súilleabháin, *Small States at the United Nations: Diverse Perspectives, Shared Opportunities* (International Peace Institute, New York, 2014) 3 with a discussion on the definitional challenge; The Commonwealth Small States (accessed 20 Jun. 2024).
3. The World Bank in Small States (accessed 20 Jun. 2024), The Commonwealth Small States (accessed 20 Jun. 2024), the Institute of Small and Micro States (accessed 20 Jun. 2024); *see* for the range of definitions Súilleabháin, *supra* n. 2, p. 3 and Forum of Small States at the United Nations (accessed 20 Jun. 2024), established by Singapore in 1992 which includes states with a population of 10 million or less. *See* regarding academic discussion: Finizio, *supra* n. 1, p. 3.
4. *See*, The Commonwealth Small States (accessed 20 Jun. 2024), examples include Jamaica, Papua New Guinea, Namibia; World Bank (accessed 21 Jun. 2024).
5. World Bank (accessed 21 Jun. 2024).
6. *See* Finizio, *supra* n. 1, pp. 5 et seq.; *see also* regarding the following listed challenges Martin Bush, *Climate Change Adaptation in Small Island Developing States* (Wiley & Sons 2018) 28 et seq.
7. 12,000 people in Tuvalu, 2.99 million people in Jamaica – *see* World Bank (accessed 21 Jun. 2024).
8. Compare GDPs: Bahrain USD 37.8 billion and Brunei USD 13.57 billion compared to Fiji USD 4.98 billion or Samoa USD 832.9 million (source World Bank – accessed 24 Jun. 2024).
9. Some states are archipelagos dispersed over a broad ocean area (e.g., Kiribati has an area of 810 km^2 distributed in 35 atolls and islands spread over 3.6 million km^2 of ocean) World Bank (accessed 21 Jun. 2024).

than the European Union countries.[11] To exercise their power, however, small states must navigate their inherent vulnerabilities to ensure survival and economic success.[12] Collaboration, for example, in the form of multilateral and bilateral arrangements, can provide small states with the necessary resilience framework.[13] To illustrate how small states can benefit from multilateral dispute frameworks, this chapter will assess two international dispute settlement mechanisms, an existing one that small states have successfully used in their struggle against climate change and one that is, at this point in time, still theoretically but has garnered support from Commonwealth small states.

II CLIMATE CHANGE: THE INTERNATIONAL TRIBUNAL FOR THE LAW OF THE SEA

Before focusing specifically on the power of collaboration, it should be noted that international courts and tribunals established through treaties and other integration processes can enable small states with limited capabilities to effectively resolve disputes with larger or more powerful states. Using binding dispute resolution mechanisms often offers small states a way to break free from the cycle of stalemate in frustrated negotiations. Such mechanisms can also facilitate the peaceful resolution of highly sensitive and complex issues, including nuclear proliferation, environmental protection, territorial sovereignty,[14] and maritime delimitation,[15] in accordance with international law principles. Small states, one could say creatively, have been framing environmental concerns in a manner that enables these claims to be adjudicated before tribunals such as the International Court of Justice.[16] However, the leverage international courts and tribunals can provide small states is dependent on that small states are actually using the available dispute resolution mechanisms. The obstacle to the

10. Some of the states, especially SIDS, are among the most remote in terms of distance to the nearest international market, e.g., the Pacific Islands.
11. Forty-two of the UN Member States are small states, using the here advanced population definition.
12. Baldur Thorhallsson, 'Small States and the Changing Global Order: What Small State Theory Can Offer New Zealand Foreign Policymaking' in Anne-Marie Brady (ed.) *Small States and the Changing Global Order* (Springer, 2019) 379, 384 who also points out that in addition to mentioned structural limitations, small states commonly have modest military capabilities compared to larger states.
13. Note that this chapter narrowly focusses on small (island) states and their ability to use international dispute frameworks. *See*, for example, in regard to international environmental dispute resolution Tim Stephens, 'The Settlement of Disputes in International Environmental Law' in Erika Techera et al. (eds) *Routledge Handbook of International Environmental Law* (Routledge, 2020) Chapter 7.
14. *See* the border dispute between Guyana and Venezuela currently before the International Court of Justice International Court of Justice (icj-cij.org) (accessed 26 Jun. 2024).
15. *See*, for example, Dispute concerning Delimitation of the Maritime Boundary between Mauritius and Maldives in the Indian Ocean, ITLOS, Case No. 28, 28 Apr. 2023: International Tribunal for the Law of the Sea: *Dispute concerning delimitation of the maritime boundary between Mauritius and Maldives in the Indian Ocean (Mauritius/Maldives)* (itlos.org) (accessed 26 Jun. 2024).
16. *Certain Phosphate Lands in Nauru, Nauru v. Australia*, Preliminary Objections, Judgment, (1992) ICJ Rep 240 (Preliminary Objections, Judgment).

utilisation lies in their limited financial and human resources and often in the lack of institutional knowledge regarding the dispute mechanisms available for a particular issue.[17]

Limited resources, the lack of institutional knowledge and the power imbalances between small (island developing) states and larger states make collaborations between small states particularly important to overcome their individual resource and capacity constraints. Small states have gained particular momentum regarding the climate change crisis. They have played a key role in climate change negotiations, driving important milestones in climate action through various negotiating blocks, such as the Alliance of Small Island States (AOSIS), the G77, and the High Ambition Coalition. They have been the driving force behind loss and damage discussions and the establishment of a fund for responding to loss and damage at COP27.[18] They have also been instrumental in keeping the 1.5°C target in the Paris Agreement, arguing that a 2°C limit would put their countries at very high risk of impacts.[19]

Climate change affects small states and in particular SIDS disproportionately to their contribution to the climate crisis, i.e., they are low-emitting countries.[20] As already indicated, SIDS face significant environmental challenges, such as land degradation, biodiversity loss, and coastal and marine pollution.[21] These challenges are aggravated by factors like population growth and urbanisation.[22] Climate change further intensifies these challenges. Its impacts include sea-level rise, altered precipitation patterns, more frequent and severe extreme weather events, ocean acidification, and coral bleaching which have adverse effects on island communities.[23] Those effects include changes in precipitation, and higher temperatures contribute to the spread of vector-borne diseases. Ocean acidification negatively impacts fisheries, while increased storm activity and rising sea levels threaten coastal infrastructure and agriculture – both crucial, even on larger mountainous islands. Decreased agricultural productivity and fishing not only undermine food security but also affect employment

17. *See* regarding ideas how to combat the limited capacity of small states: Brian McGarry, 'Cost-Efficiency in Inter-State Dispute Settlement' in Petra Butler et al. (eds) *Integration and International Dispute Resolution in Small States* (Springer, 2018) 319.
18. *See* Kate Abnett, 'Explainer: COP27: What Is "Loss and Damage" Funding, and Who Should Pay?' *Reuters*, 20 Nov. 2022.
19. Small Islands propose 'below 1.5°C' global goal for Paris Agreement – AOSIS (accessed 26 Jun. 2024).
20. Aideen Foley, 'States of "Knowing": Uncertainty, Ambiguity and Risk in SIDS Climate Change Impacts' in S Mocanda et al. (eds) *Small Island Developing States* (Springer, 2021) 13, 14; Carola Betzold, 'Adapting to Climate Change in Small Island Developing States' 133 (2015) Climate Change 481, 481 https://doi.org/10.1007/s10584-015-1408-0.
21. *See* Md Nurul Momen & Marzina Begum, 'Small Island Development States (SIDS): Nexus of Environment and Sustainable Livelihood' in Leal Filho et al. (eds) *Partnerships for the Goals. Encyclopedia of the UN Sustainable Development Goals* (Springer, 2021).
22. *See* Md Nurul Momen & Marzina Begum, 'Small Island Development States (SIDS): Nexus of Environment and Sustainable Livelihood' in Leal Filho et al. (eds) *Partnerships for the Goals. Encyclopedia of the UN Sustainable Development Goals* (Springer, 2021).
23. *See* IPCC, 'Ch 3: Oceans and Coastal Ecosystems and Their Services' in Sixth Assessment Report: *Climate Change 2022: Impacts, Adaptation and Vulnerability* (2022).

and income, exacerbated further by declines in tourism following events such as cyclones.[24]

In summary and in the words of the United Nations Secretary-General, Antonio Guterres, 'SIDS are a test case for climate justice and financial justice.'[25] To achieve climate justice, SIDS formed a number of multilateral partnerships, such as the AOSIS[26] or the Commission of Small Island States on Climate Change and International Law (COSIS).[27] It was the latter that asked the International Tribunal for the Law of the Sea (ITLOS) for an advisory opinion in 2022 on:

> What are the specific obligations of State Parties to the United Nations Convention on the Law of the Sea ('UNCLOS'), including under Part XII:
>
> (a) to prevent, reduce and control pollution of the marine environment in relation to the deleterious effects that result or are likely to result from climate change, including through ocean warming and sea level rise, and ocean acidification, which are caused by anthropogenic greenhouse gas emissions into the atmosphere?
> (b) to protect and preserve the marine environment in relation to climate change impacts, including ocean warming and sea level rise, and ocean acidification?[28]

The significant finding of the Tribunal was its acknowledgement that greenhouse gas emissions constitute pollution of the marine environment under the UNCLOS.[29] Finding the nexus of greenhouse gas emissions and pollution was motivated by the SIDS' unique experience in regard to ocean degradation and its impact on blue economy.[30] Without the SIDS experience, their determination, and collaboration, it is unlikely that the Tribunal would have been asked to decide on the nexus at this point in time.

The Tribunal also concluded that parties to the Convention bear substantive and specific responsibilities to mitigate the impacts on the oceans arising from their greenhouse gas emissions. These obligations apply universally, encompassing both the high seas and maritime areas falling under a state's jurisdiction. Additionally, states must adopt measures necessary to implement international standards established by competent organisations like the International Maritime Organization (IMO) and

24. *See* Martin Bush, *Climate Change Adaptation in Small Island Developing States* (Wiley & Sons 2018) regarding coastal marine ecosystems, pp. 32 et seq.
25. Opening Ceremony of the Fourth International Conference on SIDS (SIDS4), 27 May 2024, Antigua and Barbuda.
26. AOSIS – Alliance of Small Island States (accessed 26 Jun. 2024).
27. Commission of Small Island States on Climate Change and International Law (cosis-ccil.org) (accessed 26 Jun. 2024).
28. International Tribunal for the Law of the Sea, 'Request for an Advisory Opinion submitted by the Commission of Small Island States on Climate Change and International Law – Advisory Opinion' (21 May 2024) Case No. 31, 5 – reproducing.
29. International Tribunal for the Law of the Sea, 'Request for an Advisory Opinion submitted by the Commission of Small Island States on Climate Change and International Law – Advisory Opinion' (21 May 2024) Case No. 31, paras 159 et seq.
30. *See*, for example, UNDP, *Blue Economies and Nature-Based Solutions for Enhanced Climate Action in Latin America and the Caribbean Small Island Developing States*, Report (October 2023).

International Civil Aviation Organization (ICAO). These actions must be grounded in the best available scientific knowledge and international rules and standards. The Tribunal underscored the importance of key international legal frameworks such as the UN Framework Convention on Climate Change and the Paris Agreement.

The Tribunal's opinion is not only significant regarding its findings on the substantial issues but also important as a manifestation of how small states/SIDS can drive change, in particular when they collaborate. It is noteworthy that the initiative for COSIS spans from the Pacific Islands to the Caribbean, with the aim 'to promote and contribute to the definition, implementation, and progressive development of rules and principles of international law concerning climate change, including, but not limited to, the obligations of States relating to the protection and preservation of the marine environment and their responsibility for injuries arising from internationally wrongful acts in respect of the breach of such obligations'.[31] The proceedings attracted the involvement of many well-known international law academics and international law firms.[32] This speaks to the ability of small states when collaborating and forming a critical mass to be able to capture the attention of the mainstream and to enlist their help.[33]

III ACCESS TO COMMERCIAL JUSTICE: A MULTILATERAL DISPUTE RESOLUTION FRAMEWORK

A Introduction

The Commission of Island States on Climate Change and International Law and its request for an Advisory Opinion submitted to ITLOS is an example of small states' ability to collaborate on the international plan to achieve a common goal. The following will discuss the opportunity for the Caribbean and Pacific Island small states' groups to develop a respective multilateral dispute resolution framework to provide reliable access to commercial justice for foreign businesses and to enable easier intra-country trade among local businesses.

In the realm of international commercial dispute resolution, small states confront challenges such as insufficient human (legal) resources, limited financial capacity to

31. About – Commission of Small Island States on Climate Change and International Law (cosis-ccil.org) (accessed 26 Jun. 2024).
32. International Tribunal for the Law of the Sea, 'Request for an Advisory Opinion Submitted by the Commission of Small Island States on Climate Change and International Law – Advisory Opinion' (21 May 2024) Case No. 31, para. 38.
33. Another example is Monica Feria-Tinta representing the Institute of Small and Micro States regarding the Advisory proceedings on the Climate Emergency and Human Rights in the Inter-American Court of Human Rights MFT-Amicus.pdf (twentyessex.com & Institute of Small and Micro States (ismsworld.com) (accessed 26 Jun. 2024)). In 2023, Vanuatu led a global coalition that resulted in the historic UN Resolution requesting the International Court of Justice(Obligations of States in respect of Climate Change (icj-cij.org) (accessed 25 Jun. 2024)) to hold polluting countries legally accountable for failing to tackle the climate emergency (77th Session (29 Mar. 2023) GA/12497, 'Request for an advisory opinion of the International Court of Justice on the obligations of States in respect of climate change').

invest in the legal sector, and a well-resourced judiciary.[34] Existing methods for resolving cross-border disputes through national court litigation present significant risks for businesses involved in international trade. These risks include potential conflicts between national laws, the presence of biased, inefficient, or inexperienced decision-makers, inconsistent and overlapping court proceedings across different countries, and formidable barriers to enforcing judgments. These shortcomings hinder cross-border trade and investment, sometimes depriving parties of fair access to justice. Developing small states, which are often disadvantaged participants in the market, feel the effects of these deficiencies more acutely. Many developing small states are not members of the international treaties that allow for the enforcement of their judgments or arbitral awards abroad or for the domestic enforcement of foreign judgments and foreign awards (an issue not exclusive to developing small states, albeit one where developed states are typically better equipped and financed to negotiate such agreements). Where small states have become members of the relevant treaties, they often lack the capacity to adequately implement them since the legal profession and the judiciary frequently do not have access to the jurisprudence and scholarship necessary. Consequently, foreign investors encounter significant risks of prolonged delays and inadequate legal recourse in disputes. These factors contribute to a heightened perception of risk for businesses, thereby restricting trade and deterring foreign direct investment (FDI).

Intra-small states' trade is also hindered by the lack of coherent dispute resolution frameworks. In the Commonwealth Pacific Islands, for example, small states cross-border dispute resolution has its roots in the common law. Due to the different colonisation and de-colonisation histories, the common law, however, has developed differently in the various jurisdictions. That, for a number of Pacific Island countries, the London-based Judicial Committee of the Privy Council continues to act as the court of last resort[35] adds to the divergence of the common law in the region.

B The Cross-Border Commercial Dispute Resolution Framework

A cross-border commercial dispute resolution framework that has been discussed in the literature is the bilateral or multilateral arbitration treaty (BAT/MAT).[36] The core idea is to replace the current default dispute resolution framework of litigation in business-to-business (B2B) cross-border commercial disputes with a default framework based on the principles of international commercial arbitration in participating jurisdictions. A default B2B dispute resolution framework (Framework) that would harness the advantages of international commercial arbitration and, depending on the

34. *See* Petra Butler & Anna Dziedzic, *Judicial Diversity in Small Commonwealth States* (Commonwealth Secretariat, 2022) Executive Summary.
35. For the Pacific region, these are the following independent states and dependent territories: the Cook Islands, Kiribati, Niue, and Tuvalu. *See* Judicial Committee of the Privy Council https://www.jcpc.uk/docs/jurisdiction-of-the-jcpc.pdf (accessed 16 Dec. 2024).
36. Gary Born, 'BIT's, BAT's and Buts', 10 (2013) Rev Bras Arb 138 https://doi.org/10.54648/rba 2013031; Gary Born, 'Integration and Dispute Resolution in Small States' in Petra Butler et al. (eds) *Integration and Dispute Resolution in Small States* (Springer, 2018) 10.4.1.

region, mediation would mitigate the current pitfalls of cross-border litigation, such as the possibility of parallel proceedings, the potential difficulty of enforcement of a judgment, the lack of the finality of the first instance judgment, the lack of choice of the decision-maker (i.e., the fear that the foreign judge is not neutral), the costs due to the need of layering of counsel, and the complexity and uncertainty of the proceedings for a party due to the lack of a uniform procedural law.[37] The framework would apply to: (i) commercial contractual disputes and (ii) between entities and nationals of the signatory states to the Framework. The Commonwealth Study of International Commercial Arbitration surveyed stakeholders on whether such a framework would be desirable. The majority of respondent governments to the survey indicated a preference for a specialised regional B2B cross-border dispute resolution mechanism.[38] A total of 94% of respondents to the university survey thought that a regional dispute resolution regime for B2B disputes would be valuable.[39] The majority of respondents to the judges, arbitrator, and counsel surveys also indicated a preference for a specialised regional B2B cross-border dispute resolution regime.[40] There was also considerable support by arbitral institutions for such a regime.[41]

C Application of the Framework

The Framework would assure foreign businesses and investors that their disputes would be resolved fairly and efficiently, and any outcome will be enforceable. The Framework would serve as a substitute for local courts which are often less experienced in cross-border matters and/or have a high workload, resulting in a considerable backlog of cases.[42] Currently, parties, of course, may opt for courts in a neutral third-party country to settle their international disputes instead of relying on local courts. This approach, however, is not suitable for developing small states and their businesses or their foreign business partners. A judge in London may not be well versed in the commercial dynamics of the taro trade between Samoa and Fiji. Decision-makers selected under the Framework, in line with common principles of arbitrator selection, on the other hand, would be selected based on their specific expertise and familiarity with the relevant region and business sector. Businesses in Pacific Island countries would be able to select an 'arbitrator' with particular regard to their customary competence.[43] This will result in disputes being managed in a more

37. Petra Butler & Campbell Herbert, 'Access to Justice v Access to Justice for Small and Medium-Sized Enterprises. The Case for Bilateral Arbitration Treaty' 26 (2014) NZULR 186, 198 et seq. https://doi.org/10.26686/wgtn.12617339.v1.
38. Petra Butler & Dharshini Prasad, *A Study of International Commercial Arbitration in the Commonwealth* (Commonwealth Secretariat, 2020) 4.7.2.
39. *Supra* n. 38.
40. *Supra* n. 38.
41. *Supra* n. 38.
42. For example, Gregory Lige, 'A Case Study on Increased Backlog Cases in PNG' *Papua New Guinea Studies* (24 May 2024).
43. *See* for a discussion on the importance of custom/kastom: Petra Butler & Christoph Katerndahl, 'Kastom: A Public Policy Exception under the New York Convention on the Recognition and

expert and efficient fashion and will result in a cost reduction. Furthermore, the Framework would provide especially foreign businesses with greater certainty in the enforceability of decisions under the Convention on the Recognition and Enforcement of Foreign Arbitral Awards (1958).[44] Pacific Island countries would thereby be able to reassure investors that the outcomes of their legal actions will yield a tangible result. This has the potential to contribute to the economic growth of Pacific Island countries by making them a more attractive destination to do business.

The advantage of the implementation of the Framework between the Pacific Island countries, i.e. a regional Framework, would be that the Framework can be adapted according to the contracting states' particular circumstances and needs. The Pacific Island countries could define, for example, the category or type of disputes that would be subjected to the Framework. Importantly, as already mentioned, the Pacific Islands could include rules regarding the importance of custom regarding 'arbitrator' selection and/or traditional procedures. It would allow to include elements of mediation in the dispute resolution process, too, leaving adjudicative 'arbitration' as the mechanism of last resort. This might be seen by many as more akin to the traditional way of dispute resolution in the Pacific Islands. The Framework would support the existing regional trade agreements, such as the Pacific Islands Countries Trade Agreement.[45] The regional trade agreements aim to increase trade of goods and services among Pacific Island countries, i.e., encourage cross-border business relationships which in turn will lead to increased cross-border disputes. The trade agreements even though encouraging cross-border business relationships do not contain any B2B dispute resolution mechanism. A gap the Framework could fill. Given that the Framework is based on the principles of international commercial arbitration, i.e., is a-national or neutral, the Framework would ensure that cross-border B2B disputes are resolved in the spirit of the trade agreements, namely as barrier-free as possible.

Lastly, from the viewpoint of the Pacific Island countries, adopting the Framework would lead to reduced costs associated with maintaining the judiciary and alleviating case backlogs.[46] National courts could concentrate on handling domestic disputes and reinforcing local legal frameworks. This shift could also lessen the expenditure and resources required for resolving complex international disputes that necessitate the application of foreign laws. At the same time, the Framework would introduce the principles of international arbitration, i.e., an alternative way to solve disputes, to local lawyers, thereby indirectly enhancing the overall excellence of the local legal profession.

Enforcement of Foreign Arbitral Awards' 7 (2018) Indian Journal of Arbitration Law, 104 https://doi.org/10.2139/ssrn.3270313.

44. *See* for a discussion regarding the application of the New York Convention in relation to BATs: Gary Born, 'Integration and Dispute Resolution in Small States' in Petra Butler et al. (eds) *Integration and Dispute Resolution in Small States* (Springer, 2018) 10.4.1.
45. *See* for an overview of the trade agreements in the Pacific Islands: Treaty Collection | Pacific Islands Forum Secretariat (accessed 1 Jul. 2024).
46. *See also* discussion in Petra Butler & Anna Dziedzic, *Judicial Diversity in Small Commonwealth States* (Commonwealth Secretariat, 2022).

D Summary

Small states and their businesses are generally ill-equipped to deal with the inadequacies of international commercial litigation in dealing with disputes. The ability of small states to collaborate on a deep and sophisticated level as evidenced in regard to climate change evidences that small states, such as the Pacific Island countries, would have the capacity to combat the inadequacies of international commercial litigation to allow their economies to grow and to take part more easily in global trade. The presented Framework would harness the advantages of international commercial arbitration and, depending on the region, mediation, would mitigate the current pitfalls of cross-border litigation.

IV CONCLUSION

Small states, despite being often the most disadvantaged members of the global community, have the advantage of being more agile and better able to collaborate than their larger siblings. Their pioneering collaboration contributed to holding the causers of climate change accountable and has been direction-setting regarding measures to combat climate change and the climate change discourse. Their success should encourage small states to adopt decisive action regarding a default B2B dispute resolution framework that would mitigate the current pitfalls of cross-border litigation by harnessing the advantages of international commercial arbitration and, depending on the region, mediation. Such a dispute resolution framework would allow small states to grow their economies and take part more easily in global trade. In turn, a growing economy will provide small states with more resources to combat climate change.

CHAPTER 7

Maintaining Speed: Promoting and Advancing Gender Diversity in International Arbitration*

*Carolyn B. Lamm & Jennifer A. Ivers***

Over the past decade, tremendous progress has been made in advancing the role of women as counsel and as arbitrators in international arbitration. While much has been accomplished, significant work remains to progress and promote the role of women in arbitration. This chapter evaluates the status of women as counsel and arbitrator in arbitration, assesses the reasons why women face barriers in advancing in those roles, and examines reforms and measures taken to address such barriers in recent years. It concludes by urging all members of the arbitration community, including those in law firms, arbitral institutions, public and private entities, litigation funders, and other organizations, to continue to highlight and undertake efforts on gender diversity to maintain speed in efforts to advance women in arbitration going forward.

Diversity, equity, and inclusion efforts have been the subject of discussion and debate for numerous years. Such discussions have extended to the international arbitration community, which historically has been criticized as a field reputed as "pale, stale, and male."[1]

---

* The views expressed in this chapter are those of the authors and do not necessarily reflect the views of White & Case LLP or its clients.

** The authors wish to thank Olivia Rosenzweig and Kiara Williams for their assistance in preparing this chapter.

1. Joseph Mamounas, *Does "Male, Pale, and Stale" Threaten the Legitimacy of International Arbitration? Perhaps, But There's No Clear Path to Change*, 1, https://arbitrationblog.kluwerarbitration.com/2014/04/10/icca-2014-does-male-pale-and-stale-threaten-the-legitimacy-of-international-arbitration-perhaps-but-theres-no-clear-path-to-change/ (accessed Dec. 16, 2024);

From the perspective of gender diversity, these criticisms are not unfounded. Historical data confirms that, as of 1990, women represented a mere 1% of total arbitrator appointments—a percentage that remained in the single digits until 2012.[2] Likewise, women represented only 20% of all lawyers in the United States and less than 20% of all lawyers in Germany as of the early 1990s.[3]

Happily, however, we have witnessed tremendous progress over the past decade. Over the course of a decade from 2012 to 2021, the proportion of women appointed as arbitrators doubled, rising from 12.5% of all appointments in 2012 to 26.1% in 2021,[4] while the proportion of women as lawyers in the United States has increased more modestly, rising from 33% in 2012 to 37% in 2021.[5] Women in Germany similarly comprise 37% of all lawyers in Germany as of 2023.[6]

Such progress has taken an incredible effort by numerous actors in the legal field. Those efforts should by all means proceed going forward, as the importance of diversity cannot be underestimated. Among other benefits, it has repeatedly been shown that diversity enhances the decision-making process of a group or team. As one study found, executive teams in the top quartile for gender diversity were 25% more likely to experience above-average profitability than their peer companies, while executive teams containing over 30% women are significantly more likely to outperform teams with a lower percentage of women.[7] Studies further have shown that more inclusive teams make better business decisions up to 87% of the time and make

---

see also Matteo M. Winkler & Mikaël Schinazi, *No Longer "Pale, Male, and Stale"? Approaching Diversity and Inclusiveness in International Arbitration, in* Liber Amicorum Guillermo Aguilar Álvarez, 2 (Nigel Blackaby, W. Michael Reisman, Cecilia Azar, Carlos Dávalos & Luis Alberto Aziz eds, 2023).

2. Int'l Council for Commercial Arb., *Report of the Cross-Institutional Task Force on Gender Diversity in Arbitral Appointments and Proceedings 2022 Update*, Appendix E, Table E.1, https://cdn.arbitration-icca.org/s3fs-public/document/media_document/ICCA-Report-8u2-electronic3.pdf (accessed Dec. 16, 2024).
3. Am. Bar Ass'n, *Profile of the Legal Profession*, 22, https://www.abalegalprofile.com/demographics.html#:~:text=The%20gender%20numbers%20have%20changed,Brent%2C%20in%201648%20in%20Maryland (accessed Dec. 16, 2024); Bundesrechtsanwaltskammer [Federal Bar Association of Germany], *Anteil der Rechtsanwältinnen Seit 1970* [*Proportion of Female Lawyers Since 1970*], https://www.brak.de/fileadmin/04_fuer_journalisten/statistiken/2023/1970-2023-Anteil-RAinnen.pdf (accessed Dec. 16, 2024).
4. Int'l Council for Commercial Arb., *Report of the Cross-Institutional Task Force on Gender Diversity in Arbitral Appointments and Proceedings 2022 Update*, 27, 30, https://cdn.arbitration-icca.org/s3fs-public/document/media_document/ICCA-Report-8u2-electronic3.pdf (accessed Dec. 16, 2024).
5. Am. Bar Ass'n, *ABA National Lawyer Population Survey*, 4, https://www.americanbar.org/content/dam/aba/administrative/market_research/2022-national-lawyer-population-survey.pdf (accessed Dec. 16, 2024).
6. Bundesrechtsanwaltskammer [Federal Bar Association of Germany], *Anteil der Rechtsanwältinnen Seit 1970* [*Proportion of Female Lawyers Since 1970*], https://www.brak.de/fileadmin/04_fuer_journalisten/statistiken/2023/1970-2023-Anteil-RAinnen.pdf (accessed Dec. 16, 2024).
7. McKinsey & Co., *Diversity Wins: How Inclusion Matters*, 3, https://www.mckinsey.com/~/media/mckinsey/featured%20insights/diversity%20and%20inclusion/diversity%20wins%20how%20inclusion%20matters/diversity-wins-how-inclusion-matters-vf.pdf (accessed Dec. 16, 2024).

decisions twice as fast,[8] including because of the creativity and innovation generated from diverse employees.[9] Diverse teams are also able to retain their team members longer, which contributes to building more effective decision-making processes.[10]

These findings translate directly to decision-making on arbitral panels. Diverse panels allow for more cultural insight, a bridge in understanding gaps, and an added layer of richness in the arbitration process,[11] thereby benefitting the parties in the arbitral process through an enhanced decision-making process.

This chapter examines two of the largest roles that women play in the international arbitration community: counsel and arbitrator. We evaluate the status of women in each role, followed by an assessment of the reasons why women face barriers in progressing as counsel and as arbitrators, as well as reforms and measures taken to address those barriers in recent years that have contributed to progress already made. We conclude by urging the arbitral community to continue to highlight and undertake efforts on gender diversity to continue progress going forward.

We note that while this chapter focuses on gender diversity specifically, we highlight and encourage the promotion of diversity in all forms, including with respect to race, ethnicity, nationality, age, disability, sexual orientation, and socio-economic factors. We also take note of the importance of studies and analyses on the intersectionality of gender and other forms of diversity, for example, women of color and LGBTQ+ women within arbitration.[12]

I RETAINING AND PROMOTING WOMEN AS COUNSEL IN INTERNATIONAL ARBITRATION

Within international arbitration, counsel is the most common and prevalent role, with lawyers primarily working through law firms, large and small. In light of limited data with respect to women in international arbitration or international dispute resolution practices specifically, as well as limited data about the retention of women in law firms on a global or even regional basis, we look to the status of the retention of women in law firms in a small sample of countries to briefly assess the current status of women in law firms.

8. Erik Larson, *New Research: Diversity + Inclusion = Better Decision Making at Work*, https://www.forbes.com/sites/eriklarson/2017/09/21/new-research-diversity-inclusion-better-decision-making-at-work/?sh=10a436534cbf (accessed Dec. 16, 2024).
9. Sylvia Ann Hewlett, Melinda Marshall & Laura Sherbin, *How Diversity Can Drive Innovation*, https://hbr.org/2013/12/how-diversity-can-drive-innovation (accessed Dec. 16, 2024).
10. Steve Leigh, *Why Diverse Work Environments Are Vital for Staff Retention*, https://www.peoplemanagement.co.uk/article/1797243/why-diverse-work-environments-vital-staff-retention (accessed Dec. 16, 2024).
11. Tariq Sheikh, *Diversity and Inclusion in International Arbitration: A Trend or a Necessity?*, https://www.linkedin.com/pulse/diversity-inclusion-international-arbitration-trend-necessity-sheikh/ (accessed Dec. 16, 2024).
12. *See, e.g.*, Kabir A.N. Duggal & Rekha Rangachari, *Gender, Race, or Both? The Need for Greater Consideration of Intersectionality in International Arbitration*, *in* Diversity in International Arbitration (Shahla F. Ali, Filip Balcerzak, Giorgio Colombo & Joshua Karton eds, 2022).

In the United States, women make up slightly more than half of all law students as of 2023.[13] That proportion carries over to associates at U.S. law firms (50.3%) but drops at the partner level, with women comprising 33.3% of non-equity partners and 23.7% of equity partners.[14] Even these numbers at the partner level, however, do represent progress; in comparison, as of 2013, 27.6% and 16.5% of non-equity and equity partners, respectively, were women.[15]

According to the Solicitors' Regulation Authority in the United Kingdom, as of 2023, 53% of all lawyers in law firms were women, while only 37% of partners were women—an increase from 32% in 2015.[16] In Australia, the percentage of women partners in leading commercial law firms totaled 33.5% as of July 2023,[17] although women made up around 60% of associates and special counsels in Australian law firms overall.[18] In Germany, while women comprised 34.37% of lawyers as of 2017, they made up only 10.7% of equity partners that year.[19]

While this chapter does not present the opportunity to comprehensively evaluate the status of the retention of women in law firms throughout the world, it is evident that, although women now make up a substantial—if not equal—proportion of lawyers in at least some countries, women still do not reach to the top of their profession, including as equity partners at law firms, at equal rates to their male counterparts. Below, we evaluate some of the hurdles that women face in advancing their careers at law firms and how such hurdles have been and can continue to be addressed going forward.

Women frequently cite pay disparity between men and women, particularly at the equity partner level, as reason for their departure from firms. One study of U.S. partners in 2018 revealed that men partners earned an average of USD 1.13 million per year, while women partners earned an average of only USD 784,000.[20] Another study

13. Susan L. Krinsky, *Incoming Class of 2022: A Major Advance in Diversity, More Work to Do*, https://www.lsac.org/blog/incoming-class-2022-major-advance-diversity-more-work-to-do (accessed Dec. 16, 2024).
14. NALP, *2023 Report on Diversity in U.S. Law Firms*, Table 7, Table 9, https://www.nalp.org/uploads/Research/2023NALPReportonDiversityFinal.pdf (accessed Dec. 16, 2024).
15. NALP, *2023 Report on Diversity in U.S. Law Firms*, Table 7, https://www.nalp.org/uploads/Research/2023NALPReportonDiversityFinal.pdf (accessed Dec. 16, 2024).
16. Solics. Regul. Auth., *Diversity in Law Firms' Workforce*, https://www.sra.org.uk/sra/equality-diversity/diversity-profession/diverse-legal-profession/ (accessed Dec. 16, 2024).
17. Michael Pelly & Edmund Tadros, *Female Partners Surge at Top Law Firms (to One Third)*, https://www.afr.com/companies/professional-services/women-partners-surge-at-top-law-firms-to-one-third-20230704-p5dlne (accessed Dec. 16, 2024).
18. Michael Pelly, *Female Lawyers to Wait Another Decade for Partner Equality*, https://www.afr.com/companies/professional-services/female-lawyers-to-wait-another-decade-for-partner-equality-20220705-p5az4z (accessed Dec. 16, 2024).
19. Ulrike Schultz, *Haben Frauen in der Anwaltschaft Schlechte Karten?* [*Do Women in the Bad Have Bad Cards?*], 225-226, https://www.brak-mitteilungen.de/media/BRAK_2018_05.pdf (accessed Dec. 16, 2024); *see also* Marcus Schriefers, *New Study Reveals Advances and Challenges for Female Attorneys in Germany*, https://www.uianet.org/en/news/new-study-reveals-advances-and-challenges-female-attorneys-germany (accessed Dec. 16, 2024).
20. Jeffery Lowe, *2020 Partner Compensation Survey*, 10, https://www.acc.com/sites/default/files/2021-02/MLA%202020%20Partner%20CompensationSurvey.pdf (accessed Dec. 16, 2024).

by the National Association of Women Lawyers found that, while women associates and non-equity partners received an average of 95 % of the compensation of men in the same positions in 2020, women equity partners earned only 80 % of that earned by men equity partners.[21] Indeed, 92 % of law firms in that study reported that the highest-paid attorney at the firm was a man.[22] In another 2019 report, 28 % of the women surveyed reported being "extremely" or "somewhat" dissatisfied with their compensation, compared to only 12 % of men, while 38 % of women reported being "dissatisfied" with the method by which compensation is determined—as compared to only 17% of men.[23]

A number of countries have implemented legislation to combat the pay discrepancies in law firms in particular. In 2023, Australia passed legislation that required law firms with more than hundred employees to publicly disclose their gender pay discrepancies.[24] This requirement follows similar pay transparency legislation enacted in the United Kingdom in 2017 and the European Union in 2021.[25] In the United Kingdom, for example, the imposition of a pay transparency requirement for large law firms has led many firms to adopt internal policies to further address this issue, including increasing the transparency of all partners' pay and expanding the gender diversity of newly appointed partners.[26]

Harassment in the workplace also plays a factor. In one study, over half of the surveyed women lawyers at law firms had experienced unwanted sexual conduct at the workplace, compared to just 6% of men—although over one-quarter of women decided not to report that conduct.[27] To address such issues, the Commission on Women in the Profession at the American Bar Association has promoted a number of ways for firms to tackle this issue, such as holding training sessions about sexual harassment as part of new lawyer orientations, publishing yearly reviews of the firm's

---

21. Lauren Rikleen, *Women Lawyers Continue to Lag Behind Male Colleagues*, 7, https://www.nyipla.org/images/nyipla/Programs/2018December6/NAWL2015SURVEY_FINAL.pdf (accessed Dec. 16, 2024).
22. *Ibid.*
23. Roberta Liebenberg & Stephanie Scharf, *Walking Out the Door: The Facts, Figures, and Future of Experienced Women Lawyers in Private Practice*, 6, https://www.americanbar.org/content/dam/aba/administrative/women/walkoutdoor_online_042320.pdf (accessed Dec. 16, 2024).
24. Alasdair Pal, *Australia Passes Law Forcing Firms to Disclose Gender Pay Gap*, https://www.reuters.com/world/asia-pacific/australia-passes-law-forcing-firms-disclose-gender-pay-gap-2023-03-29/ (accessed Dec. 16, 2024); *see also* Christopher Niesche, *Law Firms in Australia Will Have to Report Gender Pay Gaps*, https://www.law.com/international-edition/2023/05/14/law-firms-in-australia-will-have-to-report-gender-pay-gaps/?slreturn=20240324153642 (accessed Dec. 16, 2024).
25. Alasdair Pal, *Australia Passes Law Forcing Firms to Disclose Gender Pay Gap*, https://www.reuters.com/world/asia-pacific/australia-passes-law-forcing-firms-disclose-gender-pay-gap-2023-03-29/ (accessed Dec. 16, 2024).
26. Law Soc'y, *Firms Using Gender Pay Gap Reporting to Drive Positive Change*, https://www.lawsociety.org.uk/contact-or-visit-us/press-office/press-releases/firms-using-gender-pay-gap-reporting-to-drive-positive-change (accessed Dec. 16, 2024).
27. Roberta Liebenberg & Stephanie Scharf, *Walking Out the Door: The Facts, Figures, and Future of Experienced Women Lawyers in Private Practice*, 8, https://www.americanbar.org/content/dam/aba/administrative/women/walkoutdoor_online_042320.pdf (accessed Dec. 16, 2024).

harassment policies, hosting targeted training for firm leaders who are in charge of policy enforcement, creating methods for identifying harassment, and establishing a safe and open environment for the topic of sexual harassment to be addressed.[28] In Australia, as well, many legal institutions and law firms have implemented workplace training programs aimed at addressing sexual harassment in their institutions, including introducing "no bystanders" rules, which create reporting requirements for employees who experience or become aware of sex-based harassment in their workplaces.[29]

Care-taking responsibilities are another factor that seriously impact the retention of women, as experienced women lawyers are far more likely than their male counterparts to carry the full responsibility of arranging childcare, leaving work for childcare purposes and providing daytime and evening childcare.[30] To address childcare issues, a number of U.S. law firms have introduced initiatives that assist lawyers with the financial and administrative challenges involved in taking leave from work after having a child, such as gender-neutral paid parental leave policies and free access to parental leave coaching.[31] Indeed, a 2017 McKinsey survey on women in law firms found that most U.S. law firms offered parental leave that exceeded government requirements, as well as emergency backup childcare services.[32]

Another way to address the increased responsibilities faced by women is by creating more flexibility for both men and women to better schedule their work around their caregiver responsibilities.[33] The global pandemic compelled all workplaces, including law firms, to adapt to a more remote workplace, leading to a spike in remote and flexible work arrangements. In the years since the peak of the pandemic, many employers continue to allow more flexible work arrangements, as compared to

28. Am. Bar Ass'n Comm'n on Women in the Pro., *Zero Tolerance Program Toolkit: Identifying and Combating Sex-Based Harassment in the Legal Profession*, 7, https://www.americanbar.org/content/dam/aba/administrative/women/zerotolerance-brochure-download2018.pdf (accessed Dec. 16, 2024).
29. Hannah Wootton, *We've Got a Long Way to Go on Harassment, Bullying: Law Firms*, https://www.afr.com/companies/professional-services/we-ve-got-a-long-way-to-go-on-harassment-bullying-law-firms-20210422-p57les (accessed Dec. 16, 2024).
30. Roberta Liebenberg & Stephanie Scharf, *Walking Out the Door: The Facts, Figures, and Future of Experienced Women Lawyers in Private Practice*, 12, https://www.americanbar.org/content/dam/aba/administrative/women/walkoutdoor_online_042320.pdf (accessed Dec. 16, 2024); Amy Diehl, Amber L. Stephenson & Leanne M. Dzubinksi, *Research: How Bias Against Women Persists in Female-Dominated Workplaces*, https://hbr.org/2022/03/research-how-bias-against-women-persists-in-female-dominated-workplaces (accessed Dec. 16, 2024).
31. *See, e.g.*, Danielle Nichole Smith, *White & Case Revamped Parental Leave Policy for 2018*, https://www.law360.com/articles/1102075/white-case-revamped-parental-leave-policy-for-2018 (accessed Dec. 16, 2024).
32. Marc Brodherson, Laura McGee & Mariana Pires dos Reis, *Women in Law Firms*, 9, https://www.mckinsey.com/~/media/mckinsey/featured%20insights/gender%20equality/women%20in%20law%20firms/women-in-law-firms-final-103017.ashx (accessed Dec. 16, 2024).
33. Int'l Council for Commercial Arb., *Report of the Cross-Institutional Task Force on Gender Diversity in Arbitral Appointments and Proceedings 2022 Update*, 198-199, https://cdn.arbitration-icca.org/s3fs-public/document/media_document/ICCA-Report-8u2-electronic3.pdf (accessed Dec. 16, 2024).

pre-pandemic times, although at increasingly lower rates.[34] Many employers, for example, have pushed to get their employees back into the physical office, which often is viewed as more productive, promoting collaboration and allowing for more mentorship opportunities.[35]

Another underlying reason for the lack of retention of women at law firms lies in women's failure to receive recognition for their work. As one American Bar Association study reported, 46% of women "extremely" or "somewhat" dissatisfied with the recognition received, as compared to 15% of men.[36] While such concerns may be addressed on an individualized basis, including coaching sessions and training on how lawyers can promote and champion themselves,[37] other solutions include for law firms to prioritize recognizing legal teams over individuals as a way to spread the credit across multiple lawyers,[38] as well as to ensure that legal teams set expectations at the outset, in order to ensure clearer standards for all attorneys as well as an easier way to recognize successes.[39]

Throughout their careers, women also face significant unconscious bias, which permeates multiple areas of an attorney's practice, including hiring, compensation, performance evaluation, and promotion.[40] One way to address bias in the workplace is by acknowledging and recognizing its existence. Employers can shine a light on the issue, including through training programs for their employees. The state of California in the United States, for example, requires one unit of bias training in the twenty-five hours of continuing education required by attorneys every three years.[41]

---

34. Herbert Smith Freehills, *Future of Work 2023: Remote and Flexible Working*, https://www.herbertsmithfreehills.com/insights/reports/future-of-work-report-2023/fow-2023-remote-and-flexible-working (accessed Dec. 16, 2024); Jessica R. Blaemire, *Analysis: Lawyer Work-From-Home Options Decrease During Endemic*, https://news.bloomberglaw.com/bloomberg-law-analysis/analysis-lawyer-work-from-home-options-decrease-during-endemic (accessed Dec. 16, 2024).
35. *Ibid.*
36. Roberta Liebenberg & Stephanie Scharf, *Walking Out the Door: The Facts, Figures, and Future of Experienced Women Lawyers in Private Practice*, 5, https://www.americanbar.org/content/dam/aba/administrative/women/walkoutdoor_online_042320.pdf (accessed Dec. 16, 2024).
37. WorkLife L. UC Hastings Coll. of the L., *Effective Policies and Programs for Retention and Advancement of Women in the Law*, 6, https://worklifelaw.org/publications/Effective-Policies-and-Programs-for-Retention-and-Advancesment-of-Women-in-the-Law.pdf (accessed Dec. 16, 2024).
38. WorkLife L. UC Hastings Coll. of the L., *Effective Policies and Programs for Retention and Advancement of Women in the Law*, 28, https://worklifelaw.org/publications/Effective-Policies-and-Programs-for-Retention-and-Advancement-of-Women-in-the-Law.pdf (accessed Dec. 16, 2024).
39. Anna Jaffe, Grace Chediak, Erika Douglas & Mackenzie Tudor, *White Paper: Retaining & Advancing Women in National Law Firms*, 48, https://judicialstudies.duke.edu/sites/default/files/centers/judicialstudies/panel_1-retaining_and_advancing_women_in_national_law_firm_stanford_white_paper_may.pdf (accessed Dec. 16, 2024).
40. Elizabeth M. Manno & Karen M. Richardson, *Viewpoint: How Unconscious Bias Keeps Women from Advancing at Law Firms*, https://www.bizjournals.com/washington/news/2023/10/24/women-diversity-law-bias-nawl.html (accessed Dec. 16, 2024); Kylie Ora Lobell, *How to Tackle Unconscious Biases*, https://www.alanet.org/legal-management/2021/july-august/features/how-tot-tackle-unconscious-bias (accessed Dec. 16, 2024).
41. Sonoma Cnty. Bar Ass'n, *New Implicit Bias Education Now Required for All Attorneys*, https://www.sonomacountybar.org/?blAction=showEntry&blogEntry=106361&pg=Blog (accessed Dec. 16, 2024).

In addition to addressing the individual issues noted above, one key way to assist women in advancing their careers is to ensure that women lawyers have mentors (those who provide guidance and share knowledge) and sponsors (those in a position to advocate for and promote more junior colleagues), which enhances the likelihood of women succeeding in their careers.[42] Indeed, women have reported that the investment in mentorship from employers provides a supportive work environment that builds self-awareness, which in turn increases employee engagement.[43]

One reason for the increase in women as counsel in recent decades may have resulted from the multitude of women-focused professional legal networks that provide mentoring programs and networking opportunities. Within the arbitration community alone, for example, ArbitralWomen has played a key role in advancing women since it was informally created in 1993 and officially founded as a non-profit organization in 2005.[44] Bringing together women in the dispute resolution community, ArbitralWomen provides a wide variety of services to advance the interests of women practitioners, enable networking, provide mentoring, organize conferences, assist in professional development, and liaise with other organizations to further the interests of its members.[45] Recent programs, for example, include a Mentorship Programme to connect younger practitioners with more experienced attorneys, "Young ArbitralWomen Practitioners," a networking initiative for female lawyers under 40, and "ArbitralWomen SpeedNet events," which offer speed networking opportunities in cities around the world to help female attorneys form new connections.[46] Other initiatives likewise promote networking among women arbitration practitioners, such as Arbitration Lunch Match, which has brought together more than 1,500 women in arbitration across fifty-three cities globally.[47]

Other programs aimed at providing mentorship opportunities for young professional women and other minority groups in the international arbitration field include the American Society of International Law's Women in International Law Interest Group Mentoring Program ("WILIG"), the Young International Council for Commercial Arbitration ("ICCA") Mentoring Program, the Hong Kong International Arbitration

42. Tammy D. Allen, Lillian T. Eby, Mark L. Poteet, Elizabeth Lentz & Lizzette Lima, *Career Benefits Associated with Mentoring for Proteges: A Meta-Analysis*, 89 J. Applied Psych. 127, 130-132 (2004) https://doi.org/10.1037/0021-9010.89.1.127; *see also* Sylvia Ann Hewlett, with Kerrie Peraino, Laura Sherbin & Karen Sumberg, *The Sponsor Effect: Breaking Through the Last Glass Ceiling*, 8, https://www.wearethecity.com/wp-content/uploads/2014/10/The-Sponsor-Effect.pdf (accessed Dec. 16, 2024).
43. Anna Sutton & Cecile Crobach, *Improving Self-Awareness and Engagement Through Group Coaching*, 20 Int'l J. Evidence Based Coaching & Mentoring, 35, 37 (2022).
44. ArbitralWomen, *About ArbitralWomen*, https://www.arbitralwomen.org/aw-outline/ (accessed Dec. 16, 2024).
45. *Ibid.*
46. ArbitralWomen, *Young ArbitralWomen Practitioners*, https://www.arbitralwomen.org/young_arbitralwomen_practitioners/ (accessed Dec. 16, 2024); *see also* Int'l Council for Commercial Arb., *Report of the Cross-Institutional Task Force on Gender Diversity in Arbitral Appointments and Proceedings 2022 Update*, 186, https://cdn.arbitration-icca.org/s3fs-public/document/media_document/ICCA-Report-8u2-electronic3.pdf (accessed Dec. 16, 2024).
47. Arbitration Lunch Match, https://arbitrationlunch.com/ (accessed Dec. 16, 2024).

Centre ("HKIAC") Women in Arbitration, and the Institute for Transnational Arbitration ("ITA") Young Mentorship Program, among others.[48] Law firms have also been doing their part to create mentorship programs specifically aimed at female practitioners, including, for example, White & Case LLP's Global Women's Initiative, which offers coaching and partner sponsorship opportunities for women attorneys, among other programs.[49] White & Case LLP also offers individual and group coaching sessions for its women attorneys,[50] which contribute to empowering women, improving performance, enhancing management and leadership skills, and building confidence.[51]

By directly addressing the specific hurdles that women face in their careers (whether through targeted training on harassment or unconscious bias, providing more transparency in salaries, or offering emergency childcare and caregiver services), and by providing programs to further assist women (whether through mentorship or coaching programs), law firms have and should continue to take a variety of steps to support women lawyers in advancing their careers. Such measures should be applauded and continue to be expanded upon going forward, with the goal of enhancing the retention of women at the highest levels of counsel in international arbitration.

II APPOINTING WOMEN AS ARBITRATORS IN INTERNATIONAL ARBITRATION PROCEEDINGS

Another significant indicator of the status and advancement of women in international arbitration can be measured by the proportion of women being appointed as arbitrators. We are honored to be the Chair and a Member of the ICCA Cross-Institutional Task Force on Gender Diversity in Arbitral Appointments and Proceedings, which for the first time compiled and analyzed statistics on the appointment of women as arbitrators from a multitude of arbitral institutions.[52] Following its initial Report in 2020,[53] the Task Force released an Update in 2022, which evaluated data provided by twenty-six arbitral institutions, including eleven arbitral institutions from Latin America, from 2015 to 2021.[54]

The overall data collected by the Task Force demonstrates significant progress in the surveyed arbitral institutions. As of 2015, only 12.6% of all arbitrator appointments were of women. This number steadily increased to 19.7% in 2017, to 22.8% in 2019,

48. Int'l Council for Commercial Arb., *Report of the Cross-Institutional Task Force on Gender Diversity in Arbitral Appointments and Proceedings 2022 Update*, 165-166, 186-190, https://cdn.arbitration-icca.org/s3fs-public/document/media_document/ICCA-Report-8u2-electronic3.pdf (accessed Dec. 16, 2024).
49. White & Case, *Advancing Women*, https://www.whitecase.com/diversity/advancing-women (accessed Dec. 16, 2024).
50. *Ibid.*
51. *See, e.g.*, Allaya Cooks-Campbell, *29 Benefits of Coaching for Individuals and Businesses*, https://www.betterup.com/blog/benefits-of-coaching (accessed Dec. 16, 2024).
52. Int'l Council for Commercial Arb., *Report of the Cross-Institutional Task Force on Gender Diversity in Arbitral Appointments and Proceedings 2022 Update*, v, https://cdn.arbitration-icca.org/s3fs-public/document/media_document/ICCA-Report-8u2-electronic3.pdf (accessed Dec. 16, 2024).
53. *Ibid.*, at xi.
54. *Ibid.*, at 23-24.

to 26.1% in 2021.[55] The Task Force further evaluated data on whether women were more frequently appointed by the parties, the co-arbitrators, or by institutions.[56] Institutions notably appoint a significantly higher percentage of women than co-arbitrators or the parties, with 37.9% of all appointments made by the institutions being of women in 2021.[57] Indeed, these relatively high numbers have continued in at least some institutions over the last two years. The London Court of International Arbitration ("LCIA"), for example, reported that 45% of its institutional appointments in 2022 were of women,[58] while the International Centre for Settlement of Investment Disputes ("ICSID") reported that 51% of its appointments in 2023 were of women.[59]

The high percentage of women appointments by the institutions is a contrast against other appointments, with 27.1% of co-arbitrator appointments of women, and a mere 17.9% of party appointments of women.[60] Looking at the data in another manner, based on the total number of women appointed, in 2021, institutions appointed approximately one-half of all women arbitrators, one-third being appointed by parties, with the others appointed by co-arbitrators.[61]

While women clearly have been appointed in increasing percentages over the years, it remains that a substantially lower number of women are being appointed in international arbitration proceedings. Below, we evaluate some of the hurdles that women face in obtaining arbitrator appointments and how such hurdles have been and can continue to be addressed going forward.

One of the main hurdles to the appointment of women as arbitrators, at least historically, is more limited access to information about qualified women who could and should be considered as candidates for an arbitral appointment. Simply put, women cannot be appointed if they are not known to those in a position to appoint arbitrators.

Women can seek to individually promote themselves through networking, participating in conferences, and promoting their own qualifications. Mentors can assist more junior women lawyers in obtaining speaking roles at hearings and promoting them to the arbitration community, while those who organize conferences can take steps to ensure that women are equally represented on panels, as keynote speakers, and as moderators. Indeed, several organizations have adopted policies to ensure diversity on their conference panels.[62]

55. *Ibid.*, at 25-26.
56. *Ibid.*, at Table 8, 39.
57. *Ibid.*
58. London Ct. of Int'l Arb., *2022 Annual Casework Report*, 22, https://www.lcia.org/News/lcia-news-annual-report-on-2022-updates-on-the-lcia-court-and.aspx (accessed Dec. 16, 2024).
59. Int'l Ctr. for Settlement of Inv. Disp., *ICSID Releases 2023 Caseload Statistics*, https://icsid.worldbank.org/news-and-events/news-releases/icsid-releases-2023-caseload-statistics (accessed Dec. 16, 2024).
60. Int'l Council for Commercial Arb., *Report of the Cross-Institutional Task Force on Gender Diversity in Arbitral Appointments and Proceedings 2022 Update*, Table 8, 39, https://cdn.arbitration-icca.org/s3fs-public/document/media_document/ICCA-Report-8u2-electronic3.pdf (accessed Dec. 16, 2024).
61. *Ibid.*, at 87.
62. Under its Gender Balance Pledge, for example, the ICC is committed to increasing gender diversity in panels at conferences in which the ICC participates. *See* Int'l Chamber of Com.,

On a broader scale, over the past several years, various organizations have created databases and programs that assist in identifying qualified women candidates. For example, Mute Off Thursdays, together with the Global Arbitration Review ("GAR") and Burford Capital, have prepared a "Compendium of Unicorns: A Global Guide to Women Arbitrators," with the purpose of making it easier for users to identify suitable candidates for appointments.[63] The Equal Representation in Arbitration ("ERA") Pledge further maintains a global database of women arbitrators who are involved with the Pledge; provides a Female Arbitrator Resources Tool, which lists arbitrator profile sources (including those focused on women arbitrators); and offers more personalized assistance from the ERA Search Committee, which provides tailored proposals for arbitrator candidates.[64] ArbitralWomen also maintains a member database of over 1,200 women dispute resolution practitioners, which is searchable by name and country of residence,[65] while Women Way in Arbitration ("WWA") LATAM likewise maintains a member database of over hundred practitioners searchable by name and country.[66]

Moreover, lists of arbitrators by institutions more frequently include filters for gender. The HKIAC, for example, includes a filter to search for arbitrators by "Identify as Female," "Identify as Male," "Non-binary," or "Prefer not to say" on its Panel and List Arbitrators.[67] The GAR Arbitrator Research Tool likewise has filters for "male" and "female" arbitrators.[68]

In addition to adding filters, directories that maintain arbitrator—or, more broadly, attorney—profiles can encourage the inclusion of women therein. For example, Arbitrator Intelligence, which collects and analyzes information on over thousand arbitrators,[69] launched a Diversity Campaign in 2021 to collect more information and make it easier to identify and appoint more diverse arbitrators.[70]

World Business Women's Gender Balance Pledge, https://iccwbo.org/news-publications/policies-reports/icc-gender-balance-pledge/ (accessed Dec. 16, 2024).

63. Global Arbitration Review, *Compendium of Unicorns: A Global Guide to Women Arbitrators*, https://globalarbitrationreview.com/guide/compendium-of-unicorns-global-guide-women-arbitrators/1st-edition (accessed Dec. 16, 2024).
64. Equal Representation in Arb. Pledge, *Search for Female Arbitrators*, https://www.arbitrationpledge.com/arbitration-search (accessed Dec. 16, 2024).
65. ArbitralWomen, *Directory of ArbitralWomen Dispute Resolution Practitioners*, https://www.arbitralwomen.org/members-directory/ (accessed Dec. 16, 2024).
66. Women Way in Arb. LATAM, *List of Members Associated with WWA*, https://wwarb.org/directorio.php (accessed Dec. 16, 2024).
67. H.K. Int'l Arb. Ctr., *HKIAC Panel and List of Arbitrators*, https://www.hkiac.org/arbitration/arbitrators/panel-and-list-of-arbitrators (accessed Dec. 16, 2024).
68. Glob. Arb. Rev., *Arbitrator Research Tool*, https://globalarbitrationreview.com/tools/arbitrator-research-tool (accessed Dec. 16, 2024).
69. Arb. Intel., *Frequently Asked Questions*, https://arbitratorintelligence.vercel.app/faq (accessed Dec. 16, 2024); Arb. Intel., *About Us*, https://arbitratorintelligence.vercel.app/about (accessed Dec. 16, 2024).
70. Kluwer Arb. Blog, *The Missing Link in Progress to Greater Diversity: Your Feedback about Diverse Arbitrators: Arbitrator Intelligence 2021 Diversity Campaign*, https://arbitrationblog.kluwerarbitration.com/2021/09/13/the-missing-link-in-progress-to-greater-diversity-your-feedback-about-diverse-arbitrators-arbitrator-intelligence-2021-diversity-campaign/ (accessed Dec. 16, 2024).

Yet another hurdle to the appointment of women as arbitrators is that diversity often is not the top priority—or any priority—in considering appointments. Particularly given the significantly lower percentage of women appointed by parties in an arbitration, the parties themselves—whether a multinational corporation, a small local entity, or a government—can encourage their counsel to at least consider the appointment of women as their appointed arbitrator. Indeed, several companies expressly consider diversity in selecting outside counsel[71] and could expand on these commitments to encourage the appointment of women as arbitrators as well. Entities can also publicly announce their commitment to gender and other forms of diversity by signing on to various commitments, such as the Ray Corollary Initiative[72] and the ERA Pledge.[73]

Prior to any dispute arising, public and private sector entities also can include an express clause in their contracts, such as the following sample clause provided by JAMS: "The parties agree that, wherever practicable, they will seek to appoint a fair representation of diverse arbitrators (considering gender, ethnicity and sexual orientation), and will request administering institutions to include a fair representation of diverse candidates on their rosters and list of potential arbitrator appointees."[74] In investment arbitration, States likewise can take action through express language in treaties. The 2021 Model Bilateral Investment Treaty of Canada, for example, "encourage[s]" the disputing parties "to consider greater diversity in arbitrator appointments, including through the appointment of women."[75] Under the 2019 Model Bilateral Investment Treaty of the Netherlands, the appointing authority, which is to appoint all members of a tribunal constituted under that treaty, "shall strive for gender and geographic diversity."[76]

In-house counsel in both the public and private sectors thus can take on a more active role in encouraging and mandating diversity; at the same time, outside counsel can encourage their clients to do so as well, highlighting the many benefits of diverse tribunals, as discussed above. By continuing to shine a light on diversity issues and by taking advantage of the increased number of resources now available to identify qualified diverse candidates, the parties and their counsel can continue to increase the proportion of women appointed as arbitrators.

71. *See* Int'l Council for Commercial Arb., *Report of the Cross-Institutional Task Force on Gender Diversity in Arbitral Appointments and Proceedings 2022 Update,* 145-146, https://cdn.arbitration-icca.org/s3fs-public/document/media_document/ICCA-Report-8u2-electronic3.pdf (accessed Dec. 16, 2024).
72. Ray Corollary Initiative, *Take the RCI Pledge,* https://raycorollary.org/take-the-rci-pledge/ (accessed Dec. 16, 2024).
73. Equal Representation in Arb. Pledge, *Take the Pledge,* https://www.arbitrationpledge.com/take-the-pledge (accessed Dec. 16, 2024).
74. JAMS, *Diversity and Inclusion Clause for Arbitration Agreements and Contracts,* https://www.jamsadr.com/inclusion-clause#:~:text=The%20parties%20agree%20that%2C%20wherever,rosters%20and%20list%20of%20potential (accessed Dec. 16, 2024).
75. 2021 Model FIPA, Agreement Between Canada and __ for the Promotion and Protection of Investments, Art. 30, https://www.international.gc.ca/trade-commerce/trade-agreements-accords-commerciaux/agr-acc/fipa-apie/2021_model_fipa-2021_modele_apie.aspx?lang=eng#sec-a (accessed Dec. 16, 2024).
76. Netherlands Model Investment Agreement, Art. 20(2), https://investmentpolicy.unctad.org/international-investment-agreements/treaty-files/5832/download (accessed Dec. 16, 2024).

As noted above, the arbitral institutions as a whole already have made significant progress in the appointment of women, in some cases appointing more women than men as arbitrators.[77] Such progress is likely a result of multiple organizations implementing policies that prioritize diversity, such as by requiring the identification of diverse candidates during the appointment process, and/or ensuring that at least one diverse candidate is included on candidate lists.[78] Other institutions, such as the Tashkent International Arbitration Centre, have adopted lists of factors to consider in the appointment process to enhance diversity.[79] Law firms similarly can adopt policies to ensure that they consider diversity in the appointment process, using templates such as the ERA Pledge Checklist of Best Practices for the Selection of Arbitrators.[80]

Another way that organizations can measurably prioritize diversity is through monetary investments. One prominent example is the Burford Equity Project, which utilizes a USD 150 million pool of capital to finance commercial litigation and arbitration matters led by female and racially diverse lawyers in order to provide these groups with more leadership opportunities to advance their careers and close the diversity gaps.[81] In another approach, the Move the Needle Fund has given four prominent law firms the opportunity to create aggressive metrics-based diversity goals, experiment with research-based methods to achieve them, and publicly report their progress.[82] Most recently, in March 2024, the American Arbitration Association-International Centre for Dispute Resolution Foundation and the JAMS Foundation announced a grant of USD 750,000 to increase efforts at advancing diversity among

77. Int'l Council for Commercial Arb., *Report of the Cross-Institutional Task Force on Gender Diversity in Arbitral Appointments and Proceedings 2022 Update*, 31-32, https://cdn.arbitration-icca.org/s3fs-public/document/media_document/ICCA-Report-8u2-electronic3.pdf (accessed Dec. 16, 2024); Int'l Ctr. for Settlement of Inv. Disp., *The ICSID Case Load: Statistics*, 23, https://icsid.worldbank.org/sites/default/files/publications/ENG_The_ICSID_Caseload_Statistics_Issue%202024.pdf (accessed Dec. 16, 2024).
78. *See* Int'l Council for Commercial Arb., *Report of the Cross-Institutional Task Force on Gender Diversity in Arbitral Appointments and Proceedings 2022 Update*, 126-129, https://cdn.arbitration-icca.org/s3fs-public/document/media_document/ICCA-Report-8u2-electronic3.pdf (accessed Dec. 16, 2024) (detailing the various approaches of the institutions to increase diversity in appointments).
79. Tashkent Int'l Arb. Ctr., *Tashkent International Arbitration Centre (TIAC) at the Chamber of Commerce and Industry of Uzbekistan and TIAC45 Launch the TIAC Diversity Toolkit to Assist the TIAC Court and Secretariat in Making Institutional Arbitrator Appointments*, https://www.tiac.uz/media (accessed Dec. 16, 2024); Int'l Council for Commercial Arb., *Report of the Cross-Institutional Task Force on Gender Diversity in Arbitral Appointments and Proceedings 2022 Update*, 129, https://cdn.arbitration-icca.org/s3fs-public/document/media_document/ICCA-Report-8u2-electronic3.pdf (accessed Dec. 16, 2024).
80. Equal Representation in Arb., *The ERA Pledge Constitution of the Arbitral Tribunal: Checklist of Best Practices for the Selection of Arbitrators*, https://assets.website-files.com/58a4313f62641fda6d995826/5fa3cfad308ce4cda9ba39ba_08424_PG_DR_ERA%20France%20guidelines%20pdf_V4.pdf (accessed Dec. 16, 2024).
81. Burford, *Introducing the Equity Project*, https://www.burfordcapital.com/insights-news-events/insights-research/introducing-the-equity-project/ (accessed Dec. 16, 2024).
82. Diversity Lab, *Move the Needle Fund*, https://www.mtnfund2025.com/ (accessed Dec. 16, 2024).

arbitrators and mediators, including providing tools and research supporting diversity.[83]

Finally, one of the key issues that women and other diverse attorneys face in obtaining their first arbitral appointment lies in a general aversion against appointing an individual for the first time.[84] Preferred candidates for arbitrator positions are often those with prior experiences as arbitrators, creating a significant barrier for new and more diverse candidates, including women, to enter the candidate pool.[85]

There are a number of measures that can be taken to address this aversion. Professional networking and mentorship groups geared toward women and young lawyers, as discussed above, create more visibility for traditionally underrepresented groups and can assist individuals in obtaining their first appointments. Women and other diverse candidates seeking their first appointments also can get their name in front of arbitral institutions, which may be more likely to take a chance on a first-time candidate, than are parties. On an institutional level, reconsidering minimum experience requirements for arbitral appointments can also allow the candidate pool to expand by taking away one of the barriers for more diverse candidates to try to break into the pool of qualified arbitrators.[86]

By addressing the hurdles that women face in obtaining their first and subsequent appointments as arbitrators, including through the adoption of diversity policies, public pronouncements or monetary investments in diversity initiatives, and professional groups aimed at promoting women, the arbitration community can continue to progress in the appointment of women as arbitrations. Tremendous progress has been made within merely the last ten years, but more certainly remains to be done.

III CONCLUSION

Despite the progress made over the past decade in particular, the retention of women as counsel and the appointment of women arbitrators remain a serious issue, and the international arbitration community must maintain speed in continuing to promote diversity efforts for women as both counsel and arbitrator. Work must continue to address the hurdles that women face throughout their careers as counsel, including unconscious bias, harassment, lower pay, and caregiver responsibilities. Initiatives and programming to address these ongoing issues, whether through mentorship, executive coaching, pay transparency, or firmwide training should be a priority for law firm partners and senior management.

83. Matt Perez, *2 Arbitration Bodies Donate $750K for Diversity Efforts*, https://www.law360.com/internationalarbitration/articles/1815132?nl_pk = 5e24c5a4-3466-4654-bb0d-0e7391ac29e7&utm_source = newsletter&utm_medium = email&utm_campaign = internationalarbitration&utm_content = 2024-03-20&read_main = 1&nlsidx = 0&nlaidx = 2 (accessed Dec. 16, 2024).
84. *See* Lucy Greenwood & C. Mark Baker, *Getting a Better Balance on International Arbitration Tribunals*, 28 Arb. Int'l 653, 658 (2012) https://doi.org/10.1093/arbitration/28.4.653.
85. *See* Catherine Rogers, *The Vocation of the International Arbitrator*, 20 Am. U. Int'l L. Rev. 957, 967-968 (2005).
86. Catherine Drummond, *The Party-Appointment Process: Addressing Barriers to Equal Opportunities for Women in the Appointment of Ad Hoc Adjudicators, in* Identity and Diversity on the International Bench: Who Is the Judge? 89, 91 (Freya Baetens ed., 2020).

Work must also continue to address the ongoing difficulties of women obtaining their first and subsequent arbitral appointments and should remain top-of-mind not only for outside counsel and arbitral institutions but also for co-arbitrators, in-house counsel, litigation funders, and the parties to any commercial or investment arbitration. Those appointing arbitrators should take full advantage of the wide variety of increasingly available resources that highlight qualified, diverse candidates, and in-house and outside counsel should push one another to do more. The importance of sustained effort by individuals throughout the arbitration field cannot be minimized.

In this regard, the Cross-Institutional Task Force (supported by the leaders in the field, including ICCA, White & Case LLP, Three Crowns LLP, Freshfields Bruckhaus Deringer, the ERA Pledge, ArbitralWomen, and fourteen arbitral institutions on the Task Force itself) must continue its work—as must many others highlighted herein. The sustained efforts and support of the entire arbitration community are essential. We applaud the progress and look forward to continued significant effort.

CHAPTER 8
Addressing Diversity in International Arbitration

Kabir Duggal & Kevin W. Gray[*]

This chapter considers the recent developments in scholarship on diversity, inclusion, equity, and belonging in international arbitration and attempts to update the work of previous scholars writing in the field.[1] *It begins by, first, examining ways in which diversity and inclusion should be understood in the context of international arbitration. It then provides an examination of recent attempts to increase diversity in the field. The chapter then concludes with a discussion of where advances have been made and where more work remains to be done to increase the presence of underrepresented groups.*

'Diversity doesn't look like anyone. It looks like everyone' – Karen Draper

I INTRODUCTION

The emergence of international arbitration as the preferred method for international dispute resolution brings with it a growing collective awareness of the underlying

---

* The authors thank Marc Morros Bo and Anna Regina Cruz Regalado for their excellent research assistance. This paper draws, in part, on previous work by Dr Duggal. For further details, *see* Kabir Duggal & Amanda Lee, *A 360-Degree, Kaleidoscopic View of Diversity and Inclusion (or the Lack Thereof) in International Arbitration*, 33:1 American Review of International Arbitration (2023); Kabir Duggal, Amanda Lee, Annabel Maréchal & Archismita Raha, *Diversity and Inclusion (or Lack Thereof) in International Arbitration: Investor-State Arbitration in the Spotlight*, American Review of International Arbitration (November 2024); Kabir A.N. Duggal & Rekha Rangachari, *Gender, Race, or Both? The Need for Greater Consideration of Intersectionality in International Arbitration*, in Sustainable Diversity in Arbitration (Shahla Ali, Filip Balcerzak, Giorgio F. Colombo, Joshua Karton, eds) (Elgar, 2022). Naturally, any mistakes remain the authors' own.

1. For the purposes of this chapter, we use 'diversity' as the concept to encompass diversity, inclusion, equity, and belonging.

diversity and inclusion issues confronting international arbitration.[2] For one, the selection and appointment of arbitrators have figured prominently in the discussions on the lack of diversity in arbitration. Arbitrator appointments are dominated by members of a limited demographic group, comprising largely white senior members of the profession from the global north,[3] while underrepresented groups like women, members of racialized groups, and people with visible disabilities remain underrepresented as arbitrators.[4] Additionally, while data about individuals' sexual orientations, non-visible disabilities, or socio-economic class origin is less available, anecdotal evidence would appear to suggest under-representation as well.

Multiple theories exist to explain the lack of diversity.[5] According to Professor Won Kidane, key criteria for the selection of arbitrators include 'familiarity with the applicable law, the cultural competence to understand the facts, and the scholastic aptitude, temperament, and integrity to apply the facts to the law and render a fair judgment'.[6] This 'invariably le[]d to the concentration of almost all of the world's leading arbitrators in the developed world of the West for five decades when the parties in fact come from diverse cultures around the world'.[7] While much has been said about the lack of diversity in the selection and appointment of arbitrators, particularly in reference to gender disparity, diversity, and inclusion issues impacting arbitration on various levels, the lack of diversity is not solely explainable in those terms. Any analysis must also consider the concentrations of socio-economic power in the West and risk aversion on the part of parties to a dispute. Few studies exist on the influence of those two causal vectors. Those that do exist suggest that it may be rational to hire repeat players and not to diversify.[8]

The reality is that international arbitration continues to expand its reach not only in terms of the growing number of international disputes resolved through arbitration

2. For the purposes of this chapter, unless otherwise indicated, international arbitration refers to both international commercial arbitration and investor-state arbitration.
3. Joseph Mamounas, *ICCA 2014. Does 'Male, Pale, and Stale' Threaten the Legitimacy of International Arbitration? Perhaps, but There's No Clear Path to Change*, Kluwer Arbitration Blog (10 Apr. 2014), https://arbitrationblog.kluwerarbitration.com/2014/04/10/icca-2014-does-male-pale-and-stale-threaten-the-legitimacy-of-international-arbitration-perhaps-but-theres-no-clear-path-to-change/ (accessed 16 Dec. 2024).
4. L. Yves Fortier, *Diversity in International Arbitration*, 39:2 Arbitration International 226 (2023) https://doi.org/10.1093/arbint/aiad020.
5. We use the word 'diversity' as a proxy for a number of different terms, including DEI, diversity and belonging.
6. Won L. Kidane, *The Culture of International Arbitration*, 285, 286 (OUP, 2017).
7. Won L. Kidane, *The Culture of International Arbitration*, 285, 286 (OUP, 2017) (Kidane observed that the criteria for the selection of arbitrators must at a minimum bear a substantial resemblance to the work performed by arbitrators); Kidane also cites to Crook: John Crook, Fact-Finding in the Fog: Determining the Facts of Upheavals and Wars in Inter-State Disputes, in *The Future of Investment* Arbitration 313, 314 (Catherine A. Rogers & Roger P. Alford, eds) (2009) (according to Crook, 'should they pause to reflect, most international lawyers would likely accept the thought that the science and art of deciding legal disputes involves at least three inter-related components. The first two involve determining the relevant law and the relevant facts. Then comes stage three – applying the law to the facts').
8. Vidhan K. Goyal, Joshua Madsen & Wei Wang, *Knowing is Power: The Value of Judge-Lawyer Familiarity* (16 Jun. 2021). HKUST Business School Research Paper No. 2020-019 (SSRN), https://ssrn.com/abstract=3666263 (accessed 16 Dec. 2024).

but also as to the subject matter and issues submitted by parties for resolution. In this regard, for arbitration to maintain its legitimacy as an effective and responsive dispute resolution mechanism, there is a strong argument to be made that it must reflect the diversity of the commercial landscape within which parties to an arbitration interact and operate.[9]

The question of how to adequately address diversity and inclusion issues has become increasingly complex and requires both a multi-faceted and intersectional approach. In the context of international arbitration, issues relating to diversity can involve several different dimensions including: (i) gender; (ii) race, ethnic, linguistic, or national origin; (iii) age; (iv) disability; (v) sexual orientation; (vi) socio-economic factors; and (vii) educational and professional background.[10] As will be discussed below, each of these dimensions must also be understood through an intersectional lens. The next sections of the chapter provide a general overview of how issues of diversity and inclusion in international arbitration should be understood, recent efforts and developments aimed at addressing these issues and evaluate what work remains to be done.

II UNDERSTANDING DIVERSITY AND INCLUSION IN INTERNATIONAL ARBITRATION

This section begins by considering how diversity and inclusion should be understood in the arbitral context. Verna Myers has described the relationship between diversity and inclusion as follows: '[d]iversity is being invited to the party; inclusion is being asked to dance'.[11] Myers' oft-cited line has sparked a creative discussion on how to reimagine the conversation on diversity and inclusion. As a starting point, questions of diversity ultimately boil down to an analysis of 'the representation or composition of various social identity groups in a workgroup, organization, or community'.[12] In simpler terms, diversity is variation and considers specific attributes such as race, ethnicity, culture, gender, gender identity and expression, sexual orientation, socio-economic status, religion, spirituality, disability, age, national origin, immigration status, and language, among others.[13]

9. Stephan W. Schill, *Conceptions of Legitimacy of International Arbitration*, in Practicing Virtue: Inside International Arbitration 106, 110 (David D. Caron et al., eds) (OUP, 2015); Freya Baetens, *Identity and Diversity on the International Bench: Implications for the Legitimacy of International Arbitration*, in Identity and Diversity on the International Bench 1, 11 (Freya Baetens, ed.) (OUP, 2020).
10. Kabir Duggal and Amanda Lee, *A 360-Degree, Kaleidoscopic View of Diversity and Inclusion (or the Lack Thereof) in International Arbitration*, 33:1 American Review of International Arbitration (2023).
11. Janet H. Cho, *Diversity Is Being Invited to the Party; Inclusion Is Being Asked to Dance*, https://www.cleveland.com/business/2016/05/diversity_is_being_invited_to.html (accessed 16 Dec. 2024).
12. American Psychological Association, *Equity, Diversity, and Inclusion Framework*, 12, https://www.apa.org/about/apa/equity-diversity-inclusion/framework.pdf (accessed 16 Dec. 2024).
13. American Psychological Association, *Equity, Diversity, and Inclusion Framework*, 14, https://www.apa.org/about/apa/equity-diversity-inclusion/framework.pdf (accessed 16 Dec. 2024).

Although related to diversity, inclusion is a distinct value. Inclusion contributes to the full realization of diversity and enables diversity to thrive; it does more.[14] If '[d]iversity is the "what"; inclusion is the "how." Diversity focuses on the makeup of your workforce [...], and inclusion is a measure of culture that enables diversity to thrive'.[15] As Andrés Tapia has stated, '[d]iversity is the mix, inclusion is making the mix work'.[16] An inclusive environment is one which 'offers affirmation, celebration, and appreciation of different approaches, styles, perspectives, and experiences, thus allowing all individuals to bring in their whole selves (and all of their identities) and to demonstrate their strengths and capacity'.[17]

Beyond merely opening the profession to other candidates, diversity and inclusion in arbitration potentially serve goals intrinsic to the proper functioning of the arbitral system. Diversity and inclusion may play an essential role in maintaining the legitimacy of the arbitral process by bringing different perspectives to the proceedings or being able to view the contracting parties and the contractual framework within a wider social, religious, or cultural perspective.[18] On this theory, diversity impacts the quality of decision-making, with different perspectives resulting in better decisions.[19]

A Diversity as a Dynamic Concept

Professor Joshua Karton has observed that the discourse surrounding diversity has been largely one-dimensional, focusing on the issue of fairness within the profession.[20] Instead, he argues that diversity should be understood across four dimensions, each of which addresses a particular goal or interest: (1) diversity in the service of equity and equality within the profession; (2) diversity in the service of fairness to the parties through diversity of expertise and cultural competence; (3) diversity in the service of legitimacy of the arbitration system through representativeness of the arbitrator pool;

14. ADP, *Diversity and Inclusion: What's the Difference, and How Can We Ensure Both?*, https://www.adp.com/spark/articles/2019/03/diversity-and-inclusion-whats-the-difference-and-how-can-we-ensure-both.aspx (accessed 16 Dec. 2024).
15. ADP, *Diversity and Inclusion: What's the Difference, and How Can We Ensure Both?*, https://www.adp.com/spark/articles/2019/03/diversity-and-inclusion-whats-the-difference-and-how-can-we-ensure-both.aspx (accessed 16 Dec. 2024).
16. Andrés Tapia, *The Inclusion Paradox: The Obama Era and the Transformation of Global Diversity* 12 (Hewitt, 2009).
17. American Psychological Association, *Equity, Diversity, and Inclusion Framework*, 14, https://www.apa.org/about/apa/equity-diversity-inclusion/framework.pdf (accessed 16 Dec. 2024).
18. Paula Hodges, May Tai & Elizabeth Kantor, *Inside Arbitration: Diversity – What Has Been Done So Far and Can the Arbitration Community Do More?*, Herbert Smith Freehills – Insights, https://www.herbertsmithfreehills.com/insights/2022-02/inside-arbitration-diversity-what-has-been-done-so-far-and-can-the-arbitration-community-do (accessed 16 Dec. 2024).
19. Vikrant Pachnanda, *Importance of Diversity While Forming an Arbitration Tribunal*, India Law Journal (2023), https://indialawjournal.org/importance-of-diversity-while-forming-an-arbitration-tribunal.php (accessed 16 Dec. 2024).
20. Joshua Karton, *Diversity in Four Dimensions*, in Sustainable Diversity in Arbitration (Shahla Ali, Filip Balcerzak, Giorgio F. Colombo, Joshua Karton, eds) 6, 19 (Elgar, 2022) (the diversity discourse in international arbitration 'has focused on the issue of fairness within the profession – not to the exclusion of other dimensions of diversity, but to the extent that it has 'crowded out' those other dimensions from the conversation').

and (4) diversity as tending to promote higher-quality decisions.[21] Ultimately, as Professor Karton suggests, diversity is best understood as a trajectory rather than a destination.[22]

In a similar vein, Yas Banifatemi, in her opening address at the 2023 Paris Arbitration Week, characterized diversity as a moving target.[23] According to Banifatemi, as society changes, the goals of representation change to reflect these societal values. Understanding diversity as a dynamic goal, rather than as a static endpoint, allows for the expansion of the diversity conversation.

Additionally, Banifatemi argued that diversity serves as 'a proxy for equality'.[24] This is less clear and may point to an under-explored concern with the diversity literature (one that is beyond the scope of this chapter). An unequal distribution of the burdens and benefits of society is prima facie evidence of a lack of equality.[25] However, the converse is not true. A diverse society can be unequal in many different ways, not all of which can be captured by referring to diversity. Understanding the demand for equality requires a broader understanding of the social structures which lead to inequality.

B An Intersectional Approach to Diversity

One critique of the discourse on diversity in arbitration is that it 'often converges around some single diversity characteristics such as race or gender in isolation'.[26] However, as Professor Kimberlé Crenshaw has argued, human identity is defined by 'the interconnected nature of social categorizations such as a race, class, and gender'.[27]

21. Joshua Karton, *Diversity in Four Dimensions*, in Sustainable Diversity in Arbitration (Shahla Ali, Filip Balcerzak, Giorgio F. Colombo, Joshua Karton, eds) 6, 8 (Elgar, 2022).
22. Joshua Karton, *Diversity in Four Dimensions*, in Sustainable Diversity in Arbitration (Shahla Ali, Filip Balcerzak, Giorgio F. Colombo, Joshua Karton, eds) 6, 20 (Elgar, 2022).
23. Andrew Mizner, *PAW2023: Diversity Concerns in Focus for Arbitration's Future*, Commercial Dispute Resolution, https://parisarbitrationweek.com/wp-content/uploads/2023/09/4--cdr_270323_1_paw2023-diversity-concerns-in-focus-for-arbitrations-future-andrew-mizner-cdr-article.pdf (accessed 16 Dec. 2024).
24. Andrew Mizner, *PAW2023: Diversity Concerns in Focus for Arbitration's Future*, Commercial Dispute Resolution, https://parisarbitrationweek.com/wp-content/uploads/2023/09/4--cdr_270323_1_paw2023-diversity-concerns-in-focus-for-arbitrations-future-andrew-mizner-cdr-article.pdf (accessed 16 Dec. 2024).
25. *See, e.g.*, John Rawls, *A Theory of Justice, Revised Edition* (Harvard, MA: Harvard University Press, 1999).
26. Ksenia Polonskaya, *Diversity in the Investor-State Arbitration: Intersectionality Must Be a Part of the Conversation*, 19 Melbourne J Int'l Law 259, 296 (2018) (Polonskaya refers to diversity in investment arbitration in particular, but the discussion on intersectionality nevertheless applies to international arbitration as a whole).
27. Kimberlé Crenshaw, *Demarginalizing the Intersection of Race and Sex: A Black Feminist Critique of Antidiscrimination Doctrine, Feminist Theory and Antiracist Politics*, 1989:1 University of Chicago Legal Forum 139, 140 (1989) https://doi.org/10.1093/oso/9780198782063.003.0016 (Crenshaw, in defining intersectionality, describes the experience of African American women as existing at the intersection of race and sex – how the challenge that they experience cannot be adequately described by a single axis consideration only race or only sex); *see also*, Merrill Perlman, *The Origin of the Term 'Intersectionality'*, Columbia Journalism Review (23 Oct. 2018), https://www.cjr.org/language_corner/intersectionality.php (accessed 16 Dec. 2024); Rachel

Those categories create 'overlapping and interdependent systems of discrimination or disadvantage; a theoretical approach based on such a premise'.[28] Professor Ksenia Polonskaya stated that:

> [t]here is no appreciation of [the] overlap. As a result, candidates with overlapping identities are 'invisible' on investment arbitration panels, in statistical reports and in academic discourse. Such an approach is methodologically and analytically problematic because it reveals the trap of conventional thinking about 'gender' as a unifying characteristic that has a potential to trump other characteristics and promotes a vision that *all* women face equal obstacles in accessing arbitral seats.[29]

Multiple factors produce inequality and must be analysed together. This is fundamentally the insight offered by the discourse on intersectionality.

As Professors Fabri and Stoppioni argue in this book, an intersectional approach in international investment law would show not only how different identities interact to produce inequality but also how the traditional manner in which international investment arbitration has been practised has the potential to exclude different points of view.[30]

III ADVANCES AND RETREATS IN THE APPOINTMENT OF DIVERSE ARBITRATORS

This next section considers where in international arbitration progress has been made as well as where institutional practices impede inclusion. Parties choose arbitration through their freedom to contract and through the principle of party autonomy. The most distinct example of party autonomy at work is the process of selecting and appointing arbitrators. This is not to suggest that diversity and inclusion are restricted only to the appointment of arbitrators. Quite the contrary, the quest for equal representation exists at every stage of the arbitral process. However, looking at the appointment of arbitrators for time provides a unique lens for us to analyse whether the pool of arbitrators has become more representative of the global constituents it represents.

There can be no doubt, as with much of the legal field, 'the role of arbitrator has traditionally been occupied by men, just as the wider legal profession and the business world have traditionally been dominated by men'.[31] Parties remain reluctant to appoint

Pears, *At a Crossroads with Intersectionality*, Globe Law and Business and the Centre for Legal Leadership, 136 (2nd ed., Globe Law and Business, 2022).

28. Kimberlé Crenshaw, *Demarginalizing the Intersection of Race and Sex: A Black Feminist Critique of Antidiscrimination Doctrine, Feminist Theory and Antiracist Politics*, 1989 University of Chicago Legal Forum 139, 140 (1989).
29. Ksenia Polonskaya, *Diversity in the Investor-State Arbitration: Intersectionality Must Be A Part of the Conversation*, 19 Melbourne J Int'l Law 259, 296 (2018).
30. Hélène Ruiz Fabri & Edoardo Stoppioni, 'Reforming the Reform? Taking Intersectionality Seriously'.
31. Jessica Foley, *Opening Our Eyes to Stereotypes: An Argument Against Gender-Blind Arbitral Appointments*, International Arbitration in England: Perspectives in Times of Change (Gregory Roy Fullelove et al., eds), 21 (Kluwer Law International, 2022).

the unknown diverse arbitrators, expressing a preference for white, male arbitrators who are senior in the profession.[32] Further, these arbitrators have high social capital[33] and have generally attended the best schools in their respective jurisdictions accompanied with a Master's degree from top universities in key arbitral jurisdictions, come from families with significant economic advantages, and have worked at the upper tiers of the legal profession.

There has historically been bias (conscious or unconscious) against women as arbitrators 'caused by the mismatch between the perceived attributes of women and the attributes perceived as required for success as an arbitrator'.[34] This is based on the so-called lack of fit theory.[35] Even those individuals who hold no explicit biases may fall foul of the 'lack of fit' effect. Although overall percentages are improving, arbitration users are less inclined to select women as arbitrators because the bias works at an unconscious level.[36]

In 2020, the Cross-Institutional Task Force on Gender Diversity in Arbitral Appointments and Proceedings of the International Council for Commercial Arbitration (ICCA) released a report (ICCA Reports No. 8) examining the appointment of women. The ICCA categorized the causes of lack of gender diversity, which are equally applicable to the lack of racial and ethnic diversity into two broad categories: insufficient experience and insufficient appointments. Moreover, it identified structural barriers to obtaining experience or being appointed. As ICCA Reports No. 8 noted, such barriers include:

> [F]inancial barriers, social class, lack of flexibility, a culture of exclusivity and unconscious bias[, including gender stereotyping]. These reasons are not limited to the international arbitration community at large but also affect those based in emerging jurisdictions like the Caribbean, Latin America and Africa although these

32. Kabir Duggal & Amanda Lee, *A 360-Degree, Kaleidoscopic View of Diversity and Inclusion (or the Lack Thereof) in International Arbitration*, 33:1 American Review of International Arbitration (2023) at 18 (the ability of parties to choose arbitrators is one of the cornerstones of arbitration. However, historical party reluctance to appoint diverse arbitrators persists. There are many reasons for this, including: (1) the supposed lack of exposure and/or availability of insufficient information about diverse arbitrators; (2) the impact of unconscious bias; and (3) the confidentiality of many arbitrations).
33. Pierre Bourdieu & Loic Wacquant, *An Invitation to Reflexive Sociology* (Polity, 1992).
34. Jessica Foley, *Opening Our Eyes to Stereotypes: An Argument Against Gender-Blind Arbitral Appointments*, International Arbitration in England: Perspectives in Times of Change (Gregory Roy Fullelove et al., eds), 21 (Kluwer Law International, 2022).
    https://www-kluwerarbitration-com.prx.law.columbia.edu/document/KLI-KA-Fullelove-2022-Ch02#n17 (accessed 16 Dec. 2024).
35. Jessica Foley, *Opening Our Eyes to Stereotypes: An Argument Against Gender-Blind Arbitral Appointments*, International Arbitration in England: Perspectives in Times of Change (Gregory Roy Fullelove et al., eds), 21 (Kluwer Law International, 2022), citing to Madeline Heilman, *Gender Stereotypes and Workplace Bias*, 32 Research in Organizational Behavior 116 (2012).
36. Jessica Foley, *Opening Our Eyes to Stereotypes: An Argument Against Gender-Blind Arbitral Appointments*, International Arbitration in England: Perspectives in Times of Change (Gregory Roy Fullelove et al., eds), 21, section 2.05 (Kluwer Law International, 2022).

emerging jurisdictions have only begun to develop arbitration in the last few decades.[37]

An update to the ICCA Reports No. 8, published in 2022, expanded the list to what it would call 'leaks in the pipeline'. These are lower rates of retention of women in private practice, the promotion of fewer women to senior ranks within an organization, and the lack of availability of opportunities (or the awareness of opportunities) for women to attain visibility in the profession. Another important factor was likely the existence of informational barriers: those with the power to appoint arbitrators were frequently unaware of available talented female candidates.[38]

Nonetheless, gender diversity in arbitral tribunals has continued to increase, although we are still far from our goal of parity. The proportion of female arbitrator appointees has risen from 12.6% in 2015 to 26.1% in 2021 globally. The same is true when looking at the whole number of cases administered by arbitral institutions. In particular, in cases administered by the ICAC and the London Court of International Arbitration (LCIA) during 2021, 37.9% of the total 483 arbitrators of the ICAC and 31.6% of 449 arbitrators at the LCIA. Data from other tribunals lagged behind. The percentage of female appointees at the International Centre for Dispute Resolution (ICDR), International Centre for Settlement of Investment Disputes (ICSID), and the Stockholm Chamber of Commerce (SCC) was 26.2%, 27.2%, and 28.7%.

The statistics, while suggesting some improvement, are potentially misleading. Much of the increase is attributable to the actions of institutions rather than parties. According to the 2021 statistics from the LCIA and SCC, nearly half of all arbitrators chosen by those two institutions were women (47.4% and 49.5%, respectively). Because party autonomy is central to arbitration, parties may choose to retain for themselves the ability to choose arbitrators. Statistics from the LCIA indicate that institutions themselves are about twice as likely to appoint women as arbitrators as compared to parties themselves.[39] Both parties and co-arbitrators selected a notably lower percentage of women arbitrators. The LCIA reports that women comprised only 22% of party-appointed arbitrators in 2020, 16% in 2021, and 19% in 2022. Co-arbitrators selected women 30% of the time in 2020, 33% in 2021, and 23% in 2022.

Moreover, there has been a recent increase in the percentage of arbitrators selected by parties or by other co-arbitrators, alongside a concomitant reduction in appointments by arbitral institutions themselves. As a result, efforts to promote diversity through arbitration institutions have become less effective. As helpful as

37. D'Andra A. Johnson & Theominique D. Nottage, *Diversifying the Dominant Demographics in International Arbitration: The How, the Why and the ('Maybe') Solution*, in Sustainable Diversity in Arbitration (Shahla Ali, Filip Balcerzak, Giorgio F. Colombo, Joshua Karton, eds) (Elgar, 2022).
38. International Council for Commercial Arbitration, *Report of the Cross-Institutional Task Force on Gender Diversity in Arbitral Appointments and* Proceedings, 2022 Update https://cdn.arbitration-icca.org/s3fs-public/document/media_document/ICCA-Reports-no-8-Gender-Diversity-2022-update.pdf (accessed 16 Dec. 2024).
39. LCIA, *2020 to 2022 Annual Casework Reports*, https://www.lcia.org/lcia/reports.aspx (accessed 16 Dec. 2024).

those initiatives may be, their impact will be reduced if parties choose arbitrators themselves and prevent institutions from doing so.

IV RECENT INITIATIVES TO INCREASE DIVERSITY

Several recent initiatives have attempted to advance diversity in arbitration.[40] Arbitral Women was founded thirty years ago to advance gender parity in the profession.[41] Regional organizations have also followed suit: Women Way in Arbitration was founded in Latin America.[42] Women in Arbitration was launched by the Hong Kong International Arbitration Centre (HKIAC) in 2018.[43]

Additionally, the Equal Representation in Arbitration (ERA) Pledge was authored in 2015.[44] It was designed 'to increase, on an equal opportunity basis, the number of women appointed as arbitrators in order to achieve a fair representation as soon practically possible, with the ultimate goal of full parity'.[45] To address additional disparities in the arbitral space, its sister pledge, the Equal Representation, was launched for signature in 2022, with a goal of increasing 'the number of women appointed as expert witnesses in dispute resolution procedures worldwide'.[46]

On racial equality and intersection, the Racial Equality for Arbitration Lawyers (REAL) group appears at the forefront of such efforts. According to its web page, 'REAL is a group of global lawyers practicing in international arbitration and striving to achieve racial equality for arbitration lawyers' since 18 January 2021.[47] The two core goals of REAL are 'advocacy' for underrepresented groups and 'access' for those who may not have opportunities to become part of the arbitral community. REAL has offered over 150 scholarships to people from all around the world.

A second initiative is the Rising Arbitrator Initiative (RAI), created in 2021. RAI focuses on age diversity and is aimed at supporting arbitration practitioners under 45 'who either have already received their first appointment as arbitrator or have at least seven years of professional experience in […] international arbitration by inter alia creating a support network and encouraging best practices'.[48]

---

40. These initiatives are discussed in greater detail in Carolyn B. Lamm & Jennifer A. Ivers, 'Maintaining Speed: Promoting and Advancing Gender Diversity in International Arbitration', in this book.
41. Arbitral Women, https://www.arbitralwomen.org (accessed 16 Dec. 2024).
42. Women Way in Arbitration, www.wwarb.org/ (accessed 16 Dec. 2024).
43. HKIAC, *Women in Arbitration*, https://www.hkiac.org/women-arbitration-wia (accessed 16 Dec. 2024).
44. Equal Representation in Arbitration, http://www.arbitrationpledge.com/ (accessed 16 Dec. 2024).
45. Equal Representation in Arbitration, *Commentary to the Pledge*, http://www.arbitrationpledge.com/about-the-pledge (accessed 16 Dec. 2024).
46. Equal Representation for Expert Witnesses Pledge, https://www.expertwitnesspledge.com/ (accessed 16 Dec. 2024).
47. Racial Equality for Arbitration Lawyers, *What Is REAL?*, https://letsgetrealarbitration.org/#eluid0d45c7d5 (accessed 16 Dec. 2024).
48. Rising Arbitrators Initiative, *About Rising Arbitrators Initiative (RAI)*, https://risingarbitratorsinitiative.com/page/about-us.htm (accessed 16 Dec. 2024).

The ICCA has also adopted important diversity initiatives. Its Diversity and Inclusiveness Committee promoted the publication of the report 'Cross-Institutional Task Force on Gender Diversity in Arbitral Appointments and Proceedings', which 'brings together representatives leading international arbitration institutions, law firms and gender diversity initiatives' to analyse the gender gap in the field.[49] An important innovation was the development of a database containing the names of potential female arbitrators and female counsels. Additionally, the ICCA partnered with the Arbitration Committee of the International Bar Association to develop a 'diversity checklist' that might be adopted when organizing arbitration conference.[50]

Many stakeholders have adopted voluntary pledges aimed at promoting diversity in international arbitration. With more than 830 signatories globally by 2022, the 2021 Pledge for Equal Representation for Expert Witnesses (ERE Pledge) is expected to have similar success to its sister 2015 Pledge for Equal Representation in Arbitration (ERA Pledge).[51] Today, the ERA Pledge, which was designed to draw attention to the under-representation of women on international arbitration tribunals, has 5,576 signatories, including both organizations and individuals.[52] Similarly, the International Chamber of Commerce (ICC) released its Centenary Declaration in January 2023, pledging 'diversity, equity, and inclusion for all stakeholders in dispute resolution as one of its ten main objectives for the next century'.[53]

Arbitral centres have also adopted either formal rules or informal guidance aimed at increasing representation. In 2022, the ICC released its Note to National Committees and Groups on the proposal of Arbitrators ('Note'). Adherence to the content of the Note was not mandatory. Instead, it 'encouraged' inclusive behaviour in the appointment of arbitrators. The Note stated that '[w]hen proposing arbitrators, Committees and Groups are encouraged to consider diversity, broadly defined, including but not limited to racial, ethnic, cultural, generational, and gender diversity'. The encouragement was also extended to the creation of 'nomination commissions' for proposing arbitrators to the ICC Court, the members of which 'should reflect the diversity, broadly defined, of the arbitration community in the Committee's country or in the Group's territory, including but not limited to racial, ethnic, cultural, generational, and gender diversity. Committees and Groups should make best efforts to achieve and maintain gender parity in their Nominations Commissions'. The model letters to parties,

49. International Council for Commercial Arbitration, *Inclusion and Diversity*, https://www.arbitration-icca.org/inclusion-and-diversity (accessed 16 Dec. 2024).
50. International Bar Association, International Council for Commercial Arbitration, *IBA Arbitration Committee/ICCA Conference Diversity Checklist*, https://cdn.arbitration-icca.org/s3fs-public/document/media_document/IBA%20AC%20%E2%80%93%20ICCA%20Conference%20Diversity%20Checklist.pdf (accessed 16 Dec. 2024).
51. Shreya Jain, *2022 Year in Review: Diversity in the Mainstream*, Kluwer Arbitration Blog, https://arbitrationblog.kluwerarbitration.com/2023/02/12/2022-year-in-review-diversity-in-the-mainstream/ (accessed 16 Dec. 2024).
52. Equal Representation in Arbitration, *Time for Change*, http://www.arbitrationpledge.com/ (accessed 16 Dec. 2024).
53. Shreya Jain, *2022 Year in Review: Diversity in the Mainstream*, Kluwer Arbitration Blog, https://arbitrationblog.kluwerarbitration.com/2023/02/12/2022-year-in-review-diversity-in-the-mainstream/ (accessed 16 Dec. 2024).

co-arbitrators, appointing authorities, and ICC national committees were amended to incorporate similar language by the end of 2022.[54]

Additionally, to encourage opportunities for younger members of the profession, the International Institute for Conflict Prevention and Resolution (CPR) adopted its Young Lawyer Rule. Under that rule, tribunals have the discretion to permit junior lawyers to examine witnesses and give submissions if both lead counsel and the client agree.[55] The CPR has followed up on this by introducing the so-called Diversity & Inclusion Model Clause that allows parties to pre-commit to a selection of a diverse neutral in a three-person tribunal.[56]

Some institutions have gone further and formally amended their rules. Both the Scottish Arbitration Centre and the Belgian Centre for Arbitration and Mediation (CEPANI) have introduced specific requirements concerning diversity into their rules. Article 8.1 of the Rules of the Scottish Arbitration Centre, 2022 provides that '[i]n proposing or appointing any arbitrator under the Rules, the parties, their counsel, any appointed arbitrator and the Centre shall have regard to the Equal Representation in Arbitration Pledge and [the above seen] R.E.A.L'.[57] The 2023 Arbitration Rules of the Belgian Centre for Arbitration and Mediation (CEPANI) require 'considerations of diversity and inclusion' to be taken into account in appointing or confirming the arbitral tribunal.[58]

V ARE THESE INITIATIVES WORKING?

These initiatives have spotlighted different dimensions of diversity, and we are seeing slow incremental change. For example, increasingly, women have been nominated to important roles in international arbitration. Claudia Salomon became President of the ICC in July 2021, making an important milestone in international arbitration. She is the first woman selected to serve as President of the ICC Court in its almost hundred-year

54. Shreya Jain, *2022 Year in Review: Diversity in the Mainstream*, Kluwer Arbitration Blog, https://arbitrationblog.kluwerarbitration.com/2023/02/12/2022-year-in-review-diversity-in-the-mainstream/ (accessed 16 Dec. 2024).
55. International Institute for Conflict Prevention & Resolution, *2018 CPR Non-Administered Arbitration* (2018), rule 12.5 ('In order to support the development of the next generation of lawyers, the Tribunal, in its discretion, may encourage lead counsel to permit more junior lawyers with significantly less arbitration experience than lead counsel to examine witnesses at the hearing and present argument. The Tribunal, in its discretion, may permit experienced counsel to provide assistance or support, where appropriate, to a lawyer with significantly less experience during the examination of witnesses or argument. Notwithstanding the contents of this Rule 12.5, the ultimate decision of who speaks on behalf of the client in an arbitration is for the parties and their counsel, not the Tribunal').
56. International Institute for Conflict Prevention & Resolution, Diversity Commitment Clause, https://drs.cpradr.org/model-clauses/arbitration-model-clauses/diversity-focus (accessed 16 Dec. 2024).
57. Shreya Jain, *2022 Year in Review: Diversity in the Mainstream*, Kluwer Arbitration Blog, https://arbitrationblog.kluwerarbitration.com/2023/02/12/2022-year-in-review-diversity-in-the-mainstream/ (accessed 16 Dec. 2024).
58. Shreya Jain, *2022 Year in Review: Diversity in the Mainstream*, Kluwer Arbitration Blog, https://arbitrationblog.kluwerarbitration.com/2023/02/12/2022-year-in-review-diversity-in-the-mainstream/ (accessed 16 Dec. 2024).

history.[59] This appointment was part of a series of high-profile appointment of women in the arbitral space. Lucy Reed was appointed head of the Singapore International Arbitration Centre (SIAC) in 2021. Jackie van Haersolte-van Hof was appointed head of the LCIA in 2014. Justice Bridget M. McCormack was appointed as the President and CEO of the American Arbitration Association-ICDR in 2022. Similarly, Gabrielle Kaufmann-Kohler was appointed the first female President of the ICCA.[60]

Nonetheless, there are clouds on the horizon. First, in light of recent changes in American law and pushback against diversity initiatives, many law firms are becoming less rather than more diverse.[61] Second, it is unclear if the benefits are equally spread among all equity-seeking groups. Commentators have argued that 'the main beneficiaries of the closing gender gap are white women based in Europe or North America'.[62] This mirrors the broader discourse that it is white women who have benefited most from affirmative action.[63] This highlights the need for greater consideration of intersectionality. Indeed, the update to ICCA Reports No. 8 in 2022 expressly noted: 'there is much work to be done to address diversity and inclusion in international arbitration in terms of ethnicity, nationality, geography, race, religion, age, and sexual orientation, among others, as well as how these factors intersect with each other'.[64]

Finally, little data is available on whether diversity is being achieved with respect to members of the LGBTQ community, the disabled community, or other equity-seeking groups. Moreover, law is an inherently conservative profession. Firms hire from the best law schools, who in turn recruit from the best undergraduate programmes or best high schools and colleges. Such students are hardly representative of national diversity.[65] These schools' student bodies privilege those from wealthy families, including those who can pay for the best educational programmes for their

59. ICC, *Claudia Salomon Becomes President of ICC Court*, Arbitration, https://iccwbo.org/news-publications/news/claudia-salomon-becomes-president-of-icc-court/ (accessed 16 Dec. 2024).
60. ICCA, *Historic Treasures*, https://www.arbitration-icca.org/historic-treasures (accessed 16 Dec. 2024).
61. National Association for Law Placement, 'Report on Diversity in U.S. Law Firms', January 2024 at 1, https://www.nalp.org/report_on_diversity (accessed 16 Dec. 2024); Joe Mille, *Biggest US Law Firms Hired Fewer Diverse Candidates amid DEI backlash*, Financial Times, 7 Mar. 2024, https://www.ft.com/content/df5f4d76-3a37-40f6-8bee-6161f56b6af7 (accessed 16 Dec. 2024).
62. Nobumichi Teramura, Luke Nottage & James Tanna, *Declining Professional Diversity in International Arbitration*, Kluwer Arbitration Blog, https://arbitrationblog.kluwerarbitration.com/2022/04/03/declining-professional-diversity-in-international-arbitration/ (accessed 16 Dec. 2024); Jiran Nasir Gore, *2021 In Review: Continued Strides in Favor of Diversity and Sustainable Development in International Arbitration*, Kluwer Arbitration Blog, https://arbitrationblog.kluwerarbitration.com/2022/02/27/2021-in-review-continued-strides-in-favor-of-diversity-and-sustainable-development-in-international-arbitration/ (accessed 16 Dec. 2024).
63. Tim Wise, *Is Sisterhood Conditional? White Women and the Rollback of Affirmative Action*, 10:3 NWSA Journal 1 (1998) https://doi.org/10.2979/nws.1998.10.3.1.
64. ICCA, *Report of the Cross-Institutional Task Force on Gender Diversity in Arbitral Appointments and Proceedings*, 2022 Update, 5.
65. Both admissions data and anecdotal evidence suggest that racially diverse candidates are hardly representative of racial groups as a whole. *See, e.g.*, Max Larkin, *Harvard Has Become More Racially Diverse, But Most Of Its Students Are Still Really Rich*, WBUR, https://www.wbur.org/news/2018/10/24/harvard-diverse-wealth (accessed 16 Dec. 2024); Editorial, 'Most Black Students at Harvard Are From High-Income Families', *The Journal of Blacks in Higher Education* (2006), https://www.jbhe.com/news_views/52_harvard-blackstudents.html (accessed 16 Dec. 2024).

children and the best linguistic training.[66] Little data is available on pathways for the economically less privileged. As a community, we should aspire to provide fair opportunities for all participants.

VI CONCLUSION: THE WAY FORWARD

There is evidence that international arbitration may be facing a legitimacy crisis. While international commercial arbitration has continued to grow, investment arbitration has been criticized as corrupt or underinclusive. *The New York Times* Magazine, in a rarity for international arbitration, recently featured a full-length article on the question of corruption in arbitration, focusing on the annulment of the award in *Nigeria v. P&ID*.[67] Recent investment agreements have excluded arbitration entirely[68] or severely curtailed its reach.[69]

Legitimacy in this alternative dispute resolution mechanism is essential for ensuring its survival. One way this can occur is through providing for legitimacy in the selection of participants in the process.

This chapter has aimed at assessing the current status of diversity and inclusion in international arbitration. It began with the assumption that diversity and inclusion could lead to increased legitimacy. Achieving diversity and inclusion in the field is not only an ethical matter or an improver to the decision-making quality but also a key to arbitration's future.

The international community has continued to use four main channels to advance equality. First, initiatives, such as ArbitralWomen, the ERA and ERE pledges, REAL, RAI, and the ICCA have been at the forefront of the fight against discrimination through the establishment of a network of arbitrators from equity-seeking groups. Second, arbitration institutions have consciously chosen to incorporate diversity considerations into nomination for leadership roles. Third, organizations have adopted specific pledges to encourage parties to take into account considerations of diversity and inclusion when appointing expert witnesses, arbitrators, and others. Fourth, arbitral institutions have begun to adopt specific rules requiring consideration of equity in appointing arbitrators.

No single approach is likely to solve the problem. Moreover, structural barriers, such as high entry costs into the profession of law, will remain endemic.

---

66. Yves Dezalay & Bryant G. Garth, *Dealing in Virtue: International Commercial Arbitration and the Construction of a Transnational Legal Order* 25 (University of Chicago, 1998).
67. Susannah Moody, *The Most Severe Abuses of the Arbitral Process: UK Court Overturns Mega-award on Grounds of Fraud*, Global Arbitration Review, https://globalarbitrationreview.com/article/the-most-severe-abuses-of-the-arbitral-process-uk-court-overturns-mega-award-grounds-of-fraud (accessed 16 Dec. 2024); Jesse Barron, *How Two Irish Businessmen Almost Took Nigeria for $11 Billion*, 9 Feb. 2024, https://www.nytimes.com/2024/02/09/magazine/nigeria-corruption-michael-quinn-brendan-cahill.html (accessed 16 Dec. 2024).
68. The Transatlantic Trade and Investment Partnership would have replaced ISDS with a trade court. However, it never came into existence.
69. *United States-Mexico-Canada Agreement* (2020), text available at: https://ustr.gov/usmca (accessed 16 Dec. 2024).

Finally, arbitration's diversity and inclusion problem is hardly unique. Other areas of legal practice face a similar situation. However, arbitration is unique in one way: it depends in large part on whether participants view it as legitimate. For arbitration to continue to exist, companies and individuals must continue to choose arbitration as their preferred dispute resolution method over other dispute resolution alternatives, most notably, litigation. Indeed, this is especially true in a world where arbitration is being employed in regions of the world outside the global north.

CHAPTER 9

The Role of Professional Organizations in International Arbitration: International Bar Association

Chiann Bao & Amr Omran

Professional organizations play a pivotal role in international arbitration. They shape legal values, develop arbitral best practice, and provide platforms for cross-fertilization among diverse legal systems. This piece focuses on the International Bar Association (IBA), a distinguished and lauded institution formed in the second half of the twenty-first century with the aim of fostering the administration of justice and rule of law globally. Throughout its Arbitration Committee, the IBA has instilled frameworks to evaluate impartiality and independence in arbitral proceedings, streamlining the taking of evidence in a hybrid system of dispute settlement and disseminating knowledge through the sharing of information and recommendations influencing the field, to name a few of its many contributions to the field. From a socio-legal lens, the IBA has been perceived as a 'distinctive value provider' and its frameworks carry precedential value that contribute to the standardization and harmonization of international best practices in international arbitration. It is within the IBA's innovative character of tackling complex issues in the arbitral landscape that inspired its streams of reforms with a vision of creating a resilient, more effective dispute settlement body.

I INTRODUCTION

Professional organizations impact the field of international arbitration in ways in which traditional actors, including the parties themselves, cannot. Generally, these professional organizations are membership-based and therefore self-selecting. Any standing such organizations have received over the years is a result of many factors, in particular, the professionalization of international arbitration and the initiative of the members themselves to address current issues facing the legal landscape.

This chapter highlights the role of the Arbitration Committee of the International Bar Association ('IBA') ('Committee'), which 'focuses on laws, practice and procedures relating to the arbitration of transnational disputes. Through its conferences, publications and projects, the Committee seeks to share information about international arbitration, promote its use and improve its effectiveness'.[1] The Committee aims to serve as a positive institutional 'role model', offering a vision of the conduct of international arbitration from the vantage point of its diverse membership. It is this forward-thinking element coupled with its self-initiating membership base and collaborative culture that makes the IBA inherently innovative.

II THE ROLE OF THE IBA IN INTERNATIONAL ARBITRATION

The origins of the IBA can be traced to its founding in 1947 inspired by the then recently established United Nations and accompanying vision, with the intention of instilling the rule of law and the administration of justice around the globe.[2] This overarching mission aligns directly with the aim of international arbitration as a dispute resolution process developed to resolve cross-border disputes.

The composition of the IBA has also changed over the years and today comprises not only the world's bar associations and law societies but also individual lawyers and law firms. Such constituency is more reflective of the international arbitration community which in turn benefits more directly the work of the international arbitration ecosystem.[3] Its present membership comprises more than eighty thousand individual international lawyers from law firms around the globe and around 190 bar associations and law societies spanning more than 170 countries.

III THE IBA IN REFORMING ARBITRATION

The Committee has served as an influential force behind arbitration reform for almost three decades. Perhaps its most notable contribution is the suite of published guidelines and rules now widely adopted by arbitration users and even national courts.[4] Notwithstanding their 'soft law' status, the *IBA Rules on the Taking of Evidence in*

---

1. *See* the Committee's webpage: IBA, *Arbitration Committee*, https://www.ibanet.org/unit/Dispute+Resolution+Section/committee/Arbitration+Committee/3010 (accessed 16 Dec. 2024).
2. IBA, *IBA Practical Guide on Business and Human Rights for Business Lawyers* (2016), at 7, https://www.ibanet.org/MediaHandler?id=d6306c84-e2f8-4c82-a86f-93940d6736c4 (accessed 16 Dec. 2024).
3. IBA, *About the IBA*, https://www.ibanet.org/About-the-IBA (accessed 16 Dec. 2024).
4. *W Ltd v. M SDN BHD* [2016] EWHC 422 (Comm): '[t]he 2014 IBA Guidelines make a distinguished contribution in the field of international arbitration. Their objective, to assist in assessing impartiality and independence, is to be commended' following on to state '[i]t is therefore with diffidence that I say that the present case suggests there are weaknesses in the 2014 IBA Guidelines in two inter-connected respects'.

International Arbitration (incepted in 1999) and the *IBA Guidelines on Conflicts of Interest in International Arbitration* (first adopted by the IBA Council in 2004 and most recently revised and adopted in 2024) in particular have been widely accepted not only domestically but also internationally.[5] Originally envisaged for users of international commercial arbitration, such soft law instruments have also been more broadly 'codified' in investment arbitration as well.[6] The prolific reach of the IBA suite of soft law reflects the precedential value and in turn contribution to the standardization or harmonization of international best practices in international arbitration. The IBA's efforts in that respect have had a significant impact on arbitral practice as we know it today:

> One thing that deserves to be highlighted is the harmonization of procedural aspects of arbitration. The discrepancy in procedural expectations that we saw much more frequently before as compared with today owes to the successful harmonization of certain areas of procedure [which] is a result of the growth, the increase in the number of cases and also the years of experience and exposure by

5. Many courts around the world have recognized the value and relevance of IBA rules and guidelines; *see, e.g., China State Construction Engineering Corporation v. CJSC INTEKO and MISK Ltd*, Svea Court of Appeal, 10 Apr. 2013, Case No. T 2484-11, in which the Court held that: ('[i]n the present case, CSCEC has to a large extent relied on the guidelines issued by [the IBA]. Even if these guidelines are not directly applicable they can, considering that the present case relates to international arbitration, be of some interest'); Swiss Supreme Court, 4A_506/2007, 20 Mar. 2008, para. 3.3.2.2: '[the IBA Guidelines on Conflicts of Interest in International Arbitration] admittedly have no statutory value … yet they are a precious instrument, capable of contributing to harmonization and unification of the standards applied in the field of international arbitration to dispose of conflict of interests … and such an instrument should not fail to influence the practice of arbitral institutions and tribunals'; *W Ltd v. M SDN BHD* [2016] EWHC 422 ('the present arbitration is international, and parties often choose English Law in an international context. Thus the role of this Court has an international dimension. I therefore prefer to consider the 2014 IBA Guidelines, as I have done, and explain why I do not, with respect, think they can yet be correct'); *see also supra* n. 4. Some courts in the Middle East have also sought guidance from IBA instruments. For example, the Egyptian Court of Cassation has relied on the 2014 *IBA Guidelines on Conflicts of Interest in International Arbitration* (the '2014 IBA Guidelines') in multiple decisions to determine whether the impugned arbitrator conduct met the necessary threshold for setting aside arbitral awards under Egyptian law for lack of independence and/or impartiality. The Court acknowledged the worldwide legitimacy of the 2014 IBA Guidelines considering that they are 'used as a guide by the judiciary in many countries'; *see* Egyptian Court of Cassation, Petitions Nos 7913 and 13996 of JY91 (Commercial and Economic Circuit), 9 May 2023 (citing to the Green List of the 2014 IBA Guidelines); Egyptian Court of Cassation, Petition No. 13892 of JY81 (Commercial and Economic Circuit), 22 Feb. 2022 (citing to the Orange List of the 2014 IBA Guidelines); Egyptian Court of Cassation, Petition No. 10103 of JY86 (Commercial and Economic Circuit), 23 Apr. 2019 (holding that the facts of the case do not constitute any form of conflict of interest under the 2014 IBA Guidelines).
6. *See, e.g.*, Comprehensive Economic and Trade Agreement Between Canada, of the one part, and the European Union and its Member States, Art. 8.30, providing that '[the parties] shall comply with the International Bar Association Guidelines on Conflicts of Interest in International Arbitration or any supplemental rules adopted pursuant to Article 8.44.2', https://investmentpolicy.unctad.org/international-investment-agreements/treaty-files/3593/download (accessed 16 Dec. 2024); *see also* United States–Mexico–Canada Agreement, Art. 14.D.6(5), providing that 'Arbitrators appointed to a tribunal for claims submitted under Article 14.D.3.1 shall: (a) comply with the International Bar Association Guidelines on Conflicts of Interest in International Arbitration, including guidelines regarding direct or indirect conflicts of interest, or any supplemental guidelines or rules adopted by the Annex Parties', https://ustr.gov/sites/default/files/files/agreements/FTA/USMCA/Text/14-Investment.pdf (accessed 16 Dec. 2024).

> professionals around the world from diverse cultures. So, certainly the contributions of the IBA Arbitration Committee in creating soft law is a part of that.[7]

As leading arbitration practitioners explain, '[t]he development of soft law in arbitration illustrates the vitality of the epistemic community and the cross fertilization between its different components, practitioners, arbitral institutions and professional organizations', adding that '[t]his is how arbitration progresses and evolves'.[8] Apart from the development and dissemination of rules and guidelines, another major contribution of the Committee has been the promotion of diversity and inclusion in the arbitration community.[9]

The Committee has also served as a thought leader, shaping the wider arbitration community through seminars and conferences and other wide-reaching channels.[10] In particular, the establishment of an annual 'arbitration day' in 1997 – thanks to the efforts of David Rivkin and Dr Wolfgang Kühn – represented a milestone for the arbitration community.[11] In fact, the arbitration world at the time was much smaller and there was a perceived need for international arbitration to be 'more international'.[12] The founders of the Arbitration Day sought to achieve that goal by working to 'make the procedure more accessible for those entering the field and for those without any prior experience, and ... make it more attractive to companies to use international arbitration, and ... expand the geographic scope of international arbitration'.[13]

Another key benefit of this yearly gathering of arbitration practitioners from around the world has been 'introducing international procedural and substantive law rules into international arbitration ... by adopting civil law procedure, common law procedure, and civil law and common law material law' as well as by 'borrow[ing] good ideas from the ICC International Court of Arbitration and other institutions'.[14]

The annual IBA Arbitration Day remains a key event on the arbitration calendar which brings together practitioners from around the world to discuss important topics of the day. In addition, the Arbitration Days are often used 'as an opportunity to road

---

7. Sally Harpole, *Video Contribution to the Committee on Occasion of the 25th Annual IBA Arbitration Day in Singapore* (2024).
8. Alexis Mourre, 'About Procedural Soft Law, the IBA Guidelines on Party Representation and the Future of Arbitration', in: Patricia Louise Shaughnessy & Sherlin Tung (eds), *The Powers and Duties of an Arbitrator: Liber Amicorum Pierre A. Karrer*, 239, at 241 (Kluwer Law International 2017), citing Gabrielle Kauffman-Kohler, *Soft Law in International Arbitration: Codification and Normativity*, 1 J. Int'l Disp. Settlement, 283, at 295 (2010) https://doi.org/10.1093/jnlids/idq009.
9. Dominique Brown-Berset, *Video Contribution to the Committee on Occasion of the 25th Annual IBA Arbitration Day in Singapore* (2024).
10. Luke Nottage, 'International Arbitration and Society at Large', in: Stefan Kröll, Andrea K. Bjorklund & Franco Ferrari (eds), *Cambridge Compendium of International Commercial and Investment Arbitration*, 389, at 416 (Cambridge University Press 2023).
11. Since its inception, the IBA Arbitration Day was a great success, with the inaugural edition taking place in New York on 25 Sep. 1997 with approximately two hundred participants, and speakers from eleven countries and four continents; Wolfgang Kühn, *Video Contribution to the Committee on Occasion of the 25th Annual IBA Arbitration Day in Singapore* (2024); David W. Rivkin, *Video Contribution to the Committee on Occasion of the 25th Annual IBA Arbitration Day in Singapore* (2024).
12. Rivkin, *supra* n. 11.
13. *Ibid*.
14. Kühn, *supra* n. 11.

test and explore the issues that will subsequently appear in materials for the IBA'.[15] From a socio-legal lens, the development of such an event has influenced the 'culture of arbitration' and indeed is now an integral part of the same.[16]

Finally, as a self-initiating membership body, the Committee could not have the success it has today without the contribution of its members who represent practitioners from both common and civil law systems. Structurally organized with sub-committees engaging in initiatives aimed at improving the specific area of that sub-committee, the intellectual capital of each of these groupings is unmatched. Through the collective efforts of members of these smaller groups, the Committee can impact more meaningfully as a neutral platform with the broad mission to promote best practices in international arbitration. The following instruments are noteworthy in this regard.

Guidelines for Drafting International Arbitration Clauses (2010). Inherent in the name, these guidelines are designed to assist users with drafting effective arbitration clauses which embody the parties' wishes, unambiguously. The guidelines are prescribed to ensure that users are aware of the essential elements of an effective arbitration clause and at the same time understand choices in alternative drafting while retaining the validity of the clause.[17]

Guidelines on Party Representation in International Arbitration (2013). These guidelines aim to ensure that parties in international arbitrations have a streamlined set of professional conduct rules reflective of international best practices (in contrast with domestic professional conduct rules) and have a reference point in understanding what it means to act with integrity and honesty in international arbitration proceedings and refrain from unnecessary delay or expense, which often take the form of dilatory tactics aimed at obstructing the course of the arbitral proceedings.[18]

Rules on the Taking of Evidence in International Arbitration (2020). Prepared in 1999, the IBA sought to strike common ground between the common and civil law practices of evidentiary requirements in international arbitration.[19] These rules are flexible and are designed for use in conjunction with institutional or ad hoc rules governing international arbitrations. For example, on the issue of protecting privilege within documents in the course of preparing for arbitral proceedings, as a general point, document production in international arbitration is considerably more limited than in proceedings within common law jurisdictions. The success of these rules is evidenced by their widespread use throughout the world as 'best practice'.

---

15. Judith Gill, *Video Contribution to the Committee on Occasion of the 25th Annual IBA Arbitration Day in Singapore* (2024).
16. Alexis Mourre, 'Arbitral Institutions and Professional Organizations as Lawmakers', in: Jean Engelmayer Kalicki & Mohamed Abdel Raouf (eds), *ICCA Congress Series No. 20: Evolution and Adaptation – The Future of International Arbitration*, 86, at 92 (Kluwer Law International 2019).
17. IBA, *IBA Guidelines for Drafting International Arbitration Clauses* (2010), https://www.ibanet.org/MediaHandler?id=D94438EB-2ED5-4CEA-9722-7A0C9281F2F2 (accessed 16 Dec. 2024).
18. IBA, *IBA Guidelines on Party Representation in International Arbitration* (2013), https://www.ibanet.org/MediaHandler?id=6F0C57D7-E7A0-43AF-B76E-714D9FE74D7F (accessed 16 Dec. 2024).
19. IBA, *IBA Rules on the Taking of Evidence in International Arbitration* (2020), https://www.ibanet.org/MediaHandler?id=def0807b-9fec-43ef-b624-f2cb2af7cf7b (accessed 16 Dec. 2024).

Guidelines on Conflicts of Interest (2024). Since their issuance in 2004, the guidelines gained global acceptance within the international arbitration community and, as held by the 2015 Queen Mary survey, it is hailed as one of the most frequently used soft instruments by arbitration practitioners.[20] Arbitrators and counsel refer to the guidelines when making decisions about prospective appointments and disclosures in arbitration, while arbitral institutions and national courts regularly consult the guidelines when considering challenges to arbitrators.[21] The famous 'traffic-light' guidance influences decisions made about disclosure by an arbitrator or challenge to an arbitrator's appointment through three lists of specific categories of situations that arise in international arbitration practice – designated 'Red', 'Orange', and 'Green', respectively.[22]

As these guidelines form the framework for arbitrator relationships, when challenges are raised, such guidelines will invariably be mentioned in the resulting decision by the institution or judgment in the courts. Having a firsthand understanding as to how the guidelines are applied in practice enhances the influential value of the guidelines. With such information, parties seeking to challenge arbitrators are able to better anticipate the likelihood of success of any challenge. International Centre for Settlement of Investment Disputes (ICSID) in particular has stated that '[w]hile the IBA Guidelines on Conflicts of Interest are not binding, they may serve as useful references in a challenge under the ICSID Convention'.[23] The growing investment arbitration jurisprudence supports this proposition that, while non-binding,[24] they are non-binding in proceedings constituted under it.[25]

---

20. Queen Mary International Arbitration Survey, Improvements and Innovations in International Arbitration (2015), at 35, https://arbitration.qmul.ac.uk/media/arbitration/docs/2015_International_Arbitration_Survey.pdf (accessed 16 Dec. 2024); *see also* Queen Mary International Arbitration Survey: Current and Preferred Practices in the Arbitral Process (2012), at 11, https://arbitration.qmul.ac.uk/media/arbitration/docs/2012_International_Arbitration_Survey.pdf (accessed 16 Dec. 2024).
21. *IBA Guidelines on Conflicts of Interest in International Arbitration* (2024), https://www.ibanet.org/document?id=Guidelines-on-Conflicts-of-Interest-in-International-Arbitration-2024 (accessed 16 Dec. 2024).
22. The 'Green' list outlines categories that, when assessed objectively, do not give rise to a conflict of interest and therefore no disclosure is necessary for such categories. The 'Orange' list sets out categories that, depending on the facts of a particular case, may give rise to justifiable doubts regarding an arbitrator's impartiality and independence and hence disclosure is warranted (albeit the arbitrator may continue if there is no objection). The 'Red' list identifies categories that, depending on the facts, give rise to justifiable doubts surrounding the impartiality and independence of an arbitrator. *See also IBA Guidelines on Conflicts of Interest in International Arbitration* (2024), at 1: '[t]he innovative traffic-light system of red, orange and green lists has become a worldwide norm in many respects. Practitioners apply the Guidelines as a default; most arbitration institutions and even courts also refer to them as an essential set of principles in the field. The need for such Guidelines is unchallenged'.
23. ICSID Convention, *Procedure of Disqualification of the Arbitrator*, https://icsid.worldbank.org/procedures/arbitration/convention/disqualification/2022 (accessed 16 Dec. 2024); *see also* Margaret Moses, *The Role of the IBA Guidelines on Conflicts of Interest in Arbitrator Challenges*, Kluwer Arbitration Blog, 23 Nov. 2017.
24. *Ayat Nizar Raja Sumrain and others v. State of Kuwait*, ICSID Case No. ARB/19/20, Decision on the Claimant's Proposal to Disqualify Prof. Zachary Douglas and Mr. V.V. Veeder, 2 Jan. 2020, para. 109; *Raiffeisen Bank International AG and Raiffeisenbank Austria d.d. v. Republic of Croatia (I)*, ICSID Case No. ARB/17/34, Decision on the Proposal to Disqualify Stanimir

IV THE IBA AS A VALUE PROVIDER

In his seminal article on sociological perspective on international arbitration, Gaillard categorizes 'value providers' as international organizations (United Nations body, the Conference on Trade and Development (UNCTAD), United Nations Commission on International Trade Law (UNCITRAL), Organisation for Economic Co-operation and Development (OECD), etc.), non-governmental organizations (NGOs), 'Clubs' (International Council for Commercial Arbitration (ICCA)), academic institutions specializing in international arbitration, and professional organizations (IBA) under one monolithic grouping. With a more nuanced understanding of the Committee, one might appreciate that, in fact, the Committee reflects characteristics of all of these groupings and operates in order to 'provide guidance as to the way international arbitration should develop and arbitral social actors should behave'.[26] In recognizing this unique role, Professor Gaillard lauded the IBA as a 'distinctive value provider' which plays a 'major role in the field of international arbitration in developing rules or guidelines on a number of features of the international arbitration procedure'.[27]

This role of the IBA has been acknowledged by other 'value providers' as well. In general, professional organizations operating at the national and international levels are increasingly well connected and regularly coordinate efforts based on shared policy objectives (and sentiments towards reform). Such partnerships between professional organizations are also built on providing what each organization specializes in and forming a symbiotic relationship on such terms.

For example, in recent years, the IBA, through the Committee, has obtained observer status and regularly participates in UNCITRAL meetings, especially in Working Group III. UN Conference on Trade and Development also recognizes contributions from the IBA and engages with its work from time to time.

Most recently, the Committee has established a joint initiative with Jus Mundi. Such partnership aims to make accessible data on IBA-branded soft law by collecting non-confidential commercial arbitration awards and related documents to these awards.[28] This project reflects the complementary advantages that the two entities possess, one in the power of the collective membership base and its thought leadership and the other in the prominence of an accelerating technological application in international arbitration.

Alexandrov, 17 May 2018, para. 85; *Eiser Infrastructure Limited and Energía Solar Luxembourg S.à r.l. v. Kingdom of Spain*, ICSID Case No. ARB/13/36, Decision on the Kingdom of Spain's Application for Annulment, 11 Jun. 2020, para. 226.

25. *Alpha Projektholding GmbH v. Ukraine*, ICSID Case No. ARB/07/16, Decision on Respondent's Proposal to Disqualify Arbitrator Dr. Yoram Turbowicz, 19 Mar. 2010, para. 56.
26. Emmanuel Gaillard, *Sociology of International Arbitration*, 31(1) Arb. Int'l 1, 7 (2015) https://doi.org/10.1093/arbint/aiv021.
27. *Ibid.*, at 9.
28. Jus Mundi, *An Exclusive Partnership to Promote Accessibility in Commercial Arbitration*, https://jusmundi.com/en/partnership/iba (accessed 16 Dec. 2024); *see also* the introduction of the IBA Arbitration Library on Jus Mundi, https://jusmundi.com/en/iba-arbitration-library (accessed 16 Dec. 2024).

V CONCLUSION

As highlighted in the pioneering analysis of the sociology of arbitration 'Dealing in Virtue',[29] the development and legitimacy of international arbitration have been significantly influenced by the interplay between various legal traditions and institutions. Indeed, institutions such as the IBA have developed into a de facto lawmaker by consensus. As a former co-chair of the Committee, Alexis Mourre explains, '[t]he Arbitration Committee of the International Bar Association (IBA) is a perfect example of an institution having gained a central role in the arbitration community by its ability to create high-quality rules that have become widely used in practice. There is, in other words, a marketing versant of the rule-making exercise that may contribute to an undesired proliferation of rules'.[30] With such a recognized role in the international arbitration ecosystem, the Committee must ensure that its members represent the many voices of international arbitration and be prepared to engage in reform initiatives so that international arbitration can continue to thrive despite changing times.

29. Yves Dezalay & Bryant Garth, *Dealing in Virtue International Commercial Arbitration and the Construction of a Transnational Legal Order* (University of Chicago Press 1996).
30. Mourre, *supra* n. 16, at 88.

CHAPTER 10

Why Dispute Resolution Institutions Must Be Governed with a Purpose, and Why They Must Continuously Reform Themselves

Maria Fernanda Garza & Michael McIlwrath

For a compendium about reforming arbitration reform, it is appropriate to pose threshold questions about the nature of institutions that offer dispute resolution services (DRS): What is the purpose that they serve? And to whom is an institution accountable with respect to whether and how it accomplishes its purpose in a world experiencing rapid changes? In this chapter, the authors – the outgoing Chair of the International Chamber of Commerce (ICC) and the outgoing Chair of the ICC's DRS – explain how governance plays a role in the continuous evolution of the world's leading provider of global DRS.

Practitioners would be forgiven for assuming that arbitration institutions exist for the purpose of disputes. Or, more cynically, that they exist to provide gainful work to lawyers and arbitrators. Yet these statements describe the service that institutions provide and how they provide them. They do not address the ultimate purpose, i.e., the reason *why* an institution would be created and exists to resolve disputes. Arbitration practitioners would benefit from understanding the real purpose that an institution aims to serve. And, more importantly, when institutions engage in arbitration reform, as they should from time to time to adapt to changes in the markets in which they operate, those reforms should be aligned and support the reasons for which the institution exists. And that is the job of an institution's governance.

Although international arbitration as a tool of global governance has been discussed in the literature,[1] a topic that is rarely addressed directly is how they are governed themselves.

The authors of this chapter are familiar with the governance of the International Chamber of Commerce (ICC), the organisation perhaps most recognised globally for its international Dispute Resolution Services (DRS). With this chapter, we hope to shed light on how the ICC's DRS help sustain the ICC's core objectives and how ICC's governance structure drives its dispute services to continuously adapt to global changes in order to continue to meet the organisation's objectives.

I GOVERNANCE AND PURPOSE

The governance of an institution should consider how well it is achieving the organisation's purpose today and whether it will need to change to achieve it in the future. By way of an example from an unrelated field, consider a ferry service for transporting passengers by sea from place A to place B and back. Obviously, the ferries must be seaworthy and well maintained, i.e., that they are operationally sound. If the ferry company fails to demonstrate that it can safely carry passengers to their destination, no one will take its ferries. But if it meets the passengers' expectations, those who need to get from place A to B and back will use the ferry, possibly because many live in one location and work in the other. The ferry will prosper if there are people who need to get from A to B and back, and the ferry is the most reliable and efficient way to achieve this. If, instead, the ferry's passengers discover a better way to meet their needs of A to B travel, perhaps by taking an automobile over a bridge, then they may begin preferring that over the ferry.

The board or governing body of the ferry company must ensure not only that its operations are sound but also that the service it provides is better than other available options. If the company succeeds in these areas, it will prosper as the preferred method for transporting passengers from A to B and back.

Institutions that provide DRS face a similar situation. The parties that use their services – the ones who pay the bills – typically come to them through the disputes clauses of commercial contracts and the rules they specify. Once in a dispute, what they experience of the institution will be its operations, i.e., how the institution employs its rules to get parties to a result of their dispute. If the processes are robust and the institution's employees capably administer proceedings under its rules, then parties will feel they are in safe hands as they travel from the inception of their dispute to an award.

But providing a high-quality service is no guarantee that parties will prefer the institution's rules to resolve their disputes. Just as ferry passengers may begin to prefer

1. *See, e.g.*, C.J.W. Baaij, Hiding in Plain Site: The Power of Public Governance in International Arbitration, Harvard Int'l Law J. Volume 60, Number 1, Winter 2019, https://journals.law.harvard.edu/ilj/wp-content/uploads/sites/84/HILJ_601_4_Baaij.pdf (accessed 16 Dec. 2024); S. Nappert, https://academic.oup.com/edited-volume/35422/chapter-abstract/303175967?redirectedFrom=fulltext (accessed 16 Dec. 2024).

other means of getting from A to B, parties will choose the institution only so long as it appears the best option to achieve their goal of dispute resolution. They may select the rules of another institution or the courts if they feel they offer a superior means of addressing their needs.

Thus, the governance of an institution must be concerned with both its operations – meaning its capability of competently discharging the service of administering a dispute resolution service – and how it is positioned with respect to other means of resolving disputes that parties may choose. Or, to return to our example of a ferry service, how should the company react if it learns that the people who use its service might soon have access to flying cars? Should it do nothing and wait to see if its passengers opt to use flying cars instead of ferries, or should the ferry service begin to consider whether and how it might adapt if flying cars become widely adopted?

While this may sound like science fiction, it is not far from what recent advancements in Artificial Intelligence ('AI'), notably generative AI, is currently posing to the future DRS. In an informal poll of arbitration institutions conducted in May 2024, only two out of the eleven respondents indicated that they are not presently considering whether or how to adopt AI. Of the other nine responding institutions, five indicated that this is something they are presently considering, and four stated that they have already begun to adopt AI in varying degrees.[2]

A Why Institutions Must Undergo Periodic Reform, and the Pressure They Face to Continuously Evolve

The reforms or innovations of peer institutions are hardly the only motivator for institutions to question whether they should change. Institutions must continuously consider innovations adopted by national courts, often to expand access to justice. The introduction of AI into the procedures of the national courts is likely to be the next innovation to which arbitration must pay heed.

For example, in Mainland China, courts have been introducing new technologies for a number of years. In Singapore, the courts are investigating the adoption of generative AI to assist in deciding certain 'arithmetical' aspects of disputes, according to the country's Chief Justice:

> Consider simple civil matters that *do not require significant normative judgment*, but involve *largely arithmetical issues that can be appropriately resolved through the application of common patterns* – for example, maintenance applications in family proceedings. …
>
> *We are … continuing to study the possible use of AI to support adjudication in such simple civil cases. Existing AI models can identify an appropriate outcome in such cases with reasonable reliability, and this could both speed up the process and lower the cost of dispute-resolution for these cases. It would also free up judicial*

2. M. Osadchiy et al., *Are Arbitral Institutions Using Artificial Intelligence? The State of Play in Adopting AI*, Kluwer Arbitration Blog, https://arbitrationblog.kluwerarbitration.com/2024/05/08/are-arbitral-institutions-using-artificial-intelligence-the-state-of-play-in-adopting-ai/ (accessed 16 Dec. 2024).

> *resources that can then be channelled to more complex matters. All of this can significantly enhance access to justice* (emphasis added).[3]

If courts begin to adopt AI to 'speed up the process and lower the cost of dispute resolution', it will not be possible for arbitration institutions to ignore the innovation for long. First, institutions may simply find they will require the support of new technology to handle their case load using their available resources. Second, and more important, the expectations of parties may evolve based on their experience in courts, especially if they are found to offer a comparable (if not superior) solution in terms of time and cost. As the legal bar rises, so too must the capabilities of dispute resolution institutions.

And, naturally, party experiences with other institutions and the courts are not the only things with which, from a governance perspective, institutions must keep pace.

With the digital transformation, norms can change quickly, and entrenched practices can be rapidly disrupted almost overnight. Perhaps, the best example is the widespread adoption of remote hearings in arbitration brought on by the Covid-19 pandemic. While remote meeting technology was widely available and in use by many companies before the pandemic, it was only when parties, counsel, and arbitrators were forced to choose between suspending dispute resolution altogether or adopting the new technology that it rapidly found its way into regular practice.[4]

And, similarly from a governance perspective, institutions must pay heed to changes in societal norms. Institutions are, like all other organisations, responsible for ensuring their hiring. Their retention practices reflect the diversity of the societies in which they operate. And arbitration institutions may also consider their relationship with the environment and whether they can assist in combatting climate change through carbon-reducing initiatives. Indeed, the field of arbitration is aided in this by a dedicated organisation, the Campaign for Greener Arbitrations, which provides standards and tools for arbitrations to be conducted through sustainable practices, such as corresponding electronically and encouraging the use of remote meeting technology.[5]

II THE ICC AND ITS DRS

The current president of the ICC International Court of Arbitration, Claudia Salomon, aptly captured the objective of ICC DRS in a recent speech. In paraphrasing law and technology guru Richard Susskind, she stated that patients do not go to neurosurgeons

3. Singapore Justice Sundaresh Menon, 'Legal Systems in a Digital Age: Pursuing the Next Frontier', speech given at 3rd Annual France-Singapore Symposium on Law and Business, 11 May 2023, available at https://www.judiciary.gov.sg/news-and-resources/news/news-details/chief-justice-sundaresh-menon-speech-delivered-at-3rd-annual-france-singapore-symposium-on-law-and-business-in-paris-france (accessed 16 Dec. 2024).
4. E. Friedman & M. McIlwrath, *The Future of International Arbitration Isn't Over Yet, in* International Arbitration and the Covid 19 Revolution (M. Scherer, N. Bassiri, M. Abdel Wahab, eds, Kluwer Law Int'l 2020).
5. *See* https://www.greenerarbitrations.com / (accessed 16 Dec. 2024).

because they want their heads cut open; they go because they want health. And parties do not come to the ICC because they want an arbitral process; they come 'because they want a resolution'.[6]

Providing resolution is the means by which ICC achieves the purpose of its DRS, whether by arbitration, mediation, or the other services that ICC DRS provides.

Since the organisation's inception over hundred years ago, ICC's purpose has been to promote international commerce. In establishing the ICC in the wake of World War I, the ICC's founders believed they were contributing towards a more stable international framework that would reduce the risk of future great wars by encouraging trade between countries. They spoke about peace through commerce and called themselves 'Merchants of Peace'.

The ICC Commission on Arbitration (now Arbitration and ADR) was created almost immediately after the ICC's establishment. The ICC Court of Arbitration was established the following year, in 1923. The core values that led to the ICC's foundation remain as present as ever in ICC DRS today, and it continues to evolve as international commerce evolves.

III THE GOVERNANCE STRUCTURE FOR ICC AND ITS DRS

The ICC is managed by an Executive Board, whose members are highly experienced international business leaders from around the world. As mandated by its Executive Board, the ICC is currently pursuing a number of initiatives aimed at, among other things, strengthening multilateralism in commerce and developing policies and practices to aid small- and medium-sized enterprises (SMEs).[7] The ICC Executive Board is widely viewed as the voice of the international business community.

The ICC Executive Board has a number of committees, one of which is the Governing Body for DRS. Its mandate is to ensure dispute services advance ICC's objectives and preserve the organisation's reputation as the premier institution for providing parties with a resolution to their commercial disputes.

While the Governing Body reviews the overall caseload and financial results of the dispute services, it does not monitor (nor have access to) individual cases. Neither does the ICC's Executive Board. It is of particular importance at ICC that the Court of International Arbitration remains at all times completely independent in the conduct and management of cases.

Instead, the Governing Body focuses, as its name indicates, on governance. Its responsibilities include the preparation of business plans and policy proposals and oversight of implementation of changes of strategic importance. The body's sixteen

6. C. Salomon, 'Maslow's Hammer', keynote speech at Tel-Aviv Arbitration Week 2023.
7. The ICC has for a number of years endeavoured to provide SMEs with greater access to the tools of international trade considering their importance to the global business and employment and under-representation in cross-border commerce. As noted by the World Economic Forum in a note of 16 Jan. 2023, 'SMEs account for more than 90% of businesses and more than 50% of employment worldwide, yet their participation in international trade is limited.' https://www.weforum.org/agenda/2023/01/why-supporting-smes-is-critical-for-a-global-trade-stability-and-and-a-more-inclusive-economy (accessed 16 Dec. 2024).

members are drawn from leaders in different areas relevant to assisting ICC DRS in achieving ICC's objectives: the Chair and Secretary General of the ICC, the President and Secretary General of the International Court of Arbitration, a member of ICC's Executive Board, a member of ICC's Finance Committee, plus ten individuals recognised internationally as leaders in the field of international arbitration and alternative dispute resolution, of which four must be senior in-house counsel, three from private practice, one senior legal professional with substantial experience in the use of information technologies, and two members who are globally recognised leaders in the judiciary, academia, or public service.

The Governing Body oversees all of ICC's DRS, not just arbitration. The ICC International Centre for ADR offers a range of services that can be used separately, successively or even concurrently with arbitration to meet the need to provide parties with the best available option for achieving a resolution. The ICC's ADR team provides mediation, expertise/expert appointments, a specialised procedure for trade finance instruments (called Docdex), dispute boards which assist in avoiding or overcoming disagreement and disputes during the performance of a contract, and the ICANN New gTLD Dispute Resolution, which is a programme aiming at protecting and supporting a stable Internet. The ICC's International Centre for ADR is also responsible for ICC's renowned student competition, Mediation Competition Week, which is held each year, contributing to the spread of innovative forms of resolving commercial conflicts.

IV CONCLUDING WORDS: GOVERNANCE AS CONSTANT EVOLUTION AND REFORM

To return to our initial queries about purpose and accountability of an arbitration institution, we hope that we have provided with answers and the relevance of governance. For the ICC, its Governing Body exists to ensure the institution's DRS remain true to the purpose and objectives of ICC and that they are accountable to the international business community, as represented by ICC's Executive Board.

Beyond that, governance of arbitration institutions is hardly a task of ensuring that all the parts of the organisation are functioning as they should, although that is also an important function of governance. With arbitration, governance must also include keeping pace with the time as well as seeing around corners and assisting an institution in defining its future of resolving disputes.

CHAPTER 11

Intra-continental Trade: Catalyst for New Voices in Regional Institutions in Latin America and the Caribbean

Daniel Ávila II

The evolution of arbitration in Latin America and now the Caribbean can be attributed to the increase in trade flows throughout the region. This chapter explores this evolution, particularly focusing on the proliferation of regional arbitral institutions and their role in handling disputes arising from the increased commerce. It also traces historical developments from the disfavoring of international arbitration under the so-called Calvo Doctrine to the embrace of free trade and globalization in the twentieth century, leading to the promulgation of arbitration-friendly national law and the rise of regional arbitration centers.

The analysis highlights the increased trust in submitting these disputes to regional arbitration institutions as evidenced by the findings of the Institute for Transnational Arbitration's (ITA's) Guides to Latin American Arbitral Institutions in 2011 and 2023. It also addresses the increasing gender diversity among arbitrators in Latin America and the Caribbean, showcasing efforts by institutions to promote diversity through various initiatives.

Lastly, it explores the emergence of new voices in arbitration, particularly in the Caribbean, where multiple new centers have opened their doors and have integrated new aspects to their arbitration rules to meet the growing demand for diversity in arbitration. Overall, the chapter underscores the significant role of regional arbitral institutions in advancing arbitration initiatives and supporting the region's integration into the global arbitration landscape amidst challenges such as the resurgence of protectionist attitudes from several Latin American countries.

I INTRODUCTION

In 2011, the Institute for Transnational Arbitration (ITA), Americas Initiative, announced that the "*era of Latin American arbitral institutions ha[d] arrived.*"[1] This "era" included over 160 regional arbitral institutions that were identified all across the Latin America region with many opening their doors between 1997 and 2002.[2] A table included in the 2011 Inaugural Survey of Latin American Arbitral Institutions (the "2011 ITA Guide") displayed the correlation between the opening of these institutions and the signing of the New York Convention and local arbitral laws occurring in the 1980s and 1990s, leading to more trade in the region.[3]

As "horizontal" investments[4] in Latin America continue, an increased demand for dispute resolution services to settle disputes related to these investments also continues to increase. Parties have now gained more confidence in using these institutions to settle disputes in the region and in including regional institutions in arbitration agreements arising out of these investments and their inclusion in commercial contracts.

Although international institutions such as the International Chamber of Commerce ("ICC") and the International Centre for Dispute Resolution ("ICDR") have continued to register the majority of the international arbitration disputes in Latin America, local and regional arbitral institutions have continued to grow in number in Latin America—and now in the Caribbean—leading to a proliferation of options for arbitration in the region.

This chapter analyses relevant historical developments of arbitration and trade in the region, as well as identifies the key findings from the ITA's 2023 Guide to Latin American Arbitral Institutions (the "2023 ITA Guide") showing that new voices are being developed in Latin American arbitration.

II HISTORICAL BACKGROUND

Historically, the use of international arbitration for the settlement of disputes between parties of different countries had been disfavored in Latin America, largely driven by the "Calvo" doctrine, which emerged at the end of the nineteenth century as Latin American diplomats sought to refuse diplomatic protection to foreign investors under international law.[5] At its core, the doctrine provided that disputes brought by foreign investors should be resolved exclusively in the national courts where the investment

1. *See* 2011 ITA Guide to Latin American Arbitral Institutions, p. 3.
2. *See ibid.*, at p. 11.
3. *See ibid.*, at p. 7.
4. For example, investment from Colombia to Ecuador rather than from the United States to Ecuador.
5. John P Bowman, *The Panama Convention and Its Implementation under the Federal Arbitration Act*, 11 *Am. Rev. Int'l Arb.* 1 (2000) https://doi.org/10.54648/rba2004047.

was located as opposed to any other forum, including arbitration.[6] Arbitration was seen as being in conflict with the concept of exclusive reliance on local courts and local law.[7]

That, however, slowly started to change, beginning with 1965, when countries in the Americas began signing treaties for the enforcement of arbitral awards. For instance, the Washington Convention establishing the International Centre for Settlement of Investment Disputes (ICSID),[8] the Convention on the Recognition and Enforcement of Foreign Arbitral Awards (the "New York Convention"),[9] and the 1975 Inter-American Convention on International Commercial Arbitration (the "Panama Convention"). The United Nations Commission on International Trade Law ("UNCITRAL") subsequently promulgated its Model Arbitration Law in 1985, with Mexico being the first country in the region to adopt it in 1993. Other countries followed suit as they sought to modernize their arbitration laws.

During the late 1980s and 1990s, governments in the region privatized and liberalized their economies, as they embraced free trade and globalization in an effort to attract foreign investment. Countries in the region ratified investment protection treaties that allowed foreign investors to seek recourse to arbitration, thus effectively putting an end to the Calvo doctrine. As disputes began to emerge, flowing from the privatization of enterprises that had taken place, few regional centers had the international experience to handle those disputes. As a result, most parties opted to arbitrate their disputes in forums such as the ICC or the ICDR. Over the course of the next decade, as the region continued to embrace free trade and globalization, regional centers matured, and many countries in Latin America developed suitable arbitration infrastructures.

III INCREASED TRADE WITHIN THE REGION

A review of the increase in arbitral institutions in the region must also be analyzed next to the backdrop of the trade happening in the region. As arbitration institutions continued to open within the region between 1998 and 2002, trade also increased within the region, showing a direct correlation between the confidence to trade and to invest in the region, given arbitral institutions being able to handle any disputes that may arise (Figure 11.1).[10]

6. Arturo Muñoz & Daniel Ávila II, *Localising Cross-Border Disputes: The Growing Appeal of Regional Arbitral Centres in Latin America and the Caribbean* in The Guide to Arbitration in Latin America (Second Edition).
7. *Ibid.*
8. It should be noted, however, that the first Latin American country to sign the Washington Convention was not until 1981, which was Paraguay.
9. The New York Convention was signed in 1958 and entered into force in 1959.
10. Graph reproduced by Reed Smith LLP from data provided in Manuel Pastor & Carol Wise, *Good-Bye Financial Crash, Hello Financial Eclecticism: Latin American Responses to the 2008-09 Global Financial Crisis*, Journal of International Money and Finance, 200-217 (2015) https://doi.org/10.1016/j.jimonfin.2014.11.019.

Figure 11.1 Trade in Latin America (Goods Only) (1980-2013)

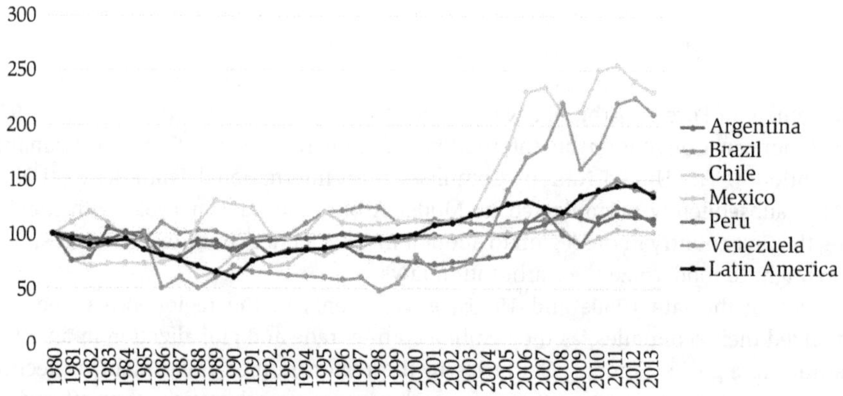

Ten years later, at the same time, with the release of the 2011 ITA Guide, the Inter-American Development Bank ("IDB") published a report showing a continuing rise in trade from the Latin American region (Figure 11.2).[11]

Figure 11.2 Growth of Total LATAM Exports (January 2008-October 2012)

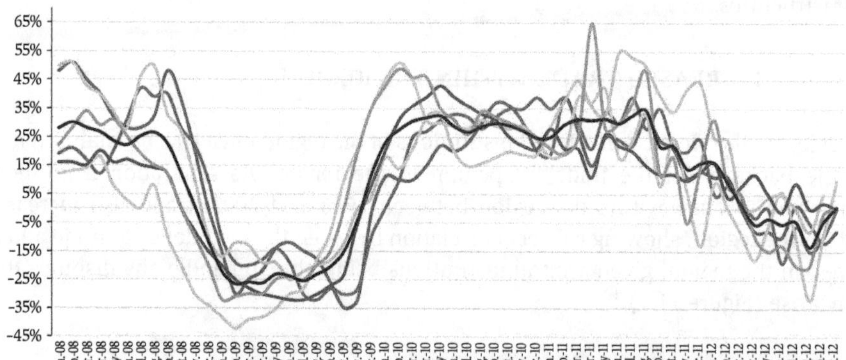

This "era" of increased trade within the region continued even after the COVID-19 pandemic, where the IDB reported that trade within Latin America and the Caribbean not only returned to levels before the pandemic but, in fact, also increased significantly (Figure 11.3).[12]

11. Graph reproduced by Reed Smith LLP from data provided in DB, Latin American Trade Trend Estimates 2012, p. 1.
12. Graph reproduced by Reed Smith LLP from data provided in IDB Trade Trend Estimates in Latin America and the Caribbean 2022, p. 6.

Figure 11.3 Imports from Latin America and the Caribbean and the World (2019-2021)

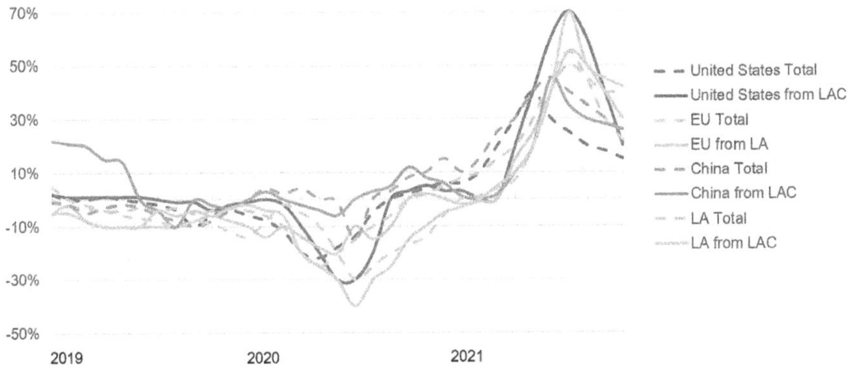

What does this all mean? It is no coincidence that the growth in trade within Latin America and the Caribbean lead to more disputes and the demand that local and regional arbitration institutions manage those disputes. This was further displayed from the results of the ITA Guide to Latin American Arbitral Institutions in 2011 and later in 2023.

IV THE ITA GUIDE TO LATIN AMERICAN ARBITRAL INSTITUTIONS

In 2011, the ITA surveyed the use of regional centers in Latin America.[13] This same guide was recently updated in 2023. The initial survey concluded that the region's embracing of free trade and globalization in the 1990s was correlated with the significant resort to regional institutions to resolve disputes.[14] The 2011 ITA Guide reported that a little more than half of Latin America's arbitral institutions were established between 1997 and 2002.[15] The latest 2023 ITA Guide reported that at least seven new institutions opened their doors since 2011.[16] Below is a review of key findings from the 2023 ITA Guide on Latin American Arbitral Institutions.[17]

13. ITA 2011 Inaugural Survey of Latin American Institutions (ITA Survey), p. 3.
14. *Ibid.*, p. 12.
15. *Ibid.*, p. 11.
16. *See* ITA Guide to Latin American Institutions 2023. The institutions surveyed in the 2023 Guide provided numbers from 2021, as the survey was conducted in December of 2022.
17. The ITA's Americas Initiative was established in 2003 originally focusing on Latin America. This was later expanded in 2018 to Canada and 2021 to the Caribbean. The ITA Americas Initiative's methodology for the 2023 ITA Guide included initially identifying 170 regional institutions across the Americas. The editorial team then surveyed members across Latin America via ITAFOR to identify the three most used institutions in each country. The editorial team then made a selection from this group according to the size of each jurisdiction. Arriving at fifty institutions, the editorial team sent out surveys to these institutions and received responses from thirty institutions in twenty countries.

V GENDER DIVERSITY

Regional arbitral institutions in Latin America are increasingly gaining more experienced and diverse arbitrators on their rosters. In 2012, the International Council for Commercial Arbitration ("ICCA") organized a Cross-Institutional Task Force on Gender Diversity in Arbitral Appointments and Proceedings (the "ICCA Report"). The ICCA Report aimed to identify the number of women arbitrators appointed in 2011 according to their nationality, and it found that 12.9% of the total women appointments by international institutions held nationalities from Latin America and the Caribbean,[18] the majority of these being in ICC proceedings.[19]

The ICCA Report also identified the trend in appointments by *regional* institutions. The ICCA Report found that the average proportion of women arbitrator appointments in Latin America and the Caribbean was greater than the overall average reflected in the global assessment—20.2% compared to 12.9%.[20] In comparison, the findings of the 2023 ITA Guide indicate that the majority of the arbitration institutions responded that at least 26% of their cases had at least one woman as an arbitrator on a tribunal.[21] Despite these efforts, the majority of institutions responding to the Survey noted that less than 25% of their domestic and international arbitrator lists contain female arbitrators.[22] Thus, although there seems to be a rise in women arbitrator appointments since 2011, less than a quarter of the members of arbitration lists are female.

However, it should be noted that the Centro de Mediación y Arbitraje de la Cámara Nacional de Comercio de la Ciudad de México ("CANACO Mexico"); the Centro de Solución de Conflictos ("CSC Panama"); and the Centro Nacional de Arbitrajes S.A. ("CNA Chile") all responded that the *majority* of their disputes have at least one woman as an arbitrator on the tribunal. The CSC Panama also responded that the majority of their disputes had a woman arbitrator as the chair or the sole arbitrator of the tribunal. The CAM Santiago reported 113 cases where a woman was appointed to the tribunal.

With respect to rosters, the domestic rosters seem to have more women arbitrators listed than international rosters that exist in these regional institutions.[23] The findings of the 2023 ITA Guide also indicate that in Latin American arbitrations, while at least one woman sits on a tribunal in over 50% of the cases (as reported by some institutions), it is still rare for a woman to be a sole arbitrator or the president of an arbitration panel. The majority of the institutions responded that in less than 25% of tribunals, the president of the tribunal or the sole arbitrator was a female. These numbers indicate an increase in the appointment of female arbitrators both on rosters

18. *See* ICCA organized a Cross-Institutional Task Force on Gender Diversity in Arbitral Appointments and Proceedings, p. 66.
19. *See Ibid.*
20. *See Ibid.*
21. *See* ITA Guide to Latin American Institutions 2023, p. 14.
22. *See Ibid.*
23. *See Ibid.*

and on panels since the last Survey. While progress has been made, these findings confirm that there is still work to be done to foster gender diversity in these institutions.

Institutions also provided responses with respect to their ongoing diversity initiatives. Here, the Centro de Arbitraje de Mexico S.A. de C.V. ("CAM Mexico") noted that, internally, when the institution is tasked with appointing an arbitrator, the internal commission must include at least one woman in the proposal of arbitrators sent to the *Consejo General*.

The Camara de Comercio de Santiago ("CAM Santiago Chile") reported several diversity initiatives. For example:

- In 2019, CAM Santiago incorporated twenty-six professional women in its list of arbitrators and organized a webinar in 2020 titled "*Mujeres cruzando fronteras: desafíos en la gestión de conflictos*" where the institution agreed to the Equal Representation in Arbitration (ERA) Pledge.
- In the context of International Women's Day, the Santiago Arbitration and Mediation Center launched the institution's mentoring program for young arbitrators (AJCAM) called "*Mujeres líderes en arbitraje.*" This program featured fourteen mentees and thirteen mentors, all women, with the aim of connecting the female members of CAM Santiago's roster of young arbitrators with prominent female lawyers with arbitration experience.
- In June 2021, CAM Santiago launched the first edition of its mentoring program for new professionals. Unlike the program above, this one was not specifically aimed at women but at the best speakers of the CAM Santiago 2021 VIs Pre Moot. The mentor for this first edition was Sabina Sacco, and two of the three mentees were female students.
- In June 2021 and 2022, the Santiago Chamber of Commerce ("CCS") and CAM Santiago launched a new mentoring program on "Legal and Negotiation Tools for Women Entrepreneurs."
- During the second half of 2022, CAM Santiago launched a new mentoring program for young arbitrators. Although this program is not aimed exclusively at women, it had a high female participation. The Center's executive director, Macarena Letelier, is also director of ERA Pledge LATAM and Woman Way in Arbitration.

These initiatives all show the focus on promoting new "voices" in international arbitration across the Latin American region through diversity-focused initiatives.

VI PARTY STATUS

Arbitral institutions in Latin America routinely resolve complex and multifaceted disputes. These disputes increasingly involve cross-border disputes with foreign parties, and they require consideration and assessment of public international law and civil and common law issues. These disputes are also regularly administered in more than one language. The majority of institutions responding to the 2023 ITA Guide reported that their cases primarily include domestic parties.[24] However, it should be noted that this does not take into consideration that many of the "domestic" disputes may be related to subsidiaries of multinational companies operating in the territory.

Some institutions did report administering almost half of their cases with foreign entities. For example, the Centro Empresarial de Conciliación y Arbitraje in Venezuela ("CECA Venezuela") and Centro de Arbitraje de la Cámara de Caracas, Venezuela ("CACC Venezuela") both recorded between 26% and 50% of cases as international cases.

Although the majority of cases identified in the Survey involve private entities, an increasing number of cases involve public entities. This finding is consistent with the evolution of the practice and the use of arbitration in the region. For example, in Peru, public procurement contracts (including State construction contracts) and public-private partnership contracts are mandatorily referred to arbitration.[25] This is consistent with responses from institutions such as El Centro Nacional e Internacional de Arbitraje de la Cámara de Comercio in Lima, Peru ("CCP Panama"), who recorded between 51% and 75% of all cases in 2021 as cases with public parties.

Overall, there was an increase in participation in arbitration in regional institutions by foreign and public entities compared to the 2011 ITA Guide where it was reported that foreign parties made up 12% and public parties made up 5% of the disputes.[26] These results may indicate that multinational companies are continuing to utilize regional centers to handle their disputes—or simply that there is an increase in adding these institutions in commercial agreements locally. With respect to States or State-owned entities, the results indicate an increased trust in the arbitration process. This support by State and State-owned entities can be beneficial to the growth of the region. It should be noted, however, that this may require additional guarantees of transparency when a State entity is a party. For example, in the context of arbitration in Brazil, Article 2(3) of the Brazilian Arbitration Act provides that arbitration involving public entities is subject to the transparency principles.[27]

VII SEAT AND VENUE OF THE ARBITRATION

The seat of the arbitration can be important for purposes of enforcement, vacatur and interim measures, among others. It is vital, for example, to have support from the courts at the seat of the arbitration to enforce interim measures such as preserving assets to ensure your arbitration award is not a "pyrrhic victory."[28] Whether the seat

24. 2023 ITA Guide to Latin American Arbitral Institutions, p. 15.
25. Pascal Hollander, Sofia Martins & Jus Mundi, *Peru, Country-by-Country Guides to Arbitration*, 3 (2018) (updated June 2021).
26. Cf. 2011 ITA Guide, pp. 11-12 to 2023 ITA Guide to Latin American Arbitral Institutions, p. 15.
27. *See* Brazilian Arbitration Act, Art. 2(3).
28. *See* International Arbitration Focus: *How to Avoid a Pyrrhic Victory in International Arbitration*, Reed Smith.com (2023), available at https://www.reedsmith.com/-/media/files/perspectives/2023/reed-smith-international-arbitration-focus-12-2023-pyrrhic-victory.pdf?rev=6176494719ce480eaa672285c750e9fa&hash=DE0B602CA1108E02902DA90F063F3600 (accessed Dec. 16, 2024).

allows third-party subpoenas may also be important when critical documents are in the custody of third parties.[29] The 2023 ITA Guide included a country indicator,[30] showing that some countries have less favorable arbitration laws and performance indicators related to ease of business compared to others, showing the importance of choosing the right seat.

The venue, in contrast, is simply where the arbitration hearing will be held. The venue may differ from the location of the seat of the arbitration depending on where the parties and tribunal agree to have the hearing.

For most (if not all) of the institutions surveyed, the seat of arbitration was the same as the country of the institution.[31] In fact, less than 10% of registered cases of arbitral institutions in Latin America had the seat other than the institution's country in 2021.[32] The same results were for the *venue* of the arbitration. This may demonstrate the focus of the regional Latin American institutions as servicing local disputes rather than cross-border disputes seated outside of the continent. Moreover, the low number of arbitration cases in 2021 with a different venue (in addition to the "seat") than the country of the institution might be due to the pandemic and travel restrictions adopted to prevent the spread of COVID. The increase of remote proceedings after the pandemic has continued not only in the major institutions but also in Latin America as a whole. Many institutions in the region have provided for the use of remote proceedings in their arbitration rules. The responses regarding arbitrator requirements, on the other hand, seem to lean more in favor of international influence in cases registered in these institutions.

Arbitrator Requirements

Party autonomy is key in arbitration, and autonomy in selecting an arbitrator forms an additional incentive for foreign trade and investment. The selection of arbitrators is a critical step in an arbitration, as it increases the confidence of the participants in fair, neutral proceedings. The results of the 2023 ITA Guide indicate that 90% of the arbitration institutions do not have the requirement for an arbitrator to be a national of the State where the institution is located.[33] In another survey question, 29% of the institutions indicated that a license to practice in the jurisdiction is needed for arbitrators sitting in *domestic* cases, whereas only 10% have indicated a similar requirement for international arbitrations. This shows the openness of the Latin American jurisdictions to international disputes.[34]

It is worth highlighting the varying responses from the different institutions. For example, the Centro de Arbitraje y Mediación Paraguay ("CAMP Paraguay") reported only requiring roster selections for domestic cases but not for international cases. Some

29. *See Ibid.*
30. 2023 ITA Guide to Latin American Arbitral Institutions, p. 11.
31. *Ibid.*, at p. 16.
32. *See Ibid.*
33. *See Ibid.*, p. 17.
34. *See Ibid.*

institutions, such as the Tribunal de Arbitraje General de la Bolsa de Comercio de Buenos Aires ("Bolsa de Comercio Argentina"), responded that the arbitrators must be nationals of the country where the institution is listed.[35] For domestic cases, the Camara de Comercio de Medellin ("CCM Colombia"), the Bolsa de Comercio Argentina, the Centro Internacional de Conciliación y Arbitraje de la Cámara de Comercio Costarricense Norteamericana ("AmCham Costa Rica"), and CANACO Mexico all require the arbitrators to be licensed to practice law in that country. The CCM Colombia and the Centro de Arbitraje y Mediación Cámara De Comercio De Quito ("CAM Quito Ecuador") reported that for international cases, parties must select from the roster as well absent an agreement.

Although the majority of the institutions did not have a separate roster for international cases, the ones that did included the CCM Colombia, the AmCham Costa Rica, the CSC Panama, the Câmara de Conciliação Mediação e Arbitragem Brazil, and the CAM Quito Ecuador.

These responses show the focus on allowing parties to choose arbitrators outside of the jurisdiction when the dispute is not solely between local parties. Whether the dispute is actually between "local" or "domestic" parties or simply a subsidiary of a multinational is not clearly tracked, however. This could be an issue for a multinational companies' subsidiary being classified as a "domestic" company and being forced to apply the domestic arbitration rules or having to select from an arbitrator on the domestic roster. Consequently, there may be a need to modernize how these disputes are being registered to better understand the players at hand.

VIII PRELIMINARY MEASURES AND EMERGENCY PROCEEDINGS

As discussed above regarding the arbitral seat, preliminary measures can provide protection to safeguard a party's substantive rights prior to an arbitral proceeding commencing or even during the pendency of the proceeding (but prior to the issuance of a final award). When national courts are unavailable, nor best suited, or incapable of hearing the dispute at hand, an emergency arbitrator may provide this preliminary relief.

In 2019, the ICC Arbitration and ADR Commission issued a Report on Emergency Arbitrator Proceedings. This report indicated that among the first emergency applications filed with the ICC, 30% came from Latin America and the Caribbean.[36] This high demand shows the particular relevance of such emergency relief to parties from this region. The 2023 ITA Guide reported that all arbitral institutions in Latin America allow for both emergency arbitrators and preliminary measures.[37]

35. The Tribunal de Arbitraje General de la Bolsa de Comercio de Buenos Aires reported having a standing arbitration tribunal.
36. *See* ICC Arbitration and ADR Commission Report on Emergency Arbitrator Proceedings, p. 37 (2019).
37. 2023 ITA Guide to Latin American Arbitral Institutions, p. 19.

IX ARBITRATION RULES

Consistent arbitration rules may be beneficial, in particular in the context of jurisdictions where arbitration is still developing, as they provide predictability to the users, who may relate to their experience from other institutions and courts interpreting and applying similar rules. Surprisingly, the majority of the institutions responded that their arbitration rules did *not* derive from the Model UNCITRAL Model Rules.

Although most of the institutions applied the same rules to both domestic and international arbitration, there were several institutions which had separate set rules for each, for instance, CAM Santiago Chile, Bolsa de Comercio Argentina, CCM Colombia, Camara de Comercio de Bogota Colombia ("CCB Colombia"), Camara de Comercio de Cali Colombia ("CCC Colombia"), and the Arbitration Mediation Court of the Caribbean in Barbados ("Arbitration Court of Barbados").

With respect to conflict-of-interest rules, the majority of the institutions answered that the institution had its own conflict of interest rules. Some, however, follow the International Bar Association (IBA) Rules on Conflicts of interest, including CAM Mexico, Câmara de Mediação e Arbitragem Empresarial ("CAMARB Brasil"), CAM Ecuador, CACC Venezuela, AmCham Quito Ecuador, and the Arbitration Court of Barbados. The Cayman International Mediation and Arbitration Centre ("CI-MAC") indicated that its rules contain commitments[38] to increase diversity, equity, and inclusion in the selection of arbitrators.

X DISPOSITIVE MOTIONS

A procedural tool conventionally associated with domestic litigation, dispositive motions have become more common in certain jurisdictions within the Latin American region and in international arbitrations at large in response to the demand for more efficiency in arbitration proceedings and costs.

In the past, international arbitration tribunals have been skeptical of dispositive motions for fear of an award being challenged for issues with due process under the New York Convention, in the event a party submitted that it had not been given a fair opportunity to "present its case."[39] This attitude has now changed, given that institutions have added rules on dispositive motions, subsequently upheld by courts.[40] With written submissions in arbitration proceedings continuing to increase in size, some have noted that international arbitration may be losing its competitive edge in resolving

38. This includes the Green Pledge regarding environmentally sustainable practices, the ERA Pledge, and the Ray Corollary Initiative.
39. *See, e.g.*, ICC Case No. 11413 (December 2001), 21 ICC Intl. Ct. Arb. Bull. 34 (2010) (noting that ICC Rules and Section 33 of the English Act were both discussed ensuring the parties were given a reasonable opportunity to present their case).
40. *See, e.g.*, ICDR Rule 23 (March 2021).

disputes quickly and quietly.[41] A Queen Mary Survey published in 2018 found that dispositive motion procedures should be utilized in several industry-related disputes, including banking and finance, construction/infrastructure, energy (oil& gas), and technology, among others (Figure 11.4).[42]

Figure 11.4 Which of the Following Improvements and Innovations Would Make International Arbitration More Suitable for Resolving Cross-Border Disputes in These Industries and Sectors?

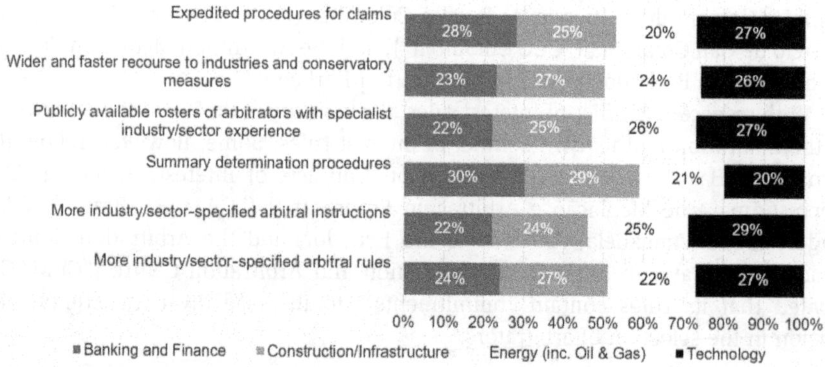

The same survey in 2021 found that 61 % of the participants would be willing to do without unlimited length of written submissions (Figure 11.5).[43]

41. *See* Caline Mouawad & Elizabeth Silbert, *A Case for Dispositive Motions in International Commercial Arbitration* 78 (Kluwer Law 2015, Vol. 2, Issue 1), ("Practitioners and parties have criticized international arbitration in the recent years for losing its competitive edge of resolving disputes swiftly").

42. Graph reproduced by Reed Smith LLP from data provided in Queen Mary University of London, 2018 International Arbitration Survey: *The Evolution of International Arbitration* (2018), available at arbitration.qmul.ac.uk.

43. Graph reproduced by Reed Smith LLP from data provided in Queen Mary University of London, 2021 International Arbitration Survey: *Adapting Arbitration to a Changing World* (2021), available at arbitration.qmul.ac.uk.

Figure 11.5 If You Were a Party or Counsel, Which of the Following Procedural Options Would You Be Willing to Do Without If This Would Make Your Arbitration Cheaper or Faster?

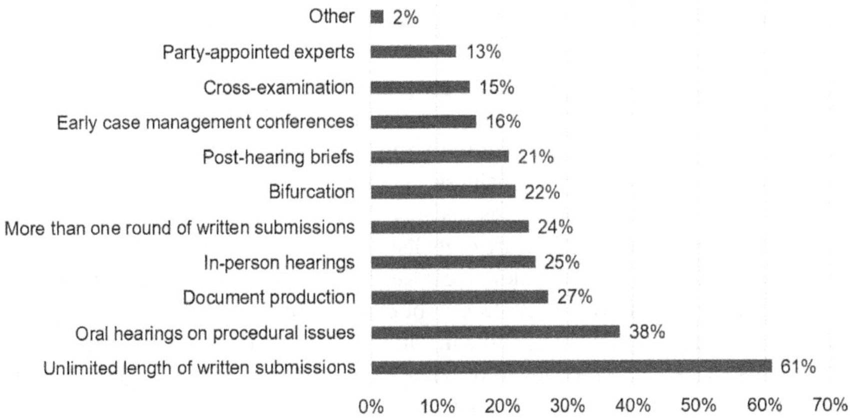

As explained above, in response to this, several international arbitration institutions have amended their rules to provide expressly for the authority for dispositive motions.[44] Notwithstanding this, many arbitral tribunals have found the authority to grant dispositive motions in the arbitrator's duty to run an "expeditious" arbitration and to avoid "unnecessary delay or expense."[45]

Surprisingly, in the Latin American jurisdictions that participated in the 2023 ITA Guide, the majority of the institutions responded that they *do* allow dispositive motions.[46] When permitted, these motions are sometimes limited to being raised in the initial stages of a dispute (akin to a motion to dismiss).[47]

Certain institutions reported that a party can bring a dispositive motion at *anytime*. These included the Centro de Conciliación y Arbitraje Comercial de CAINCO in Bolivia ("CAINCO Bolivia"), CAMARB Brazil, and the Arbitration Court of Barbados. The Centro Empresarial de Conciliación y Arbitraje (CEDCA) in Venezuela, the CAM Quito Ecuador, and the CACC Venezuela reported only allowing dispositive motions at the commencement of the arbitration.

Best practices include detailed case-by-case analysis prior to bringing these motions with the objective of determining the likely success of the motion, along with the overall impact on time and cost of the proceeding.

44. *See, e.g.*, Hong Kong International Arbitration Centre 2018 Rules, Art. 43 (allowing for tribunals to make early determinations of law or fact where "such points of law or fact are manifestly without merit"); *see also, e.g.*, 2020 LCIA Rules, Rule 22.1 ("Early Determination"); *see also, e.g.*, U.S. Revised Uniform Arbitration Act, § 15(b)("[a]n arbitrator may decide a request for summary disposition of a claim or particular issue").
45. *See* Charlie Caher & Jonathan Lim, *Summary Disposition Procedures in International Arbitration*, 2.
46. 2023 ITA Guide to Latin American Arbitral Institutions, p. 18.
47. *Ibid.*

XI THE NEW VOICES IN CARIBBEAN ARBITRATION

As trade increased in the Caribbean region,[48] new "voices" emerged in these jurisdictions to meet the demand. The majority of the participating institutions reported being established between 1995 and 2004. However, over 20% were established after 2000, and several institutions were established after the release of the last 2011 ITA Guide—all from the Caribbean.

This is consistent with the focus on promoting arbitration in the Caribbean, including the ITA's own Caribbean Task Force launched in 2021 as part of the Americas Initiative. As a result of this pro-arbitration approach, the region's emerging markets are adjusting to the new global business climate. The Caribbean region is a very attractive location to host arbitrations because of its neutral geography at the crossroads of the Americas and the mixture of its legal regimes, covering both common and civil law.[49] The ITA Caribbean Task Force's Report and Recommendations showcases the diversity within the Caribbean alone.[50] For example, there are six official languages in the region—English, Spanish, French, Dutch, Haitian Kreyol, and Papiamentu. There are also three different legal systems: common law in the English-speaking countries; civil law in the Spanish-speaking, French-speaking, and Dutch-speaking countries; as well as a hybrid system in St. Lucia and Guyana.[51]

The Caribbean region has also witnessed the creation of several arbitration institutions, the first being the BVI International Arbitration Centre, established in 2013.[52] The Dominican Republic, Cuba and Haiti have arbitration centers which have been operating for several years, such as the Centre for Alternative Dispute Resolution of the Chamber of Commerce and Production of Santo Domingo and the Haiti Chamber of Conciliation and Arbitration, the Cuban Court of International Commercial Arbitration, respectively.[53] Recently, arbitration centers have been created in the Cayman Islands, Jamaica, Barbados, Trinidad and Tobago, and Guadeloupe, such as: CI-MAC, Jamaica International Arbitration Centre, Arbitration and Mediation Court of the Caribbean, Dialogue Solutions Limited, Dispute Resolution Foundation, OHADAC Regional Arbitration Centre, respectively.[54]

Although several arbitral institutions in the Caribbean have opened their doors, it is still reported that the majority of the international arbitration disputes are being submitted to the ICC, London Court of International Arbitration (LCIA), and to a lesser

48. *See supra*, Figure 11.3 Imports from Latin America and the Caribbean and the World (2019-2021).
49. *See* Francois Lassalle & Hana Doumal, *International Arbitration in the Caribbean*, GAR, *The Arbitration Review of the Americas 2023* (Jul. 29, 2022), available at https://globalarbitrationreview.com/review/the-arbitration-review-of-the-americas/2023/article/international-arbitration-in-the-caribbean#footnote-032 (accessed Dec. 16, 2024).
50. Calvin Hamilton, Hon. Barry Leon & Theominique D. Nottage, *Final Report of Caribbean Task Force* (Jun. 12, 2023).
51. *Ibid.*
52. *Ibid.*
53. *Ibid.*
54. *Ibid.*

extent the ICDR.[55] Thus, whether these institutions will support international arbitrations at a high demand is still undetermined.

XII CONCLUSION

As explained at the outset, the era of regional arbitral institutions is here to stay. As trade arising out of the Latin America region (including the Caribbean) increased, new voices have emerged in the region not just through the establishment of new arbitration institutions but by the increased appointments of diverse arbitrators—in particular women—in Latin American-based arbitrations. The rise of regional centers and female appointments in Latin America is, to a large extent, part of the broader story of initiatives focusing on increasing diversity arbitration. Statistics are helpful, as they may shed light on what the future may hold. Regional centers are increasingly managing a higher volume of disputes, including those of larger value and with a progressively more international scope.

Although there are indications of continued trust in arbitration by States and State entities, there are also indications of a resurgence of the Calvo doctrine in the horizon, with more States denouncing ICSID, bilateral investment treaties, and offers to submit disputes to investor-state arbitration under national law.[56]

Thus, regional institutions hold a significant role in advancing these initiatives, as they possess an advantage over foreign counterparts in advocating for arbitration. They may also be more successful in delivering a targeted message to their local business networks, legal practitioners, and judiciary.[57] Today, arbitration is not merely an unfamiliar concept imposed by foreign investors; rather, it has become firmly established and thrives as an inherent element of the landscape.

55. *See* Hon. Barry Leon, Calvin Hamilton & Theominique Nottage, *A New Dawn: Sunrise of Caribbean Arbitration as ITA Launches Initiative to Support its Development* (Dec. 8, 2023), available at https://arbitrationblog.kluwerarbitration.com/2023/12/08/a-new-dawn-sunrise-of-caribbean-arbitration-as-ita-launches-initiative-to-support-its-development/ (accessed Dec. 16, 2024).
56. *See, e.g.*, ICSID, *Honduras Denounces the ICSID Convention* (Feb. 29, 2024), available at https://icsid.worldbank.org/news-and-events/communiques/honduras-denounces-icsid-convention (accessed Dec. 16, 2024); *see also* Aurelie Skrobik, *Ecuadorians Reject Bid to Seduce Foreign Investors*, inkstickmedia.com (Apr. 25, 2024), available at https://inkstickmedia.com/ecuadorians-reject-bid-to-seduce-foreign-investors/ (accessed Dec. 16, 2024).
57. *See, e.g.*, IA Reporter, *Caribbean Court of Justice Set out its Views on Enforcement of Foreign Arbitral Awards in Region* (Jul. 31, 2013), available at https://www.iareporter.com/articles/caribbean-court-of-justice-set-out-its-views-on-enforcement-of-foreign-arbitral-awards-in-region/ (accessed Dec. 16, 2024).

CHAPTER 12

Regionalization of Bilateral Investment Treaty Practice in Latin America: The Case of Brazil's ACFIs and the MERCOSUR Investment Protocol

Facundo Pérez-Aznar

Brazil is one of the largest economies that has never ratified a traditional bilateral Investment treaty (BIT). However, since 2015, Brazil has pursued a policy of concluding Agreements on Cooperation and Facilitation of Investments (ACFIs), which put emphasis on investment facilitation and dispute prevention and exclude investor-state dispute settlement (ISDS). In line with this policy, in 2017, MERCOSUR States Parties signed the Investment Cooperation and Facilitation Protocol Intra-MERCOSUR (ICFP), which draws significantly on ACFIs. Its emergence represents a step towards regionalizing the Brazilian rationale towards foreign investments while generating different challenges for MERCOSUR and its State Parties. These challenges include the coexistence of two investment regimes in MERCOSUR and in the region, the impact of MERCOSUR's regionalization of Brazil's ACFI model as an alternative to classical international investment agreements (IIAs), the interaction of the MERCOSUR Investment Protocol with existing MERCOSUR dispute settlement mechanisms, and the implementation of the Protocol at the national level of MERCOSUR States Parties. This chapter analyses these challenges and proposes some venues to face them.

I INTRODUCTION

Latin American governments have a long history of regionalizing their foreign investment policies – from policy synchronization in nineteenth-century treaties of friendship, commerce and navigation (with similar patterns, e.g., by excluding consular jurisdiction), through adoption of the Calvo Doctrine and the Calvo Clause, to the late twentieth-century turn towards bilateral investment treaties (BITs). By the end of the 1990s, Latin American countries had entered into 316 BITs (of which 57 were within the region),[1] and 14 of them had ratified the Convention on the Settlement of Investment Disputes Between States and Nationals of other States (ICSID Convention).[2] By the mid-1990s, another regionalization trend had appeared: regional Free Trade Agreements (FTAs) with investment chapters, most of them modelled on the North American Free Trade Agreement (NAFTA),[3] starting with the Colombia-Mexico-Venezuela FTA signed in 1994.[4]

In the twenty-first century, criticism of BITs and their investor-state dispute settlement (ISDS) mechanisms has led many countries to consider alternative approaches, which implied a sort of de-regionalization or re-regionalization. Differing 'Pacific' and 'Atlantic' approaches to economic integration in Latin America have affected investment regionalization as well.[5] Those adopting the 'Pacific' approach favour market opening and liberalization, with a smaller role for political and social components of economic integration and overall acceptance of international investment agreements (IIAs). The 'Atlantic' countries, by contrast, are generally more protectionist, focus on integration beyond economic aspects (including political and social issues), and reject traditional investment treaties.[6]

As for de-regionalization and re-regionalization, most Latin American countries have refined their policy approaches to BITs or FTA investment chapters, based on their experience gained in investment agreement negotiations, investment litigation and multilateral discussions. Some countries withdrew from the ICSID Convention[7]

1. The number of BITs concluded by Latin American countries by decade are the following: 1960s: 3, 1970s: 4; 1980s: 23, 1990s: 316, 2000s: 125, 2010s: 49. Of those figures, the number BITs concluded between countries in the region, by decade also, are the following: 1960s: 0, 1970s: 0, 1980s: 1, 1990s: 57, 2000s: 20, 2010s: 9. Source: https://investmentpolicy.unctad.org/international-investment-agreements (accessed 16 Dec. 2024).
2. The number of ratifications to the ICSID Convention by Latin American countries by decade are the following: 1960s: 1, 1970s: 0, 1980s: 4, 1990s: 9, 2000s: 3, 2010s: 1. Source: https://icsid.worldbank.org/sites/default/files/ICSID-3.pdf (accessed 16 Dec. 2024).
3. The number of FTAs with investment chapters concluded by Latin American countries by decade are the following: 1990s: 9, 2000s: 27, 2010s: 29. Of those figures, the number of FTAs concluded between countries in the region, by decade also, are the following: 1990s: 6, 2000s: 6, 2010s: 12. Source: https://investmentpolicy.unctad.org/international-investment-agreements (accessed 16 Dec. 2024). It has to be noted that some of these FTAs are plurilateral.
4. FTA between Colombia, Mexico and Venezuela (signed 13 Jun. 1994, entered into force 1 Jan. 1995). The investment chapter of this agreement is available at https://investmentpolicy.unctad.org/international-investment-agreements/treaty-files/2432/download (accessed 16 Dec. 2024).
5. Rodrigo Polanco Lazo, 'Regional and Preferential Agreements: The "Pacific" and "Atlantic" Styles in Latin America', in Benedict Kingsbury, David M. Malone, Paul Mertensкötter, Richard B. Stewart, Thomas Streinz & Atsushi Sunami (eds), *Megaregulation Contested: Global Economic Ordering after TPP* (Oxford University Press, 2019), 623-649.
6. *Ibid.*
7. Bolivia denounced the ICSID Convention in 2007, Ecuador in 2009 and Venezuela in 2012. Ecuador ratified the ICSID Convention again in 2021. Source: https://icsid.worldbank.org/about/member-states/database-of-member-states (accessed 16 Dec. 2024).

and terminated some or all of their BITs.[8] Argentina gave serious consideration to withdrawing from the ICSID Convention, terminating its BITs and having domestic tribunals review arbitral awards, but ultimately remained in the BIT regime.[9] There were also regional initiatives, such as the creation of a Centre for the Settlement of Investment Disputes within the failed Union of South American Nations (UNASUR).[10]

Brazil took another path. Brazil is one of the largest economies never to have ratified a traditional BIT. Even though Brazil negotiated BITs in the 1990s,[11] these treaties' domestic approval was discontinued due to opposition in the Brazilian National Congress.[12] Since 2015, instead, Brazil has pursued a policy of concluding Agreements on Cooperation and Facilitation of Investments ('ACFI' or 'CIFA').[13]

The ACFI model departs significantly from a traditional BIT. Its pillars are: (i) emphasis on investment facilitation and dispute prevention; (ii) limited substantive provisions (national treatment, most-favoured nation and direct expropriation clauses, excluding classical standards such as fair and equitable treatment, full protection and security, and protection against indirect expropriation); (iii) encouragement of sustainable development and corporate social responsibility practices by foreign investors; and (iv) state-to-state dispute settlement only.

---

8. Bolivia has terminated twenty-one of its twenty-two BITs (with Argentina, Austria, Belgium-Luxembourg, Chile, China, Cuba, Denmark, Ecuador, France, Germany, Italy, Korea, the Netherlands, Paraguay, Peru, Romania, Spain, Sweden, Switzerland, United Kingdom and United States). Ecuador has terminated twenty-six of its twenty-eight BITs (with Argentina, Bolivia, Canada, Chile, China, Cuba, the Dominican Republic, El Salvador, Finland, France, Germany, Guatemala, Honduras, Italy, the Netherlands, Nicaragua, Paraguay, Peru, Romania, Spain, Sweden, Switzerland, United Kingdom, United States, Uruguay, Venezuela). Source: https://investmentpolicy.unctad.org/international-investment-agreements (accessed 16 Dec. 2024).
9. Facundo Pérez Aznar, 'La protección de inversiones extranjeras en la Argentina: sus orígenes, la negociación de los tratados de inversiones y sus primeros impactos', in *Liber Amicorum* (forthcoming).
10. *See* María Gabriela Sarmiento, *The UNASUR Centre for the Settlement of Investment Disputes and Venezuela: Will Both Ever See the Light at the End of the Tunnel?* 17 JWIT 658 (2016) https://doi.org/10.1163/22119000-12340008.
11. Brazil signed fourteen BITs between 1994 and 1999: Brazil-Portugal BIT (signed 9 Feb. 1994), Brazil-Chile BIT (signed 22 Mar. 1994), Brazil-United Kingdom BIT (signed 19 Jul. 1994), Brazil-Switzerland BIT (11 Nov. 1994), Brazil-France BIT (signed 21 Mar. 1995), Brazil-Finland BIT (signed 28 Mar. 1995), Brazil-Italy BIT (signed 3 Apr. 1995), Brazil-Denmark BIT (signed 4 May 1995), Brazil-Venezuela BIT (signed 4 Jul. 1995), Brazil-Korea BIT (signed 1 Sep. 1995), Brazil-Germany BIT (signed 21 Sep. 1995), Brazil-Cuba BIT (signed 26 Jul. 1997), Brazil-Netherlands BIT (signed 25 Nov. 1998), Brazil-Belgium-Luxembourg Economic Union BIT (signed 6 Jan. 1999).
12. *See* Daniela Campello & Leany Lemos, *The Non-Ratification of Bilateral Investment Treaties in Brazil: A Story of Conflict in a Land of Cooperation*, 4 RIPE 1055, 1086 (2016) https://doi.org/10.1080/09692290.2014.987154.
13. On the Brazilian approach in general, *see* Michelle Ratton Sanchez Badin & Fabio Morosini, 'Navigating Between Resistance and Conformity with the International Investment Regime: The Brazilian Agreements on Cooperation and Facilitation of Investments (ACFIs)', in Fabio Morosini & Michelle Ratton Sanchez Badin (eds), *Reconceptualizing International Investment Law from the Global South* (Cambridge University Press, 2017), 219-250. *See also* Henrique Choer Moraes, *Em defesa da vanguarda: a participação do Brasil nas discussões da UNCITRAL sobre a reforma dos Mecanismos de Solução de Controvérsias Investidor-Estado* (Fundação Alexandre de Gusmão, 2023).

Since 2015, Brazil has concluded seventeen ACFI-type treaties.[14] The first ACFIs, signed with African countries in 2015 (Angola, Mozambique and Malawi, in chronological order), set out the core ACFI elements.[15] A second group of agreements signed with Latin American countries (Mexico, Colombia, Chile and Peru) follow the ACFI template, adding a wider range of regulatory carve-outs (such as explicit exceptions), anti-corruption provisions, detailed regulation of state-to-state arbitration, and refinement of some provisions. A third approach is the 2020 Brazil–India Investment Cooperation and Facilitation Treaty (ICFT), which brings to the IIA world a blend of Brazil's and India's model investment agreements even though the dispute prevention and settlement provisions are Brazilian-style.[16]

While the core ACFI features outlined above are present in all seventeen agreements, the more recent treaties are in many ways more detailed and broader in coverage. The developments in these ACFIs reflect a natural evolution in thinking about ACFIs, the negotiations between particular treaty partners, and the change of administrations in Brazil during the last decade.

In line with Brazil's treaty practice, on 7 April 2017, MERCOSUR (in Spanish *Mercado Común del Sur*) States Parties signed the Investment Cooperation and Facilitation Protocol Intra-MERCOSUR ('ICFP' or 'Investment Protocol').[17] The ICFP draws significantly on the Brazilian model ACFI. Its emergence represents a step towards the regionalization of the Brazilian model, although it also includes provisions not found in previous ACFIs.[18] By entering into the Protocol, MERCOSUR Member

14. As of February 2024, Brazil has concluded fourteen ACFIs and three agreements with ACFI-type provisions: Brazil-Mozambique ACFI (signed 30 Mar. 2015), Brazil-Angola ACFI (signed 1 Apr. 2015, entered into force 28 Jul. 2017), Brazil-Mexico ACFI (signed 26 May 2015, entered into force 7 Oct. 2018), Brazil-Malawi ACFI (signed 25 Jun. 2015), Brazil-Colombia ACFI (signed 9 Oct. 2015), Brazil-Chile ACFI (signed 23 Nov. 2015), Brazil-Peru Economic and Trade Expansion Agreement (ETEA) (signed 29 Apr. 2016), Intra-MERCOSUR Cooperation and Facilitation Investment Protocol (signed 7 Apr. 2017, entered into force 30 Jul. 2019), Brazil-Ethiopia ACFI (signed 11 Apr. 2018), Brazil-Suriname ACFI (signed 2 May 2018), Brazil-Chile FTA (signed 21 Nov. 2018, entered into force 25 Jan. 2022), Brazil-Guyana ACFI (signed 13 Dec. 2018), Brazil-United Arab Emirates (UAE) ACFI (signed 15 Mar. 2019), Brazil-Morocco ACFI (signed 13 Jun. 2019), Brazil-Ecuador ACFI (signed 25 Sep. 2019), Brazil-India ACFI (signed 25 Jan. 2020), Brazil-Sao Tome and Principe ACFI (signed 27 Aug. 2023).
15. Nathalie Bernasconi-Osterwalder & Martin Dietrich Brauch, *Comparative Commentary to Brazil's Cooperation and Investment Facilitation Agreements (CIFAs) with Mozambique, Angola, Mexico, and Malawi* (International Institute for Sustainable Development, September 2015), 1-17, https://www.iisd.org/system/files/publications/commentary-brazil-cifas-acfis-mozambique-angola-mexico-malawi.pdf (accessed 16 Dec. 2024).
16. Martin Dietrich Brauch, *The Best of Two Worlds? The Brazil–India Investment Cooperation and Facilitation Treaty* (International Institute for Sustainable Development, 10 Mar. 2020), https://www.iisd.org/itn/en/2020/03/10/the-best-of-two-worlds-the-brazil-india-investment-cooperation-and-facilitation-treaty-martin-dietrich-brauch/ (accessed 16 Dec. 2024).
17. Investments Cooperation and Facilitation Protocol Intra-MERCOSUR (signed 7 Apr. 2017, entered into force for Brazil and Uruguay 30 Jul. 2019, for Argentina 24 Nov. 2020).
18. For a first analysis of the agreement, *see* Facundo Perez Aznar & Henrique Choer Moraes, *The MERCOSUR Protocol on Investment Cooperation and Facilitation: Regionalizing an Innovative Approach to Investment Agreements*, EJIL: Talk! (12 Sep. 2017) https://www.ejiltalk.org/the-mercosur-protocol-on-investment-cooperation-and-facilitation-regionalizing-an-innovative-approach-to-investment-agreements/ (accessed 16 Dec. 2024). Some of the ideas developed in this chapter are based on that earlier work.

States have opted for governing their mutual relations based on this model. In addition, the Protocol borrows the existing MERCOSUR dispute settlement mechanisms, which include a permanent appellate body. In doing so, the Protocol goes beyond prior ACFIs and moves towards institutionalization of investment dispute settlement, a topic at the core of current discussions on IIA reform.

The ICFP has implications at the investment policy level, raising interesting challenges. The challenges include the coexistence of two investment regimes in MERCOSUR and in the region, the impact of MERCOSUR's regionalization of Brazil's ACFI model as an alternative to classical IIAs, how the MERCOSUR ICFP interacts with existing MERCOSUR dispute settlement procedures and mechanisms, and the implementation of the Protocol at the national level of MERCOSUR States Parties.

This chapter addresses these challenges as follows. The following section discusses attempts to regulate investments in MERCOSUR, including creation of MERCOSUR and its treaty-making power, the process towards a (partial) common investment policy, and the failed first attempt at regionalizing BITs. The section after that discusses the successful approach of regionalizing the ACFI model. It analyses the 2017 ICFP and follow-on initiatives, covering protections and obligations for investors, institutional governance and the dispute prevention mechanism, MERCOSUR dispute settlement, and MERCOSUR negotiations with third states. I conclude by summing up the benefits and challenges of regionalizing in MERCOSUR based on the ACFI model.

II MERCOSUR AND THE ATTEMPTS TO REGULATE INVESTMENTS

A The Creation of MERCOSUR and Its Treaty-Making Power

MERCOSUR was created in 1991 when Argentina, Brazil, Paraguay, and Uruguay signed the Treaty of Asunción, aiming to create the Common Market of the South ('MERCOSUR').[19] In 1994, MERCOSUR was institutionally restructured by the Ouro Preto Protocol ('OPP') and became a subject of international law.[20] The establishment of a common market still remains a future goal since MERCOSUR's progress has been limited to the formation of an incomplete customs union.[21] MERCOSUR's present structure is explicitly intergovernmental and not supranational. Its organs are required to make their decisions by consensus and in the presence of all States Parties. In general, each State Party must implement MERCOSUR decisions by incorporating them into its domestic legal order.

19. Treaty for the Establishment of a Common Market between the Argentine Republic, the Federative Republic of Brazil, the Republic of Paraguay and the Eastern Republic of Uruguay (signed 26 Mar. 1991, entered into force 29 Nov. 1991) 2140 UNTS 257 ('Treaty of Asunción'). For a general overview on MERCOSUR in English, *see* Jan Peter Schmidt, 'MERCOSUR' in *The Max Planck Encyclopedia of International Law*, https://opil.ouplaw.com/home/mpil (accessed 16 Dec. 2024). *See* also Marcelo Toscano Franca Filho, Lucas Lixinski & Maria Belén Olmos Giupponi (eds), *The Law of Mercosur* (Hart Publishing, 2010).
20. Additional Protocol to the Treaty of Asunción on the Institutional Structure of MERCOSUR (signed 17 Dec. 1994, entered into force 15 Dec. 1995) 2145 UNTS 298 ('Ouro Preto Protocol').
21. Schmidt, *supra* n. 19.

According to the Treaty of Asunción, the Common Market implies the 'free circulation of goods, services and productive factors between countries', the establishment of 'common external tariff', the adoption of 'a common commercial policy', the 'coordination of macroeconomic and sectoral policies', and the commitment of the States Parties to 'harmonize their legislation' in the relevant areas.[22]

The Treaty of Asunción obligates States Parties to adopt a 'common commercial policy'. This means, among other things, that States Parties cannot negotiate FTAs individually, except for trade agreements concluded with Latin American countries in the framework of the Latin American Integration Association ('LAIA' or, in Spanish, 'ALADI'). In 2000, MERCOSUR States Parties 'reaffirmed' their commitment to jointly negotiate trade agreements with third countries in which tariff preferences are granted and to abstain from engaging in any new bilateral preferential agreements or new trade preferences under LAIA.[23] MERCOSUR States Parties must negotiate trade agreements *en bloc*.[24] MERCOSUR has recently engaged in FTA negotiations with the European Union (EU), the European Free Trade Association ('EFTA') and Singapore, as I will discuss below.

'Investment policy' is not mentioned in the MERCOSUR's constituent treaties. That explains in part why, until recently, investment provisions were generally non-existent or minimal in the FTAs concluded by MERCOSUR and why States Parties have concluded investment treaties individually since the 1990s and have kept doing so until now.[25] However, as it will be developed in the following sections, there have been different attempts to develop a (partial) common investment policy in MERCOSUR.

B Attempts at a (Partial) Common Investment Policy

At the beginning of the 1990s, MERCOSUR States Parties tried to design a comprehensive regional scheme for the promotion and protection of foreign direct investment (FDI) within the region. In 1992, a working group received a mandate to prepare drafts of two different 'framework agreements' on the issue of FDI.[26] While one of them

22. Treaty of Asunción, Art. 1.
23. MERCOSUR/CMC/DEC. No. 32/00 (29 Jun. 2000).
24. MERCOSUR negotiated trade agreements with Bolivia and Chile in 1996, the Southern African Customs Union in 2000, Mexico in 2002, India and the Andean Community in 2004, Peru in 2005, Cuba in 2006, Egypt and Israel in 2010, and Colombia in 2017. The text of these agreements is available at https://www.mercosur.int/relacionamiento-externo/red-de-acuerdos/ (accessed 16 Dec. 2024).
25. Argentina signed sixty-one BITs. Paraguay signed twenty-four BITs between 1978 and 2001 and two since 2017. Uruguay signed thirty-seven BITs between 1985 and 2022. Brazil signed fourteen BITs between 1994 and 1999 and Brazil has signed fourteen ACFIs and three agreements with ACFIs-type provisions since 2015. Information available at the UNCTAD Investment Policy Hub – International Investment Agreements Navigator, https://investmentpolicy.unctad.org/international-investment-agreements (accessed 16 Dec. 2024).
26. Minutes of Subgroup No. 4 – Fiscal and Monetary Policies Related to Trade (16 and 17 Mar. 1992) ('The delegations agreed, given the particular characteristics of the aforementioned Agreements and their consequent asymmetry, to submit to the Common Market Group for consideration that their treatment be analysed by a Group of Experts that specifically evaluates the issue'); MERCOSUR/GMC/RES. No. 20/92 (25 Jun. 1992), Art. 1 ('To create a Commission

would regulate foreign investments within MERCOSUR members, the other would regulate foreign investments coming to MERCOSUR from third countries. The preparation of the drafts took almost two years.

In 1994, the Common Market Council ('CMC') adopted in January the Colonia Protocol for the Mutual Protection and Promotion of Investments in MERCOSUR ('Colonia Protocol' or 'CP'),[27] which regulated foreign investment within the region, and in August the Buenos Aires Protocol on the Protection and Promotion of Investments Coming from States Not Parties to MERCOSUR ('Buenos Aires Protocol' or 'BAP'),[28] which regulated foreign investments from third countries. These protocols never entered into force. The CP was ratified only by Argentina, and the BAP was ratified by Argentina, Paraguay and Uruguay.[29] Unlike the future Investment Protocol, those protocols required ratification by all the MERCOSUR States Parties to enter into force. I will analyse the content of these protocols in the next section.

Besides signing the Colonia and BAPs, States Parties never abandoned the possibility of negotiating BITs individually with third countries. Paraguay had already signed a BIT with France in 1978 and another with the UK in 1981 and resumed the policy of signing BITs in 1992 until 2001, and later concluded BITs with the United Arab Emirates in 2017 and Qatar in 2018, with a total of twenty-six BITs signed.[30] Uruguay started to sign BITs in 1985, with a BIT with Ecuador, and will continue signing BITs until our days with a total of thirty-seven BITs signed plus FTAs with investment chapters with Mexico, the US and Chile.[31] Argentina started to sign BITs in 1990 with the treaty with Italy and will continue signing treaties until 2001, with a total of fifty-eight BITs, and from 2016 it would re-start signing BITs.[32] Brazil started to sign BITs in 1994, the first being with Portugal, and would follow that policy until 1999, with a total of fourteen BITs signed but not ratified, and in 2015 started the policy of signing ACFIs.[33]

within Working Subgroup No. 4 that will have the objective of carrying out studies and formulating recommendations on promotion and reciprocal protection of investments'); MERCOSUR\CMC\DEC No. 9/93 'Adjustment of the Schedule of Las Leñas' ('Working Subgroup No. 4 – Fiscal and Monetary Policies Related to Trade ... 5.1.2 Preparation of an intra-zone framework agreement ... 5.2.2 Preparation of an extra-zone framework agreement ...').

27. MERCOSUR/CMC/DEC. No. 11/93 (17 Jan. 1994), which includes the Colonia Protocol for the Promotion and Reciprocal Protection of Investments in MERCOSUR (signed 17 Jan. 1994) ('Colonia Protocol').
28. MERCOSUR/CMC/DEC. No. 11/94 (5 Aug. 1994), Buenos Aires Protocol on the Promotion and Protection of Investments from States that are not part of MERCOSUR (signed 5 Aug. 1994) ('Buenos Aires Protocol').
29. The Colonia Protocol was ratified only by Argentina (Decree No. 24891/95). The Buenos Aires Protocol was ratified by Argentina (Decree No. 24554/96), Paraguay (Decree No. 593/95) and Uruguay (Decree No. 17531/2003).
30. Information available at the UNCTAD Investment Policy Hub – International Investment Agreements Navigator, https://investmentpolicy.unctad.org/international-investment-agreements (accessed 16 Dec. 2024).
31. *Ibid.*
32. *Ibid.*
33. *Ibid.*

In 1995, MERCOSUR and the EU signed an Interregional Framework Cooperation Agreement.[34] This broad agreement focuses on cooperation in different areas, including trade, intellectual property, energy and telecommunications and investment promotion.[35] MERCOSUR countries also signed joint memorandums of understanding on trade and investment with Guyana (adopted 28 June 1999), Trinidad and Tobago (adopted 28 June 1999), and Singapore (adopted 24 September 2007).[36] The content of these agreements was however quite generic: signatories agreed to strengthen economic relations and promote investments and trade.

In 2000, the MERCOSUR Common Market Group ('CMG') established its Working Subgroup No. 12 on Investments.[37] The group had among its functions to analyse the difficulties encountered by the States Parties in the ratification of the Colonia and BAPs, monitor investment negotiations at the international level, and coordinate the positions of the MERCOSUR States Parties in the international forums in which they participate. However, there was not much progress in these areas.

This situation coincided with two developments. First, Argentina suffered one of its worst crises in 2001, stopped its policy of concluding BITs and became the number one target of ISDS claimants. Second, Brazil's government decided in 2002, after opposition in the National Congress, to withdraw the BITs it had presented for approval during the 1990s.[38]

C Characteristics of the Failed First Attempt at Regionalizing BITs

The Colonia and BAPs followed in general the classic BIT model. They never entered into force, but they were interesting experiments in how to incorporate that model into an integration process like MERCOSUR, and they were quite innovative in some respects. For these reasons, they deserve a close analysis.

The 1994 CP was a sort of regional BIT attempting to regulate investments intra-zone within MERCOSUR. It included classical BIT treatment provisions: fair and equitable treatment, full protection, national and most-favoured-nation treatment (CP, Article 3), expropriation and compensation (CP, Article 4) and transfer of funds (CP, Article 4).

The provision on the settlement of disputes between contracting parties in the CP provided that disputes would be submitted to the procedures established by the Brasília Protocol (which had established the dispute settlement mechanism available

34. Interregional Framework Cooperation Agreement between Mercosur and the EU (adopted 15 Dec. 1995, entered into force 1 Jul. 1999). Available at: http://www.sice.oas.org/tpd/mer_eu/negotiations/Framework1995_e.pdf (accessed 16 Dec. 2024).
35. *Ibid.*, Art. 12 ('Promotion of investment').
36. Memorandums of understanding between MERCOSUR and Guyana on trade and investment (adopted 28 Jun. 1999), Memorandums of understanding between MERCOSUR and Trinidad y Tobago on trade and investment (adopted 28 Jun. 1999), Memorandums of understanding between MERCOSUR and Singapore on trade and investment (adopted 24 Sep. 2007). The text of the agreements is available at https://www.mre.gov.py/tratados/public_web/ConsultaMercosur.aspx (accessed 16 Dec. 2024).
37. MERCOSUR/GMC/RES. No. 13/00 (5 Apr. 2000), Art. 2.
38. Ratton Sanchez Badin & Morosini, *supra* n. 13, at 240.

in MERCOSUR at that time) or to the system that would be established in its replacement (CP, Article 8). As regards dispute resolution between an investor and a host contracting party, the Protocol provided that if consultations could not resolve a dispute the investor could choose to submit it to one of the following procedures: (i) the courts of the host party; (ii) international arbitration under the ICSID Convention or an ad hoc arbitral tribunal under the United Nations Commission on International Trade Law (UNCITRAL) rules; or (iii) a permanent dispute settlement system for individual claimants to be eventually established in MERCOSUR (CP, Article 9).

The 1994 BAP extra-zone investment agreement attempted to regulate FDI into MERCOSUR from third states. Rather than a BIT-type agreement, the Protocol was a real framework agreement establishing some general obligations and guidelines for MERCOSUR States Parties. It functioned as a unilateral declaration in favour of investors from third states.

The BAP highlighted 'the need to harmonize' the legal principles to be applied by each of the States Parties to investments from third states 'in order not to create differential conditions that distort the flow of investments' (BAP, Preamble). The States Parties would undertake to grant investments from third states a 'treatment no more favourable than that established in this Protocol' (BAP, Article 1). In line with this, the general treatment to be agreed upon by each State Party with third states would 'not recognize benefits and rights greater than those recognized to the investor in the following regulatory bases' (BAP, Article 2). As substantive provisions, the Protocol included fair and equitable treatment, full protection and security, national treatment, most-favoured nation, expropriation and compensation, transfer of funds and subrogation (BAP, Article 2). The States Parties would undertake to exchange information on the negotiation of IIAs with third states and to carry on consultations between them in advance on substantial modifications to the treatment agreed in any future agreement (BAP, Article 3).

Concerning the settlement of disputes between a State Party and a third state, the Protocol briefly provided that disputes would, as far as possible, be resolved through diplomatic channels and by arbitration (BAP, Article 2.G). Concerning disputes between an investor from a third state and a host State Party, the Protocol provided that if consultations could not resolve disputes, the investor may choose to submit it: (i) to the courts of the host State Party, or (ii) to international arbitration (either an ad hoc arbitral tribunal or an international arbitration institution) (BAP, Article 2.H). Interestingly, the Protocol provided that the arbitral body would decide based on the provisions of the 'concluded agreement', the law of the host State Party and the terms of any particular agreements concluded in relation to the investment (*ibid.*).

As mentioned, this agreement required the ratification of all the States Parties in order to enter into force, something that never happened. In 2010, the CMC 'derogated' these agreements.[39] Nevertheless, the Buenos Aires agreement seems a very interesting attempt to coordinate and establish some framework to the BITs that State Parties were negotiating individually.

39. MERCOSUR/CMC/DEC. No. 30/10 (16 Dec. 10).

D The Successful Second Attempt: Regionalizing Based on the ACFI Model

In 2007, in Brazil, the CAMEX Council of Ministers approved general guidelines for negotiation of investment agreements, which suggested first, to renegotiate investment agreements within MERCOSUR; second, to prioritize negotiation of new investment agreements with South American countries; and third, to negotiate investment agreements with extra-regional countries in connection with broader commercial arrangements.[40]

In 2010, the MERCOSUR CMC instructed Working Subgroup No. 12 on Investments to submit a proposal for an investment agreement intra-MERCOSUR in 2011.[41] The instructions included a short set of 'guidelines for the conclusion of an investment agreement in MERCOSUR'. The guidelines stated that the main obligations to be included in the future agreement were national treatment, expropriation, transparency, national regulations, key personnel and transfer of capital. The guidelines omitted any reference to other substantive standards such as fair and equitable treatment, full protection and security and most-favoured nation. The guidelines referred to state-to-state dispute resolution based on the Olivos Protocol (OP), with no reference to ISDS. The guidelines also provided that the treaty could enter into force bilaterally without requiring ratification by all four States Parties. The same CMC decision 'derogated' the previous CMC decisions that in 1994 had approved the Colonia and BAPs.

Negotiations within MERCOSUR then stalled because of opposition from Argentina.[42] At the time, Argentina faced a tidal wave of investment claims and views within Argentina were divided on what to do with its FDI regime. However, many of the guidelines in the 2010 CMC decision would be reflected in the future Investment Protocol.

In 2013, the Chamber of Foreign Trade (CAMEX) approved a draft ACFI to be negotiated with selected African countries.[43] Brazil launched ACFI negotiations in 2015.[44] On 7 April 2017, MERCOSUR States Parties approved the ACFI-inspired Investment Protocol,[45] which was signed the same day. The Investment Protocol entered into force for Uruguay and Brazil on 30 July 2019 and for Argentina on 24 November 2020, while Paraguay has not yet ratified it.[46] Unlike the 1994 Protocols, the ICFP entered into force as soon as it had two ratifications (ICFP, Article 26.1). I will

40. Ratton Sanchez Badin & Morosini, *supra* n. 13, at 244.
41. MERCOSUR/CMC/DEC. No. 30/10 (16 Dec. 10).
42. *See* Nicolás M. Perrone & Gustavo Rojas de Cerqueira César, 'Brazil's Bilateral Investment Treaties: More Than a New Investment Treaty Model?' (Columbia FDI Perspectives, Perspectives on Topical Foreign Direct Investment Issues No. 159, 26 Oct. 2015), https://ccsi.columbia.edu/content/no-159-brazils-bilateral-investment-treaties-more-new-investment-treaty-model-nicolas-m (accessed 16 Dec. 2024).
43. Ratton Sanchez Badin & Morosini, *supra* n. 13, at 246.
44. *Ibid.*, at 236.
45. MERCOSUR/CMC/DEC. No. 03/17 (7 Apr. 2017).
46. In Uruguay, the Protocol was approved by Law No. 19635 (13 Jul. 2018), in Brazil it was approved by Legislative Decree No. 187 (20 Dec. 2018), in Argentina it was approved by Law No. 27,527. The information on the status of the Protocol is available at https://www.mre.gov.py/tratados/public_web/ConsultaMercosur.aspx (accessed 16 Dec. 2024).

analyse the content of the Investment Protocol and its implications in the following sections.

III REGIONALIZATION IN PRACTICE: THE 2017 INVESTMENT PROTOCOL AND ITS IMPLICATIONS

A The Search of Balance Between Protections and Obligations for Investors

In terms of investor protections and obligations, the 2017 MERCOSUR Investment Protocol largely follows the ACFIs concluded by Brazil with Latin American countries. So, most of the features of Brazilian ACFIs are found in the MERCOSUR Protocol, although it also adds provisions or commitments not found in some of the previous ACFIs.

The Protocol's purpose is to promote cooperation between the States Parties to facilitate direct investment that enables sustainable development (ICFP, Article 1). For this reason, the contracting states seek to establish a strategic association in matters of investment and a normative framework that allows the promotion of investments and strengthens contacts between investors and governments (ICFP, Preamble). This language appears in many ACFIs.

The Protocol includes relatively limited definitions of investment and investor. The definition of investment includes objective criteria that are not found in the first ACFIs: 'the commitment of capital, the objective of establishing a lasting interest, the expectation of profit or utility and the assumption of risks' (ICFP, Article 3.3). It also includes a non-exhaustive positive list of investments, which includes equity, property rights, debt instruments and a negative list that excludes from the definition public debt, portfolio investments, pecuniary claims arising exclusively from commercial contracts and pre-establishment costs and obligations. At the same time, the pre-establishment phase of investments is not covered (ICFP, Article 4.3). The definition of 'investor' covers legal persons constituted under and within its domicile and with substantial business activities in the territory of another State Party and that has made an investment in another State Party (ICFP, Article 3.4).

The substantive provisions included in the Protocol are limited. They include 'access to justice' and 'due process' (ICFP, Article 4.1 and 4.2), which do not appear in previous ACFIs.[47] Since the first ACFI, Brazil has consistently rejected standards found in traditional BITs, such as fair and equitable treatment, full protection and security and indirect expropriation. Yet, while the ACFIs signed with African countries ignored these provisions, the Brazilian agreements with Latin American countries adopted a more active dismissal of such standards by excluding from dispute settlement those standards agreed with a third Party.[48] The MERCOSUR Protocol goes in this same

47. The closest references in prior ACFIs are to 'denial of justice' and 'due process' in the Brazil-Colombia ACFI, Art. 4.2 and 4.3.
48. *See, e.g.*, Brazil-Colombia ACFI, Art. 5.3.b; Brazil-Chile ACFI, Art. 6.3.b; and Brazil-Mexico ACFI, Art. 6.3.a.

direction but innovates in the acquis of the ACFIs by explicitly rejecting from its scope the standards of 'fair and equitable treatment' and 'full protection and security' (ICFP, Article 4.3).

The Protocol also expressly excludes the protection against indirect expropriation (ICFP, Article 6.6) in a language similar to that found in the agreements with Latin American countries.[49] In contrast, the provisions on expropriation included in the first ACFIs were silent on indirect expropriation.

The non-discrimination provision is also limited compared with standard BIT clauses. It provides for national treatment and most-favoured-nation treatment but is limited to the 'conditions of competition' (ICFP, Article 5.1 and 5.2).[50] The Protocol clarifies in line with Brazilian ACFIs that the non-discrimination provision shall not apply to incorporate substantive or dispute settlement provisions not contained in the Protocol (ICFP, Article 5.7).

One interesting standard included in the article on transparency, and which appears also in many Brazilian ACFIs, is that States Parties shall ensure that all measures affecting investment must be 'administered in a reasonable, objective and impartial manner, in accordance with its legal system' (ICFP, Article 8.1).[51] This standard of reasonableness, objectiveness and impartiality appears to be quite broad, although it is attached to the legal system of each State Party.

The Protocol recalls the inherent right of States Parties to regulate (ICFP, Preamble) and includes numerous exceptions and carve-outs, such as tax measures (ICFP, Article 10), measures adopted with respect to the financial sector (ICFP, Article 11), and measures aimed at preserving public order, international peace and security, the protection of essential security interests (ICFP, Article 12.1). The Protocol also excludes from its protection investments made with capital of illicit origin or where acts of corruption or illegal acts are verified (ICFP, Article 15.2). The agreement also ensures that investments are carried out in accordance with labour, environment, or health in that State Party (ICFP, Article 16.1) and that States Parties will not modify its labour, environment, or health standards to stimulate investment in its territory (ICFP, Article 16.2).

The Protocol also includes different provisions related to investors' obligations or responsibilities. It has been noted that 'BITs have arguably focused too much on investors' rights, to the detriment of the rights of host states to regulate their economy and establish limits to investors' conduct',[52] so ACFIs attempt to balance this situation. In line with this, the Protocol innovates by including an article relating to the 'investor obligations' (ICFP, Article 13), using language similar to a provision appearing in the Qatar-Argentina BIT signed in 2016. It provides that investors 'must comply with all

49. *See* Brazil-Chile ACFI, Art. 7.5; Brazil-Peru ETEA, Art. 2.7.6; and Brazil-Ecuador ACFI, Art. 5.7. The ACFI with Colombia is silent in this respect (*see ibid.*, Art. 6).
50. References to 'condition of competition' appeared already in the ACFIs with Colombia (Art. 5.1 and 5.3) and with Mexico, Art. 5.1 and 5.2.
51. This provision by contrast does not appear in the ACFIs concluded with India and Ethiopia.
52. Geraldo Vidigal & Beatriz Stevens, *Brazil's New Model of Dispute Settlement for Investment: Return to the Past or Alternative for the Future?* 19 JWIT 475, 511 (2018) https://doi.org/10.1163/22119000-12340100.

laws and regulations, as well as the policies established by the host State Party regarding the investment' (ICFP, Article 13.1).

Corporate Social Responsibility is one of the goals of the treaty. In line with numerous ACFIs, the Protocol provides that investors 'shall strive to achieve the highest possible level of contribution to the sustainable development of the host State Party, through the adoption of socially responsible practices, based on the voluntary principles' (ICFP, Article 14.1) and lists those principles.

As mentioned, most of those provisions appear in numerous ACFIs signed by Brazil. By contrast, for the other MERCOSUR States Parties, in some cases, this is the first time that some of those issues are included in IIAs (in addition to the provisions on institutional governance and dispute prevention that are a novelty for them), and it may imply expanding disciplines that were not covered by BITs before and adapting some structures at the national level to comply with the Protocol.

B Institutional Governance and Dispute Prevention (Levels 1 and 2)

Each ACFI creates two types of institutions to govern the agreement: (i) national focal points or 'ombudsmen', which operate at the investor-state (national) level of each state party and provide government assistance to investors from the other party and (ii) a joint committee, which operates at the state-to-state (international) level and is composed of government representatives from each of the parties.[53]

Concerning dispute prevention and settlement, the ACFIs operate at three interrelated levels: (i) Level 1 – investor-state at the national level through the national focal points, (ii) Level 2 – state-to-state at the international level before the joint committee, (iii) Level 3 – state-to-state dispute settlement (arbitration) also at the international level.[54]

The MERCOSUR Protocol follows a similar structure to ACFIs in this regard, with two main variations. First, the Joint Committee will act within the structure of MERCOSUR. Second, state-to-state dispute settlement is institutionalized and takes place before the 'procedures and mechanisms' available in MERCOSUR. I will develop these aspects in the next paragraphs.

Institutional Governance: National Focal Points and Joint Committee

It has been noted that ACFIs can be seen 'as a possible return to the pre-BITs phase of politicized investment protection' and that they 'allow[] for a degree of political control over disputes by home states'.[55] This goes in line with the prevention and mitigation mechanisms of international investment disputes developed by the World Bank and discussed at the UNCITRAL WGIII.[56]

53. Ratton Sanchez Badin & Morosini, *supra* n. 13, at 226.
54. *Ibid.*, at 232.
55. Vidigal & Stevens, *supra*, n. 52, at 511.
56. *See* World Bank, Retention and Expansion of Foreign Direct Investment, Political Risk and Policy Responses (2019) and World Bank, Managing Investor Issues through Retention Mechanisms (2021).

In line with prior ACFIs, the Protocol puts forward the institutional layout for the main rationales of the ACFI – cooperation and investment facilitation – by establishing national focal points and a Joint Committee. First, the Protocol mandates each MERCOSUR State Party to designate a National Focal Point or 'Ombudsman' (ICFP, Article 18.1).[57] The National Focal Points have the primary responsibility to support investors from other States Parties in its territory (ICFP, Article 18.1). Among its tasks, the National Focal Points: (a) interact with the National Focal Points of the other States Parties; (b) evaluate possible suggestions and proposals from another State Party regarding investments or investors of this State Party and recommend, when pertinent, actions to improve the investments environment; (c) seek to prevent investment disputes in coordination with the competent government authorities; (d) provide information on national regulations; (e) report to the Joint Committee on its activities and actions, when it deems it necessary and endeavour to comply with its guidelines (ICFP, Article 18.3). The National Focal Points exercise their responsibilities in relation to investments even when they have not started to operate in the territory of the host State Party (ICFP, Article 18.5).[58] The States Parties are mandated to adopt the necessary measures for their National Focal Points to carry out their functions (ICFP, Article 18.4).

Second, the Protocol establishes the creation of a MERCOSUR Investment Joint Committee, which is in charge of administering the Protocol. The Joint Committee will be made up of the representatives of the MERCOSUR States Parties and shall meet at least once a year (ICFP, Article 17.1 and 17.2). Among its functions, the Joint Committee will: (a) supervise the application and execution of the Protocol and, if necessary, make recommendations to the States Parties for its modification; (b) discuss issues relevant to investment in the States Parties; (c) coordinate the implementation of cooperation and facilitation programmes; (d) consult the private sector and civil society for their views on specific issues related to its work; (e) prevent disputes relating to investments of the States Parties to resolve them amicably; and (f) coordinate the implementation of the 'Agenda for Cooperation and Facilitation of Investments' (ICFP, Article 17.3). When appropriate, the Joint Committee will consult the private sector and civil society and invite them to participate in its meetings (ICFP, Article 17.3 and 17.4).

57. The MERCOSUR Investment Protocol provides that States Parties may modify their National Focal Points designated in this Protocol (ICFP, Art. 18.1). In the resent agreement with Singapore, it is stated that the focal points or Ombudspersons of the MERCOSUR States Parties (which would act also as focal points for the purposes of the MERCOSUR Investment Protocol) are: (a) for Argentina, *Dirección Nacional de la Promoción de Inversiones (DNPRI)* (National Directorate for Investment Promotion of the Ministry of Foreign Affairs, International Trade and Worship); (b) for Brazil, *Ombusdman de Investimentos Diretos (OID) da Câmara de Comércio Exterior (CAMEX)* (Ombudsman of Direct Foreign Investment (DIO) of the Foreign Trade Board); (c) for Paraguay, *Subsecretaría de Estado de Industria del Ministerio de Industria y Comercio* (Sub-secretariat of Industry of the Ministry of Industry and Commerce); (d) for Uruguay, *Asesoría de Política Comercial del Ministerio de Economía y Finanzas* (Trade Policy Advisory of the Ministry of Economy and Finance). *See* FTA between MERCOSUR and Singapore (signed 7 Dec. 2023), Annex 9-B.

58. This is notwithstanding that the pre-establishment phase is not covered by the Protocol (ICFP, Art. 4.3), as already mentioned.

One of the particularities of the MERCOSUR Joint Committee, unlike joint committees under the ACFIs, is that it will be created in the framework of an integration organization such as MERCOSUR. In 2021, the MERCOSUR States Parties agreed that the Joint Committee would be constituted within the institutional structure of MERCOSUR and instructed the GMC to make the necessary adjustments for that purpose.[59] It was agreed that the SGT No. 12 on Investments will assume this function, starting its activities from the Protocol's entry into force for all State Parties.[60] This will happen when Paraguay ratifies the Protocol. This brings the challenge for investors and States Parties of having that body functioning when that last ratification will take place.

The Institutional Governance in the Protocol is reinforced by two additional obligations for States Parties: the exchange of information and the cooperation between agencies in charge of investment promotion.

On the one hand, the Protocol provides that States Parties, through the Joint Committee and their National Focal Points, shall exchange information on business opportunities, procedures and requirements for investments (ICFP, Article 19.1). For that purpose, States Parties will provide, when requested and when that is feasible and in accordance with its national law, in particular, information on the different points of relevance for the promotion of foreign investments including: (a) investment programmes; (b) public policies and legal frameworks; (c) legal framework for investment; (e) customs procedures and tax regimes; (f) statistics; (g) infrastructure; and (h) social, labour, immigration and exchange legislation; among others (ICFP, Article 19.2). At the same time, the Protocol mandates for the treatment of protected information (ICFP, Article 20).

On the other hand, the Protocol provides that States Parties shall encourage their competent agencies or entities in matters of investment promotion[61] to, *inter alia*: (a) share information to encourage investment; (b) collaborate in the development of investment attraction policies; (c) identify areas of business opportunities; and (d) exchange experiences related to investment promotion and organize joint activities to attract investments (ICFP, Article 22.1). The Protocol has a meticulous provision on this aspect that does not appear with the level of detail in other agreements.[62] This reflects the broader goal of MERCOSUR as an integration bloc.

Level 1: National Focal Points and the Example of Brazil

As mentioned, the Protocol mandates each State Party to designate a National Focal Point or 'Ombudsman', which has the primary responsibility to support investors from

59. MERCOSUR/CMC/ACTA No. 03/21 (28 Sep. 2021).
60. MERCOSUR/SGT No. 12/ACTA No. 01/22 (6 Jun. 2022).
61. According to the Investment Protocol, the agencies or entities competent in matters of investment promotion of the States Parties are: (i) in Argentina, the Argentine Investment and International Trade Agency, (ii) in Brazil, the Brazilian Agency for the Promotion of Exports and Investments – Apex Brazil, (iii) in Paraguay, the Investment and Export Network – REDIEX and (iv) in Uruguay the Instituto Uruguay XXI (ICFP, Art. 22.2).
62. Cf. Brazil-Chile ACFI, Art. 23; Brazil-Colombia ACFI, Art. 21; Brazil-UAE ACFI, Art. 23; and Brazil-Ecuador ACFI, Art. 23.

other States Parties in its territory (ICFP, Article 18.1). National Focal Points operate at the investor-state (national) level of each State Party and, among other responsibilities, seek to prevent investment disputes in coordination with the competent government authorities (ICFP, Article 18.3). Resorting to the National Focal Point is not a prerequisite to resort later to the dispute prevention procedure before the Joint Committee.

Here, I will focus on the implementation of this requirement in Brazil since it has a very developed implementing regulation, in line with all the ACFIs concluded by that country, that could serve as a model for other States Parties in MERCOSUR. It must be noted, however, that the ACFI model is the only model for Brazil's investment agreements. For other states, implementation is more complex due to their participation in ACFIs and classic BITs.

In Brazil, the Ombudsman is linked to an intergovernmental body – the CAMEX. CAMEX aims to formulate, adopt, implement and coordinate policies and activities relating to foreign trade and direct foreign investments in Brazil and Brazilian investments abroad.[63] Thus, it has a very important role in formulating Brazil's Foreign Trade Policies. CAMEX is composed of ten bodies, which include the National Investment Committee (CONINV) and the Direct Investment Ombudsman (DIO).[64]

CONINV was created in 2016. It is a forum for discussion and elaboration of investment policies. Among its functions, CONINV 'aims to formulate proposals and recommendations to CAMEX intended at promoting and facilitating' foreign investments in Brazil and Brazilian investments abroad.[65] CONINV's functions include to 'monitor the implementation, by the respective bodies, of the recommendations made by the Direct Investment Ombudsman (DIO) for the solution of questions received from foreign investors'.[66]

The DIO was established in 2016 within the Executive Secretariat of CAMEX.[67] The DIO comprises the executive secretary of CAMEX, a secretariat, an advisory group of representatives of different ministries, and a network of focal points comprising fifty agencies and entities of the federal and sub-federal public administration.[68] Among its competencies, the DIO supports and guides investors, recommending solutions to their grievances and proposing to public agencies possible improvements in the legislation or administrative procedures.[69] Under this mechanism, investors can submit: (i) requests ('*consultas*') to clarify general doubts about legislation and administrative

63. Decree No. 11.428 (2 Mar. 2023), Art. 1.
64. *Ibid.*, Art. 2.
65. CAMEX Internal Regulation (29 May 2022), Art. 84, https://www.gov.br/mdic/pt-br/assuntos/camex/colegiados/regimento-interno-da-camex (accessed 16 Dec. 2024).
66. *Ibid.*, Art. 89.IV.
67. Decree No. 8.863/16 (28 Sep. 2016), Art. 1.
68. *Ibid.*, Art. 3 and 'Direct Investment Ombudsman', presentation done by the General Coordination of Investment Policies, Brazilian Foreign Trade Board (CAMEX) at the Forum on Dispute Prevention in Investor-State Dispute Settlement, 7 Jul. 2023, Vienna International Centre, https://uncitral.un.org/sites/uncitral.un.org/files/media-documents/uncitral/en/2023071.ppt.pdf (accessed 16 Dec. 2024).
69. Decree No. 8.863/16, Arts 2 and 4, and CAMEX Internal Regulation, Art. 104.

procedures related to the investments and (ii) enquiries (‘*questionamentos*’) to seek solutions to the situations related to some government agency in the concrete cases that are affecting an investment.[70]

The applicable regulation establishes the procedure to be followed. The Executive Secretary of CAMEX may establish a Grievance Settlement Body (‘*Grupo de Solução de Questionamentos*’ or ‘GSQ’) to assist the DIO in responding to enquiries presented by an investor.[71] The GSQ will be composed of representatives of public entities related to the matter being questioned, representatives of ministries and coordinated by the executive secretary of CAMEX. Public entities must contribute to the DIO in clarifying and resolving the question. After the group’s final analysis, the DIO prepares the final report, including recommendations and potential solutions. The final report is sent to the respective agency or entity involved in the grievance.[72] The DIO cannot respond to claims involving disputes that are before local tribunals in Brazil.[73]

Concerning the assessment of the system, between 2019 and 2023, there have been a total of thirty-four attendances (twenty-one requests and thirteen enquiries). Of those thirty-four attendances, thirty attendances were answered while four remained inert (meaning that investors do not send complementary information requested by the DIO). The attendances involved a wide range of economic sectors, such as mining, oil and gas, energy, industry, finance and telecommunications.[74]

Level 2: Dispute Prevention Procedure Before the Joint Committee

As mentioned, concerning dispute prevention and settlement, the ACFIs operate at three interrelated levels: (i) Level 1 – investor-state at the national level through the focal points, (ii) Level 2 – state-to-state at the international level before the joint committee, and (iii) Level 3 – state-to-state dispute settlement. A similar structure is followed in the Investment Protocol.

The Dispute Prevention Procedure is carried out before the Joint Committee by the States Parties involved in the potential dispute. Among its functions, the Joint Committee supervises the application and execution of the Protocol, carries on consultations with the private sector and civil society to have their views on specific issues related to its work, and prevents disputes relating to investments of the States Parties to resolve them amicably (ICFP, Article 17.3).

If a State Party considers that a specific measure adopted by another State Party constitutes a violation of the Protocol, it may initiate a dispute prevention procedure within the Joint Committee (ICFP, Article 23.1). To initiate the procedure, the

70. *Ibid.*, Art. 2.2 and CAMEX Internal Regulation, Art. 105. *See* https://www.legisweb.com.br/legislacao/?id=405049 (accessed 16 Dec. 2024).
71. Decree No. 8.863/16, Art. 7 and CAMEX Internal Regulation, Arts 109.7, 121.4, 122, 123 and 124.
72. *Ibid. See also* CAMEX Resolution No. 43 (DIO’s Internal Regulation) (4 May 2020).
73. CAMEX Resolution No. 43 (4 May 2020), Art. 2.
74. *See* ‘Direct Investment Ombudsman’, *supra* n. 68.

interested State Party must submit to the Committee an initial brief that allows it to evaluate the difference (ICFP, Article 23.2.a). The initial brief must include at least: (i) the States Parties involved; (ii) the object of the difference; (iii) a description of the background that gave rise to the difference; (iv) legal grounds for the allegation of violation; and (v) evidence of the alleged facts (*idem.*).

The Joint Committee will convene a meeting within thirty days from the date of the submission (ICFP, Article 23.2.b). Whenever relevant to the examination of the measure in question, the Committee may invite other interested parties to appear before it (ICFP, Article 23.4). The Committee will have a period of sixty days from the date of the first meeting (extendable by agreement between the States Parties involved) to evaluate the initial brief, try to reach a solution and prepare a report (ICFP, Article 23.2.c). Thus, the Joint Committee must deliver a recommendation in general within ninety days from the initiation of the proceedings. The report shall include, among other elements: (i) the identification of the States Parties directly involved; (ii) a description of the measure in question and the alleged violation of the Protocol; and (iii) a summary of the conclusions reached by the States Parties directly involved (ICFP, Article 23.2.d).

If the measure in question affects a specific investor: (a) the initial brief of the State Party initiating the procedure must identify the affected investor; (b) the Joint Committee may invite the representatives of the affected investor to participate in its meetings; (c) in the event that the investor breached the legal system of the host State Party these breaches shall be recorded in the report; and (d) a State Party may deny that a dispute previously submitted to a dispute settlement mechanism provided for in other agreements be submitted again to the mechanisms established in this Protocol (ICFP, Article 23.3).

The records of the meetings held within the scope of the Dispute Prevention Procedure and all related documentation shall be confidential, except the report submitted by the Committee (ICFP, Article 23.5).

If the difference is not resolved under an established deadline (i.e., a total of ninety days), the dispute may be 'submitted to the dispute settlement procedures and mechanisms in force in MERCOSUR', in accordance with Article 24 of the Protocol (ICFP, Article 23.2.e).

As mentioned, the MERCOSUR SGT No. 12 on Investments will assume the function of acting as the Investment Protocol's Joint Committee, starting its activities from the entry into force of the Protocol for all State Parties. This will occur once Paraguay ratifies the Protocol. This creates a challenge since the Protocol is already in force for Argentina, Brazil and Uruguay. Until the ratification by Paraguay, those states would not have access to the functions to be performed by the Joint Committee, including the dispute prevention function, which is a prerequisite to resorting to the dispute settlement procedures. In the meantime, investors may need to explore (mainly through their states) alternative dispute resolution mechanisms or invoke the Protocol standards before domestic tribunals in the host state.

C Dispute Settlement Before MERCOSUR's Procedures and Mechanisms (Level 3)

One of the particularities of ACFIs is the WTO-inspired adjudication provisions.[75] This is explained in part due to the fact that '[w]hen Brazil began to frame new investment policy proposals in the early 2010s, the officials involved had expertise in international economic law and long experience in trade law, but they were outsiders to arbitration'.[76] The positive experiences that influenced ACFIs also derived from state-to-state management or settlement of disputes in MERCOSUR: 'the experience gained [in MERCOSUR] from addressing and/or solving disputes at the consultations stage is far from negligible' and this experience 'exposed Brazilian officials to the permanent practice of alternative (i.e. non-judicial) methods'.[77] This makes the blend between ACFIs and MERCOSUR dispute settlement provisions that appear in the Investment Protocol even more innovative.

The Protocol provides that if the claim is not resolved under the dispute prevention mechanism before the Joint Committee in the established time periods, i.e., usually ninety days (Level 2), the dispute may be submitted to the dispute settlement 'procedures and mechanisms' in force in MERCOSUR (Level 3) (ICFP, Article 23.2(e)). This is one of the main innovations of the Protocol, in comparison to Brazilian ACFIs, which provide for ad hoc state-to-state arbitration. For this reason, it is helpful to start the analysis with an overview of MERCOSUR's dispute settlement mechanisms.

Background: MERCOSUR's Dispute Settlement Mechanisms

Dispute settlement in MERCOSUR[78] was governed first by Annex III of the Treaty of Asunción which established a non-coercive and diplomatic dispute settlement system, and then by the Brasília Protocol for the Settlement of Disputes, which provided a three-step dispute resolution mechanism, the last step comprising state-to-state arbitration.[79]

In 2002, the MERCOSUR States Parties adopted the Olivos Protocol for the Settlement of Disputes in MERCOSUR ('Olivos Protocol' or 'OP'), which entered into force in 2004 and established the dispute settlement system applicable until today.[80] The OP is complemented by the 'Implementing Regulations of the Olivos Protocol for

75. Vidigal & Stevens, *supra*, n. 52, at 491-493.
76. Anthea Roberts & Taylor St John, *The Originality of Outsiders: Innovation in the Investment Treaty System*, 33(4) EJIL 1153, 1171 (2023) https://doi.org/10.1093/ejil/chac065.
77. Martino Maggetti & Henrique Choer Moraes, 'The Policy-Making of Investment Treaties in Brazil: Policy Learning in the Context of Late Adoption', in Claire A. Dunlop et al. (eds), *Learning in Public Policy* (Palgrave Macmillan, 2018), at 306.
78. For a general overview of the MERCOSUR dispute settlement system in English, *see* Paula Wojcikiewicz Almeida, 'MERCOSUR Dispute Settlement System', in *The Max Planck Encyclopedia of International Law*, https://opil.ouplaw.com/home/mpil (accessed 16 Dec. 2024).
79. Brasilia Protocol for the Settlement of Disputes in MERCOSUR (signed 17 Dec. 1991, entered into force 22 Apr. 1993) 2145 UNTS 252.
80. Olivos Protocol for the Settlement of Disputes in MERCOSUR (signed 18 Feb. 2002, entered into force 1 Jan. 2004) 2251 UNTS 243.

the Settlement of Disputes in MERCOSUR', whose last version was adopted by MERCOSUR/CMC/DEC. No 05/22 ('CMC 05/22') in 2022.[81]

The OP provides first for a three-stage dispute settlement procedure between States Parties: (i) direct negotiations (OP, Articles 4 and 5); (ii) ad hoc state-to-state arbitration; and (iii) the possibility to appeal before the Permanent Appeals Court ('PAC', in Spanish Tribunal Permanente de Revisión or 'TPR') (OP, Articles 9 to 38). There is also the possibility to resort directly to the PAC with the agreement of the states party to the dispute (OP, Article 23). In this sense, one of the most significant achievements of the OP is the establishment of the PAC, a permanent judiciary body with its seat in Asunción, Paraguay.[82] The PAC has a dual jurisdiction: it decides disputes of a legal nature that are submitted to it by MERCOSUR States Parties, and it delivers advisory opinions on legal questions at the request of the States Parties altogether, their highest courts, or the organs of the MERCOSUR authorized to make such a request for advisory jurisdiction.[83] The adjudicative and advisory mechanisms under the OP have been used only in a limited number of cases: two arbitral awards by ad hoc tribunals and six awards of the PAC.[84]

The OP also provides for two alternative dispute resolution procedures: (i) the optional intervention of the CMG, which requires the agreement of the states party to the dispute (OP, Articles 6 to 8); and (ii) the possibility for natural and legal persons to initiate 'individual claims', first before the national group of the CMG (individual-home state level), then before the CMG (state-to-state level) and then before a group of experts, which ultimately requires the consensus of MERCOSUR's States Parties (OP, Articles 39 to 44).

In addition, alternative dispute resolution mechanisms are available for States Parties in MERCOSUR outside the OP. On the one hand, the OPP established the 'General Procedure for Claims before the MERCOSUR Trade Commission', which consists of two levels of dispute settlement, first before the MERCOSUR Trade Commission ('MTC') and in a second step before the CMG (OPP, Article 21 and Annex). On the other hand, an informal procedure, the 'Consultation Mechanism', was elaborated before the MTC by Directive No. 13/95, replaced by Directive No. 17/99 in 1999.[85] The 'Consultation Mechanism' is the most used dispute settlement mechanism in MERCOSUR. By 2010, more than five hundred consultations had been presented since 1995.[86] The high amount of consultation submitted appears to be maintained.[87]

81. MERCOSUR/CMC/DEC No. 05/22 ('CMC 05/22') 'Implementing Regulations of the Olivos Protocol for the Settlement of Disputes in MERCOSUR' (20 Jul. 2022).
82. *See* Marianne Klumpp, 'MERCOSUR, Permanent Appeals Court', in *The Max Planck Encyclopedia of International Law*, https://opil.ouplaw.com/home/mpil (accessed 16 Dec. 2024).
83. Advisory opinions are regulated by Arts 3 to 14 of CMC 05/22.
84. The awards of the MECOSUR dispute settlement mechanisms are available at https://www.tprmercosur.org/es/sol_contr_laudos.htm (accessed 16 Dec. 2024).
85. MERCOSUR/CCM/DIR No. 17/99 'Consultation Mechanism in the MERCOSUR Trade Commission, Text Updated According to Resolution CMG No. 20/18'.
86. Nadine Susani, 'Dispute Settlement', in Marcelo Toscano Franca Filho, Lucas Lixinski, & Maria Belén Olmos Giupponi (eds), *The Law of Mercosur* (Hart Publishing, 2010), at 76-77.
87. The minutes of the MTC meetings are available at https://documentos.mercosur.int (accessed 16 Dec. 2024). Some examples of recent minutes where numerous consultations were listed are

Apart from the very limited access for individuals to the 'individual claims' mechanism just analysed (which is an alternative dispute resolution procedure), currently, the MERCOSUR's adjudicatory system leaves no room for access to justice in the case of individuals, although the PAC Secretariat would have the human resources and well-defined structure to provide mediation and arbitration services for individuals.[88] The only additional option for individuals is to pursue claims through proceedings before national courts (where they could invoke the Investment Protocol), and then supreme courts may resort to the PAC through the mechanism of advisory opinions.[89]

Dispute Settlement Provisions in the Investment Protocol

Under ACFIs, the dispute prevention procedure before the joint committee is a mandatory step before arbitral proceedings. The Protocol follows the same logic and provides that if a claim is not settled under the dispute prevention mechanism before the Joint Committee in the established time period (usually ninety days) or if there is no participation of a State Party involved in the dispute in the meetings of the Joint Committee, the dispute may be submitted to the 'dispute settlement procedures and mechanisms in force in MERCOSUR' (ICFP, Articles 23.2.e and 24.1).

Article 24 of the Protocol provides that disputes may be submitted by any of the States Parties involved in the dispute 'in accordance with the provisions of this article' (ICFP, Article 24.1). That article, which acts as *lex specialis* covers three situations.

First, it provides for a five-year limitation period: the Protocol may be invoked to address a dispute related to investments provided that a period of more than five years has not elapsed from the date on which the State Party first knew or should have known the facts that gave rise to the dispute (ICFP, Article 24.2).

Second, certain obligations are excluded from the dispute settlement mechanism.[90] It may not be subject to the dispute resolution mechanism: (i) the provisions on corporate social responsibility, which establish certain duties for investors, (ii) the part of the provision on corruption and illegality, which mandates States Parties to take measures to prevent and combat those situations, and (iii) the part of the provision on investments and the environment, labour and health, where it mandates States Parties not to stimulate investment by lowering labour, environmental or health standards (ICFP, Article 24.3). In addition to those exclusions, the article on security exceptions provides that measures adopted under it will not be subject to the dispute settlement provisions of the Protocol (ICFP, Article 12.2).

---

the following MERCOSUR/CCM/ACTA No. 05/2019, MERCOSUR/CCM/ACTA No. 06/2020, and MERCOSUR/CCM/ACTA No. 03/21.

88. Juan Manuel Rivero Godoy, *Servicios de arbitraje y mediación: desafíos y posibilidades en el Mercosur*, in 7 Secretaría del TPR del MERCOSUR – Aportes Académicos 15, 20 (2022).
89. Wojcikiewicz Almeida, *supra* n. 78.
90. Ratton Sanchez Badin and Morosini note with respect to some ACFIs with similar provisions that 'It is not clear then if this exclusion from arbitration as a contentious system means their exclusion from the amicable dispute prevention system also.' *See* Ratton Sanchez Badin & Morosini, *supra* n. 13, at 231.

Third, the election of dispute prevention and settlement under the Investment Protocol implies a renunciation to proceedings under other investment agreements. The Protocol provides that a dispute relating to an investment that has been submitted to the dispute prevention procedure 'and' dispute settlement between the States Parties under the Protocol may not be submitted to the arbitration procedures established in BITs or other agreements with provisions relating to investment to which the States Parties are or become parties (ICFP, Article 24.4).

Interaction of the Investment Protocol and MERCOSUR's Mechanisms on Dispute Settlement

There are different challenges and open questions concerning the Protocol's interaction with the dispute settlement procedures and mechanisms in force in MERCOSUR. I address some of them in the next paragraphs.

First, the Protocol refers to dispute settlement 'procedures and mechanisms' in force in MERCOSUR. This would imply that not only the 'procedures' provided for in the OP would be available (i.e., direct negotiations, ad hoc stat-to-state arbitration, proceedings before the PAC, intervention by the CMG and individual claims) but also MERCOSUR dispute settlement 'mechanisms' inside and outside that protocol. This would include, *inter alia*, first 'mechanisms' included in the Protocol, i.e., mechanisms related to technical aspects (OP, Article 2) and advisory opinions (OP, Article 3) and second 'mechanisms' outside the Protocol, such as the 'General Procedure for Claims' and the 'Complain Mechanism' before the MTC, already mentioned.

Second, the interaction of the provisions in the Protocol and MERCOSUR's procedures and mechanisms would imply that after the parties resort to the dispute prevention procedure before the Joint Committee (ICFP, Article 17.3.e), they should resort again to a political stage of direct negotiations before resorting to state-to-state arbitration or they could resort to other political alternative dispute resolution procedures and mechanisms, such as intervention by the CMG or individual claims (both under the OP), or to 'General Procedure for Claims' or 'Complaint Mechanism' (outside the OP).

Third, the OP provides a shorter period for settling disputes than ACFIs (in addition to the ninety days for the dispute prevention mechanism). The OP provides for: (i) fifteen days of direct negotiations (OP, Article 5.1), (ii) thirty days for the constitution of the arbitral tribunal (OP, Article 10), (iii) sixty days for the arbitral tribunal to render its award, which can be extended for a maximum period of thirty days (OP, Article 16), with the possibility of (iv) appeal for review, which can last other seventy-five days (OP, Articles 17 and 21). This is considerably shorter than the time periods in the ACFIs. For instance, the ACFI with Ecuador provides for: (i) three months for the parties to the dispute to appoint an arbitrator each, (ii) another three months for the two members to appoint the president of the tribunal, and (iii) six months for the tribunal to render its award.[91] So, an arbitral tribunal in MERCOSUR

91. Brazil-Ecuador ACFI, Arts 25.6 and 25.10.

would have two to three months to render its award versus the six months of the tribunals under the ACFIs.

Lastly, MERCOSUR dispute settlement mechanisms were explicitly created to settle trade disputes. This is clear from the remedies provided for in the OP. That agreement provides that if a state party to a dispute does not comply with an arbitral award, the other party to the dispute will have the power to apply 'temporary compensatory measures', 'such as the suspension of concessions or other equivalent obligations, aimed at obtaining compliance with the award'. The OP further states that the State Party benefited by the award 'will seek, first of all, to suspend the concessions or equivalent obligations in the same sector or sectors affected' (OP, Article 31.2). Thus, the OP provides retaliatory compensation on the part of the winning party, not reparatory compensation on the part of the losing party.

However, this appears to be in line with most ACFIs, which focus on compliance rather than compensation. Rather than reparation, ACFIs 'aim to restore the value of the investment and ensure [investors] take their projects forward'.[92] The ACFIs with Mexico, Colombia, Chile, Peru, and Ecuador provide that the main objective of the arbitration is to bring the challenged measure into conformity with the agreement.[93] However, some ACFIs, like those with Mexico, Colombia and Ecuador, declare that the arbitration tribunal may also determine the existence of damages to the investor and the amount of compensation.[94]

These challenges may justify the adoption of implementing regulations directed specifically to disputes under the Investment Protocol to address the particularities of state-to-state investment disputes better.

D Regionalization and MERCOSUR Treaty Negotiations with Third Parties

One of the challenges that MERCOSUR States Parties face is negotiating investment provisions with third countries, given that they have ACFI-based agreements, as in the case of the MERCOSUR Investment Protocol, together with classical BITs (this last except for Brazil). As it can be seen from the content of the recent FTAs concluded by MERCOSUR, the ACFI-type provisions have had an *in crescendo* influence in those agreements.

MERCOSUR–EU trade talks date back to the 1990s.[95] Since then, negotiations were stopped and relaunched several times due to different factors. On 28 June 2019,

92. Vidigal & Stevens, *supra*, n. 52, at 511.
93. *See* Brazil-Mexico ACFI, Art. 19.2; Brazil-Colombia ACFI, Art. 23.2; Brazil-Chile ACFI, Art. 7.3, Brazil-Peru ETEA, Art. 2.21.2, Brazil-Ecuador ACFI, Art. 25.2.
94. According to ACFIs with Mexico, Colombia and Ecuador, the parties may request the arbitral tribunal to determine the amount to be compensated, and the compensation shall be transmitted by the State Party to the affected investor, with the deduction of the arbitration costs. *See* Brazil-Mexico ACFI, Art. 19.2; Brazil-Colombia ACFI, Art. 23.14; Brazil-Ecuador ACFI, Art. 25.13.c.
95. For a sequence of the main developments and documents involving the MECOSUR and EU negotiations, *see* MERCOSUR-European Union, Background and Negotiations available at http://www.sice.oas.org/tpd/mer_eu/mer_eu_e.asp (accessed 16 Dec. 2024).

MERCOSUR and the EU reached an 'agreement in principle' for a comprehensive trade agreement.[96] There is no 'investment chapter' in the agreement, although at the same point, there were discussions on such a chapter, but focused on the promotion and establishment phase of investments.[97] However, there are different provisions dealing with investments in that FTA. The agreement covers investment liberalization ('establishment'), in both the services and non-services sectors, and it provides for market access and national treatment.[98] The parties recognize the right to regulate and agree that they should not lower labour or environmental standards to attract trade and investment.[99] The agreement furthermore grants the 'free movement of capital relating to direct investments' with regard to transactions on the capital and financial account of the balance of payments.[100] However, the agreement does not include investment protection standards or investment dispute settlement mechanisms specifically dealing with investments.

So, the impact of the ACFIs or the Investment Protocol is somewhat limited in the agreement with the EU, perhaps because the mandate on investments was rather limited, and the negotiations were well advanced when the Brazilian ACFIs' negotiations started and the Investment Protocol was adopted. Another factor that may have influenced the negotiations is that three of the four MERCOSUR members already had BITs with numerous EU Member States (Argentina nineteen BITs, Paraguay twelve BITs and Uruguay thirteen BITs).

By contrast, in the subsequent FTAs negotiated by MERCOSUR, the impact appears to be much higher. On 23 August 2019, the Member States of the EFTA and of MERCOSUR concluded in substance the negotiations on an FTA.[101] The agreement includes a chapter on 'investments', which grants non-discriminatory rights of establishment ('commercial presence') in economic sectors included in the schedules. The chapter also reaffirms the Parties' right to regulate and includes a provision on the corporate social responsibility of enterprises. The chapter foresees that investors can

96. *See* New EU-Mercosur trade agreement: The agreement in principle (Brussels, 1 Jul. 2019). Available at https://policy.trade.ec.europa.eu/eu-trade-relationships-country-and-region/countries-and-regions/mercosur/eu-mercosur-agreement_en (accessed 16 Dec. 2024).
97. *See* First Meeting of the EU-Mercosur biregional negotiations committee (6-7 Apr. 2000) ('General principles and objectives of trade negotiations [include t]he encouragement of an open and non-discriminatory investment climate') and Mercosur-European Union, Mercosur's Completed Offer on Investment (24 Sep. 2004) ('The offer remains conditional on the final text of the Investment Chapter of the Mercosur-EU agreement, as well as on the other Chapters affecting investment where definition is still pending'). Available at http://www.sice.oas.org/tpd/mer_eu/mer_eu_e.asp#:~:text=MERCOSUR%20and%20the%20European%20Union,as%20of%201%20July%201999 (accessed 16 Dec. 2024).
98. EU-Mercosur Association Agreement, Chapter 'Trade in Services and Establishment', Arts 2 and 3. The text of the agreement is available at https://policy.trade.ec.europa.eu/eu-trade-relationships-country-and-region/countries-and-regions/mercosur/eu-mercosur-agreement/text-agreement_en (accessed 16 Dec. 2024).
99. EU-Mercosur Association Agreement, Chapter 'Trade and Sustainable Development', Art. 2.
100. EU-Mercosur Association Agreement, Chapter 'Current Payments and Capital Movements', Art. 1.
101. The text of the agreement is not public yet. *See* EFTA Secretariat, 'Conclusion in Substance of the EFTA – MERCOSUR Free Trade Negotiations' (24 Aug. 2019), https://www.efta.int/sites/default/files/documents/legal-texts/free-trade-relations/mercosur/2019-08-24-EFTA-Mercosur-Chapter-Description-of-FTA.pdf (accessed 16 Dec. 2024).

submit enquiries to the national focal points. In the chapter on 'institutional provisions', a joint committee is established, comprising of representatives of each party, to supervise and administer the agreement and to oversee its further development. The chapter on 'dispute settlement' provides for state-to-state amicable resolution under the consultation mechanisms and arbitration.[102]

Even though the FTA with the EU influenced to some extent the one with EFTA (the negotiations in the last years were carried out in parallel), the impact of the Investment Protocol appears to be much higher on the latter. One factor that may have influenced this is that the network of IIAs between blocs was rather limited: from the four EFTA Member States, only Switzerland had concluded BITs with Argentina, Paraguay and Uruguay.

The impact is even higher in FTA MERCOSUR-Singapore concluded in 2023.[103] The agreement includes a chapter on 'investments' but focused on 'commercial presence' (rather than on 'investments' per se), understood as 'any type of business establishment within the territory of a State Party, for the purpose of performing an economic activity'.[104] As regards substantive standards, the chapter provides for national treatment, access to justice and due process of law and the treatment due to payments and transfers.[105] Concerning the administration of the chapter and the facilitation of investments, it provides that it will be administered by the Subcommittee on Investment under the Joint Committee, mandates the establishment of national focal points, and creates dispute prevention and mediation mechanisms.[106]

An important aspect of the agreement with Singapore is that (in an annex) it includes a set of obligations that apply to all the contracting parties except Argentina.[107] Unlike the chapter, the annex is focused on 'investments' (with a definition focused on property rights) and not on 'commercial presence'.[108] It includes provisions on the treatment of investments which includes 'manifestly abusive treatment', 'discrimination in matters of law enforcement', direct expropriation and compensation for losses.[109] The chapter on dispute settlement provides for dispute settlement mechanisms between the parties (i.e., state-to-state): consultations, the intervention of the Joint Committee and arbitration.[110]

As can be seen, the agreement with Singapore incorporates many of the Investment Protocol's features while excluding Argentina from an important part of those features. A factor of relevance is that neither of the MERCOSUR members has a BIT

102. *Ibid.*
103. FTA between MERCOSUR and Singapore (signed 7 Dec. 2023). The text of the agreement is available at https://www.mercosur.int/acuerdo-de-libre-comercio-entre-el-mercosur-y-la-republica-de-singapur/ (accessed 16 Dec. 2024).
104. FTA MERCOSUR – Singapore, Art. 9.1.(a). The chapter applies to measures affecting: (a) juridical or natural persons in respect of a commercial presence and (b) commercial presence of such juridical or natural persons, Art. 9.2.
105. FTA MERCOSUR – Singapore, Art. 9.3, 9.5 and 9.10.
106. FTA MERCOSUR – Singapore, Art. 9.13, 9.14 and 9.15.
107. The chapter includes an Annex on 'Additional Investment Provisions for Brazil, Paraguay, Uruguay and Singapore' (i.e., excluding Argentina).
108. FTA MERCOSUR – Singapore, Annex, Art. 9-A.3.
109. FTA MERCOSUR – Singapore, Annex, Art. 9-A.4, 9-A.5 and 9-A.2.
110. FTA MERCOSUR – Singapore, Art. 18.2, 18.6, 18.7 and 18.8.

with Singapore. The fact that Argentina does not have an agreement with Singapore would imply that it preferred to avoid having strong investment obligations in the agreement.

IV CONCLUSION

Regionalization of the Brazilian ACFI model in MERCOSUR has many positive aspects. The ACFI model emphasizes investment facilitation and dispute prevention, which can improve the overall climate for FDI and influence the development of institutional mechanisms both within each MERCOSUR member and at the MERCOSUR level. At the same time, that regionalization brings different challenges.

The first challenge is the coexistence of two investment regimes in MERCOSUR and in the region. On the one hand, there is the ACFI-based regime of the MERCOSUR ICFP and Brazil's ACFIs. On the other, there is the regime in the other countries' investment agreements, based on classical BIT protection (i.e., classical substantive standards plus ISDS). All indications are that this coexistence is here to stay.

Governments in the region thus face challenges in their treaty planning and implementation. For instance, MERCOSUR's investment negotiations must take into account both competing regimes. MERCOSUR's agreement with Singapore, with its special provisions for some MERCOSUR members, is an example of this. Another consequence is that MERCOSUR has no common policy in international fora such as UNCITRAL Working Group III on ISDS Reform, and each MERCOSUR State Party speaks for itself, although they agree on many issues.[111]

The second challenge is the impact of MERCOSUR's regionalization of Brazil's ACFI model as an alternative to classical IIAs. Brazil's National Congress asserted concerning the MERCOSUR Investment Protocol that 'for the Brazilian Party, this Protocol represents another step towards the consolidation of this model of agreements'.[112] The presence of ACFI-type provisions in MERCOSUR FTAs with third states (such as EFTA and Singapore) reinforces this potential trend. Yet, it is not clear whether other states can adopt the Brazil ACFI model overall in their investment policies. The concept exists of exempting some states including Brazil from ISDS, but other states are also attempting to include ACFI-type provisions in some of their investment treaty negotiations (as in the Angola-EU Sustainable Investment Facilitation Agreement).[113] Should countries be expected to follow a single consistent approach in their investment law-making? The answer so far appears to be in general on

111. On Brazil's participation at the UNCITRAL WGIII, *see* Roberts & St John, *supra* n. 76, at 1172-1176 and Choer Moraes, *supra* n. 13.

112. Relatório Câmara dos Deputados, Comissão de Relações e de Defensa Nacional, *Projecto de Decreto Legislativo No. 1.010, de 2018*, https://www.camara.leg.br/proposicoesWeb/prop_mostrarintegra?codteor=1695132&filename=Tramitacao-PRL%201%20CREDN%20=%3E%20PDC%201010/2018 (accessed 16 Dec. 2024).

113. Sustainable Investment Facilitation Agreement between the EU and the Republic of Angola (signed 17 Nov. 2023). The object of the agreement is to facilitate the 'attraction, expansion and retention' of investments for the purposes of economic diversification and sustainable development (Art. 1). The agreement includes, *inter alia*, the following provisions dealing with

the negative since countries that have concluded ACFIs with Brazil keep concluding traditional BITs.

The third challenge is how MERCOSUR's ICFP interacts with existing MERCOSUR dispute settlement procedures and mechanisms, which were targeted at resolving trade disputes but have been seldom used and have no provisions for state-to-state investment claims. Since Brazil's ACFIs were conceived of in a trade dispute settlement context, the ACFI-model ICFP may be compatible with the trade-oriented MERCOSUR dispute settlement mechanisms, but MERCOSUR may need to adopt implementing regulations addressed specifically to the particularities of state-to-state investment disputes. In recent years, almost all intra-MERCOSUR disputes have been resolved not through MERCOSUR adjudication but by diplomatic negotiation or alternative dispute resolution. If a comparable situation prevails for state-to-state investment disputes, MERCOSUR may need to reinforce alternative dispute resolution options for its members.

The fourth challenge relates to the implementation of the Protocol at the national level. Brazil has already adopted an innovative implementing regulation, which could provide a model for the other States Parties. But the ACFI model is the *only* model for Brazil's investment agreements. For other states, implementation is complicated by their participation both in ACFIs and in classic BITs. A country with BITs may have a concern that a prevention mechanism at the local level could have a negative impact on the host state's position in potential BIT disputes.

The final challenge is of relevance for cross-border FDI within MERCOSUR. Cross-border investments among the states that have ratified the Protocol benefit immediately from the substantive obligations in the Investment Protocol. Yet, after all four MERCOSUR states ratify the Protocol, the Protocol's Joint Committee will start functioning and this can affect the dispute prevention and dispute settlement mechanisms available for states parties. Investors may need to explore (mainly through their states) alternative dispute resolution mechanisms or invoke the Protocol standards before domestic tribunals in the host state.

These observations concur with a more general one: the difficulty states face when trying to design a consistent investment policy or bring about policy change. The evidence demonstrates that it is not sufficient for a government to have experience in concluding investment agreements and defending investment claims or to have wise and expert negotiators and policy makers. To achieve real change requires all that, plus a sustained political will. For the MERCOSUR countries, and developing countries generally, that political will remains indispensable.

treatment: most-favoured-nation treatment (Art. 4), the 'administ[ration] in a reasonable, objective and impartial manner' of measures affecting investments (Art. 6), and transparency obligations (Arts 9 and 10). Concerning the governance of the agreement, each party shall establish investment facilitation focal points (Art. 22), and the parties establish a Committee on Investment Facilitation (Art. 43). As regards dispute avoidance and settlement, the treaty provides for consultations, mutually agreed solutions, mediation, and state-to-state arbitration (Arts 36 to 41). The treaty includes numerous provisions on sustainable development and carve-outs.

CHAPTER 13

ASEAN Centrality in Investment Arbitration Rulemaking

Jeffrey (Chieh) Lo & Pasha L. Hsieh[*]

This chapter explores the central role of the Association of Southeast Asian Nations (ASEAN) in shaping investment arbitration rulemaking in the Asia-Pacific and beyond. Built upon the principle of ASEAN centrality, the ASEAN Economic Community (AEC) and the Regional Comprehensive Economic Partnership (RCEP) have energized an Asia-wide consensus on investment reforms. Pivotal features of recent ASEAN-led investment provisions on investment liberalization, facilitation, and investor-state dispute settlement (ISDS) demonstrate the pragmatic incrementalism of ASEAN's legalization approach. Collectively, these developments will contribute to the emergence of new Asian regionalism and enrich international investment law.

I INTRODUCTION

International investment law has been facing a strong backlash recently. Critics argue that the abstract, vague substantive treatment standards, along with the investor-state dispute settlement (ISDS) mechanism, have hindered states' sovereign right to regulate and ability to adopt socially beneficial policies.[1] To safeguard policy spaces, countries have adopted diverse "reform options," ranging from terminating their international

* We are grateful for the research grants provided by the Jean Monnet Chair Program and the Ministries of Education of Singapore and Taiwan.

1. *See, e.g.*, Gus Van Harten, *Perceived Bias in Investment Treaty Arbitration*, *in* The Backlash Against Investment Arbitration: Perceptions and Reality 433, 433-445 (Claire Balchin et al. eds, 2010).

investment agreements (IIAs) to implementing modernized substantive and procedural rules.[2] The United Nations Commission on International Trade Law (UNCITRAL) also entrusted Working Group III to identify the insufficiencies of the current regime and explore procedural reforms for ISDS.[3]

While the development of international investment law has mostly been driven by Western countries, Asia's influence has increased due to its growing importance in the global economy, enhanced regionalism, and sophistication in international investment rulemaking.[4] At the center of Asia's escalating status lies the economic integration process led by the Association of Southeast Asian Nations (ASEAN) based on the principle of "ASEAN centrality."[5] This principle ensures the bloc's indispensable role in the regional architecture including security and economic regionalism.

The ASEAN Economic Community (AEC) and the "ASEAN Plus One" free trade agreements (FTAs) with major regional economies have constructed the legal regimes of new Asian regionalism, which led to the Regional Comprehensive Economic Partnership (RCEP).[6] The importance of RCEP is self-explanatory when looking at the economic scale it represents. As the world's largest FTA, the fifteen RCEP parties encompass ASEAN, China, Japan, Korea, Australia and New Zealand, representing 30% of global GDP and 26.2% of foreign direct investment flows.[7]

RCEP members, including ASEAN countries, are parties to various IIAs that comprise investment chapters of FTAs and bilateral investment treaties (BITs). Several RCEP parties are frequent respondents or home states of claimant investors in investment treaty arbitrations. According to the United Nations Conference on Trade and Development's (UNCTAD's) latest statistics, ASEAN as a bloc entered into fourteen IIAs and thirteen of them are in force.[8] Notably, Singapore and Indonesia are parties of more than hundred IIAs.[9] In terms of known investment treaty arbitration,

2. To clarify, the authors use the term "reform options" broadly to refer to the host state's response to the perceived flaws in the substantive investment protection provisions or the ISDS mechanism. UNCTAD compiled the so-called reform options in its 2015 World Investment Report and its "reform package" in 2018. However, these options were in existence before the abovementioned works of UNCTAD and had been employed by newer generation IIAs. *See* UNCTAD, *UNCTAD's Reform Package for the International Investment Regime*, 3, 32-70 (2018), https://investmentpolicy.unctad.org/uploaded-files/document/UNCTAD_Reform_Package_2018.pdf (accessed Dec. 16, 2024).
3. Malcolm Langford et al., *Special Issue: UNCITRAL and Investment Arbitration Reform—Matching Concerns and Solutions: An Introduction*, 21 J. World Invest. & Trade 16, 172-177 (2020) https://doi.org/10.1163/22119000-12340171.
4. Junji Nakagawa, *Introduction, in* Asian Perspectives on International Investment Law, 1 (Junji Nakagawa ed., 2019); *see also generally* Kenneth J. Vandevelde, *Bilateral Investment Treaties: History, Policy, and Interpretation*, 19-74 (2010).
5. ASEAN Centrality is a guiding principle enshrined in the ASEAN Charter and thereafter was reiterated in the ASEAN Framework for the RCEP to acknowledge the RCEP as "an ASEAN-led process."
6. Joint Leaders' Statement on the RCEP (Joint Leaders' Statement on the RCEP) (2020).
7. UNCTAD, *World Investment Report 2021: Investing in Sustainable Recovery*, 6 (2021).
8. *Investment Dispute Settlement Navigator and International Investment Agreements Navigator*, United Nations Conference on Trade and Development Investment Policy Hub, https://investmentpolicy.unctad.org (accessed Dec. 16, 2024).
9. *Ibid.*

ASEAN countries have been respondents in thirty-six cases.[10] They include some high-profile disputes such as *Amco v. Indonesia* and *SGS v. Philippines*.[11]

ASEAN states were also the home states of the claimants in seventeen cases. The respondent states in these cases include other ASEAN countries, India and Taiwan.[12] These developments demonstrate the increasing involvement in the international investment regime of ASEAN countries. Notwithstanding their presence at multilateral forums such as Working Group III, the Asian countries have not formed a common position on reform directions.[13] Hence, this chapter sheds light on Asian approaches to investment rulemaking critical to the development of international arbitration.

II ASEAN CENTRALITY IN NEW ASIAN REGIONALISM

Before delving into the legal architecture of ASEAN integration, it is essential to grasp the context of current global trends. Echoing the first wave of regionalism in the 1950s and 1960s, ASEAN was established as a geopolitical alliance aiming to contain the potential expansion of the communist bloc.[14] However, along with the changing geopolitical environment, ASEAN gained new momentum in the second wave of regionalism in the 1980s and 1990s.[15] The competition from the deeper economic integration in Europe and North America, represented by the European Union (EU) and the North American Free Trade Agreement (NAFTA), motivated ASEAN to accelerate on a similar course.[16] A major milestone was the signing of "ASEAN Plus Three," which established a framework subsequently expanded to include "ASEAN Plus Six" members, with the addition of Australia, India, and New Zealand.[17]

The most recent wave of regionalism came after the 2000s. New Asian regionalism highlighting this third wave of regionalism emerged. The underpinning structure of this new Asian regionalism is the framework of ASEAN's internal and external

10. *Ibid.*
11. *Amco Asia Corporation and others v. Republic of Indonesia*, ICSID Case No. ARB/81/1 & *SGS Société Générale de Surveillance S.A. v. Republic of the Philippines*, ICSID Case No. ARB/02/6.
12. *Id.* The case against Taiwan was brought by a Singaporean investor for the alleged breach of the Singapore-Taiwan FTA. *See generally* Jeffrey (Chieh) Lo, *A Story of TWO DISPUTES: (Potential) Investment Claims That Hit Taiwan under Singapore-Taiwan FTA (ASTEP)*, 38 Chinese (Taiwan) YB Int'l L. 138, 149-55 (2020) https://doi.org/10.1163/9789004501638_007.
13. *See* submissions from Asian governments, United Nations Commission on International Trade Law: Working Group III: Investor-State Dispute Settlement Reform, https://uncitral.un.org/en/working_groups/3/investor-state (accessed Dec. 16, 2024).
14. Jagdish Bhagwati, *Termites in the Trading System: How Preferential Agreements Undermine Free Trade*, 29-32 (2008).
15. One significant change is that after the collapse of the Soviet bloc in the 1990s, ASEAN opened the door for former communist foes—Cambodia, Laos and Vietnam and therefore expanded its reach. *See* Siow Yue Chia & Michael G. Plummer, *ASEAN Economic Cooperation and Integration: Progress, Challenges and Future Directions*, 1-4 (2015); Asian Development Bank Institute, *ASEAN 2030: Toward a Borderless Economic Community*, 4-7 (2014).
16. Richard Baldwin, "A Domino Theory of Regionalism," NBER Working Paper Series, No. 4465 (1993), at 2-5; Rodolfo C. Severino, *Southeast Asia in Search of an ASEAN Community: Insights from the Former ASEAN Secretary-General*, 222-223 (2006).
17. It covers ten ASEAN countries, China, Japan and Korea.

economic integration.[18] The structure encompasses the establishment of AEC in 2015 and the signing of RCEP in 2020.[19] In this latest wave of regionalism, a new approach reflecting ASEAN members' pragmatic incrementalism emerged. This approach features a higher degree of legalization while allowing for structural flexibility, which is widely different from the strategy employed by ASEAN members in the first and second waves of regionalism. At that time, ASEAN members used to rely on the so-called ASEAN way, which is a strategy emphasizing collective and consensual decision-making among the members. As a result, the international instruments promoting regional integration concluded among the ASEAN members at that time were mostly of a non-binding, soft-law nature and therefore were deemed as having a lower degree of legalization.

This traditional view no longer offers a sufficient account of ASEAN's new approach. The first feature of the new strategy, namely "the higher degree of legalization," in the context of investment rulemaking, is reflected through the use of hard-law instruments to establish core legal obligations among ASEAN members or contracting parties. In this respect, the investment rules under the AEC, the ASEAN Plus Six FTAs and the RCEP all impose clear hard-legal obligations to enhance the level of investment liberalization and protection. The new rules also addressed the ambiguity that existed in the previous instruments such as the 1987 Agreement for the Promotion and Protection of Investments (commonly known as the ASEAN Investment Guarantee Agreement, IGA) and the 1998 Framework Agreement on the ASEAN Investment Area (AIA). These hard-law instruments increased the certainty of the legal regime and enhanced the level of investment protection as well as liberalization in the region.

However, these instruments also allow for sufficient flexibility for contracting parties. The approach of the RCEP and the AEC investment/trade-in-service liberalization negotiation provide significant examples. With regard to the RCEP, the investment chapter incorporates country-specific requirements concerning the protected investments. RECP parties also postponed the negotiation for an ISDS mechanism to secure the benefit of other less contentious matters. For the AEC's investment/trade-in-service liberalization, packages of commitments were made in rounds of negotiations, gradually increasing the level of liberalization in the region.

Similarly, these instruments employed various designs to safeguard contracting parties' regulatory spaces. Examples may be found in the unique, narrow formulation of fair and equitable treatment (FET), the linking of the definition of expropriation with domestic law, and the inclusion of investment facilitation and investment promotion provisions under the RCEP and the AEC. These designs mitigate ASEAN Member States' or contracting parties' concern over the possible restraint on sovereignty and therefore successfully enlisted their support over time. At first glance, this approach might seem to produce fewer results in the short run. Yet, in the long run, this strategy has proven to be more pragmatic and can yield greater results. How these features are

18. Pasha L. Hsieh, *New Asian Regionalism in International Economic Law*, 107-11 (2022).
19. ASEAN concluded six "ASEAN Plus One" FTAs sequentially with seven economies, including China, Japan, India, Korea, Australia, New Zealand, and Hong Kong.

reflected in investment rulemaking under the AEC, the ASEAN Plus Six FTAs and the RCEP will be discussed in detail below.

III ASEAN'S INVESTMENT REGIME

The creation of the AEC in 2015 is a key milestone of ASEAN's internal regionalism.[20] Under AEC Blueprint 2025, the AEC aims to build "a more unified market" by facilitating "the seamless movement of goods, services, investment, capital and skilled labour."[21] Investment protection and liberalization are no doubt key areas of the AEC. Two instruments of particular importance are the ASEAN Comprehensive Investment Agreement (ACIA) and the ASEAN Trade in Services Agreement (ATISA). The ACIA governs the protection and liberalization of investments in agriculture, fishery, forestry, manufacturing, mining, and quarrying sectors, as well as related service sectors.[22] The ATISA regulates the liberalization of investment in service sectors.[23]

A Investment Protection

The ACIA modernizes the international rules for intra-ASEAN investments. Signed in 2009, the ACIA replaces and consolidates the IGA and AIA.[24] As a single instrument covering intra-ASEAN investment protection and investment liberalization, the ACIA avoided the ambiguity of the legal relations between the IGA and AIA.[25] Moreover, the ACIA implements various reform options to balance investment protection and host states' right to regulate.[26]

Starting from the protected investments under the ACIA, ASEAN members opted for a broad, non-exhaustive, and asset-based definition of investments that encompasses "every kind of asset."[27] Compared with the strict approach under the IGA, the ACIA significantly broadens the scope of protection.[28] Based on US IIA practices, the ACIA excludes assets that lack "the characteristics of an investment," including the commitment of capital, the expectation of gain or profit, or the assumption of risk.[29] Certain one-off transactions are also excluded from the definition of investment.[30]

20. Charter of the Association of Southeast Asian Nations (2007), Arts 1(1) and 3.
21. ASEAN Economic Community Blueprint 2025 (2015) (AEC Blueprint 2025), para. 7.
22. ASEAN Comprehensive Investment Agreement (2009) (ACIA), Art. 3(3).
23. ASEAN Trade in Services Agreement (2020) (ATISA), Arts 1-3. *See also* ASEAN, ASEAN Integration Report, 30 (2019).
24. Julien Chaisse & Sufian Jusoh, *The ASEAN Comprehensive Investment Agreement: The Regionalisation of Laws and Policy on Foreign Investment*, 67-68 (2016).
25. For instance, in *Yaung Chi Oo Trading Pte Ltd v. Government of the Union of Myanmar*, 30 ILM 15, the relations between ASEAN's previous intra-investment pacts had become an issue.
26. For the "options" of IIA reform, *see* UNCTAD, *supra* n. 2.
27. ACIA, Art. 4(c).
28. ASEAN Investment Guarantee Agreement (IGA), Arts 1(3) and 2(1).
29. ACIA, Art. 4(c), n. 2.
30. ACIA, Art. 4(c), n. 3.

The protected investor under the ACIA includes natural and juridical persons of an ASEAN member. While a foreign-owned or controlled enterprise is entitled to the ACIA's protection if it is incorporated in an ASEAN country, the ACIA requires such enterprise to maintain "substantive business operations" in an ASEAN member.[31] This "denial of benefit" provision prevents non-ASEAN investors from free-riding the ACIA's protection.[32]

More recent designs are incorporated into the ACIA's substantive protection provisions. Its provision of FET is deliberately narrow. The host country is in breach of FET under the ACIA only where there is a "denial of justice in legal and administrative proceedings."[33] A further clarification is also added that a breach of other provisions of the ACIA or other international agreements does not constitute a breach of the FET or full protection and security provision in itself.[34] This unique formulation perhaps reflects the concerns of ASEAN members on the expansive scope of FET developed by the investment arbitral jurisprudence, which significantly reduced the scope of protection but allowed more certainty for the host states.[35]

Although national treatment (NT) and most-favored-nation (MFN) treatment under the ACIA extends to both the pre- and post-establishment stages, the ISDS mechanism does not apply to the pre-establishment phase.[36] Moreover, the MFN clause of the ACIA does not apply to ISDS proceedings in other agreements.[37] This is a response to the unfavorable development of arbitral jurisprudence.[38] Importantly, expropriation is an area where the ACIA safeguards the host state's regulatory spaces. The ACIA, modeled after newer US IIAs, provides clearer rules of what constitutes expropriation, the conditions under which expropriation may be lawfully made, and the standards of compensation.[39] An annex is provided to further clarify the scope of the provision.[40] Less commonly seen in other IIAs, however, is a footnote that ties "any measure of expropriation relating to land" back to the definition and procedural requirement of Member States' respective laws and regulations.[41]

Finally, the ACIA maintains the treaty-based arbitration as the ISDS mechanism between the ASEAN members. To increase certainty, the ACIA incorporated detailed arbitration procedures applicable notwithstanding which forum the claimant

31. ACIA, Arts 3(1), 4(d) and 19; Chaisse & Jusoh, *supra* n. 24, at 76-78; Luke Nottage, *The Investment Chapter and ISDS in the TPP: Lessons from Southeast Asia*, ISEAS Yusof Ishak Institute Economics Working Paper (2017), No. 2017-2, 2-3.
32. ACIA, Art. 19.
33. ACIA, Art. 11.
34. ACIA, Art. 11.
35. Traditionally, FET has been interpreted to incorporate broader elements.
36. ACIA, Art. 5, 6 & 32(a).
37. ACIA, Art. 6, n. 4(1).
38. Wolfgang Alschner, *The Impact of Investment Arbitration on Investment Treaty Design: Myth Versus Reality*, 42(1) Yale J. Int'l L. 1, 58 (2017) https://doi.org/10.2139/ssrn.2781525, explaining the rulemaking response to arbitral decision on the scope of MFN clause.
39. ACIA, Art. 14.
40. ACIA, Annex (2).
41. ACIA, Art. 14, nn. 9-10.

chooses.[42] These provisions demonstrate a recent trend to secure more procedural certainty in investment arbitration. A major example is Article 34, which stipulates condition precedents of Member States' consent to arbitrate. In addition, characterizing the ACIA's regional focus, the ACIA listed "Regional Centre for Arbitration at Kuala Lumpur or any other regional centre for arbitration in ASEAN" as one of the forums for investment arbitration.[43]

B Investment and Services Liberalization

In terms of investment liberalization, the ACIA aims at "progressive liberalization" of existing restrictions and strengthening transparency of investment rules.[44] After the adoption of the Fourth Protocol, the ASEAN members changed the original single negative-list annex to two-annex negative lists of liberalization commitments.[45] ASEAN members indicated their current non-conforming measures in the first annex and reserved future spaces for measures in the second annex under this new formulation.[46]

For the liberalization of investment in service sectors, the ATISA that came into force only in 2021 consolidates the commitments of ASEAN members under the older 1995 ASEAN Framework Agreement on Services (AFAS).[47] The AFAS adopts a packaged, positive-list commitment structure. Service liberalization commitments were made in various rounds of negotiations. Each package of commitment would make further liberalization progress in terms of foreign equity restrictions, market access and national treatment reservations.[48]

All packages constitute an integral part of the AFAS but are not self-executing.[49] Each package of service commitments requires ratification in each Member State before it can take effect domestically. The package structure is again a representation of ASEAN's pragmatic incrementalism. While the ATISA is based on the liberalization efforts in the packages of commitments reached under AFAS, the ATISA adopts a negative-list approach, enhancing transparency for foreign investors and facilitating domestic regulatory reform.[50]

42. Zewei Zhong, *The ASEAN Comprehensive Investment Agreement: Realizing a Regional Community*, 6(1) Asian J. Comp. L. 1, 4-5 (2011) https://doi.org/10.1017/s219460780000048x.
43. ACIA, Art. 33.1(e).
44. AEC Blueprint 2025, para. 14; ACIA, Art. 1.
45. Ministry of Trade and Industry Singapore (MTI), Minister Chan Chun Sing at the 25th ASEAN Economic Ministers' Retreat in Phuket, Thailand, at 4 (2019).
46. *Ibid.*, fn. 6, 4.
47. ASEAN, n. 40, 34. The AFAS and ATISA adopt the same "modes" of commitments as the General Agreement on Trade in Services, under which Mode 3 (commercial presence) governs services provided in the form of local branches, subsidiaries, and foreign equity restrictions.
48. Jayant Menon & Anna Cassandra Melendez, *Realizing an ASEAN Economic Community: Progress and Remaining Challenges*, Asian Development Bank Working Paper Series, 7 (2015).
49. ASEAN Framework Agreement on Services (1995) (AFAS), Art. VIII.
50. Tham Siew Yean, *ASEAN Trade in Services Agreement (ATISA): Advancing Services Liberalization for ASEAN?*, ISEAS Perspective, Issue 2019 No. 54, 4-6 (2019).

C Investment Facilitation and Investment Promotion

Fortifying investment promotion and facilitation has gained some popularity as a reform option for IIAs.[51] ASEAN countries are among the earliest to incorporate investment facilitation and promotion provisions in their IIAs. For instance, the IGA and the AIA each contain certain investment promotion or facilitation elements.[52] The ACIA continued this tradition. Article 21 requires ASEAN states to increase transparency with timely notification to the AIA council of any new IIA they entered into or changes in its investment legislation. Articles 24 and 25 further urge ASEAN members to cooperate to share relevant information among Member States and investors and strengthen the capacity of Member States. These provisions move beyond traditional IIAs' formulation of attracting investments by offering protection and creating a favorable environment for investment.

IV RCEP: FORGING AN ASIAN CONSENSUS

Moving from the intra-ASEAN economic integration to a broader regional integration perspective, we now turn to the role of the RCEP in investment rulemaking. The negotiation of the RCEP as the world's largest FTA by economic scale was based on the initiative of ASEAN and was led by ASEAN rather than China.[53] The RCEP reinforces the notion of ASEAN centrality in regional frameworks.[54] The combination of hard-law rules and structured flexibility shown in the ACIA was also reflected in the RCEP.

A Pivotal Investment Rules and Commitments

Both the RCEP and the ACIA include common core pillars of investment protection, liberalization, promotion, and facilitation. Nevertheless, the RCEP employs a more cautious approach compared with ACIA.[55] The RCEP adopted the asset-based definition of investment similar to the ACIA while incorporating country-specific restrictions. For Cambodia, Indonesia, and Vietnam, an investment "admitted" refers to an

51. UNCTAD, *supra* n. 2, 23, 59-63.
52. Chaisse & Jusoh, *supra* n. 24, 48-49.
53. Parties to the ASEAN Framework for the RCEP acknowledged the RCEP as "an ASEAN-led process." *See generally* ASEAN Framework for RCEP (2011).
54. Joint Leaders' Statement on the RCEP, *supra* n. 6; Grace Ho, *RCEP Negotiators Recount Twists and Turns in 8-year Journey to World's Biggest Trade Pact*, Straits Times (Nov. 28, 2020), https://www.straitstimes.com/business/economy/rcep-negotiators-recount-twists-and-turns-in-8-year-journey-to-worlds-biggest-trade (accessed Dec. 16, 2024); Deng Xijun, *RCEP: Historic Milestone for ASEAN Centrality*, Jakarta Post (Nov. 20, 2020), https://www.thejakartapost.com/academia/2020/11/20/rcep-historic-milestone-for-asean-centrality.html (accessed Dec. 16, 2024).
55. United Nations Economic Commission for Asia and the Pacific (UNESCAP), *Asia-Pacific Trade and Investment Trends: Foreign Direct Investment Trends and Outlook in Asia and the Pacific*, 26 (2020/2021); Alicia Nicholls, *RCEP Investment Rules: Help or Hindrances to Asia's COVID-19 Recovery?* (*Afronomics Law*, Feb. 17, 2021), https://www.afronomicslaw.org/category/analysis/rcep-investment-rules-help-or-hindrances-asias-covid-19-recovery (accessed Dec. 16, 2024).

investment that "has been specifically registered or approved in writing."[56] For Malaysia and Thailand, the scope of protection is limited to "covered investments which, where applicable, have been specifically approved in writing for protection by their respective competent authorities."[57] Also, an investor can be a juridical person, but its branch is excluded from having "any right to make any claim against any" RCEP party.[58] These country-specific requirements establish closer ties between regional and domestic investment rules and restrict the scope of investment protection.

Various reform options are also adopted in substantive protection provisions. To illustrate, the uniquely narrow scope of FET under the ACIA is also adopted in the RCEP, with only slight differences in wording.[59] The RCEP further addressed that FET and full protection and security shall be accorded under the minimum standard of treatment (MST) of aliens under customary international law but does not require treatment beyond that standard.[60] Given the RCEP's unique and rather narrow formulation, it is interesting to observe the impact of this additional linkage with MST.[61]

Akin to the ACIA, the RCEP and its annex detail conditions and compensation for direct and indirect expropriation.[62] Despite the inclusion of pre- and post-establishment NT and MFN treatment, RCEP excludes "any international dispute resolution procedures or mechanisms under other existing or future international agreements" from the scope of MFN.[63] Therefore, the MFN provision cannot be utilized to import preferable ISDS mechanisms in other IIAs. These reform elements of the RCEP demonstrate an emerging consensus of Asian countries' investment rulemaking and could serve as a reference point for further harmonization.

As for investment liberalization in service sectors, the RCEP follows a unique hybrid model where the parties adopt different approaches in making commitments. Eight parties used the positive-list approach under Annex II, whereas seven other parties followed the negative-list approach by including their reservations and non-conforming measures in Annex III.[64] The eight States opting for the positive-list approach are required to transition to the negative list. In particular, Cambodia, Laos and Myanmar were granted a fifteen-year transitional period.[65]

56. RCEP, Art. 10.1(a) and n. 2.
57. RCEP, Art. 10.1(a) and n. 1.
58. *Ibid.*, fn. 10.
59. RCEP, Art. 10.5(2), "fair and equitable treatment requires each Party not to deny justice in any legal or administrative proceedings."
60. UNCTAD, *supra* n. 2, at 36; *Ibid.*, Art. 10.5(1) and (2), n. 20, and Annex 10A.
61. For a discussion of arbitral jurisprudence on the FET, *see* Campbell McLachlan et al., *International Investment Arbitration*, paras 7.102-7.239 (2017).
62. RCEP, Art. 10.13, n. 25 and Annex 10B.
63. RCEP, Art. 10.4(3); Michael Ewing-Chow & Junianto James Losari, *The RCEP Investment Chapter: A State-to-State WTO Style System for Now* (*Kluwer Arbitration Blog*, Dec. 8, 2020), http://arbitrationblog.kluwerarbitration.com/2020/12/08/the-rcep-investment-chapter-a-state-to-state-wto-style-system-for-now/ (accessed Dec. 16, 2024).
64. RCEP, Annex II—Schedules of Specific Commitments for Services and Annex III—Schedules of Reservations and Non-Conforming Measures for Services and Investment.
65. These three countries include Cambodia, Laos and Myanmar. RCEP, Art. 8.12.7.

For the liberalization in other sectors, a similar approach to the ACIA Fourth Protocol was followed. Unlike the hybrid approach for services commitments, all RCEP members must schedule their liberalization commitments for investment under the negative-list approach in Annex III.[66] Following the prevalent Western IIA practice, the "non-conforming measures" under the RCEP were made in two separate lists. List A adopts a standstill and ratchet design, which does not allow the parties to make more restrictive amendments or addition of new measures to the list. No such limitation exists for the measures in List B.[67] This allows certain parties to introduce more restrictive amendments or additions to their investment regime, provided that such changes do not fall below the levels offered at the time of the RCEP's entry into force.[68] Similar to the ACIA, the RCEP also encompasses similar investment facilitation and promotion provisions.[69]

B Omission of the ISDS Mechanism

In Asia, a trend to limit the scope of ISDS, or even to replace ISDS with other alternatives such as state courts or state-to-state proceedings, is emerging.[70] This trend influenced the negotiation of the RCEP's investment chapter. One of the salient features of the RCEP is the omission of an ISDS mechanism. The RCEP only mandates that parties commence negotiations for ISDS within two years after the pact takes effect and finalize it in three years.[71]

The decision to postpone the ISDS negotiation was not the original plan. The RCEP parties had agreed to include the ISDS mechanism back in 2015.[72] Nevertheless, differences among parties soon arose. Japan and Korea advocated for detailed provisions on ISDS, while some ASEAN countries, along with Australia and New Zealand, expressed opposition.[73] Forging a consensus on ISDS became unrealistic. The RCEP parties thus decided to save ISDS issues for a future development program. Presently, the investors may still resort to the ISDS mechanism under current IIAs such as ASEAN Plus One FTAs, as the RCEP affirms "existing rights and obligations" arising from other pacts.[74]

---

66. RCEP, Art. 10.8; UNESCAP, *Asia-Pacific Trade and Investment Trends: Preferential Trade Agreements in Asia and the Pacific: Trends and Developments*, 9-10 (2020/2021).
67. RCEP Art. 10.8; New Zealand Ministry of Foreign Affairs and Trade, *Regional Comprehensive Economic Partnership: National Interest Analysis*, 41 and 85 (2020); RCEP, Annex III—Schedules of Reservations and Non-Conforming Measures for Services and Investment.
68. RCEP, Art. 10.8(1)(C).
69. RCEP, Art. 10.16 and 10.17.
70. UNCTAD, *supra* n. 2, 55-57.
71. RCEP, Art. 10.18(1) and (2).
72. Australia's Department of Foreign Affairs and Trade (DFAT), *Regional Comprehensive Economic Partnership (RCEP): Discussion Paper on Investment*, 4 (2017).
73. Belinda Townsend, *Update on the Regional Comprehensive Economic Partnership Agreement: NGO Briefing*, 2 (2015).
74. Agreement Establishing the ASEAN-Australia-New Zealand Free Trade Area (2009), Art. 2; Agreement on Comprehensive Economic Partnership among Member States of the Association of Southeast Asian Nations and Japan (2008), Art. 10; RCEP, Art. 20.2.1(b).

V NEW REQUIREMENTS AND ALTERNATIVE MECHANISMS FOR INVESTMENT DISPUTES

In parallel with the development of the AEC and the RCEP, the evolving approaches to IIAs by key countries offer insights into ASEAN's rulemaking on investment arbitration. Recent agreements in Asia, such as the ASEAN-Hong Kong Investment Agreement, the UK-Japan FTA, and the EU-China Comprehensive Investment Agreement, notably do not include ISDS mechanisms. Instead, these IIAs only require the parties to conduct further negotiation on the ISDS mechanism.[75] Important ASEAN states such as Indonesia also began to terminate their investment agreements and adopted reform options in its recent IIAs.[76]

In the 2018 Indonesia-Singapore BIT, the cooling-off period before the investor can submit for arbitration was lengthened to one year.[77] The 2019 Indonesia-Australia FTA adopted a binding "joint interpretation" mechanism which may be triggered by any disputing party or by the tribunal on its initiative.[78] This design enhanced the contracting parties' control of the arbitral tribunal's power to apply and interpret the IIA.[79] Moreover, under the 2019 amendments to the ASEAN-Japan FTA, Indonesia, alongside the Philippines, made the host state's separate written consent a condition to the submission to the International Centre for Settlement of Investment Disputes (ICSID) arbitration.[80] This is a noteworthy deviation from the conventional ISDS mechanism where host states made a standing offer to arbitrate with prospective investors.[81]

Another line of development among ASEAN countries is a move to strengthen domestic mechanisms as an alternative to the treaty-based ISDS. Indeed, this idea has already been embodied in ACIA which specifically stipulates that apart from arbitration

75. Agreement on Investment among the Governments of the Hong Kong Special Administrative Region of the People's Republic of China and the Member States of the Association of Southeast Asian Nations (2017), Art. 22.1(e); Agreement between the United Kingdom of Great Britain and Northern Ireland and Japan for a Comprehensive Economic Partnership (2020), Art. 8.5(3); EU-China Comprehensive Agreement on Investment (CAI): List of Sections (2021), section VI, subs. 2, Art. 3, https://trade.ec.europa.eu/doclib/press/index.cfm?id=2237 (accessed Dec. 16, 2024).
76. *See* Wenny Setiawati, *ICS from South East Asia Perspective in Handbook of International Investment Law and Policy*, 2540, 2542-2547 (Julien Chaisse et al. eds. 2021).
77. Indonesia-Singapore BIT (2015), Art. 8(2); Indonesia-Singapore BIT (2018), Art. 17(1); Drew Network Asia, *The New Singapore-Indonesia Investment Treaty and What It Means for Your Business*, 9 (2021).
78. Indonesia-Australia Comprehensive Economic Partnership Agreement (2019), Art. 14.33(3); Georgios Dimitropoulos, *Investor–State Dispute Settlement Reform and Theory of Institutional Design*, 9(4) J. Int'l Dispute Settlement 535-569, 560 (2018) https://doi.org/10.1093/jnlids/idy025.
79. *See, e.g.*, Anne van Aaken, *Control Mechanisms in International Investment Law in* The Foundations of International Investment Law: Bringing Theory into Practice, 409, 410-413 (Zachary Douglas et al. eds, 2014).
80. First Protocol to Amend the Agreement on Comprehensive Economic Partnership among Japan and Member States of the Association of Southeast Asian Nations (2019), Art. 51.13(9)(a) and n. 1. The Philippines also made a similar condition under ACIA. ACIA, Art. 33(1)(b) and n. 14.
81. UNCTAD, *supra* n. 2, 49-51.

under ICSID rules, the investors may resort to regional arbitration centers or domestic courts and administrative tribunals.[82] Singapore's efforts are representative. The Singapore International Commercial Court (SICC), which is a general division of Singapore's High Court, was launched in 2015.[83] As a claim of "international" and "commercial" nature is widely interpreted, the SICC is capable of adjudicating investor-state disputes.[84] Not long after, in 2017, the Singapore International Arbitration Centre (SIAC) adopted a new set of rules dedicated to investment treaty arbitration.[85] The recent case between Sanum Investments and Laos, under the China-Laos BIT, provides preliminary evidence for the roles of the SIAC and the SICC in investment disputes.[86]

VI CONCLUSION

The chapter explores the central role of ASEAN in shaping investment rulemaking in Asia and beyond. With ASEAN's growing economic importance and the initiatives under the principle of ASEAN centrality, the investment reforms under the AEC and the RCEP mark tremendous progress toward an Asian consensus. There are pivotal features. The recent ASEAN-led investment rulemaking efforts impose hard-law obligations but grant significant flexibility to parties. This pragmatic incrementalism energizes a new ASEAN Way. The deliberate exclusion of the ISDS mechanism in the RCEP reinforces the strategy of pragmatic incrementalism, which helped prevent deadlocks in negotiations and deferred the ISDS issue for future talks.

We have also identified several common features in the choice of investment reform options by the AEC and the RCEP. Both follow the ASEAN tradition of incorporating investment facilitation and liberalization provisions. These provisions encourage parties to actively create a favorable environment. Regarding reforms in investment protection provisions, both the ACIA and the RCEP include treaty language that clarifies or limits the scope of substantive provisions. Unique formulations, such as a narrower definition of FET or tying the definition of covered investment back to national legislation, indicate ASEAN's preference to secure the host state's regulatory spaces. Additionally, there is a procedural tendency to focus on the capacity of domestic institutions to settle investment disputes. Collectively, these developments will enhance ASEAN centrality in investment arbitration rulemaking and contribute to the normative consensus in new Asian regionalism.

82. ACIA, Art. 33(1).
83. Supreme Court of Judicature Act (Chapter 322) (2007), section 18A.
84. Rules of Court, Interpretation (O. 110, r. 1); Georgios Dimitropoulos, *International Commercial Courts in the "Modern Law of Nature": Adjudicatory Unilateralism in Special Economic Zones*, 24(1) J. Int'l Eco. L., 361-379, 366-367, 377-379 (2021) https://doi.org/10.1093/jiel/jgab017.
85. SIAC, *SIAC Investment Rules* (1st ed., 2017) https://siac.org.sg/wp-content/uploads/2022/06/SIAC-Investment-Rules-2017.pdf (accessed Dec. 16, 2024).
86. *Government of Lao People's Democratic Republic (LPDR) v. Sanum Investments Ltd* [2015] 2 SLR 322; *Lao Holdings NV v. LPDR and Sanum Investments Limited v. LPDR* [2021] SGHC (I) 10.

CHAPTER 14

Managed Diversity along the Legal Silk Road: The ASEAN-Asia Relationship and International Arbitration

Mark McLaughlin & Dilini Pathirana

Efforts to foster closer economic integration often focus on the alignment of standards with respect to goods and services. The harmonization of substantive regulations mitigates the inevitable friction caused by moving assets from one jurisdiction to another. In this chapter, it is argued that international arbitration plays a similar function in the Association of Southeast Asian Nations (ASEAN)-Asia relationship. By providing a neutral and reliable forum for dispute resolution, international arbitration helps manage legal diversity by creating a 'Legal Silk Road' on which commercial parties can engage with a familiar dispute resolution process without having to engage the local court system. The provision of common procedure – as opposed to harmonized substantive rules – enables states to facilitate cross-border trade and investment without overly intruding upon domestic regulation. Moreover, this function can also be seen at the state-state level, where arbitration has an increasingly prominent role in international agreements within ASEAN and between ASEAN and Asian States.

The collection of ancient trade routes that once comprised the 'Silk Road' have come to loom large in the pursuit of modern economic integration.[1] Across Asia and the Middle East, the Silk Road concept has inspired diplomatic exchanges between nations seeking to facilitate cross-border investment, cultural interchange, and geopolitical realignment. It is a key pillar of the 'Belt and Road Initiative' (BRI), a Chinese-led initiative for

1. *Vision and Actions on Jointly Building Silk Road Economic Belt and 21st-Century Maritime Silk Road*, issued by the National Development and Reform Commission, Ministry of Foreign Affairs, and Ministry of Commerce of the People's Republic of China, 28 Mar. 2015.

economic integration encompassing overland trade routes through central Asia (the Belt) and maritime trade routes through the Indo-Pacific (the Road). Funding for large-scale infrastructure projects seeks to resurrect ancient trade routes through improving regional connectivity with a view to realizing diversified and sustainable development.[2] Its legal underpinnings derive not from 'hard law' international agreements but soft law memorandums of understanding and agreements to cooperate.[3] To a meaningful extent, the modern Silk Road is not limited to the realm of physical transport infrastructure, nor only to relations between China and its immediate neighbours. Instead, the concept has been adopted by more than 146 countries,[4] extending to a broad range of subject matters across several modes of cross-border interaction.[5]

This chapter focuses on the development of what we term the 'Legal Silk Road'. Where once international trade was facilitated by the construction of roads and railways, the inducement of cross-border business activity now relies at least as much on a legal environment that is conducive to bridging an ever-present expectation gap between manufacturers and service providers in different jurisdictions. This gap might be created by ground-up cultural differences, top-down legislative requirements, or simple variations in common business practices. In most cases, private parties and sovereign states act to bridge this gap by concluding contracts or treaties with agreed rules. However, not every future circumstance can be foreseen, nor can every change in circumstance be accounted for. Inevitably, parties find themselves in need of dispute resolution architecture. It is with this architecture, specifically the provision for international arbitration, that this chapter is most concerned.

Arbitration has a long and storied history in Asia. While correlation cannot be equated with causation, it is notable that the most prosperous territories in the region correspond with the most active centres of international arbitration. The comparative prosperity of Singapore and Hong Kong has risen in conjunction with the popularity of the Singapore International Arbitration Centre (SIAC) and the Hong Kong International Arbitration Centre (HKIAC) as venues for the settlement of disputes.[6] To that end, our central argument is that arbitration is a direct facilitator of economic exchange within the Association of Southeast Asian Nations (ASEAN) and between ASEAN Members and other Asian states. Arbitration performs a functional role in creating an invisible

2. For an examination of the BRI in the context of the UN Sustainable Development Goals, *see* Johanna P Lorenzo, 'A Path Toward Sustainable Development Along the Belt and Road', 24(3) Journal of International Economic Law, 591 (2021) https://doi.org/10.1093/jiel/jgab032.
3. Jiangyu Wang, 'China's Governance Approach to the Belt and Road Initiative (BRI): Relations, Partnership, and Law', Global Trade and Customs Journal 14 (2019) https://doi.org/10.54648/gtcj2019021.
4. Green Finance and Development Centre, 'Countries of the Belt and Road Initiative' (December, 2023), https://greenfdc.org/countries-of-the-belt-and-road-initiative-bri/ (accessed 16 Dec. 2024).
5. On functional definitions of the Belt and Road, *see* Heng Wang, 'China's Approach to the Belt and Road Initiative: Scope, Character and Sustainability', 1 Journal of International Economic Law 22 (2019), at 32 https://doi.org/10.1093/jiel/jgy048.
6. Discussing this link, *see* Philip J McConnaughay, 'The Role of Arbitration in Economic Development and the Creation of Transnational Legal Principles', 1 Peking University Transnational Law Review 9 (2013).

trade route at national and international levels that stops short of enforcing harmonization. Instead, arbitration aids in managing legal diversity.

The argument proceeds in four parts. Section I outlines the analytical framework of the Legal Silk Road as it pertains to international arbitration and the Asia-ASEAN relationship. We identify three points of confluence: national arbitration legislation in ASEAN, internal engagement through international agreements, and external engagement between ASEAN and other Asian nations. Section II analyses national arbitration law across ASEAN in the context of the United Nations Commission on International Trade Law (UNCITRAL) Model Law on International Commercial Arbitration. There are gradations of localization, with countries like Singapore aligning more strongly with international standards and jurisdictions like Laos opting for a more domestic-focused approach. Section III examines internal engagement in arbitration through ASEAN's international agreements and external engagement with other Asian nations. There is guarded inclusion of arbitration with respect to most internal ASEAN matters but more expansive reference to the process in investment agreements and treaties with external parties. Consequently, arbitration performs different functions in different fora. Finally, section IV considers the rise of mediation and online dispute resolution, arguing that the ASEAN-Asia relationship can be leveraged to influence the future of international arbitration.

I CONCEPTUALIZING THE LEGAL SILK ROAD: CONVERGENCE AND DIVERGENCE IN INTERNATIONAL ARBITRATION

Law across Asia is influenced by a complex amalgam of factors that are wrought in their own historical, religious, and cultural contexts.[7] This is equally true within ASEAN. Some elements of Islamic law are prominent in Indonesia and Malaysia but less apparent in Singapore and the Philippines.[8] The remnants of the colonial past remain embedded in many jurisdictions. ASEAN nations that were subject to British rule have largely retained a common law system, whereas the nations that were subject to French rule, such as Cambodia, have retained elements of their civil law system. As such, the region is characterized by legal pluralism.

Our framework of the Legal Silk Road is comprised of arbitration provisions within national laws in ASEAN states, intra-ASEAN agreements, and ASEAN's external agreements with other Asian nations. The legal path they create is neither uniformly smooth nor of absolute consistency but nevertheless provides a route through which passes cross-border trade and investment. This is made possible by the provision of reliable dispute resolution architecture. At the level of business-to-business disputes, the provision for international arbitration grants commercial parties the autonomy to define their joint obligations within the boundaries set by their respective states. In state-state disputes, international arbitration provides an enforcement mechanism for

7. Analysing the interaction between culture and law in Asia, *see* Jimmy Chia-Shin Hsu, *Human Dignity in Asia: Dialogue Between Law and Culture* (Cambridge University Press 2022).
8. Elizabeth Lhost, *Everyday Islamic Law and the Making of Modern South Asia* (University of North Carolina Press 2022).

mutually agreed obligations. It is against this background that international arbitration serves several critical functions within our analysis.

First, the provision of a familiar procedural forum for cross-border commerce allows parties to resolve disputes without reference to local courts, thus bypassing idiosyncrasies in legal practice that may be unfamiliar to foreign lawyers or business professionals. Arbitration laws are crafted to meet business needs while neither supplanting nor disrupting the core legal principles that apply in a more rigid court setting. Indeed, several jurisdictions across the ASEAN region have dedicated legislation that is applicable only to international arbitrations in recognition of this function.[9] To the extent that procedural complexity is a barrier to cross-border commerce, arbitration alleviates this concern without the need for an ASEAN-wide legal instrument to impose a rigidly prescriptive method of dispute resolution.

Second, provision for this procedural forum for business-to-business disputes facilitates cross-border investment and trade while leaving the different legal cultures across the region undisturbed. There is uniform recognition that each state maintains the right to define the scope of non-arbitrable issues within its own jurisdiction.[10] Gambling is legal in some countries and not others; that a common form of dispute resolution mechanism is supported does not impede these decisions, which are considered separate and distinct areas of sovereignty.

Third, the capacity of parties to appoint their own arbitrators obviates concerns of home-court advantage and performs a de-politicizing effect on cross-border disputes. This effect is often referenced (and contested) in the context of investor-state arbitration.[11] Aron Broches described the introduction of investor-state arbitration as an attempt to 'eliminate the risk of a confrontation of the host country and the national State of the investor'.[12] While this comment might best be understood in the context of the gunboat diplomacy of the colonial era, we argue that the modern iteration of international arbitration performs a similar function in the context of international agreements between ASEAN and other states. A neutral forum for the settlement of disputes between sovereign entities helps shift decision-making from governmental to adjudicatory authorities and supports a rules-based order.

The legal instruments establishing the use of international arbitration in ASEAN States support these functions to varying degrees. National arbitration laws will be evaluated for the extent to which they deviate from the UNCITRAL Model Law on International Commercial Arbitration. Despite broad convergence on the provision for arbitration within domestic legislation across the ASEAN region, the prominence of

---

9. *See*, for example, the Singapore International Arbitration Act 1994 and Singapore Arbitration Act 2001.
10. Karl-Heinz Bockstiegel, 'Public Policy as a Limit to Arbitration and Its Enforcement', 2 Dispute Resolution International 123 (2008).
11. Ibrahim Shihata, 'Towards a Greater Depoliticization of Investment Disputes: The Roles of ICSID and MIGA', 1(1) ICSID Review Foreign Investment Law Journal 1, 4 (1986) https://doi.org/10.1093/icsidreview/1.1.1.
12. Aron Broches, The Convention on the Settlement of Investment Disputes between States and Nationals of Other States, 136 Recueil des Cours 331, 343 (1972) https://doi.org/10.1163/9789004640757_014.

local factors - such as the role of local courts and requirements to utilize local arbitrators - is highly variable.

II DIVERGENCE IN NATIONAL ARBITRATION LAWS IN ASEAN: GRADATIONS OF DELOCALIZATION

Despite their inherent legal diversity, each of the ASEAN nations - Brunei, Cambodia, Indonesia, Laos, Malaysia, Myanmar, the Philippines, Singapore, Thailand, and Vietnam - has instituted provisions for commercial arbitration or alternative dispute resolution. The touchstone for international commercial arbitration standards is the UNCITRAL Model Law on International Commercial Arbitration, promulgated in 2006.[13] In essence, the Model Law proposes a largely delocalized system of arbitration, with uniform requirements for arbitration agreements and their enforcement. While space constraints prevent a comprehensive comparative analysis of all ten ASEAN countries, there are several representative examples that highlight alignment or misalignment with international standards.

Based on our analysis, there is some divergence between ASEAN states with respect to the alignment of national arbitration legislation with the UNCITRAL Model Law. Malaysia and Singapore stand out as integrating many of the Model Law provisions verbatim within domestic legislation. Malaysia's Arbitration Act of 2005, as amended, contains a definition of 'arbitration agreement', interim measures, and grounds for setting aside that track the provisions of the Model Law on those issues.[14] In line with internationally recognized standards on party autonomy, Article 13 affords the parties autonomy in the procedure for selection of an arbitrator, mirroring the flexibility contained in the Model Law.[15] Similarly, the Singapore International Arbitration Act 2004 is explicitly based on the Model Law.[16] The definition of 'international' is adopted wholesale, and the enumerated list of powers of an arbitral tribunal is substantively similar with respect to provisions on the power of tribunals to order interim measures.[17]

However, important differences remain in some key areas. The confidentiality of arbitral proceedings is not addressed by the Model Law. By contrast, Articles 22 and 23 of the Singapore International Arbitration Act provide that proceedings under the Act are to be held in private, with accompanying reporting restrictions.[18] Malaysia's Arbitration Act contains similar limitations on parties' freedom to publish, disclose or communicate information relating to the arbitration proceeding.[19] Both the Singaporean and Malaysian arbitration legislation address the immunity of arbitral

13. UNCITRAL Model Law on International Commercial Arbitration (1985), with amendments as adopted in 2006 (hereinafter 'UNCITRAL Model Law').
14. Articles 9, 19, and 37, Arbitration Act 2005 (Laws of Malaysia Act 646).
15. Article 13 Arbitration Act 2005 (Laws of Malaysia Act 646).
16. *See* the Preamble to the International Arbitration Act 1994 (Singapore) (2020 Revised Edition).
17. Articles 5, 12, and 1 International Arbitration Act 1994 (Singapore) (2020 Revised Edition); Art. 17 UNCITRAL Model Law.
18. Article 22, 23 International Arbitration Act 1994 (Singapore) (2020 Revised Edition).
19. Article 41A, 41B Arbitration Act 2005 (Laws of Malaysia Act 646).

institutions for their good faith selection of an arbitrator, while arbitrators in Singapore are not liable for 'negligence in respect of anything done or omitted to be done in the capacity of arbitrator'.[20] As such, both jurisdictions supplement the Model Law with additional provisions to support the use of cross-border commercial arbitration. To that extent, Singapore and Malaysia represent similar profiles along our Legal Silk Road.

In assessing comparative alignment with the UN Model Law, Thailand represents somewhat of a midpoint in the ASEAN context. As such, there are broad areas of alignment akin to the situation in Singapore and Malaysia. Under the Thai Arbitration Act 2002, parties are granted autonomy over arbitrator selection, international standards of impartiality shall be enforced by Thai courts, and the grounds for setting aside arbitral awards are in line with the equivalent provisions in the Model Law.[21] However, there are more significant divergences than in the Singaporean or Malaysian context. In general, the role of Thai courts in the arbitration process is expanded. Most notably, the Thai Arbitration Act does not empower arbitral tribunals to grant interim relief. Parties must, therefore, be reliant on local courts to grant interim measures, which potentially elongates arbitral disputes and is a significant departure from more arbitration-friendly jurisdictions. Should a party fail to appoint an arbitrator, this appointment must be made by a court rather than a designated appointing authority.[22] This paradigm can also be seen in the context of jurisdictional challenges. Article 24 of the Thai Arbitration Act provides that local courts will have the final decision on jurisdictional questions, even as a preliminary matter; a party may request court review within thirty days of receiving a notice of adjudication.[23] Consequently, while the Thai Arbitration Act has broad swathes of alignment with the Model Law, it retains a more prominent role for local courts.

Laos occupies the opposite pole from Singapore and Malaysia and deviates most noticeably from the Model Law in comparison to the other ASEAN states. There is no dedicated law on arbitration in Laos; provision for arbitration is contained in the Law on the Resolution of Economic Disputes.[24] Elements of the legislation indicate a degree of openness to international arbitration. For example, foreign arbitral awards may be enforced, subject to the general civil procedure law.[25] A foreign arbitrator may also administer an arbitration where one of the parties is a foreign individual or entity.[26] However, this arbitrator may only be chosen from a list prepared by Laos' Ministry of Justice, and one of the prerequisites to qualify as an arbitrator in Laos is knowledge of the local language.[27] While ad hoc arbitration is permitted in some circumstances, this remains subject to specific government approval. As such, Laos represents the least homogenous section of our Legal Silk Road.

20. Article 25A International Arbitration Act 1994 (Singapore) (2020 Revised Edition).
21. Articles 18, 19, and 40 Arbitration Act B.E.2545 (Thailand) 2020.
22. Article 18 Arbitration Act B.E.2545 (Thailand) 2020.
23. Article 24 Arbitration Act B.E.2545 (Thailand) 2020.
24. Law on the Resolution of Economic Disputes (Lao PDR) (No. 06/NA) (2010).
25. Article 52 Law on the Resolution of Economic Disputes (Lao PDR) (No.06/NA) (2010).
26. Article 5 Law on the Resolution of Economic Disputes (Lao PDR) (No.06/NA) (2010).
27. Ramandeep Bhamra, 'Lao PDR Legal Alert: New Economic Dispute Resolution Law in Effect' (*DFDL*, 12 Feb. 2019)

Despite the gradations in the delocalization of arbitration across ASEAN, there are two issues that remain highly variable: the scope of 'public policy' that circumscribes the arbitrability of disputes and the legitimacy of third-party funding. In respect of the former, this is unsurprising. The significance of the 'public policy' concept in arbitration is no less than to demarcate the material scope of permissible arbitrations. It is inextricably linked to a state's societal norms which are, by definition, highly individual. Specific national interests or perceptions of morality vary in accordance with historical, religious, and constitutional factors. Given the cultural diversity within ASEAN, it follows that 'public policy' will be the subject of inevitable ambiguity. In general, matters that engage criminal, family law, and bankruptcy are not arbitrable, but public morality varies from jurisdiction to jurisdiction.

Unlike the other provisions of the UNCITRAL Model Law, there has been no meaningful attempt to standardize definitions of public policy, neither at the United Nations nor through any ASEAN framework. This might best be described as a state of managed diversity. On the one hand, the amorphous concept of public policy injects uncertainty and unpredictability. On the other hand, this uncertainty gives sufficient latitude for states to retain their sovereign right to maintain their core values and safeguard essential morality or public interests. It is an express choice of divergence that allows for hyper-local considerations to be prevalent over considerations of harmonization.

A similar diversity can be seen in the context of third-party funding, but for different reasons. Third-party funding involves a contractual relationship whereby a commercial party agrees to pay the costs of a legal action.[28] Should the claim succeed, the funder receives a percentage of the funds awarded. Arguments in favour of allowing third-party funding are rooted in access to justice concerns; arguments against are inspired by the common law doctrines of maintenance and champerty, which considered third party funding of litigation a potential route to abuse of judicial process. The permissibility and regulation of third-party funding vary widely across ASEAN. Singapore has adopted a formalized approach through the Civil Law (Amendment) Act 2017, which abolishes the tort of maintenance and champerty.[29] Article 5B of the Act also provides that a third-party funding contract 'is not contrary to public policy or otherwise illegal by reason that it is a contract for maintenance or champerty'.[30] Parties are not compelled to disclose the commercial terms of the funding contract but must disclose the existence of this contract to the tribunal and other party to the proceedings. This comparatively permissive approach reflects Singapore's position as a leading arbitration hub in the region.

By contrast, other ASEAN countries have yet to formally recognize or regulate third-party funding in arbitration. Neither Malaysian courts nor arbitration legislation makes provision for such arrangements, although the 2023 Arbitration Rules of the Asian International Arbitration Centre (formerly known as Kuala Lumpur Regional

28. *See* generally, Lisa Bench Nieuwveld & Victoria Shannon Sahani, *Third-Party Funding in International Arbitration* (Kluwer Law International BV 2016).
29. Article 5A The Civil Law (Amendment) Act 2017 (No. 2 of 2017).
30. Article 5B The Civil Law (Amendment) Act 2017 (No. 2 of 2017).

Centre for Arbitration) do reference the use of third-party funding.[31] There are no relevant provisions directly addressing the issue in Brunei, Cambodia, Indonesia, Laos, Myanmar, the Philippines, Thailand, and Vietnam. The permissibility of third-party funding in these jurisdictions will be dependent on laws on civil procedure and whether courts consider such arrangements to be contrary to national public policy.

The diversity in the regulation of arbitration across ASEAN reflects the distinctive approaches to the role of national courts in intervening in cross-border disputes. Singapore and Malaysia tend most towards acceptance of an international, largely delocalized approach, whereas Laos tends towards an approach that favours local courts and practitioners. In all ASEAN jurisdictions, the concept of public policy provides sufficient latitude for courts to act as an obstacle to the infringement of national culture and interests. As a whole, the body of national arbitrations laws across ASEAN can be best characterized as representing managed diversity; the existence of arbitration provisions provides a common system of international arbitration, with variations reflecting a varying understanding of sovereignty along the legal silk road. A similar theme can be seen in international agreements concluded by ASEAN as a bloc.

III MANAGING DIVERSITY THROUGH INTERNATIONAL ARBITRATION: ASEAN'S INTERNAL AND EXTERNAL ENGAGEMENT

There is an observable trend towards increased formalization in dispute resolution procedures in ASEAN legal instruments since it was first established in 1967. The founding document of ASEAN, the Bangkok Declaration, recognized the 'existence of mutual interest and common problems among countries of South-East Asia' and expressed the desire to establish 'a firm foundation for common action to promote regional cooperation' based on the principles of equality and partnership.[32]

This analysis will examine the inclusion of arbitration in ASEAN international agreements and agreements concluded between ASEAN and other Asian states. While arbitration legislation seeks to smooth over divergences in legal practice between states for the benefit of private parties, the provision for arbitration within agreements concluded by ASEAN performs a different function. They circumscribe access to arbitration within the context of enforcing state-state (or not doing so) and creating enforceable obligations within the context of the investor-state relationship.

A Internal Engagement: A Guarded Approach to International Arbitration Between ASEAN States

The *Treaty of Amity and Cooperation in Southeast Asia* (the Bali Treaty) was signed in 1976 by the five founding members of ASEAN: Indonesia, Malaysia, the Philippines, Singapore and Thailand at the first ASEAN summit held in Bali. It was designed as a

31. Rule 12 AIAC Arbitration Rules 2023.
32. Preamble, The ASEAN Declaration (Bangkok Declaration) 1967.

treaty of regional security, and its provisions are limited to commitments on the peaceful settlement of disputes. This development was devised in the shadow of geopolitical tension, as Southeast Asia became a focal point of the Cold War. Against this background, the preamble to the Bali Treaty states that 'the settlement of differences or disputes between its High Contracting Parties should be regulated by rational, effective and sufficiently flexible procedures, avoiding negative attitudes which might endanger or hinder cooperation'.[33] However, its dispute settlement mechanism is limited to requiring direct negotiations (as opposed to using force) and the establishment of a High Council of ministerial representatives who will make recommendations on intractable disputes.[34] A similar approach was taken in the 1996 *Protocol on Dispute Mechanism*, which formed an integral part of the ASEAN Framework on Enhancing Economic Cooperation. It provided that economic disputes relating to ASEAN economic agreements must be resolved by consultation, good offices, conciliation, or mediation.[35] In the event that these methods failed, Article 4 of the *Protocol* establishes a procedure for a Senior Economic Officials Meeting (SEOM).[36] Matters not settled may then be raised to the SEOM, which will establish a panel to make an objective assessment of the disputes. SEOM rulings can be appealed to the ASEAN Economic Ministers, who may suspend the application of concessions under the relevant agreement.[37] This decision is final and binding on all parties to the dispute.

Arbitration was formally introduced in a limited way after the 9th ASEAN Summit held in Bali on 7-8 October 2003. The 2004 ASEAN Protocol on Enhanced Dispute Settlement resulted from this summit. It permits States that have had concessions suspended by a SEOM panel to refer the matter to arbitration.[38] This arbitration may be conducted by the original panel under the SEOM or by a panel appointed by the Secretary-General of ASEAN. This indicates that the panel and arbitration are separate and distinct processes. While the State is not permitted to seek a second arbitration, the SEOM may still decide, by consensus, to reject a request to authorize concessions, even where such a request is consistent with the arbitrator's decision.[39] As such, arbitration is introduced as one element of resolving disputes, but state representatives remain the ultimate decision-maker.

This approach is consistent with the subsequent ASEAN-wide international agreements. The *ASEAN Charter,* adopted in 2007, stipulates that Member States should rely on the peaceful settlement of disputes. Chapter VIII provides that members are expected to resolve 'all disputes' peacefully through dialogue, consultations, and negotiations, emphasizing that they establish and maintain dispute settlement mechanisms in all fields of ASEAN cooperation.[40] The precise mechanism is not specified.

33. Preamble, Treaty of Amity and Cooperation in Southeast Asia 1976.
34. Article 14 Treaty of Amity and Cooperation in Southeast Asia 1976.
35. Articles 2 and 3, Protocol on Dispute Mechanism 1994.
36. Article 4 Protocol on Dispute Mechanism 1994.
37. Article 9 Protocol on Dispute Mechanism 1994.
38. Article 16(7) ASEAN Protocol on Enhanced Dispute Settlement 2004.
39. Article 16(8) ASEAN Protocol on Enhanced Dispute Settlement 2004.
40. Chapter VIII 'Settlement of Disputes' Charter of the Association of Southeast Asian Nations 2007 (hereinafter 'ASEAN Charter 2007').

However, according to Article 23 of the Charter, disputing parties may at any time agree to resort to good offices, conciliation, or mediation to resolve the dispute with the help of the Chairman of the ASEAN or the Secretary-General of the ASEAN.[41] Disputes relating to specific ASEAN instruments should be settled through the mechanisms and procedures provided in such instruments.

An updated 2010 Protocol to the Charter more expressly provided a route by which ASEAN Member States may access and be bound by international arbitration. It applies to disputes concerning the interpretation or application of the ASEAN Charter or other ASEAN instruments that do not have dedicated dispute settlement provisions. After failure to settle through consultation, the Complaining Party may request of the Responding Party consent for the establishment of an arbitration tribunal.[42] If the Responding Party does not agree, the Complaining party may refer the dispute to the ASEAN Coordinating Council, who 'may direct the Parties to the dispute to resolve their dispute through good offices, mediation, conciliation, or arbitration'.[43] The word 'direct' indicates that it is the first stage at which a Responding Party is compelled to participate in the arbitration process. However, the process by which the ASEAN Coordinating Council will reach its decision is left to be determined by the Chairman of Council.[44] Therefore, Member States may unilaterally request arbitration but are only compelled to participate at the direction of the ASEAN Coordinating Council.

Indeed, the 2019 ASEAN Protocol on Enhanced Dispute Settlement Mechanism also requires consent before Member States enter arbitration. In other words, the protocol itself is not a basis for consent. It provides that 'expeditious arbitration within the ASEAN Economic Community as an alternative means of dispute settlement can facilitate the solution of certain disputes ... that are clearly defined by both parties'.[45] This remains subject to the 'mutual agreement of both parties' including to the procedure of the arbitration. As such, resort to compulsory arbitration is somewhat limited with regard to state-state disputes within ASEAN. Only when the ASEAN Coordinating Council intercedes on behalf of a complaining state may a party be directed to participate. Therefore, arbitration has received somewhat guarded acceptance with regard to state-state disputes. Instead, the preferred method of dispute resolution is a panel established by the SEOM, akin to the Dispute Settlement Mechanism of the World Trade Organisation. This is not the case with investment disputes.

B Engagement over Investments: A More Expansive Role for Arbitration in Investment Disputes

Under the 1987 ASEAN Investment Agreement, disputes between contracting parties shall be settled amicably or failing resolution, be submitted to the ASEAN Economic

41. Article 23 ASEAN Charter 2007.
42. Article 8 Protocol to the ASEAN Charter On Dispute Settlement Mechanisms 2010.
43. Article 9 Protocol to the ASEAN Charter On Dispute Settlement Mechanisms 2010.
44. ASEAN Protocol on Enhanced Dispute Settlement 2019.
45. Article 19 Protocol on Enhanced Dispute Settlement 2019.

Ministers for resolution.[46] Conversely, disputes between an investor and a Contracting Party may be submitted for conciliation or arbitration six months after being raised, with such election being binding on either party.[47] This is a marked departure from the dispute settlement mechanisms established by the aforementioned ASEAN instruments, which required either consent or the direction of the ASEAN Coordinating Council. Similarly, Articles 28-42 of the 2009 ASEAN Comprehensive Investment Agreement (ACIA) contain detailed provisions on the submission of investor-state disputes to arbitration.[48] The investor may opt for domestic court proceedings or arbitration. The ACIA provides that the arbitration may be administered under the International Centre for Settlement of Investment Disputes (ICSID) Convention and the ICSID Rules of Procedure for Arbitration Proceedings, the UNCITRAL Arbitration Rules, or several other forms of institutional arbitration. In both of these investment agreements, consent to investor-state arbitration is given in the signature to the treaty.

C External Engagement: Mandatory Arbitration Between ASEAN and Other Asian States

ASEAN has concluded treaties relating to economic cooperation with several other countries as a trade bloc. Our analysis focuses on agreements concluded with China, India, South Korea, and Japan. Arbitration plays a more obligatory role in the management of external relations than is apparent from the internal ASEAN agreements.

The China-ASEAN Framework on Economic Cooperation was concluded in 2002 with a view to creating a China-ASEAN Free Trade Area.[49] It contains provisions for tariff reduction or elimination on designated goods or services and identifies areas of economic cooperation, including agriculture and investment. Disputes arising under this agreement are to be settled by the subsequent 2004 Agreement on Dispute Settlement Mechanism.[50] It provides that parties should establish a Liaison Office for the purposes of administering this agreement and requires that they 'accord due consideration and adequate opportunity for consultations' over alleged failures to meet their obligations.[51] Mediation and conciliation may be part of this process.[52] Should these consultations not succeed within sixty days, Article 6 provides that the complaining state may request the appointment of an arbitral tribunal, whose function is to make an objective assessment of the dispute before it, including an examination of the facts of the case and the applicability of and conformity with the Framework Agreement.[53] Unlike the consultation provisions which include binding 'shall' language, no such

46. Article IX ASEAN Agreement for the Promotion and Protection of Investments 1987.
47. Article X(2) ASEAN Agreement for the Promotion and Protection of Investments 1987.
48. Articles 28-42 ASEAN Comprehensive Investment Agreement (ACIA) 2009.
49. Framework Agreement on Comprehensive Economic Co-Operation between the Association of South East Asian Nations and the People's Republic Of China 2002.
50. Agreement on Dispute Settlement Mechanism of the Framework Agreement on Comprehensive Economic Co-Operation between the Association of Southeast Asian Nations and the People's Republic of China 2004 (hereinafter '2004 Agreement on Dispute Settlement Mechanism').
51. Article 4 Agreement on Dispute Settlement Mechanism 2004.
52. Article 5 Agreement on Dispute Settlement Mechanism 2004.
53. Article 6 and Art. 8 Agreement on Dispute Settlement Mechanism 2004.

obligatory language exists under Article 6. However, Article 7 provides that the 'party complained against *shall* appoint an arbitrator pursuant to Article 6 with 30 days of its receipt for appointment of the arbitration tribunal'. The complaining party's appointee will act as sole arbitrator in the absence of the respondent's appointment. This is tantamount to the creation of an obligation to arbitrate upon request. The same structure of obligation is employed in the 2009 ASEAN-Japan Comprehensive Economic Partnership.[54] By contrast, the 2009 ASEAN-India Agreement on Dispute Settlement Mechanism and 2005 ASEAN-Korea Agreement on Dispute Settlement Mechanism are more explicit; Articles 6(3) and 5(3), respectively, provide that 'upon receipt of the request, an arbitral panel shall be established'.[55] Despite these differences in textual construction, their effect is the same: to give teeth to mutually agreed trade rules through binding arbitration.

As with internal ASEAN investment agreements, external agreements also mandate investor-state arbitration. The 2009 ASEAN-China Investment Agreement, 2014 ASEAN-India Investment Agreement, 2009 ASEAN Korea Investment Agreement all contain provisions for investor-state arbitration after a mandatory period of consultation negotiation. In such cases, it is in the prerogative of the investor to submit the request to an arbitration institution, which is a departure of the 'request' language of state-state agreements. This is likely the result of the fact that investors are the beneficiaries of rights granted under investment treaties but are not themselves party to those treaties.

Consequently, it is apparent that arbitration is of a changing character in the ASEAN-Asia relationship depending on the context. It is less prominent with respect to internal ASEAN agreements, although dispute settlement in this context has become increasingly formalized. By contrast, binding arbitration is commonplace in external agreements concluded with other Asian states. This may reflect the status of the latter as primarily economic relationships, whereas the former might be characterized as also political in nature. In both cases, arbitration functions as a process by which to manage legal diversity. In this context, states within ASEAN-Asia relationship can be influential in shaping the future of international arbitration.

IV THE ASEAN-ASIA RELATIONSHIP AND THE FUTURE OF INTERNATIONAL ARBITRATION

Dissatisfaction with elements of international arbitration is longstanding. The 2022 iteration of the Singapore International Dispute Resolution Academy's Survey (SIDRA Survey 2022) found that only 30% of users were satisfied with the cost of international commercial arbitration, and only 41% of users were satisfied with the speed of

54. Articles 64 and 65 Agreement on Comprehensive Economic Partnership among Japan and Member States of the Association of Southeast Asian Nations.
55. Agreement on Dispute Settlement Mechanism under the Framework Agreement on Comprehensive Economic Cooperation between the Association of Southeast Asian Nations and The Republic Of India 2009; Agreement on Dispute Settlement Mechanism Under the Framework Agreement on Comprehensive Economic Cooperation Among the Governments of the Member Countries of the Association of Southeast Asian Nations and the Republic of Korea 2005.

international arbitration.[56] Similarly, only 32% of users were satisfied with how arbitration affects the preservation of business relationships.[57] Discourse surrounding the reform of international arbitration seeks to address these issues. Our analysis focuses on two threads of reform that have been proposed to change the landscape of international arbitration: support for the use of mediation and provision for online dispute resolution. These present unique opportunities for ASEAN and Asian states to leverage their relationship to influence and benefit from a new paradigm for international dispute resolution.

It is long been observable in the realm of investor-state disputes that investors from Asian nations engage less frequently in adversarial arbitration than investors from North America or Western Europe.[58] Many theses have been advanced to explain the discrepancy, both cultural and economic.[59] We find the most convincing to be the long history of mediation and non-adversarial dispute settlement across Asia. For example, Katarungang Barangay is a system for the amicable settlement of disputes at the community level in the Philippines that is many hundreds of years old.[60] China has a long history of community in mediation that is rooted in Confucianism, which influenced similar processes in South Korea, Japan, and Vietnam.[61] These traditions remain strong today throughout ASEAN and Asian states.

Asian dispute resolution hubs like Singapore and Hong Kong are well poised to influence the global development of mediation. The Singapore Convention on Mediation (SCM) has proven a catalyst for the development of mediation law practice around the world, particularly as it was adopted alongside the UNCITRAL Model Law on International Commercial Mediation.[62] While competitors in the European Union have not yet embraced harmonized international standards in mediation, Asian states represent the plurality of current signatories of the SCM. There is already some evidence of cooperation between Asian states to promote the use of mediation; in 2019, the Singapore International Mediation Centre (SIMC), the China Council for the Promotion of International Trade (CCPIT), and the China Chamber of International Commerce Mediation Centre (CCIC) signed a memorandum of understanding to establish a Belt and Road Mediator Panel comprised of dispute resolution practitioners from China, Singapore, and other BRI countries to develop best practice for mediating

56. Nadja Alexander et al., *Singapore International Dispute Resolution Academy*, International Dispute Resolution Survey: 2022 Final Report, at 7.
57. *Ibid.*
58. Luke Nottage & J Romesh Weeramantry, 'Investment Arbitration in Asia: Five Perspectives on Law and Practice', 28 Arbitration International 19 (2012) https://doi.org/10.1093/arbitration/28.1.19.
59. *Ibid.*
60. Anna Mae R Avenido & Gil Marvel P Tabucanon, 'The Role of Mediation in Good Governance: Revisiting the Katarungang Pambarangay', 65 Ateneo Law Journal 1395 (2020).
61. Zeng Xianyi, 'Mediation in China: Past and Present', 17 Asia Pacific Law Review 1 (2009) https://doi.org/10.1080/10192557.2009.11788203.
62. United Nations Convention on International Settlement Agreements Resulting from Mediation 2018.; UNCITRAL Model Law on International Commercial Mediation and International Settlement Agreements Resulting from Mediation, 2018.

disputes.[63] ASEAN has also developed a Mediation Programme with the World Intellectual Property Organisation to offer up to 8,000 SGD for disputes where one party is an ASEAN national.[64]

Similarly, ASEAN and Asian states have demonstrated their willingness to lead the development of standards for online dispute resolution. In 2022, the ASEAN Secretariat published the ASEAN Guidelines on Online Dispute Resolution.[65] While '[a]cknowledging the heterogeneity and varying levels of maturity of consumer protection' across ASEAN, it nevertheless provides 'a common starting point to promote a certain degree of uniformity' for the development of ODR systems.[66] It offers guiding principles of accessibility, transparency and due process, and IT requirements such as interoperability and data security and privacy. Most notably, the Guidelines suggest that variances in national ODR systems 'could be remediated by consensus' and encourages cooperation among ASEAN sectoral bodies, for example, that the ASEAN Committee on Consumer Protection (ACCP) website becomes a linking point for national ODR systems.[67] To the extent that the future of arbitration will be conducted through online platforms, intra-ASEAN cooperation would be a potent tool to develop a cohesive and coherent approach to online platforms.

To that end, the ASEAN Guidelines also encourage cooperation with the wider international community. With respect to other international bodies with Asian influence, the APEC ODR Collaborative Framework would be a strong candidate for further development of the ASEAN guidelines.[68] It provides more detailed procedural rules for online disputes, which include well-defined negotiation, mediation, and arbitration stages and a Model ODR Clause for Contracts.[69] As such, the APEC ODR Framework offers a more structured, prescriptive approach than the ASEAN ODR Guidelines but encourages a more consistent approach to such disputes. Hong Kong, China, Japan, Singapore, and the United States have opted in to the APEC Framework. By adopting a closer collaboration with APEC, states may be more readily able to leverage the ASEAN-Asia relationship to have greater influence in the reform of arbitration and international dispute resolution.

V CONCLUSION

The ASEAN region's commitment to refining its dispute resolution mechanisms is akin to laying down legal infrastructure parallel to the Silk Road's physical pathways. The

63. 'SIMC and CCPIT Mediation Center establish international mediator panel to resolve BRI-related disputes', https://simc.com.sg/blog/2019/01/25/simc-and-ccpit-mediation-center-establish-international-mediator-panel-to-resolve-bri-related-disputes/ (accessed 16 Dec. 2024).
64. 'WIPO-Singapore ASEAN Mediation Programme', https://www.wipo.int/about-wipo/en/offices/singapore/news/2023/news_0011.html (accessed 16 Dec. 2024).
65. ASEAN Guidelines on Online Dispute Resolution: Options and Orientation for the Design of National ODR Systems for Consumer Protection.
66. *Ibid.*, at 2.
67. *Ibid.*, at 14.
68. APEC Collaborative Framework for Online Dispute Resolution of Cross-Border Business-to-Business Disputes.
69. *Ibid.*, Arts 6-8.

region's arbitration provisions reflect an intricate interplay between regional principles of amicable resolution and an evolving adherence to formal, rule-based mechanisms. This dynamic is indicative of ASEAN's aspirations for economic integration and legal harmonization, accommodating the diverse legal landscapes of its Member States. As the region forges ahead in an interconnected world, its dispute resolution frameworks are expected to mature further, mirroring both internal dynamics and external global trends.

Looking ahead, it is likely that ASEAN will continue to evolve its dispute resolution mechanisms towards greater formalization and rule-based systems, which will inevitably involve the development of investor-state arbitration. This is likely to occur both internally, between ASEAN States, and in conjunction with other Asian states. This evolution will likely include expanding the scope of disputes covered to address a broader range of issues, including environmental and social disputes, reflecting ASEAN's growing role in the global arena. The ongoing development of international arbitration will play a significant role in the region's efforts to entrench economic integration while maintaining legal diversity. By providing a stable and predictable legal framework for resolving disputes, ASEAN can facilitate cross-border trade and investment and contribute to the global development of investor-state arbitration.

CHAPTER 15

The Evolving Role of the European Union in International Investment Policy Reforms: Challenges, Achievements, and Future Directions

Federico Ortino

This chapter discusses the European Union's (EU's) evolving role in international investment policy reform, focusing on challenges, achievements, and future directions since the Lisbon Treaty granted the EU exclusive competence over foreign direct investment (FDI). It explores the EU's journey to develop a policy addressing critical issues in investor-State dispute settlement (ISDS), highlighting the complexity of its supranational institutional structure and the difficulties in delineating its exclusive competence. It critically analyses inward and outward-looking reforms and assesses their impact, noting that many are yet to be fully implemented due to ratification delays by Member States and ongoing multilateral discussions on ISDS reform. The chapter also suggests that future EU investment policy may increasingly focus on 'investment facilitation' as a strategy that may better align with EU's overarching values such as democracy, rule of law, and respect for fundamental rights.

I INTRODUCTION

The entry into force in December 2009 of the Lisbon Treaty marked a significant moment for the global international investment regime, as for the first time, the European Union (EU) was granted, as part of its common commercial policy, exclusive competence over foreign direct investment (FDI) (Articles 3.1 and 207 TFEU). By that time, following the 'exponential explosion' of claims brought by foreign investors under international investment treaties in the previous fifteen years, a wave of commentary had already emphasised several critical issues with regard to investor-State dispute settlement (ISDS), including the inconsistency of the growing number of arbitral decisions, arbitral tribunals' broad interpretations of investment treaties, and the lack of accountability and independence of investment treaty arbitrators. Following a conference organised at Harvard Law School in 2008, Waibel, Kaushal, Chung and Balchin edited a collection on *The Backlash Against Investment Arbitration: Perceptions and Reality*,[1] where the editors registered the existence of 'a range of serious questions [...] about the sustainability and future direction of investment arbitration ... [that] can no longer be ignored or be dismissed as esoteric criticisms by fringe groups or outsiders with no stake in the system'.[2]

Since then, the EU and its institutions have been on a journey to develop and implement an EU policy on international investment that has attempted to address many of these serious questions. This chapter aims to provide, first of all, a snapshot of the reform agenda that the EU has formulated over the course of the last fifteen years, highlighting some of the key challenges that the EU has faced in implementing such agenda, as well as the results achieved so far. The chapter also sketches some possible directions that the EU may embark on in the future, in particular moving towards alternative strategies in order to encourage foreign investment which are more in line with its overarching values such as democracy, the rule of law and respect for fundamental rights.

II COMPLEXITY OF THE EU SUPRANATIONAL INSTITUTIONAL STRUCTURE

The EU's entrance onto the global investment regime stage was not as smooth as one may have hoped. Questions regarding the scope of the newly attributed competence created the first headaches. Was the new exclusive competence limited to 'foreign direct investment' only (and thus not covering 'portfolio investment')? Was the new competence limited to 'investment liberalisation' only (and thus not covering 'investment protection')? These questions were not simply 'academic' as they had clear implications on the distribution of competences ('shared' or 'exclusive') between the EU institutions and the EU Member States, and ultimately on the shape and evolution of EU policy on foreign investment.[3]

1. Michael Waibel, Asha Kaushal, Kyo-Hwa Chung & Claire Balchin (eds), *The Backlash Against Investment Arbitration. Perceptions and Reality* (Kluwer, 2010).
2. *Ibid.*, at xxxvii. *See* further Susan Franck, 'The Legitimacy Crisis in Investment Treaty Arbitration: Privatizing Public International Law Through Inconsistent Decisions', 73 *Fordham Law Review* 1521 (2005); Zachary Douglas, 'Nothing If Not Critical for Investment Treaty Arbitration: *Occidental, Eureko, Methanex*', 22 Arbitration International 27 (March 2006) https://doi.org/10.1093/arbitration/22.1.27; Gus Van Harten, *Investment Treaty Arbitration and Public Law* (Oxford University Press, 2007).
3. *See* Piet Eeckhout & Federico Ortino, 'Towards an EU Policy on Foreign Direct Investment', in Biondi, Eeckhout & Ripley (eds), *EU Law after Lisbon* (Oxford University Press, 2012) 312.

It should be herewith emphasised that the EU institutional framework is a complex relationship between its multiple supranational institutions and the various Member States, each pursuing distinct objectives, often leading to overlapping or conflicting agendas. Among the former, the Commission is the technocratic body contributing to shaping the EU's overall strategy in particular with regard to the EU common commercial policy, and leads the negotiation of EU trade agreements; the Council represents the intergovernmental interests of the various EU Member States and plays a crucial role in EU common commercial policy as it authorises the Commission to negotiate new trade agreements on the basis of a negotiating mandate and adopts the final agreement; the Parliament represents a wider set of interests across the EU and its role in shaping EU common commercial policy, including EU trade agreements, has grown over the years; and, finally, the Court of Justice of the European Union (CJEU) ensures the correct interpretation and application of EU law.

When it comes to the Member States, they may exhibit diverse positions, including with regard to matters falling within the EU common commercial policy. For example, by the time the Lisbon Treaty entered into force, the many investment treaties concluded by EU Member States had for the most part been developed through bilateral negotiations, often between a capital-exporting country and a capital-importing country. Through such bilateral investment treaties (BITs), the latter (i.e., the host country) would ensure an increased flow of much-needed FDI into its economy, and the former (i.e., the home country) would provide its investors certain guarantees, such as against unfair, discriminatory or expropriatory measures by the host country. Furthermore, looking at the distribution of investment disputes that had by 2010 been brought against EU Member States, it was Eastern European states (such as the Czech Republic, Poland, Romania and Hungary) that had been on the receiving end of such disputes, while Western European states (such as France, Germany, Italy, and the United Kingdom) had so far been spared from investor-State treaty claims. Clearly, each Member State would now bring to the EU policy-making table each distinct investment treaty practice and ISDS experience.

Unsurprisingly, as the Commission and the Council could not agree on whether or not the new exclusive competence with regard to 'foreign direct investment' should cover all investment activities or exclude portfolio investments, the Commission eventually brought this question before the CJEU in the context of the EU–Singapore Free Trade Agreement (FTA), which had been concluded in October 2014. First, the Court interpreted the notion of FDI in a strict sense and while it found that non-direct investment is not covered by the Union's exclusive competence under Article 207 TFEU, it did regard it as 'necessary in order to achieve ... one of the objectives referred to in the Treaties', within the meaning of Article 216(1) and thus fell into the shared competences relating to the internal market.[4] Second, the Court found that since the regime governing dispute settlement between investors and states (ISDS) removes disputes from the jurisdiction of the national courts, it could not be regarded as an ancillary institutional provision, and thus it was not covered as a component of the EU

4. Opinion 2/15 of 16 May 2017, ECLI: EU:C:2017:376, para. 243.

competence.[5] As a consequence of the Court's 2/15 Opinion, any international agreements concluded by the EU covering non-direct investments and/or ISDS would have to be concluded as 'mixed agreements' and be ratified by each Member State.[6]

III THE EU REFORM AGENDA

Despite the institutional challenges referred to in the previous section, the EU developed quickly a reform agenda with regard to both the 'substance' and the dispute settlement 'procedure' of international investment treaties.

A Reform of Substantive Investment Disciplines

The initial focus of the EU was on reforming the substance of investment treaties. Negotiations on comprehensive FTAs with Canada, Singapore and Vietnam offered the EU, in particular the Commission, the opportunity to develop its own stance with regard to the substantive disciplines included in the respective chapters on investment in those three FTAs. There are two significant features of the EU reform with regard to the substantive disciplines: clarification of the scope of investment protection afforded to foreign investments and inclusion of liberalisation/pre-establishment commitments. These reforms have been, on the whole, in line with many other reforms adopted by other countries in the last two decades.

With regard to the clarification, the EU followed to some extent a similar approach that had been adopted by the United States and Canada a decade earlier, when those two countries, in the wake of several high-profile ISDS claims brought on the basis of the North American Free Trade Agreement (NAFTA),[7] had formulated new model BITs in 2004. The clarification concerned some of the core investment protection provisions that had been at the basis of many successful claims brought by foreign investors against host States, in particular the provision on expropriation, fair and equitable treatment (FET) and full protection and security (FPS). With regard to expropriation, the focus of the clarification was on the notion of 'indirect expropriation', which is now to be determined on the basis of 'a case-by-case, fact-based inquiry' that includes, among other factors, the measure's 'economic impact' and 'character' in particular 'object, context and intent'.[8] Moreover, the relevant annex clarified that 'except in the rare circumstance [...], non-discriminatory measures of a Party that are

5. *Ibid.*, para. 293.
6. For the additional challenge regarding the faith of more than 1,200 investment treaties concluded by EU Member States before the Lisbon Treaty, *see* Angelos Dimopoulos, 'The Validity and Applicability of International Investment Agreements Between EU Member States under EU and International Law', 48 *Common Market Law Review* 63 (2011) https://doi.org/10.54648/cola2011004; Nico Basener, *Investment Protection in the European Union. Considering EU Law in Investment Arbitrations Arising from Intra-EU and Extra-EU Bilateral Investment Agreements* (Nomos, 2017); Crina Baltag & Ana Stanic (eds), *The Future of Investment Treaty Arbitration in the EU. Intra-EU BITs, the Energy Charter Treaty, and the Multilateral Investment Court* (Wolters Kluwer, 2020).
7. *Metalclad v. Mexico, SD Myers v. Canada, Lowen v. USA, Methanex v. USA.*
8. *See* Annex 8-A Expropriation of EU-Canada CETA.

designed and applied to protect legitimate public welfare objectives, such as health, safety and the environment, do not constitute indirect expropriations'.

With regard to FET, the approach followed by the EU was to clarify what constitutes a breach of the obligation to provide 'fair and equitable treatment'. In this regard, the FET provision in the new EU international treaties identified an exhaustive list of possible FET breaches, which include 'denial of justice', 'fundamental breach of due process', 'manifest arbitrariness', and 'abusive treatment of investors'.[9] While the list does not refer to the frustration of the investor's legitimate expectations as a breach of the FET obligation, a reference to such a concept is indeed found in the relevant FET discipline of recent EU treaties. Accordingly, a tribunal, when applying the FET obligation, 'may take into account whether a Party made a specific representation to an investor to induce a covered investment, that created a legitimate expectation'. While there is no express reference to customary law (as one finds in many other recent investment treaties), the overall approach followed by the EU in clarifying the FET standard appears to align with how investment treaty tribunals have applied the customary minimum standard of treatment.[10]

Finally, with regard to FPS, the EU approach, in line with other recent treaty reforms, has focused on clarifying the scope of the FPS obligation by acknowledging that 'full protection and security' 'refers to the Party's obligations relating to the physical security of investors and covered investments'. This clarification thus excludes extending the FPS obligation to include 'legal protection', as some investment treaty tribunals had found, which had led to affording foreign investors 'a guarantee of stability in a secure environment, both physical, commercial and legal'.[11]

It is clear how the above clarifications all go in the direction of limiting the scope of protection afforded to foreign investments through investment treaties. Finding the right balance between granting extensive protection to investors and at the same time safeguarding host States' ability to regulate in the public interest was a challenge that the EU identified early on in its reform agenda. For example, in their Joint Statement on Shared Principles for International Investment, issued in 2012 under the auspices of the Transatlantic Economic Council, the EU and the United States recognised that 'governments should provide the highest possible level of legal certainty and protection against discriminatory, arbitrary, and otherwise unfair or harmful treatment to all investors and investments in their territories' and that 'governments can fully implement these principles while still preserving the authority to adopt and maintain measures necessary to regulate in the public interest to pursue certain public policies'.[12]

The second key feature of the EU reform of substantive disciplines in investment treaties revolves around investment liberalisation, or international commitments aimed at directly improving foreign investors' *access* to the host market (often referred to as 'pre-establishment commitments'). While again this was not a novelty per se in the world of international investment treaties (the United States had been including

9. *See* Art. 8.10 EU-Canada CETA.
10. *See*, for example, *Waste Management v. Mexico (II)*, Award, 30 Apr. 2004, para. 98.
11. *See Biwater v. Tanzania*, Award, 24 Jul. 2008, para. 729.
12. *See* EU-US Statement on Shared Principles for International Investment of 10 Apr. 2012.

such commitments since at least the 1990s), it was indeed a novelty with regard to previous European investment treaties, which principally focused on post-establishment protection only. In addition to extending the scope of the national and most-favoured-nation (MFN) treatment provisions to cover the 'establishment' of foreign investors, the EU was the first to add to its investment chapters a specific provision on 'market access', styled on the homonymous clause in the GATS (Article XVI), identifying a list of limitations (including on 'the participation of foreign capital in terms of maximum percentage limit on foreign shareholding or the total value of individual or aggregate foreign investment') that would be in principle prohibited (unless expressly exempted in the party's schedules).

B Reform of ISDS

The EU reform agenda with regard to ISDS has been, however, much more daring. It is useful here to distinguish between outward-looking (i.e., in international agreements with third countries) and inward-looking (i.e., in intra-EU agreements) reforms.

From an outward-looking perspective, the EU initial stance focused mainly on improving the transparency of the dispute settlement process, in line with increasing demands for greater transparency and participation. This was very much in line also with what other advanced economies had done already, in particular, once again, the United States and Canada. For example, the original reform of the investment dispute settlement system in the FTA signed with Canada in 2014 was based on the traditional arbitration model but provided full transparency of proceedings. However, following an EU-wide intense debate and public consultation regarding the negotiation of a new FTA, this time with the United States, the Transatlantic Trade and Investment Partnership (TTIP), the EU, in early 2015, reached the conclusion that the traditional arbitration-based model for the settlement of investor-State disputes was no longer viable in any future EU agreements.[13] In addition to the several tens of thousands of submissions to the TTIP public consultation, which were demanding the exclusion of investment protection and ISDS in the future trade and investment agreement with the US, a few government ministers in key EU Member States (such as France and Germany) were vocal in criticising ISDS, in particular. For example, Matthias Fekl, the then French Secretary of State for Foreign Trade, told EURACTIV France that he would 'never allow private tribunals in the pay of multinational companies to dictate the policies of sovereign states, particularly in certain domains like health and the environment'.[14]

Accordingly, in the second part of 2015, the 'revolutionary' Investment Court System (ICS) was elaborated, which represents a clear break from the old ISDS

13. Laura Puccio & Roderick Harte, 'From Arbitration to the Investment Court System (ICS): The Evolution of CETA Rules' *European Parliamentary Research Service* (2017), available https://www.europarl.europa.eu/thinktank/en/document/EPRS_IDA(2017)607251 (accessed 16 Dec. 2024).
14. EURACTIV, 'France and Germany to Form United Front Against ISDS' (15 Jan. 2015), available https://www.euractiv.com/section/trade-society/news/france-and-germany-to-form-united-front-against-isds/ (accessed 16 Dec. 2024).

approach and demonstrates the intent to address some of its shortcomings through the establishment of permanent, court-like tribunals.[15] Two key features of the ICS are the standing (or pre-selected) nature of the adjudicators (i.e., the disputing parties do not select them as in the case of arbitration) and the availability of an appeal mechanism to review principally errors of law by the first-tier tribunal.

The ICS was first included in the EU-Vietnam FTA (in late 2015) and in the modified EU-Canada CETA (in early 2016). In announcing the conclusion of the latter, then EU Trade Commissioner, Cecilia Malmström, acknowledged that the new ISDS was aimed to 'work like an international court' and would ensure 'that citizens can trust it to deliver fair and objective judgements' meeting 'the expectations of both the Member States and the European Parliament'.[16]

The ICS appeared to represent a backstop, developed in record time and suffering from certain shortcomings, in particular with regard to the mechanism for the enforcement of the decisions rendered on the basis of the ICS.[17] In any event, it seems quite cumbersome to develop a single-standing ICS mechanism for each bilateral FTA signed by the EU. Therefore, the EU soon pushed for the initiation of broader, multilateral discussions aimed at reforming the traditional ISDS system, ideally aimed at the establishment of a multilateral investment court, which would replace ad hoc arbitral tribunals in both past and future investment treaties. Such discussions eventually found a home within the United Nations Commission on International Trade Law (UNCITRAL) Working Group III, which was entrusted in 2017 with a broad mandate to work on possible reforms of ISDS as well as ensuring that the deliberation would be government-led, consensus-based, fully transparent and benefitting from the widest possible breadth of available expertise from all stakeholders. Specifically, the WGIII would proceed in three related but distinct phases: (i) identify and consider concerns regarding ISDS; (ii) consider whether reform was desirable in light of any identified concerns; and (iii) if the WG were to conclude that reform was desirable, develop any relevant solutions to be recommended to the Commission. The first two phases were completed in a little over two years, and the third phase is still underway; the aim is to complete the last phase by the end of 2025.[18]

The EU has taken a different approach with regard to inward-looking (i.e., with regard to intra-EU agreements) procedural reforms. Here, the European Commission and CJEU, in particular, have set out a 'crusade' against ISDS based on intra-EU

15. Wolfgang Koeth, 'Can the Investment Court System (ICS) Save TTIP and CETA?' EIPA Working Paper (2016) available https://www.eipa.eu/publications/paper/can-the-investment-court-system-ics-save-ttip-and-ceta/ (accessed 16 Dec. 2024).
16. European Commission, 'CETA: EU and Canada Agree on New Approach on Investment in Trade Agreement' Press Release (29 Feb. 2016) available https://ec.europa.eu/commission/presscorner/detail/en/IP_16_399 (accessed 16 Dec. 2024).
17. N. Jansen Calamita, 'The (In)Compatibility of Appellate Mechanisms with Existing Instruments of the Investment Treaty Regime', 18 *Journal of World Investment & Trade* 585-627 (2017) https://doi.org/10.1163/22119000-12340053.
18. All working documents of the WGIII are available online on the UNCITRAL WGIII website: https://uncitral.un.org/en/working_groups/3/investor-state (accessed 16 Dec. 2024).

investment treaties, in particular arguing that arbitration clauses in intra-EU treaties are incompatible with EU law, principally because the CJEU alone has jurisdiction to determine any (potential) issues involving the interpretation and application of EU law.[19] In this regard, it is worth noting the interventions made by the Commission as amicus curiae in investment arbitration proceedings over the years, whereby the Commission attempted to represent to the arbitral tribunal the conflicts between the investment treaty and EU law, including the impact that that conflict had on the jurisdiction of the arbitral tribunal. While arbitral tribunals regularly granted the Commission the ability to submit such amici briefs, they equally regularly rejected the legal arguments presented by the Commission.[20]

In addition, the Commission attempted to address the incompatibility between intra-EU ISDS and EU law by requiring EU Member States to terminate all their intra-EU treaties. While only a few of them actually did so (e.g., Ireland and Italy), in 2015, the Commission started the first stage of infringement procedures against five Member States (Austria, the Netherlands, Romania, Slovakia and Sweden) for failure to terminate their existing intra-EU investment treaties.[21] In 2020, the European Commission and the Member States negotiated a plurilateral agreement according to which twenty-three Member States agreed to terminate their intra-EU BITs (which also included the retroactive termination of each treaty 'sunset clause' from the moment the last intra-EU treaty signing party became a member of the EU).[22]

Finally, in the context of the modernisation of the Energy Charter Treaty (ECT), the Commission asked and obtained an express exclusion of ISDS between the members of a regional economic integration organisation (REIO). Accordingly, as the only REIO member of the ECT is the EU, all ECT-related intra-EU investment disputes would be resolved before the national courts of the host country rather than investment treaty tribunals.[23]

19. *See*, for example, Case C-284/16 *Slovak Republic v. Achmea B.V.*, 6 Mar. 2018, ECLI:EU:C:2018:158 (where the Court of Justice of the European Union ruled that the arbitration clause contained in Art. 8 of the 1991 Netherlands-Slovakia BIT has an adverse effect on the autonomy of EU law and is therefore incompatible with EU law); and C-741/19, *Republic of Moldova v. Komstroy*, 2 Sep. 2021, ECLI:EU:C:2021:655 (where the CJEU ruled that intra-EU arbitrations based in the ECT are also contrary to EU law).
20. *See* for example, *AES Summit Generation Limited v. Hungary*, ICSID Case No ARB/07/22, Award, 23 Sep. 2010, paras 3.18 et seq.; *Electrabel SA v. Hungary*, ICSID Case No. ARB/07/19, Decision on Jurisdiction, Liability and Applicable Law, 30 Nov. 2012, paras 4.89 et seq.
21. European Commission, 'Commission Asks Member States to Terminate Their Intra-EU Bilateral Investment Treaties', Press Release (18 Jun. 2015) available https://ec.europa.eu/commission/presscorner/detail/en/IP_15_5198 (accessed 16 Dec. 2024).
22. *See* Agreement for the termination of Bilateral Investment Treaties between the Member States of the European Union, SN/4656/2019/INIT, OJ L 169, 29.5.2020, pp. 1-41 (signature on 5 May 2020; entered into force on 29 Aug. 2020).
23. *See* Arts 17, 26 and 27 of the draft Agreement in Principle on the modernisation of the ECT reached on 24 Jun. 2022. The modernised ECT was adopted on 3 Dec. 2024, with the corresponding texts, as available at https://www.energycharter.org/media/news/article/the-energy-charter-conference-adopts-decisions-on-the-modernisation-of-the-energy-charter-treaty/?tx_news_pi1%5Bcontroller%5D=News&tx_news_pi1%5Baction%5D=detail&cHash=2700d60aa897f2964e644c9e66a97028 (accessed 16 Dec. 2024).

IV RESULTS SO FAR?

There is no doubt that the EU has certainly influenced the debate around reforms of the international investment system, in particular with regard to ISDS. However, results on the ground, whether with regard to intra-EU treaties or with treaties with third countries, have yet to fully materialise.

On the outward-looking front, first of all, no international investment treaty concluded by the EU has yet entered into force, or for that matter is provisionally applicable, because not all EU Member States have yet ratified them. For example, the EU-Canada CETA was signed in October 2016 and has been provisionally applicable since September 2017, with the exception of the section on investment protection and ISDS. As of January 2024, seventeen out of twenty-seven EU Member States have ratified it. The EU signed two distinct agreements with Singapore in October 2018: the Trade Agreement entered into force in November 2019, while the Investment Protection Agreement, which requires ratification by all EU Members, has not entered into force (as of February 2022, only twelve EU Member States had ratified it). Similarly, while both the EU-Vietnam Trade and Investment Protection Agreements were signed in June 2019, only the former has entered into force (August 2020). As of October 2023, only sixteen EU Member States had ratified the latter. Accordingly, most of the novel features introduced with regard to investment protection and ISDS, examined above, remain on paper.

Second, the multilateral discussions that have taken place since 2017 within UNCITRAL WGIII are still ongoing. As noted above, the EU is very much on the front line pushing for the systemic reform of traditional investor-State arbitration towards the establishment of a multilateral investment court. However, it is still very much unclear the extent of the appetite for such system reform among UNCITRAL Member States.

Third, the attempt to modernise the ECT appears to have failed, and several EU Member States and the EU have chosen the more dramatic option of withdrawing from the ECT.[24] Withdrawal will have the apparent effect that old investments will continue to be protected for twenty years pursuant to the sunset clause, while any new investments will not. Arguments have already been advanced to undermine the operation of the sunset clause,[25] and they will likely be tested in the future when any such old investments bring a claim against one of the withdrawing parties.

On the inward-looking front, the clash between international investment treaties and the EU legal system has not yet been settled, and it is played out on a daily basis in dozens of existing international arbitral or domestic judicial proceedings. For example, with only one exception,[26] no investment arbitral tribunal has accepted the

24. As of writing, the ECT Secretariat lists France, Germany and Poland as having notified their intention to withdraw in December 2022. *See* https://www.energychartertreaty.org/treaty/contracting-parties-and-signatories/ (accessed 16 Dec. 2024).
25. *See*, for example, Tibisay Morgandi & Lorand Bartels, 'Exiting the Energy Charter Treaty under the Law of Treaties', 34 *King's Law Journal* 145 (2023) https://doi.org/10.1080/09615768.2023.2196834.
26. *See Green Power K/S and Obton A/S v. Spain*, SCC Case No. V 2016/135, Award, 16 Jun. 2022.

legal arguments advanced by the EU institutions regarding the validity of intra-EU ISDS.[27] Moreover, extensive controversy has ensued among domestic courts (in the EU and outside the EU) on the relevance of the *Achmea* doctrine when it comes to anti-suit injunctions against ISDS proceedings or enforcement of investment treaty awards whether under the International Centre for Settlement of Investment Disputes (ICSID) Convention or the New York Convention.[28]

V WHAT WILL THE FUTURE BRING?

EU's underlying values are clearly set out in the EU Treaties. Article 2 TEU provides that the EU is founded on the shared values of democracy, the rule of law and respect for fundamental rights. These values also guide the development of EU investment policy, but there is clearly an open debate over how best to embed these values in the EU investment policy of the future. The EU traditional challenge of finding the right balance between affording protection to foreign investments and ensuring host States' right to regulate in the public interest has been made over the years even more difficult by several other concerns that have implications in the construction of a value-based policy on investment. These concerns include: (i) the legitimacy of the traditional ISDS system based on ad hoc arbitration, (ii) the role played by local communities in the formulation of national development policies often heavily relying on foreign investments, and (iii) the new climate change policy priorities that require the transition from fossil-based energy systems to renewable ones and thus imply the need to differentiate between different investments.

For the moment, it does not look like EU institutions are ready to give up on pursuing systemic reforms of the international investment system still principally based on investment protection, investment liberalisation and ISDS. However, there are certainly signs of fatigue, such as the failure by several EU Member States to ratify the 'modernised' Investment Protection Agreements signed by the EU and their unwillingness to endorse the reformulated ECT negotiated by the Commission over the last five years.

Short of becoming one of the 'paradigm shifters' (i.e., those who advocate for the abandoning of the traditional investment system based on protection and ISDS), it is more likely that, in the future, the EU moves its emphasis to other strategies in order to encourage foreign investment in line with its overarching values mentioned above.

27. Petros C. Mavroidis & Federico Ortino, 'Intra-EU Investment Disputes and the Monopoly Over the Interpretation of EU Law', 33 *American Review of International Arbitration* 341 (2023) https://doi.org/10.2139/ssrn.4769352.

28. *See* Steffen Hindelang et al., 'Achmea Goes to Washington' *Verfassungblog* (2023), available https://verfassungsblog.de/achmea-goes-to-washington/; Carlos Ramos-Mrosovsky & Paul M. Levine, 'Achmea in America: The United States' Amicus Brief Offers Spain Half-hearted Support' Kluwer Arbitration Blog (2024), available https://arbitrationblog.kluwerarbitration.com/2024/02/22/achmea-in-america-the-united-states-amicus-brief-offers-spain-half-hearted-support/ (accessed 16 Dec. 2024).

One such strategy that is gaining momentum is 'investment facilitation',[29] whether as an alternative or complementary approach to attract foreign investment.

Investment facilitation shifts the focus from protecting investors' rights to improving the investment climate within the host country, making the investment process smoother, more efficient and more transparent. By focusing on creating a 'procedurally' favourable business environment, nations can attract investment more effectively without compromising their regulatory sovereignty. Furthermore, investment facilitation complements investment liberalisation by addressing the operational challenges that foreign investors face within a country. It acknowledges that even in liberalised markets, investors encounter bureaucratic hurdles, legal complexities, and logistical difficulties. By improving the ease of doing business and providing a supportive ecosystem, investment facilitation ensures that foreign investors can navigate the local environment more effectively, leading to higher investment inflows as well as greater investment retention.

While investment facilitation entails a wide range of elements, three key features should be highlighted here: (i) administrative streamlining and simplification, (ii) dispute prevention or avoidance and (iii) responsible business conduct (RBC).

First, in order to eliminate redundant bureaucratic steps and to clarify the administrative framework, disciplines on streamlining and simplification of investment-related administrative procedures often provide for reasonable timeframes and costs for permit applications, strategic digitalisation, single portal submissions. Second, underscoring a move away from litigation, investment facilitation disciplines focus on more cooperative mechanisms to address investors' complaints such as mediation, consultations or institutionalised dispute avoidance procedures, through ombudspersons or national focal points mechanisms. Third, emphasising the importance of attracting and retaining sustainable investment, in line with sustainable development objectives, RBC (or Corporate Social Responsibility (CSR)) has been included in a growing number of international investment agreements, whether between and among developed countries or between and among developing countries. Referring to various instruments outlining RBC standards and principles, such as the Organisation for Economic Co-operation and Development (OECD) Guidelines on Multinational Enterprises, the UN Guiding Principles on Business and Human Rights, and the International Labour Organization (ILO) Declarations, these provisions either obligate State parties to encourage businesses to voluntarily incorporate RBC standards and principles or impose obligations on foreign investors and their investments.

29. In the context of international investment agreements, investment facilitation was introduced first of all in the new investment treaties signed by Brazil in 2015, aptly titled 'Cooperation and Investment Facilitation Agreement' (CIFA). Brazil described the goal of its CIFAs as to create incentives for reciprocal investment through intergovernmental dialogue mechanisms, with the aim of establishing rights and obligations for investors and States alike and providing an alternative institutional model for prevention and settlement of disputes. Geraldo Vidigal & Beatriz Stevens, 'Brazil's New Model of Dispute Settlement for Investment: Return to the Past or Alternative for the Future?', 19 *Journal of World Investment & Trade* 475 (2018) https://doi.org/10.1163/22119000-12340100. More recently, *see* the 2020 ASEAN Investment Facilitation Framework and the 2022 African Continental Free Trade Area (AfCFTA) Protocol on Investment.

In the last few years, the EU has played its part in supporting investment facilitation strategies at the bilateral, regional and multilateral levels. Since 2018, the EU has been one of the World Trade Organization (WTO) Members that have been discussing and negotiating the Agreement on Investment Facilitation for Development (IFD), which has just been finalised and made public in February 2024 during the WTO Ministerial Conference in Abu Dhabi.[30] Furthermore, in its 2021 Trade Policy Review, the European Commission announced its intention to pursue sustainable investment agreements with Africa and the Southern Neighbourhood, focusing in particular on investment facilitation.[31] The first result of this programme has been the conclusion of the EU-Angola Sustainable Investment Facilitation Agreement in late 2022.[32]

It is difficult to predict whether the EU will continue to pursue investment facilitation as a complementary investment policy strategy. In any event, investment facilitation requires a much more pro-active, continuous involvement by host States in adopting investment facilitation measures. Investment facilitation requires first of all an assessment of where the lack of transparency, inefficiencies and bottlenecks are found, whether at the central or local levels, when it comes to investment activities. Second, it requires a continuous monitoring of any domestic processes that may negatively affect the attraction and retainment of foreign investments. Third, investment facilitation requires technical and financial support to ensure such assessment and continuous monitoring. In this sense, the recent WTO IFD Agreement has adopted the successful special and differential treatment approach that was followed by the WTO Trade Facilitation Agreement to ensure that developing and least-developed countries are capable of actually implementing their commitments.

VI CONCLUSIONS

The EU has certainly played a role in the debate around reforms of the international investment system, adopting different strategies with regard to its relations with third countries and intra-EU relations. Its complex supranational structure has created many challenges in implementing the various components of its novel reform agenda. Moreover, it appears that one of the challenges has also been the evolving nature of the EU reform agenda, as the early endorsement of the traditional investor-State arbitration and the more recent failure to modernise the ECT appear to show. One paradox of this challenging context is that, despite the general consensus regarding the need to drastically improve the current system, lack of agreement (within and beyond the EU)

30. In February 2024, more than 120 WTO Members have finalised the Agreement on IFD (INF/IFD/W/55). *See* https://www.wto.org/english/tratop_e/invfac_public_e/invfac_e.htm (accessed 16 Dec. 2024).
31. *See* European Commission, Communication on Trade Policy Review: An Open, Sustainable and Assertive Trade Policy (18 Feb. 2021) COM(2021) 66 final, available https://policy.trade.ec.europa.eu/news/commission-sets-course-open-sustainable-and-assertive-eu-trade-strategy-2020-02-18_en (accessed 16 Dec. 2024).
32. *See* European Commission, 'EU and Angola Conclude First-Ever Sustainable Investment Facilitation Agreement' Press Release (18 Nov. 2022) available https://ec.europa.eu/commission/presscorner/detail/en/ip_22_6136 (accessed 16 Dec. 2024).

on the features of such improvement has meant that the current system has for the most part stayed the same and this has led to even more criticism from various stakeholders.[33]

33. *See* further Federico Ortino, 'ISDS and Its Transformations', 26 *Journal of International Economic Law* 177 (2023) https://doi.org/10.1093/jiel/jgac066.

CHAPTER 16

Modernization of Arbitration in China: Recent Developments of Laws, Institutions and Practices

Manjiao Chi & Zongyao Li

China's economic growth has led to a surge in demand for arbitration, yet the Arbitration Law of China (CAL) has drawn criticisms for being outdated. In response, China has proposed significant reforms of the CAL and beyond, aiming at aligning its arbitration practices with international standards. This chapter surveys recent developments of arbitration in China, highlighting the reforms reflected in the Proposed Amendment to the CAL (PACAL), some of which stem from the practice of courts and arbitral institutions. The chapter further explores evolution in two dynamic areas of arbitration, namely foreign-related arbitration and Investor-State Arbitration (ISA). China's commitment to modernizing its arbitration landscape is evident through all those efforts, conforming to the need of the Chinese state, business organizations and arbitral institutions.

I INTRODUCTION

China is an important "arbitration market." With the economic development in the past decades, Chinese enterprises have become major players in the global market, and the need for arbitration between Chinese enterprises and their business partners, both Chinese and foreign, has significantly increased. Also, China hosts a large number of arbitration institutions, and their caseloads have experienced a sharp increase in recent years.[1] In addition, Chinese enterprises have become increasingly assertive in resorting to arbitration in solving disputes, which could be shown by the increase of investor-state arbitration (ISA) cases initiated by Chinese investors against foreign governments in recent years.[2]

The Arbitration Law of China (CAL) was adopted in 1994. While the CAL plays an indispensable role in defining Chinese arbitration, it has been criticized for being outdated and cannot meet the practical need. Notably, China has recently vowed to create a sound business environment and taken steps to build Beijing and Shanghai as a prime destination for international arbitration. To achieve this goal, it seems necessary to reform the CAL. In addition, China has also taken various other measures to promote ISA and to facilitate international arbitration, especially between Mainland China and the Hong Kong Special Administrative Region (Hong Kong).

Against such a background, it makes sense to observe the latest development in arbitration relating to China. Section I is an Introduction; section II analyzes the major aspects of the reform of the CAL and its implications; section III discusses the latest developments in China's foreign-related arbitration; section IV focuses on China's latest legislative efforts in relation to ISA; section V concludes.

II THE REFORM OF THE CAL AND ITS IMPLICATIONS

The CAL was adopted during China's initial stages of transitioning to a market economy. Since its adoption, China has experienced rapid and massive economic development. However, the CAL has remained essentially unchanged, subject to two minor cosmetic amendments in 2009 and 2017, respectively.[3] Almost three decades after its adoption, many of the provisions of the CAL depart from the needs of the arbitration users and international practice today, and it is not surprising that there has been a strong call for reforming the CAL.[4]

Against this backdrop, China decided to amend the CAL. On July 31, 2021, the Ministry of Justice of China published the Proposed Amendment to the CAL (PACAL)

1. *See, e.g.*, Ministry of Justice of China, "The Influence of China's International Commercial Arbitration Institutions Is Expanding" (original in Chinese), available at https://www.moj.gov.cn/pub/sfbgw/fzgz/fzgzggflfwx/fzgzggflfw/202309/t20230911_486092.html (accessed Dec. 16, 2024).
2. *See, e.g.*, Guo Shining, Edwina Kwan & Josephine Lao, "The Rise of Chinese Investors as Claimants: What Are the Likely Impacts on International Arbitration?," available at https://www.chinalawinsight.com/2018/06/articles/dispute-resolution/the-rise-of-chinese-investors-as-claimants-what-are-the-likely-impacts-on-international-arbitration/ (accessed Dec. 16, 2024).
3. *Decision of the Standing Committee of the National People's Congress on Amending Certain Laws*, adopted on Aug. 27, 2009; *Decision of the Standing Committee of the National People's Congress on Amending Eight Laws*, adopted on Sep. 1, 2017.
4. *See, e.g.*, Weixia Gu, "Piercing the Veil of Arbitration Reform in China: Promises, Pitfalls, Patterns, Prognoses, and Prospects," 65 *American Journal of Comparative Law* 799 (2017) https://doi.org/10.1093/ajcl/avx040; Zhao Xiuwen & Lisa Kloppenberg, "Reforming Chinese Arbitration Law and Practices in the Global Economy," 31 *UD Law Review* 421 (2006) https://doi.org/10.1007/s11463-006-0017-2.

for public consultation.[5] The PACAL reflects China's attempt to systematically reform and improve the existing CAL to keep up with the needs of the arbitration users and bring the arbitration practice in China in line with international practice. It should be noted that the PACAL has not been formally adopted into law as of this writing. It is, however, on the working agenda of the Standing Committee of the National People's Congress.[6]

It bears noting that the process of "reforming" the CAL did not start with the PACAL. For the past two decades or so, the courts, in particular, the Supreme People's Court (SPC), and the arbitral institutions in China, have been instrumental in "reforming" the CAL impliedly by interpreting and applying the CAL through judicial interpretations, judgements, and arbitration practice. As detailed below, many of the key innovations in the PACAL stem from the practice of courts and arbitral institutions.

A Recognition of the Concept of the "Seat of Arbitration"

The seat of arbitration is an indispensable element in most arbitration proceedings. It determines a number of important factors in arbitration, including the nationality of an arbitral award, the *lex arbitri*, as well as the court which would have supervisory jurisdiction over an arbitration. Under the CAL, however, the concept of "*seat*" is not recognized.

In the earlier years following the promulgation of the CAL, the location of an administering institution was widely considered to carry the preponderance of weight for purposes of determining the nationality of an award, compared with the seat of arbitration.[7] Thus, in a reply issued by the SPC to the High People's Court of Shanxi Province in 2004, it was observed that an award issued by an International Chamber of Commerce (ICC) tribunal in Hong Kong was of French nationality because the ICC was an arbitral institution established in France.[8]

The courts' position has shifted in the more recent judgements. For example, in the *Brentwood* case in 2020, the Intermediate People's Court of Guangzhou Municipality confirmed that the seat of arbitration determines the nationality of the award. In that case, the Guangzhou court determined that an ICC award issued in Guangzhou may be

5. Ministry of Justice of China, Arbitration Law of the People's Republic of China (Amendment) (Draft for Comments) (original in Chinese), available at https://zqyj.chinalaw.gov.cn/h5/readmore?listType=&id=4518 (accessed Dec. 16, 2024).
6. Zhao Leji, "Working Report of the Standing Committee of the National People's Congress" (original in Chinese), available at https://npcobserver.com/wp-content/uploads/2024/03/2024-NPCSC-Work-Report_ZH.pdf (accessed Dec. 16, 2024).
7. Yang Ling, "The Seat of Arbitration: The Development of This Concept in Mainland China," 65 *Asian Disputes Review* 35, 36 (2022).
8. Letter of Reply of the SPC to the Request for Instructions on the Case of *Wei Mao International (Hong Kong) Co Ltd v. Shanxi Tianli Industrial Co Ltd* of Not Enforcing the Final Award 10334/AMW/BWD/TE of the International Court of Arbitration of International Chamber of Commerce, [2004] Min Si Ta Zi No. 6, Jul. 5, 2004.

regarded as a Chinese award (as opposed to a French award) and that such award may be enforced under applicable Chinese laws (as opposed to the New York Convention).[9]

The PACAL appears to formally recognize the concept of the seat of arbitration, thus reflecting and codifying the progress made by the courts. Specifically, it has been expressly provided, *inter alia*, that: (i) the award shall be considered to be issued at the seat of arbitration;[10] (ii) the application for setting aside an arbitral award shall be submitted to the court of the seat of arbitration;[11] and (iii) in the absence of agreement between the parties, the law governing the arbitration agreement shall be the law of the seat of arbitration.[12]

B Empowering Arbitral Tribunals to Grant Interim Relief

The CAL requires that parties to arbitration proceedings seeking interim relief from the Chinese courts must do so through the arbitral institution administering the arbitration.[13] Therefore, arbitral tribunals do not have the power to grant interim relief pursuant to the CAL.

In this respect, the arbitral institutions have sought to follow international practice by enabling the arbitral tribunals to grant interim relief to the extent possible. For example, in 2012, the China International Economic and Trade Arbitration Commission (CIETAC) arbitration rules introduced a new provision which allowed the arbitral tribunal, at the request of a party, to order any interim relief that it deems necessary or proper "*in accordance with applicable law.*"[14] As pointed out by the commentators at the time, it is doubtful that a Chinese court would give any effect to an interim relief order issued by an arbitral tribunal, given that the CAL does not provide for arbitral tribunals to issue interim relief.[15] Nevertheless, this provision illustrates how Chinese arbitral institutions have pushed the boundaries of the CAL. Indeed, it is feasible for a CIETAC arbitral tribunal seated outside of China to issue interim relief under this provision provided that it is permitted by the "*applicable law,*" i.e., the *lex arbitri*.

The PACAL explicitly permits arbitral tribunals (as well as the courts) to grant interim relief. Article 43 stipulates that before or during the arbitration proceedings, in order to safeguard the conduct of the arbitration proceedings, the ascertainment of the

9. *Brentwood Industries v. Guangdong Fa-anlong Mechanical Equipment Manufacture Co Ltd*, Intermediate People's Court of Guangzhou Municipality, [2015] Sui Zhong Fa Min Si Chu Zi No. 62, Aug. 6, 2020.
10. Article 27(2), PACAL.
11. Article 77, PACAL.
12. Article 90, PACAL.
13. Articles 28 and 46, CAL.
14. Article 21(2), CIETAC Arbitration Rules (2012).
15. William Leung, "China's Arbitration System: Changes in Light of the CIETAC Arbitration Rules 2012 and the Civil Procedure Law 2012," *79 International Journal of Arbitration, Mediation and Dispute Management* 171, 178 (2012).

disputed facts or the enforcement of the award, the parties may request the people's court or the arbitral tribunal to take provisional or urgent measures relating to the subject matter of the dispute.[16]

C Recognizing the Competence-Competence Doctrine

In essence, the competence-competence doctrine requires that arbitrators be empowered to rule on their own jurisdiction and that they are not required to stay the proceedings to seek judicial guidance.[17]

The CAL does not recognize the principle of competence-competence. It confers parallel jurisdiction upon the arbitration commission and the people's courts in resolving jurisdictional disputes while specifying that when the parties bring jurisdictional challenges before both the arbitral commission and the people's courts, the people's court shall rule on the challenge.[18] The CAL therefore diverges significantly from the principle of competence-competence in two aspects. First, it does not explicitly allow the arbitral tribunal (as opposed to the arbitral commission/institution) to rule on its jurisdiction. Second, arbitration proceedings must be suspended when any of the parties raise jurisdictional objections before the Chinese courts.

In practice, the Chinese arbitral institutions often delegate the power to decide jurisdictional issues to the arbitral tribunal. For example, the 2005 CIETAC arbitration rules introduced a mechanism which allowed, if necessary, the arbitral commission to authorize the arbitral tribunal to rule on the jurisdictional issues.[19] This has partially addressed the inconsistency between the CAL and the competence-competence doctrine. However, the effect of such clause is limited because, in practice, the parties prefer raising jurisdictional objections with the Chinese courts,[20] whose decision prevails over the decision made by the arbitral tribunal or the arbitral commission. The parties may also do so with a purpose of delaying the arbitral proceedings.

The competence-competence doctrine is unequivocally endorsed by the PACAL. According to Article 28: (i) if the parties object to the arbitral tribunal's jurisdiction, the arbitral tribunal shall make a decision; (ii) the parties may only ask the people's court to review the arbitral tribunal's decision on jurisdiction when such decision has been made by the arbitral tribunal; and (iii) the review by the people's court shall not have the effect of suspending the arbitration proceedings.[21]

16. Article 43, PACAL.
17. John Barceló III, "Who Decides the Arbitrators' Jurisdiction? Separability and Competence-Competence in Transnational Perspective" 36 *Vanderbilt Journal of Transnational Law* 1115, 1122-1124 (2003).
18. Article 20(1), CAL.
19. Article 6(1), CIETAC Arbitration Rules (2005).
20. Helen Shi, "Draft Amendment: A Big Leap for China Arbitration," Sep. 2, 2021, available at https://law.asia/draft-amendment-big-leap-china-arbitration/ (accessed Dec. 16, 2024).
21. Article 28, PACAL.

III LATEST DEVELOPMENTS IN CHINA'S FOREIGN-RELATED ARBITRATION

In general terms, the CAL established a system that is bifurcated between purely domestic arbitrations and foreign-related arbitrations in a number of aspects, and the PACAL has maintained the existing system.[22] The CAL, together with other applicable regulations and rules, typically offers greater flexibility in foreign-related arbitrations, compared to purely domestic ones. Foreign-related arbitration has often been at the forefront of promoting the development of arbitration laws and practices in China.

A The Mainland China-Hong Kong Interim Measures Arrangement

On April 2, 2019, the SPC and the Government of Hong Kong entered into the Arrangement Concerning Mutual Assistance in Court-Ordered Interim Measures in Aid of Arbitral Proceedings by the Courts of the Mainland and of the Hong Kong Special Administrative Region ("Arrangement").[23]

The Arrangement essentially empowers Mainland courts to issue interim measures in aid of arbitration proceedings seated in Hong Kong and administered by a number of institutions, including the Hong Kong International Arbitration Centre (HKIAC) and the ICC. The Arrangement has therefore practically amended the CAL (in so far as the qualified Hong Kong arbitrations are concerned), which provides no mechanism by which Chinese courts would grant interim measures in support of arbitrations seated outside of Mainland China.

According to the statistics published by the HKIAC, which is the most active institution in Hong Kong, since the Interim Measures Arrangement came into force on October 1, 2019, and as of the end of 2023, HKIAC has processed 105 applications for interim measures from Chinese courts.[24] Of the seventy decisions issued by Mainland courts of which HKIAC is aware, sixty-six granted the applications for preservation of assets upon the applicant's provision of security and only four rejected such an application.[25] These seemingly promising figures demonstrate a high likelihood of the Chinese courts granting interim measures and the added advantage for Hong Kong in China-related arbitrations compared to other jurisdictions.

Notably, the PACAL does not seek to change the position under the CAL, where courts are not empowered to grant interim measures in support of foreign arbitration or to recognize or enforce interim measures granted by foreign arbitral tribunals. It seems

22. *See*, Arts 65-73, CAL; Arts 87-93, PACAL. In the present chapter, "*foreign-related arbitration*" generally includes any arbitration that has an element that is not related to mainland China, e.g., a foreign seat or a foreign party.
23. Arrangement Concerning Mutual Assistance in Court-Ordered Interim Measures in Aid of Arbitral Proceedings by the Courts of the Mainland and of the Hong Kong Special Administrative Region, Apr. 2, 2019, available at https://www.doj.gov.hk/en/mainland_and_macao/pdf/arbitration_interim_e.pdf (accessed Dec. 16, 2024).
24. HKIAC Statistics 2023, available at https://www.hkiac.org/about-us/statistics (accessed Dec. 16, 2024).
25. *Ibid.*

that, in the foreseeable future, Hong Kong will likely continue to be the only jurisdiction outside of mainland China where arbitrations could benefit from the interim measures ordered by Chinese courts.

B Opening the Market to Foreign Arbitral Institutions

The question of whether foreign arbitral institutions can administer arbitrations in China has been a subject of a prolonged debate. The CAL does not expressly prohibit or permit an arbitration clause providing for an arbitration seated in China to be administered by a foreign institution. However, under Article 16 of the CAL, a valid arbitration agreement must contain "*a designated arbitral commission*," and the term "*arbitral commission*" (which, in its literal sense, is not significantly different from "*arbitral institution*"),[26] according to Article 10 of the CAL, only refers to those established at the municipal or provincial level and registered with the relevant authorities in China and would potentially not encompass any foreign arbitral institution.

While the Chinese courts have taken a somewhat conservative approach in the earlier years, a series of recent replies from the SPC and court decisions indicate that a consistent approach confirming the foreign arbitral institutions' ability to administer arbitrations in China has been followed. In addition to the aforementioned *Brentwood* case which enforced an ICC award issued in Guangzhou (and thus endorsing the underlying arbitration agreement providing for ICC arbitration in Guangzhou),[27] the No. 1 Intermediate People's Court of Shanghai Municipality issued a decision in 2020 confirming the validity of an arbitration agreement providing for Singapore International Arbitration Centre (SIAC) arbitration seated in Shanghai.[28] Notably, this decision was included in the SPC's ten typical court cases on judicial review of arbitration published on January 16, 2024, and in commenting on this case, the SPC specifically endorsed the Shanghai court's liberal approach in interpreting Article 16 of the CAL.[29]

In addition to the courts, the Chinese administrative authorities have also played an important role in gradually opening the market to foreign arbitral institutions. In this respect, both Beijing and Shanghai have adopted new policies, which allow foreign arbitral institutions to establish offices in designated areas and administer arbitrations.[30]

These developments have been codified in the PACAL, which: (i) removes "a designated arbitral commission" as a required element of an arbitration agreement, (ii)

26. Omar Puertas Álvarez, et al., "Can Foreign Arbitration Institutions Validly Administer Cases in Mainland China: The Last Update," 42 *Spain Arbitration Review* 119, 122-123 (2021).
27. *Brentwood Industries v. Guangdong Fa-anlong Mechanical Equipment Manufacture Co Ltd*, Intermediate People's Court of Guangzhou Municipality, [2015] Sui Zhong Fa Min Si Chu Zi No. 62, Aug. 6, 2020.
28. *Daesung Industrial Gases Co Ltd v. Praxair (China) Investment Co Ltd*, No. 1 Intermediate People's Court of Shanghai Municipality, [2020] Hu 01 Min Te No. 83, Jun. 29, 2020.
29. Bureau of Press of the SPC, The SPC Publish Cases on Judicial Review of Arbitrations, Jan. 16, 2024, https://cicc.court.gov.cn/html/1/218/62/163/2444.html (accessed Dec. 16, 2024).
30. Article 13(1), PACAL.

abandons the term "arbitral commission" and instead uses "arbitral institution,"[31] and (iii) authorizes foreign arbitral institutions to establish offices and conduct foreign-related arbitrations in China subject to certain procedural requirements.[32]

IV THE LEGISLATIVE EFFORTS FOR ENABLING ISA

China has no specialized national law on ISA, and the legal rules explicitly dealing with ISA are extremely rare. As the CAL lays down the fundamental principles and rules of arbitration in China,[33] it seems to be the law that is most closely relevant to ISA. Other relevant laws include, *inter alia*, the Civil Procedural Law of China (CPL) and the Administrative Procedural Law of China (APL).

A Legitimizing ISA Through the Reform of the CAL

It is unclear if the CAL is applicable to ISA, as ISA involves sovereign states, foreign states in particular. However, as the CAL does not explicitly exclude ISA from its ambit, it could be argued that it can be applied to ISA. That said, the CAL has two major obstacles to ISA, suggesting that ISA is impliedly banned by the CAL.

On the one hand, the CAL impliedly bans states as a party to arbitration. Chinese law requires that disputants should have the necessary capacity to be a party in arbitration. Chinese law has no explicit rules on capacity of states, especially foreign states, in legal proceedings in China. Yet, Article 2 of the CAL requires that only disputes "between citizens, legal persons and other organizations that are equal subjects" may be arbitrated.[34] Thus, to be a party to an arbitration in China, states should constitute a "legal person" or "other organization" and should be "equal subjects" with private investors.

The above requirement is unlikely to be satisfied. First, according to the *Civil Code of China* (CCC), "legal person" refers to "an institution established in accordance with law" and "shall have its name, organizational structure and premise, and property,"[35] which "can independently enjoy civil rights and undertake civil liabilities."[36] In practice, it is understood to cover enterprises and non-enterprise entities[37] but not states. Second, according to the *SPC Opinion Concerning Certain Questions on the Application of the CPL*, "other organization" refers to an "institution ... which has its own property and organizational structure but does not meet the other requirements

31. Article 12(3), PACAL.
32. *Administrative Measures for Registration of Business Offices Established by Overseas Arbitration Institutions in China (Beijing) Pilot Free Trade Zone*, Beijing Municipal Bureau of Justice, Dec. 28, 2020; *Administrative measures for Lin-gang Special Area of the China (Shanghai) Pilot Free Trade Zone*, Art. 13, Shanghai Municipal Government, Aug. 12, 2019.
33. *See* Ge Liu & Alexander Lourie, "International Commercial Arbitration in China: History, New Developments, and Current Practice," 28(3) *John Marshall Law Review* 539, 543 (1994-1995).
34. Article 3, CAL.
35. Article 58, CCC.
36. Article 57, CCC.
37. *See, e.g.*, Jiang Ping (ed.), *Civil Law* (Beijing: CUPL Press, 2nd edn 2011), at 76 (original in Chinese).

of legal person, such as foreign enterprises and social organizations."[38] By linking "other organization" to "foreign enterprise" and "social organization," it seems unlikely that this provision could be applied to deal with the legal status of states. Third, though the term "equal subjects of law" is frequently used in China, it is used in the context of civil and commercial law, where private parties to a contract can be deemed as "equal subjects of law" in legal proceedings. As ISA deals with the relationship between private parties and sovereign states, it seems unlikely for states and private investors to be treated as "equal subjects of law" in ISA.[39]

On the other hand, the CAL also denies the arbitrability of administrative disputes. Article 2 of the CAL provides that only "contractual disputes and other disputes over rights and interests in property" may be arbitrated.[40] Article 3 of the CAL further provides that "administrative disputes that shall be handled by administrative organs as prescribed by law" cannot be arbitrated.[41] According to the *APL*, "administrative disputes" means "disputes between citizens, legal persons or other organizations and state administrative organs or their personnel, arising out of the infringement of the private party's lawful rights or interests by administrative acts."[42] The APL also provides a non-exhaustive list of actionable and a list of non-actionable administrative disputes.[43] Notably, actionable administrative disputes cover eight types of administrative measures, including, *inter alia*, cancelation of government license, violation of the property rights, interference with the operation of enterprise.[44] In reality, however, administrative measures are typical reasons that give rise to disputes between investors and host states since almost all ISA cases in which an expropriation or a fair and equitable treatment clause is invoked involve allegedly illegal or irregular administrative measures of the host states.[45] In this sense, China's categorical denial of the arbitrability of administrative disputes could amount to a de facto ban of ISA in China.

In recent years, there has been a growing call that ISA should be allowed in China. First, with the implementation of the Belt and Road Initiative (BRI) since 2013, many Chinese enterprises have invested abroad. As many BRI states are politically unstable and economically underdeveloped, it is highly likely that Chinese investments will encounter risks in these states and that they may need to resort to ISA for protection. Second, over the past few decades, China has concluded over hundred

38. Article 40, *SPC* Opinions *Concerning Certain Questions on the Application of the Civil Procedural Law* (adopted at the 528th meeting of the Judicial Committee of the Supreme People's Court on Jul. 14, 1992) Fa Fa No. 22 (1992).
39. Manjiao Chi, "The ISDS Adventure of Chinese Arbitration Institutions: Towards a Dead End or a Bright Future?," 28(2) *Asia Pacific Law Review* 279, 289 (2021) https://doi.org/10.1080/10192557.2020.1856309.
40. Article 2, CAL.
41. Article 3(2), CAL.
42. Article 2, APL.
43. Articles 12 and 13, APL.
44. Article 12, APL.
45. *See* Marc Jacob & Stephan W. Schill, "Fair and Equitable Treatment: Content, Practice, Method," in Marc Bungenberg et al. (eds), *International Investment Law: A Handbook* (Baden-Baden: Nomos, 2015), at 700-763.

international investment treaties, bilateral investment treaties (BITs) in particular.[46] As most of China's BITs allow ISA, it is possible and feasible for Chinese investors to resort to ISA for treaty protection. Third, as many Chinese enterprises have grown into resourceful transnational companies and have bargaining power in developing states, they are increasingly assertive in defending their rights at the international level.[47] As a matter of fact, the recent decade has witnessed a rapid increase of ISA cases initiated by Chinese investors against their host states, including both developed and developing states.[48] Last but not least, as mentioned earlier, China has vowed to develop major cities into centers for international dispute settlement in recent years, such as Beijing and Shanghai, and allowing ISA in China seems a natural measure to achieve such a goal.

China is aware of the growing need for ISA. To allow ISA in China, the obstacles to ISA in the CAL should be removed. This is reflected in the PACAL. According to Article 2 of the PACAL, arbitral parties do not need to be "equal subjects of law." As this provision impliedly allows sovereign states to be a party in arbitration, it paves the way for ISA in China. It is also helpful for allowing some other types of arbitration in China, such as sport arbitration. According to the *Sport Arbitration Rules* adopted by the General Bureau of Sports of the People's Republic of China, parties to sport arbitration in China include "sport associations," "athlete management organizations" and "organizers of sports events."[49] As can be seen, this provision allows various types of sport or athletic organizations to be a party of arbitration, whereas such organizations are impliedly banned by the CAL due to the fact that they can hardly be deemed as "equal subjects of law" as athletes.

B The Law of State Immunity and ISA

While states are frequently involved in litigation and arbitration, no uniform rules on state immunity have been formed at the international level. Roughly speaking, though the restrictive immunity principle has been widely adopted, the absolute immunity principle is still upheld in some states.[50]

Different from some common law states that adopt the restrictive immunity principle in their national foreign state immunity laws, such as the US[51] and the UK,[52] China has held absolute immunity in case of acts of foreign states from national

46. A list of China's BITs is available at https://tfs.mofcom.gov.cn/gjk/art/2011/art_20513f4a33d64e528279070a25d63050.html (accessed Dec. 16, 2024).
47. *See* Guo Shining, Edwina Kwan & Josephine Lao, "The Rise of Chinese Investors as Claimants: What Are the Likely Impacts on International Arbitration?," available at https://www.chinalawinsight.com/2018/06/articles/dispute-resolution/the-rise-of-chinese-investors-as-claimants-what-are-the-likely-impacts-on-international-arbitration/ (accessed Dec. 16, 2024).
48. A list of these ISA cases is available at https://investmentpolicy.unctad.org/investment-dispute-settlement (accessed Dec. 16, 2024).
49. Article 3, Sport Arbitration Rules.
50. *See* generally Hazel Fox & Philippa Webb, *The Law of State Immunity* (Oxford University Press, 3rd edn 2013).
51. Foreign Sovereign Immunity Act 1976, available at https://www.law.cornell.edu/uscode/text/28/1605 (accessed Dec. 16, 2024).

jurisdiction and execution, and Chinese courts have never enforced any decisions involving public property of foreign states.[53] In the high-profile case of *Democratic Republic of the Congo and Others v. FG Hemisphere Associates LLC*,[54] the Office of the Commissioner of the Ministry of Foreign Affairs in Hong Kong Special Administrative Region, the representative of China's Central Government, issued two letters respectively to Hong Kong Court of First Instance and Court of Appeal, which clarified China's adherence to absolute immunity.[55]

China's adherence to absolute immunity has not been changed until quite recently when China adopted the Foreign State Immunity Law (FSIL). This makes it possible to enforce ISA awards against states in China. Before the adoption of the FSIL, China had a national law that deals with this issue, namely the *Law of Immunity of Assets of Foreign Central Banks of China*,[56] which allows enforcement of assets of foreign central banks located in China if the banks or their governments waive the immunity in writing or designate the assets for execution or preservation purpose.[57] As this law only deals with assets of foreign central banks, its application scope is strictly limited.

In relation to ISA, two articles of the FSIL are worth mentioning. First, according to Article 12 of the FSIL, where a foreign state has agreed with Chinese or foreign nationals to submit their investment disputes to arbitration, the foreign state shall not enjoy immunity in Chinese courts in judicial proceedings for adjudicating the validity of the arbitration agreement and the enforcement of arbitral award, among others. While such a position could be seen as a "reiteration" of the reality, it makes sense for China to legalize it in the FSIL. Second, according to Article 7 of the FSIL, foreign states shall not enjoy immunity from enforcement in Chinese courts if the foreign states engage in commercial activities. Such a position signifies that China has recognized the restrictive immunity doctrine, which is a fundamental departure from China's adherence to the absolute immunity doctrine over the past decades.

With the FSIL in place, it seems that China has paved the way for ISA to take place in China and for the enforcement of ISA awards in China, thus transforming China into an ISA-friendly jurisdiction. That being said, however, as these FSIL provisions appear quite general, it remains necessary for China to adopt further legislation or judicial guidance on the many concrete issues relating to ISA in China, such as to which level

52. Sovereign Immunity Act 1978, available at http://www.legislation.gov.uk/ukpga/1978/33 (accessed Dec. 16, 2024).
53. Xue Hanqin, "Chinese Contemporary Perspective on International Law: History, Culture and International Law," (2011) 355 *Recueil des Cours* 42, at 100-104 https://doi.org/10.1163/9789004236141.
54. *See* [2009] 1 HKLRD 410 (Court of First Instance), [2010] 2 HKLRD 66 (Court of Appeal) and FACV 5, 6 & 7/2010 (Court of Final Appeal). Available at http://www.judiciary.gov.hk/en/legal_ref/judgments.htm.
55. *See* Manjiao Chi, "The Impending Effects of the Immunity Plea on International Arbitration: China's Position Revisited," 12(1) *Asian International Arbitration Journal* 21, 36-38 (2016) https://doi.org/10.54648/aiaj2016002.
56. Adopted at the 18th Meeting of the Standing Committee of the 10th National People's Congress on Oct. 25, 2005, available at http://www.china.com.cn/chinese/PI-c/1010926.htm (accessed Dec. 16, 2024).
57. Article 1, the Foreign Bank Immunity Law of China.

of courts should Chinese or foreign investors resort to in order to enforce ISA awards, and how such awards should be enforced against foreign states by the Chinese courts. It is likely that the SPC will, at an appropriate time in the future, deliver guidelines to address these outstanding issues in the form of SPC judicial interpretation.

C Chinese Arbitration Institutions and ISA

A notable development of ISA in China is that leading Chinese arbitration institutions have started an unprecedented "ISDS adventure." As discussed above, while China has realized the need to allow ISA, Chinese arbitration institutions have also tried to step into the highly competitive Investor-State Dispute Settlement (ISDS) business for several reasons. From a legal perspective, as discussed above, since the PACAL has paved the way for ISA in China, Chinese arbitration institutions may legally deal with ISA cases in China. From a business perspective, because leading Chinese arbitration institutions have achieved historical success in commercial arbitration in the past few decades, it seems natural for them to anticipate another success in ISA. Such an expectation could be particularly attractive as many Chinese investors in BRI states tend to select Chinese arbitration institutions for dispute settlement in their investment contracts with foreign governments. From a political perspective, China has announced to "develop foreign-related rule of law" and "gain greater say in international governance." ISA in China could be deemed as a symbol of China's success in achieving these developmental goals.

Since a few years ago, leading Chinese arbitration institutions, mainly referring to CIETAC, Beijing Arbitration Commission (BAC), and Shenzhen Court of International Arbitration (SCIA), have tried to promulgate a set of arbitration rules that exclusively cater to ISA. In 2017, CIETAC published its Rules for ISA, and in 2019, BAC published its Rules for ISA, which include a set of rules for appeal, the first of its kind in the world. Though SCIA does not have a specialized set of rules for ISA, its 2016 Rules explicitly allow ISA. The SCIA has further adopted the Guidelines for the Administration of Arbitration under the United Nations Commission on International Trade Law (UNCITRAL) Arbitration Rules, which are frequently used for ad hoc ISA.

Despite the above achievements, none of these Chinese arbitration institutions has accepted any ISA cases up to the present. This could be caused by the fact that the Chinese arbitration institutions lack experience of ISA and that they also face fierce competition from the established arbitration institutions, especially the International Centre for Settlement of Investment Disputes (ICSID). Clearly, the Chinese arbitration institutions will need to prove that they are capable of handling ISA cases in order to be attractive to foreign states and investors.

V CONCLUSION

China is a rapidly growing arbitration market. Not only it hosts a large number of arbitration institutions that attract tens of thousands of arbitration cases annually but also some Chinese arbitration institutions have grown to be leading players at the global level. In recent years, China has vowed to become a prime destination of international arbitration. However, due to historical reasons, the CAL as the basic law of Chinese arbitration seems insufficiently helpful in achieving this goal.

The PACAL, which is likely to be adopted by the top legislature of China in the near future, appears to be a breakthrough. It will not only help align Chinese arbitration with the international practice but also legitimize new types of arbitration in China, such as ISA and sport arbitration. Such a reform conforms to the present needs of China and Chinese enterprises. It is also important to note that alongside the reform of the CAL, Chinese arbitration institutions have also shown a great interest in exploring some "frontiers" of business and that Chinese enterprises have also become increasingly assertive in resorting to international arbitration to protect their interests and rights.

CHAPTER 17

Foreign Investment Protection in the Context of MERCOSUR

Eduardo Grebler & Filipe Greco

This chapter seeks to analyse the current legal framework of investment protection within the Southern Common Market ('MERCOSUR'). Following a summary of the investment protection mechanism through the model Organisation for Economic Co-operation and Development ('OECD') Bilateral Investment Treaty ('BIT'), the chapter introduces the Brazilian model Agreement for the Cooperation and Facilitation of Investments ('ACFI'), from which the Protocol for Cooperation and Facilitation of Investments in MERCOSUR ('PCFI') draws its inspiration. The chapter sustains that, by neglecting the standards of substantive protection proposed by the model BIT and the investor-State dispute settlement mechanism through arbitration ('ISDS'), the ACFI and the PCFI fail to provide effective investment protection for MERCOSUR Member States.

I INTRODUCTION

The subject of foreign investment protection has been extensively debated in the last few years, with special emphasis on a possible reform of both substantive and procedural features of the investor-State dispute settlement system.

Amid that debate, Brazil has launched a new model of foreign investment protection, named 'Agreement for the Cooperation and Facilitation of Investments' ('ACFI'),[1] as an alternative to the model Bilateral Investment Treaty ('BIT')[2] drafted by the Organisation for Economic Co-operation and Development ('OECD'). Brazil is not

1. *See* Fabio Morosini & Michelle Ratton Badin, *The Brazilian Agreement of Cooperation and Facilitation of Investments (ACFI): A New Formula for International Investment Agreements?*,

a party to any BIT in force, nor has it signed the Washington Convention of 1965, which established the International Centre for Settlement of Investment Disputes ('ICSID').

The Brazilian model ACFI distances itself considerably from the traditional BIT. From a substantive perspective, the ACFI does not grant fair and equitable treatment to foreign investors, nor does it include protection against indirect expropriation; from a procedural perspective, it does not provide for access, by a foreign investor, to the dispute settlement mechanism through arbitration against a recipient State.

The Brazilian ACFI inspired the draft model of foreign investment regulation within the Southern Common Market (MERCOSUR) contained in the Protocol for Cooperation and Facilitation of Investments in MERCOSUR (PCFI). Instead of providing an offer to arbitrate, the PCFI intends to prevent conflicts involving a foreign investor and a Member State through negotiations at different administrative levels. If no negotiated settlement is reached, then the national State of the investor may sponsor its claim and submit the dispute to a State-State arbitration.

The review of the main features of both models, ACFI and PCFI, against the backdrop of the international investment protection system, purports to verify whether those instruments accomplish the goal of protecting foreign investment within the MERCOSUR region.

II BACKGROUND ON FOREIGN INVESTMENT PROTECTION

The notion of foreign investment protection has been present in international law since the early treaties of friendship, commerce and navigation were signed by the United States with some countries, with the purpose of obtaining economic and political support as they became a relevant player in international economic relations. Besides investment protection, their scope encompassed aspects such as trade, immigration, shipping, intellectual property, taxation, all of which affected the economic interests of expanding economies.[3] In the aftermath of the Second World War, foreign investment protection became still more relevant as international capital flows increased the export of capitals to countries by developed economies to countries with developing economies. The first formally structured BIT was signed by Germany and Pakistan in 1959, soon to be followed by a number of similar instruments entered by other countries.

BITs' primary purpose is to ensure protection for investments made by a foreign investor in the territory of a host State. To make it feasible, BITs generally protect the

---

https://www.iisd.org/itn/en/2015/08/04/the-brazilian-agreement-on-cooperation-and-facilitation-of-investments-acfi-a-new-formula-for-international-investment-agreements/ (accessed 16 Dec. 2024).

2. *See*, for instance, the OECD 'Draft Convention on the Protection of Foreign Property', of 1967, https://web-archive.oecd.org/2022-05-22/108412-39286571.pdf (accessed 16 Dec. 2024); *see also* the BIT signed between Germany and Pakistan, in 1959, considered one of the first 'modern' BITs: https://investmentpolicy.unctad.org/international-investment-agreements/treaty-files/1387/download (accessed 16 Dec. 2024).
3. John F. Coyle, *The Treaty of Friendship, Commerce and Navigation in the Modern Era*, 51 Columbia Journal of Transnational Law, 304-307 (2013).

foreign investor from discrimination by the host State, in relation both to other foreign investors ('most favoured nation') and to domestic investors ('national treatment'). BITs aim at: (a) the full protection and security for the investment made by the foreign investor, (b) the adequate compensation to the foreign investor in the event of expropriation of its investment, (c) the convertibility and transferability of capital, profits, dividends, and payments, without restriction, by the foreign investor.[4] By entering a BIT, the signatory States undertake to abide by those principles and rules, for the reciprocal benefit of its respective nationals.

However, there are circumstances in which conflicts arise between an investor and the host State regarding measures taken by the authorities of the latter. Despite being based on sovereignty, certain governmental measures bear an impact on investor's rights provided for in the BIT. Where the conflict fails to be resolved amicably, the investor may need to claim compensation from the host State, giving rise to a controversy that should be decided by a neutral adjudicator.

Under the principle of judicial redress prevailing in civilized nations, claims against a State may be brought before the judiciary of that same State. However, foreign investors are often reluctant to seek judicial redress by the national judiciary of the host State in view of concerns on the independence and impartiality of another branch of the same State that allegedly acted in violation of legal norms and harmed the investor's rights. It follows that foreign investors become reluctant to invest in countries in which they lack confidence on the prevalence of the rule of law. Having regard to the detrimental outcome of such circumstance to the international economic system, an independent and impartial dispute resolution process was devised by the OECD model BIT, according to which disputes involving a foreign investor and a host State should be resolved by independent and impartial adjudicators, rather than by the court system of the involved State. That is where the investor-State dispute settlement through arbitration mechanism ('ISDS') comes into play.

Many of the three-thousand-plus BITs presently in force generally follow the OECD model. However, differences do exist, deriving from the process of negotiation and the interests of countries involved in each particular treaty, the result of which is a variety of formulae that lack uniformity. To avoid that situation, economic blocs attempt to harmonize the rules of differing treaties by setting models to be followed by Member States, as in the case of MERCOSUR. That is the role of the conventions governing the investor-State arbitration mechanisms within regional blocs.

The experience drawn from the implementation of BITs during the last fifty years, particularly in disputes arising between investors and host States, led to a critical revision of the underpinnings of foreign investments worldwide. Several aspects of the ISDS mechanisms have been questioned by non-governmental organizations (NGOs), academics and international organizations as well, based mainly on the arguments of:

4. 'Developed countries responded to the threat of uncompensated expropriation by creating the bilateral investment treaty (BIT). Germany was the first to conclude such an agreement. Having lost its foreign investment because of its defeat in the Second World War, Germany was especially sensitive to the political risks to which foreign investment was exposed.' Kenneth J. Vandevelde, *A Brief History of International Investment Agreements*, 12 U.C. Davis Journal of International Law & Policy 157, 168-169 (2005) https://doi.org/10.1093/acprof:oso/9780195388534.003.0001.

(a) detriment to the States' public policies and sovereignty, (b) excessive amounts awarded as compensation for damages alleged by investors, and (c) lack of consistency on issues related to foreign investments, due to differing notions adopted by arbitral tribunals regarding, *inter alia*, the full protection, the fair and equitable treatment, the extent of damages, the criteria for calculation of investment value and the interests accruing on the amount of awarded damages.[5]

As criticism on those aspects eventually increased and became widespread, it gave way to a revision of the ISDS mechanism by some international institutions. The United Nations Commission on International Trade Law ('UNCITRAL') set up a working group to revise the norms and practices on foreign investments and to propose changes in response to challenges raised on them. Since July 2015, the UNCITRAL Working Group III has devoted itself to studying and developing alternatives for the ISDS mechanism, including the possibility of a multilateral adjudicatory body aiming at the harmonization of legal standards for both investors' and host States' rights and obligations.[6]

So far, the alternatives considered by international institutions for the reform of the investment protection system, such as the UNCITRAL and the OECD, have preserved the notion that foreign investment disputes should be resolved by an independent adjudicatory body instead of the judiciary of the host State.[7] The work undertaken by Working Group III, still in progress, has developed some alternatives for international investment protection, from both a substantive and a procedural standpoint, seeking to reach a compromise on the interests of the different stakeholders in a coherent system of worldwide acceptance.

III ARBITRATION AS A MECHANISM TO PROTECT FOREIGN INVESTMENTS

The expansion of international trade and investments in the second half of the last century gave rise to a significant increase in the number and size of investment disputes. In response to the ensuing growth of disputes, the World Bank sponsored the Washington Convention of 1965, a multilateral instrument having as its main purpose '*set[ing] up an international arbitral body to which foreign investors might have access for resolving disputes with their host governments, without having to enlist the support of their home governments to present claims on their behalf*'.[8] An arbitration centre was established – the International Center for the Settlement of Investment Disputes

5. For a comprehensive [approach] discussion of the main criticisms on international investment protection, *see*: Michel Waibel et al. (eds), *The Backlash Against Investment Arbitration* (Kluwer Law International 2010).
6. *See* Art. 2 of the 'Draft Statute of an Advisory Centre', which '*aims to provide training, support and assistance with regard to [international investment law and investor-State dispute settlement][international investment dispute resolution]*'; available at: https://uncitral.un.org/sites/uncitral.un.org/files/media-documents/uncitral/en/wp.236_advance_copy.pdf (accessed 16 Dec. 2024).
7. *See* 'Draft Statute of a Standing Mechanism for the Resolution of International Investment Disputes', at https://uncitral.un.org/sites/uncitral.un.org/files/media-documents/uncitral/en/draft_statute_of_a_standing_mechanism_sept.2023.pdf (accessed 16 Dec. 2024).
8. Antonio R. Parra, *The History of ICSID*, 18 (1st ed., Oxford University Press 2012).

(ICSID) – dedicated to adjudicating disputes involving foreign investors and States signatory to that convention.

Through the ICSID dispute settlement mechanism, a foreign investor may have direct access to a body capable of adjudicating its claims against the host State. Through that body, the international protection of foreign investments by arbitration became effective without the need for the involvement of the investor's national State in the dispute with the host State.

Following the creation of ICSID, BITs gained an international forum specialized in the adjudication of disputes arising from investment issues. A significant number of BITs generated an equally significant number of investor-State arbitration cases, evidencing that a dispute resolution mechanism was indeed necessary for the protection of foreign investments in different parts of the world.

Investor-State arbitration combines aspects of public international law and private international law, as it provides individuals and corporations with direct access to an international dispute resolution mechanism capable of rendering an enforceable award against sovereign States.[9] The system relies on the presumptive consent given by the host State upon entering the ICSID Convention for the resolution by arbitration of certain disputes with foreign investors. The consent may also be given by the national laws on the promotion and protection of foreign investments of the host State,[10] or by a BIT in force at the host State, providing foreign investors with the possibility of initiating arbitration proceedings should an investment dispute arise.[11]

IV THE BRAZILIAN APPROACH TO THE ISDS MECHANISM

Except for a brief period in the 1990s, Brazil has consistently refused to take part in the ISDS system. Between 1994 and 1996, Brazil signed fourteen BITs,[12] six of which were submitted to the Brazilian Congress for ratification;[13] however, following the election of a new Government in 2002, they were recalled from Congress before being ratified.[14]

Brazil's refusal to take part in the multilateral investment protection mechanism instituted by the ICSID Convention was due to the Government's then prevailing view that submitting the Brazilian State to a dispute resolution mechanism administered by an international institution such as the ICSID infringed national sovereignty and that

9. Zachary Douglas, *The Hybrid Foundations of Investment Treaty Arbitration*, 74 British Yearbook of International Law 151, 153 (2004) https://doi.org/10.1093/bybil/74.1.151.
10. Jan Paulsson, *Arbitration Without Privity*, 10 ICSID Review 232, 234, (1995) https://doi.org/10.1093/icsidreview/10.2.232.
11. Jeswald D. Salacuse, *The Law of Investment Treaties*, 424 (2nd ed., Oxford University Press 2015).
12. Belgium and Luxembourg, Chile, Cuba, Denmark, Finland, France, Germany, Italy, South Korea, Netherlands, Portugal, Switzerland, United Kingdom, and Venezuela.
13. *See*, for instance: Fabio Morosini & Michelle Ratton Badin, *The Brazilian Agreement of Cooperation and Facilitation of Investments (ACFI): A New Formula for International Investment Agreements?* https://www.iisd.org/itn/en/2015/08/04/the-brazilian-agreement-on-cooperation-and-facilitation-of-investments-acfi-a-new-formula-for-international-investment-agreements/ (accessed 16 Dec. 2024).
14. Rabih A. Nasser, Salem H. Nasser & Nathalie S. Sato, *Arbitragem no Novo Modelo Brasileiro de Acordos de Investimento*, 47 Revista Brasileira de Arbitragem 38, 41 (2015).

grievances against the Brazilian State should be decided by Brazilian courts of proper jurisdiction.[15]

The reasons for Brazil's stance on investment protection are apparently rooted in political positions taken by the Brazilian Congress, reflecting the position of Brazilian legal operators.[16] There has been persistent opposition to the idea that an international arbitral tribunal, set up by an international institution such as the ICSID, would have a say on the policies of the Brazilian Government.[17] That perception was synthesized on a note issued by the Ministry of Development, Industry and Commerce in 2012, stating that *'excessive litigation resulting from BITs harms both the business environment and the effort to attract investment from developing countries, as well as the regulatory capacity of the State'*. It further stated that *'preventing controversies is a better option, both for attracting and maintaining investment'*, leading to *'the inadequacy of the model of investor-State dispute resolution mechanism'*.[18]

From an economic viewpoint, opponents of the ISDS system raised the argument that, since Brazil has received a continuous flow of foreign investments for several decades, the attraction of foreign capital into the Brazilian economy did not require self-imposed restrictions to national or sub-national Governments on the treatment of foreign investments, neither subject their actions and decisions to the judgment of arbitral tribunals.

However, as compelling as such rationale might be at first sight, it does not seem to consider every economic and legal implication that ultimately affects foreign direct investments ('FDIs'). Despite the flow of FDI to Brazil remaining high, the conditions established by foreign investors for their investments may vary substantially, depending on their perception of the risks involved in their decision to invest. The trust of a foreign investor that its investments will be granted protection and security by the host State and will be treated in a fair and equitable manner, together with the certainty that, in case of possible violation of such treatment, it may seek redress by an independent and impartial adjudicatory body play a critical role on the amount to be invested, as well as on the financial conditions that will be applied to it.

From that perspective, Brazil's reluctance to provide foreign investors and investments with the assurance of full protection and security and fair and equitable treatment to FDI has negatively influenced the international legal community, which

15. Ely Caetano Xavier Jr. & José Augusto Fontoura Costa, *Expropriation in Brazil's Cooperation and Facilitation Agreements: A Failed Attempt to Think Outside the Box*, Yearbook on International Investment Law and Policy 444, 448 (2017).
16. *See* Fabio Morosini & Michelle Ratton Badin, *The Brazilian Agreement of Cooperation and Facilitation of Investments (ACFI): A New Formula for International Investment Agreements?* https://www.iisd.org/itn/en/2015/08/04/the-brazilian-agreement-on-cooperation-and-facilitation-of-investments-acfi-a-new-formula-for-international-investment-agreements/ (accessed 16 Dec. 2024).
17. *See* Leany Lemos & Daniela Campello, *The Non-ratification of Bilateral Investment Treaties in Brazil: A Story of Conflict in a Land of Cooperation*, available at: https://papers.ssrn.com/sol3/papers.cfm?abstract_id=2243120 (accessed 16 Dec. 2024).
18. Brazilian Government, available at http://www.mdic.gov.br/index.php/comercio-exterior/negociacoes-internacionais/218-negociacoes-internacionais-de-investimentos/1949-nii-acfi (accessed 16 Dec. 2024).

sees Brazil as an outcast in that scenario.[19] Countermeasures for Brazil's uncompromising stance may induce foreign investors to replace direct investments for loans in capitalizing their subsidiaries and lead the international banking system to increase interest rates, making the return of new projects less competitive as compared to other countries that offer those assurances.

V THE AGREEMENTS FOR THE COOPERATION AND FACILITATION OF INVESTMENTS

In 2015, the Brazilian Government launched a model of investment protection treaty called the 'ACFI', devised to offer an alternative to the investment protection model based on the OECD BIT. From 2015 to 2023, Brazil signed fourteen ACFIs,[20] two of which have been ratified by both signatory countries.[21]

In essence, the model ACFI purports to balance the rights and obligations of States and investors.[22] To achieve that goal, it focuses on the obligations of each of those players and on the dispute resolution mechanisms.

The Brazilian model assumes that the foreign investor should enjoy no higher protection than that granted to a Brazilian investor and that both the investor and the Government should cooperate to resolve difficulties and remove the barriers that arise during the life of the investment.

The model ACFI prohibits discriminatory measures against foreign investors and ensures that, in case of direct expropriation of investments, compensation be payable according to their fair market value. Free transferability and convertibility of funds is also ensured. However, there are substantive obligations established by the ACFI model for investors, including the duty to comply with corporate social responsibility and to employ the best efforts to contribute to the sustainable development of the host State.[23] The concept of fair and equitable treatment is expressly excluded from the ACFI model, deemed detrimental to the State regulatory power. By the same token, the ACFI model also excludes from its scope the protection against indirect expropriation.

As far as dispute resolution is concerned, a remarkable difference between the traditional OECD BIT and the Brazilian ACFI models is that the former grants the foreign investor direct access to ISDS to submit its grievances to an arbitral tribunal; under the latter, dispute resolution requires that the aggrieved investor be represented by its State of origin, initially for review by the Joint Committee and then by an arbitral tribunal, if so requested by that State.

19. Out of 193 Member States of the United Nations, a majority of 165 States have signed the Washington Convention of 1965, while 28 have not. *See* United Nations, https://treaties.un.org/pages/showDetails.aspx?objid=080000028012a925 (accessed 16 Dec. 2024).
20. Mozambique, Angola, Mexico, Malawi, Colombia, Chile, Ethiopia, Suriname, Guyana, the United Arab Emirates, Morocco, Ecuador, India and Sao Tome and Principe.
21. Mexico and Angola. *See* https://investmentpolicy.unctad.org/international-investment-agreements/countries/27/brazil (accessed 16 Dec. 2024).
22. Geraldo Vidigal & Beatriz Stevens, *Brazil's New Model of Dispute Settlement for Investment: Return to the Past or Alternative for the Future?*, 19 Journal of Investment and Trade 475, 477 (2018) https://doi.org/10.1163/22119000-12340100.
23. *Ibid.*, p. 487.

It is clear that the ACFI model adopts a *dispute prevention* approach rather than a *dispute resolution* approach. Aiming at that, the ACFI proposes the creation of two different bodies, the so-called Focal Points (or Ombudsman) and the 'Joint Committee'. The first one is a division of each party's Government, and the second one is a political body jointly composed of representatives of both parties. While the 'Ombudsman' is assigned the task of '*receiving complaints from the Government or investors of the other party and by interacting with the competent government authority, evaluating and recommending solutions*',[24] the Joint Committee has the duty of '*managing the agreement and seeking to amicably resolve any controversies that arise*'.[25]

Despite the criticism that has been addressed to the ISDS mechanism and the initiatives taken for the reform of the system, a distinctive aspect of foreign investment protection since its inception is the direct access by the foreign investor to the adjudication by arbitration of its claims against the host State, without the need for sponsorship by its State of origin. By not foreseeing such possibility, the Brazilian ACFI model distances itself from the protection granted by the traditional OECD model of BIT, leaving the investor subject to the geopolitical agenda of its State of origin.

The Focal Points and the Joint Committee provided for in the ACFI model can only make recommendations to the contracting States but have no adjudicatory powers to decide the matters brought to them. Indeed, the legal framework established by the Brazilian Ministry of Economy for the Focal Points[26] aims at '*offering support to foreign investors and Brazilian companies which intend to or already develop activities abroad, by means of consultations and seeking solutions for their enquires*'.[27]

Under those circumstances, policy considerations may prevail over the rule of law. Although the investor may resort to an institutional organism of the State to submit its pleadings and complaints, the ACFI does not provide for a mechanism for effectively avoiding or resolving disputes. As a result, where the parties do not reach an amicable solution, the sole instance to which investors may resort are the domestic courts of the host State.

Indeed, conflicts arising between foreign investors and host States will hardly be resolved amicably through negotiations assisted by the Focal Point, particularly considering that remedies foreseen in the ACFI are generally not binding. Therefore, situations such as indirect expropriation without compensation remain possible, while no mechanism exists for dispute resolution outside the host State courts.

The implementation of the few ACFIs in force since 2017 raises important concerns regarding their effectiveness. Even though the Brazilian Ombudsman – the Chamber of Foreign Trade ('CAMEX') – does not publicize information on possible complaints brought by foreign investors under ACFIs, it is generally believed that such

24. *Ibid.*, p. 52.
25. Rabih A. Nasser, Salem H. Nasser & Nathalie S. Sato, *Arbitragem no Novo Modelo Brasileiro de Acordos de Investimento*, 47 Revista Brasileira de Arbitragem 38, 52 (2015).
26. Resolution No. 43, of 4 May 2020, available at: https://www.in.gov.br/web/dou/-/resolucao-n-43-de-4-de-maio-de-2020-255374994?inheritRedirect=true&redirect=%2Fweb%2Fguest%2Fsearch%3FqSearch%3DRESOLU%25C3%2587%25C3%2583O%2520N%25C2%252%E2%80%A6 (accessed 16 Dec. 2024).
27. Resolution of the Ministry of Economy No. 43 of 4 May 2020, Art. 1.

agreements have had no real practical effect. Indeed, there has been only fourteen consultations to CAMEX regarding the treatment of foreign direct investments in Brazil.[28] No information on possible complaints of investors or requests by investors for dispute resolution through State-to-State arbitration was disclosed by the Brazilian Ombudsman.[29]

VI THE BRAZILIAN ACFI MODEL AND THE MERCOSUR PROTOCOL FOR COOPERATION AND FACILITATION OF INVESTMENTS

The 'MERCOSUR' is the South American free trade bloc, conceived in 1991 and created by the Protocol of Asunción, gathering Argentina, Brazil, Paraguay, and Uruguay, later joined by Venezuela.[30] Its announced aims are the free circulation of goods, the coordination of economic policies, the harmonization of legislation in different fields, and the levelling of international investment rules among its Member States. MERCOSUR gained its final format upon the signature of the Protocol of Ouro Preto, in 1994, having played an important political role in the relations among its Member States, notably in the first twenty years since its creation.

As far as investment protection is concerned, since its foundation, MERCOSUR has dealt with the subject from time to time but was not a priority in the agendas of its Member States. In 1994, the Treaty of Colonia[31] dealt with investments made by nationals of one Member State in the territory of another Member State but did not reach consensus among the Member States and has never come into force. Also, in 1994, the Protocol of Buenos Aires dealt with the protection of investments made by non-Member States of MERCOSUR and provided for investment arbitration but still did not come into force[32] due to the opposition of Brazil.

Twenty-five years after the foundation of MERCOSUR, the matter of investment protection within the region was raised again in 2015, this time at the initiative of Brazil. It resulted in the drafting of the 'PCFI', signed by the Member States in 2017 with the purpose of promoting investment protection and fostering investment opportunities for investors in the region.[33] The PCFI was drafted after the Brazilian ACFI model[34]

28. *See* Minutes of the General Meeting of CAMEX held on 10 Dec. 2019.
29. Document available at: https://www.gov.br/mdic/pt-br/assuntos/camex/atas-e-resolucoes/coninv/ata_4a-reuniao_coninv_redigido-pdf1.pdf/view (accessed 16 Dec. 2024).
30. Venezuela adhered to the Treaty of Asunción in July 2012.
31. Leonardo Vieira de Oliveira, *O Direito dos Investimentos no MERCOSUL e o Novo Protocolo de Facilitação e Cooperação em Investimentos*, 16 Revista da Secretaria do Tribunal Permanente de Revisão 145, 155-156 (2020).
32. *Ibid.*, p. 156.
33. *See* Ministry of Foreign Affairs International Trade and Worship of Argentina, at https://www.cancilleria.gob.ar/en/news/newsletter/new-step-encourage-intra-mercosur-investment (accessed 16 Dec. 2024).
34. In the message forwarding the PCFI to Congress, the Brazilian Ministry of External Relations informed that the PCFI was 'a version of the Cooperation and Facilitation of Bilateral Investments Agreements which Brazil has already signed with many countries adapted to MERCOSUR'.

and came into effect in July 2019; so far, it has been ratified by three of the MERCOSUR Member States.[35]

The practical effects of the PCFI are yet to be assessed. Doubts have been raised by the international community as to its efficacy, given that the PCFI, following the pattern of the Brazilian ACFI, does not grant foreign investors the right to start arbitration proceedings against the host State. Instead, it provides for dispute resolution through the submission of complaints to the Ombudsman and subsequently to a Commission formed by the State parties. The possibility of a dispute reaching the arbitration stage depends on either one of the signatory States, so the investor affected by the actions by the host State detrimental to its investment needs the support of its own national Government that holds the prerogative of starting arbitration against the host State.

The PCFI reproduces the structure of the ACFI model regarding the protection of foreign investments and the dispute settlement mechanism. It is grounded on risk and dispute mitigation mechanisms exercised by signatory States and on their agenda for cooperation and facilitation of investments.[36] The concept of 'investment' is quite limited and excludes from its scope the notions of 'fair and equitable treatment' and of 'indirect expropriation'. It introduced the principle of corporate social responsibility of investors while not providing for arbitration by an initiative of the foreign investor.[37]

Further, the PCFI established Focal Points (or ombudsmen) in each contracting party, responsible for interacting to prevent controversies and to provide information on matters related to the scope of the Protocol. In addition, the PCFI established a commission, comprised of representatives of each contracting party, responsible for administering all aspects of the agreement, including the implementation of measures for cooperation and facilitation of investments. However, the Focal Points may only provide responses to consultations and intermediate the relationship between the investor and the Host State and do not have any adjudicatory competence.

The dispute resolution mechanism contained in the PCFI is not directed to the investors but to the signatory States; thus, should a dispute arise regarding the PCFI, only the aggrieved State – not the investor – may resort to arbitration against the host State according to the dispute resolution mechanism applicable to MERCOSUR Member States.

The structure adopted in the PCFI apparently fails to offer protection to foreign investors vis-à-vis the host States, as it is limited to providing a channel for the resolution of disputes among States. It may be said that foreign investment protection as known in international investment law is absent from the PCFI, and the vindication of the investor's rights through representation by its State of origin resembles a

35. Brazil, Uruguay, and Argentina.
36. Ana Rachel Freitas da Silva & Paula Laurenne Jacobsen Valkinir. *O Potencial das Medidas de Facilitação do Protocolo de Cooperação e Facilitação de Investimentos do MERCOSUL*. 15 Revista da Secretaria do Tribunal Permanente de Revisão 11, 15-16 (2020).
37. Leonardo Vieira de Oliveira, *O Direito dos Investimentos no MERCOSUL e o Novo Protocolo de Facilitação e Cooperação em Investimentos*, 16 Revista da Secretaria do Tribunal Permanente de Revisão 145, 155 (2020). *Ibid.*, pp. 157-160.

conciliation proceeding rather than the adjudication of an investment dispute.[38] The lack of substantive protection to the foreign investor adds to the lack of an independent and impartial method of dispute resolution, making the PCFI an insufficient instrument for the protection of foreign investments in MERCOSUR.

VII CONCLUSION

The Brazilian ACFI model, from which the MERCOSUR PCFI has drawn most of its features, departs from the traditional BIT as regards the protection afforded to foreign investors, as well as the access to an adjudicatory system capable of enforcing its substantive provisions. In the balance of interests between investors and host States, the PCFI adopted the preservation of State sovereignty as a higher value than the protection of foreign investors, to the detriment of a system that has been in place for nearly six decades.

A look at the model that inspired the creation of the PCFI suggests that no results are stemming from it. No data is available as to the efficiency of the ACFI in fostering foreign investment, nor on its application to disputes involving investors and any host State. Government publicity made on the occasion of signature of each and every ACFI and of the PCFI is an indication of a political purpose rather than an effective instrument of international investment law. By denying the investor an independent and impartial dispute resolution mechanism, the ACFI and the PCFI seem to disregard the evolution of international law and the efforts for the prevalence of the rule of law.

In conclusion, foreign investment protection in MERCOSUR at present may be said to be a rhetorical tool with little effectiveness from the perspective of a foreign investor.

38. Ana Rachel Freitas da Silva & Paula Laurenne Jacobsen Valkinir, *O Potencial das Medidas de Facilitação do Protocolo de Cooperação e Facilitação de Investimentos do MERCOSUL*, 15 Revista da Secretaria do Tribunal Permanente de Revisão 11, 19 (2020).

CHAPTER 18

Preserving Perspectives: International Arbitrators in Their Own Words: Meg Kinnear Interviewed by Professor Andrea Bjorklund at the 20th ITA-ASIL Conference

Meg Kinnear, Andrea K. Bjorklund, Anamaria Marin & Filippo Zuti Giachetti

Good afternoon, everyone, and welcome to the luncheon for the 20th anniversary ITA/ASIL conference in Washington, D.C. Seeing this large crowd here is so exciting, so thanks so much to each of you for making the journey to Washington, D.C. to be here with us. I am Victoria Sahani, Associate Provost for Community and Inclusion and Professor of Law at Boston University, and I also have the honor of serving as chair of the Academic Council for the Institute for Transnational Arbitration. I previously chaired the ITA Academic Council's interview project, Preserving Perspectives: International Arbitrators in Their Own Words, and I want to recognize the current chair of the Preserving Perspectives project and vice chair of the Academic Council, Professor Crina Baltag, for her important work on this interview and all the interviews in the series. I would also like to thank the members of the Preserving Perspectives Project Committee, Professor Catharine Titi and Professor Mohamed Abdel Wahab.

I also would like to thank the chair of the ITA, Tom Sikora, and the ITA staff, led by David Winn, whom we missed seeing here in person today, for helping to bring this luncheon interview to fruition. I also would like to thank ITA's partner in organizing today's ITA/ASIL conference, the American Society for International Law. The ITA Academic Council's interview project, Preserving Perspectives: International Arbitrators in Their Own Words, is important and wholly unique among projects hosted by various international arbitration organizations worldwide in that we interview prominent international arbitrators and record the stories of their lives and careers as they themselves tell them.

Afterward, the videos of these interviews are memorialized forever on the ITA website so that future generations of international arbitration practitioners can watch and learn from them. Today's interview is extra special because this will be our first ever in-person interview during the ITA/ASIL conference. To mark this momentous occasion, we have an extra special interviewee, Meg Kinnear, Secretary-General of the International Centre for Settlement of Investment Disputes.

We are also grateful to Meg for her longstanding support and involvement in our Preserving Perspectives interview project. Meg has graciously served as the interviewer for two other interviewees during the course of the project, Albert Jan van den Berg and Carolyn Lamm. Thank you so much again, Meg, for supporting and contributing to our interview project, first as interviewer and now as interviewee.

Meg will be interviewed by Andrea Bjorklund, Professor of Law and Yves Fortier Chair in International Arbitration and International Commercial Law at McGill and a past chair of the ITA Academic Council. Andrea was the first Academic Council member and chair to carry forward David Caron's vision of the Preserving Perspectives project and develop it to its current success as a highlight of ITA's programming. Now, without further ado, the Academic Council of the Institute for Transnational Arbitration is very pleased to present our Preserving Perspectives project interview of Meg Kinnear by Professor Andrea Bjorklund of McGill.

Andrea: Thank you very much, Victoria. It is a great pleasure to be here and to see so many familiar faces and so many old friends. I have the daunting task of introducing Meg, who of course is, like many people here, in need of no introduction, especially to this crowd, but I will attempt to fill in a few of the details in her career with which you might not be as familiar.

You might know that she is a Canadian national, born and raised in Montreal, a graduate of Queen's University in Kingston, Ontario, in political science, a graduate of McGill with an LL.B., and a graduate of the University of Virginia with an LL.M. She has been called to the bars of both the District of Columbia and Ontario. Her early career, with which you might be less familiar, was in litigation representing the Government of Canada in federal and provincial courts and before administrative tribunals.

She served as Executive Assistant to the Deputy Minister of Justice of Canada from 1996 to 1999, and afterwards she led the Trade Law Bureau from 1999 to 2009, first as Director and then as Director General. As you all know, she was elected Secretary-General of ICSID in 2009 and was the first full-time Secretary-General. She is currently in her third term.

But let us go back to some of your early experience. Did you always know that you wanted to be a lawyer?

Meg: I am the nerd who has to admit yes. Basically, as soon as we realized—at about age ten—that I had no scientific aptitude, that was the next choice and I stuck with it.

Andrea: What types of experiences did you have as a young person that helped you form the core of who you are and the professional woman that you have become?

Meg: I was very fortunate to go to a very small all-girls school from grade two to grade 11. We wore tunics and the approach was everything you would think of the British tradition. But it was also an amazing place where you were really encouraged, sometimes forced, to do things like public speaking and writing and really forced to find your voice. I have to say that I have thought many times through my university career and subsequent career that my primary education gave me such a good grounding and that was a real gift. But for that, I might have gone in a different direction.

Andrea: So, you went to law school at McGill—and you are a wonderful example of the kinds of law students we now get at McGill. But when you were at McGill did you have an interest in international law or in arbitration?

Meg: I studied international political science for my undergraduate degree so I went to McGill thinking of course international law would be what I would do. I found my first general international law course very frustrating. I found it highly abstract. It seemed to me that there was never a structured analytical approach or a concrete solution to a problem. It may have just been the course I particularly took, but it steered me away from international law and more into administrative law, which in Canada is very much the study of judicial review of government bodies, government decision making, and that kind of thing. So, I focused on constitutional and administrative law.

In terms of arbitration, I am sad to say that when I went to school there was no arbitration course.

Andrea: Not even one taught by Professor Brierley?

Meg: No, no, not even. And I am really happy to say that Andrea has more than remedied that with an amazing series of courses at McGill on arbitration and created a real specialty. But when I went to law school that was not something that was being taught in Canada. So, I only picked that up later as a subset of litigation.

Andrea: So, you said that in law school you were somewhat drawn to administrative law. Did that continue when you went to the United States to do your LL.M. at Virginia?

Meg: Yes, although that was another shock for me. I had assumed that when I went to the US to study this at the master's level it would be the kind of administrative law I was used to. Again, mostly judicial review. And, at the University of Virginia, administrative law was focused on decision making in US agencies and its relationship to the American political process. So, I had to change my mindset quite a bit. It was good, it was a learning curve, but it certainly was not what I had thought I was going to be doing that year.

Andrea: So, you went back to Canada after you did your LL.M. What was your first job? What was your first law job?

Meg: In Canada we have something we call articling or a clerkship. A law student has to do the articling year before she is allowed to be called to the bar, so you have to do a year of practice under the tutelage of lawyers. I did that, and was called to the Bar of Ontario. My first job, first real job, was with the Department of Justice for Canada and it was in what they called their civil litigation section. And it had an amazing remit—Essentially we acted as the in-house lawyers for the government of Canada in all sorts of cases brought by or against the government. We were doing constitutional law, administrative law, "fender benders" when a government driver bumped into a car, all sorts of varied work, which was a wonderful experience. I have always recommended a government career, at least as part of a career, to anybody who asks how to develop litigation skills and become an advocate. The unique thing that I discovered very early on was the huge amount of responsibility and independence we were given as counsel. I recall that I would often be on my own in court with my briefcase and there would be six or eight lawyers on the other side. So, you got a huge amount of responsibility early on and it was a bit of a "sink or swim" situation, but with that kind of challenge most people swim and I swam as fast as I could.

Andrea: What part of that practice did you find the most exhilarating?

Meg: Because of my affection for administrative law, I found the administrative law work very interesting. There were all sorts of different government regulatory bodies that made various decisions under federal legislation, so I found that really interesting. And at a certain point during my early career, Canada repatriated its constitution and adopted its Charter of Rights and Freedoms for citizens. I was in the litigation section when the Charter of Rights came into effect, and all of a sudden we were faced with many people bringing cases to test the extent of protection under the Charter, and what its guarantees meant. Canada has a very interesting savings clause in its Charter, called Section 1, which basically added a proportionality test to all Charter rights, essentially saying the rights guaranteed to the individual citizen had to be balanced against reasonable legal limits imposed by the government in the name of a democratic society. This is obviously a different approach from many other countries, and certainly in the political discussions leading up to the Charter, it was meant to be different from the American system and to include what could be considered a flexibility or moderating valve. Doing that work was incredibly exciting for us, since we were on the front lines of development of our Charter.

Andrea: But it was litigation of first impression, so you really had to think on your feet.

Meg: Definitely, it was litigation of first impression with no precedents to draw on. We were often looking at the practice of "like" democracies such as the U.S. and the UK, as an indication of how a free and democratic society might balance individual and collective rights.

Andrea: What do you think is the most important skill for a litigator or counsel before tribunals to have?

Meg: I am convinced that the most difficult skill, but the most important skill, is cross-examination. When cross-examination is done well, it is a thing of beauty, but it is an extremely difficult thing to do well, and you need to do a lot of planning, a lot of preparation, and have a lot of cross-examination experience to do it well. I think that one of the things that I was lucky to do, as part of my work with the government, was to do some cases in criminal court. I did that about once a week, and they would bring you 50 dossiers and most of them were silly things, not silly I should not say that, but smaller things, like for example that somebody had sold a small amount of marijuana to somebody at the local fair, or my favorite, having too many fishing lines in the water at a time. But all of this is to say this kind of experience is where the career of litigators starts and is honed. You had to get on your feet, you got the file 10 minutes before you were pleading it, speed read through it, and then the witness was sworn in. You did not know what they were going to say or what their demeanour was so it was a really good way to create litigation instincts. As Rumpole of the Bailey would say, "You get up on your hind legs and do it."

Andrea: Did you have a mentor or mentors early in your career and what did you learn from them?

Meg: I had some amazing mentors. I think I was incredibly lucky to have terrific mentors at every stage of my career.

I worked with some of the very senior people at Canada's Department of Justice and they all had eminent careers in constitutional litigation, so that was a tremendous experience. What I learned from them was how important your theory of the case is: what do you need to prove, how do you get there and how do you pull it all together in the final argument. I think one of the things that I learned to appreciate was the importance of going to the essence of the argument: do not throw 50 things against the wall. Instead, take your five best arguments, take the ones that are really going to be taken seriously and determine the outcome, and work with those. That was a very useful lesson. Fortunately, my litigation mentors were all incredibly patient, allowing me to do submissions and cross examinations and that kind of thing, learning first-hand through experience. In terms of mentors, I also think automatically of another counsel who was at the Department of Justice with me. I think of her separately not only because she was a mentor in terms of work, but she was also a mentor in terms of how to be a professional and be a mum at the same time. She had three children and she was a bit farther ahead of me in the working mum experience. She was a tremendous mentor in terms of reassuring me that I could do this, and this whole thing was not going to come crashing to the ground. That was really important and I have to say I do not think there were a lot of people who had such a mentor, so it was extra important for that reason.

Andrea: I have had the pleasure of working with you on a couple of different projects; one of the things that I have always been struck by is your extraordinary work ethic and your ability to do so many things at once and to do them all well. I want to say that for the NAFTA book, if John [Hannaford] and I had been left to our own devices, we would still be having a glass of wine in the bar over there talking about how we were going to write that book one day, but Meg made us do it—she was the busiest person yet she was the one who was always ahead. She was the one who was always first with her chapters and with returning comments on chapters. So, did you learn that from somebody? Is that innate? Where do you think those skills come from?

Meg: Good question. I was probably the pain in the rear end who was saying get out of the bar and let's go, so it probably indicates I should learn other skills as well. I know my staff from ICSID are here and I suspect they would say sometimes they wish I would stop sending emails or coming up with new projects we had to take on. I know I learned this from my dad who was a very organized, very disciplined person, but who also did a million things at once.

Andrea: Well, in any event I have been the beneficiary of it, so thank you. Do you have any particular experience that you viewed as formative or funny, especially during a professional transition?

Meg: Yes, well there are a number, but about two weeks after I got to the Trade Law Bureau, I was told that I was Canada's representative to the Free Trade of the

Americas Agreement on the dispute settlement chapters and I literally knew absolutely nothing about this agreement. So, I dug in, and I read, and I studied. and off I went. At the time we were doing the inter-government meetings in Miami, and I remember thinking that if we worked really hard, we could get this done in the next month or so. I was very optimistic about this. I realized after lunch on the first day that we still had not got through the pleasantries of "I am so happy to see my honourable friends again," and I was itching to say "let's get on with it, we have got something to write here." But it was a good experience, and over time I realized how important relationship building is as part of the negotiation process. Now, sadly we never got the FTAA dispute settlement chapter finalized before the negotiations were abandoned, but it was a very good experience for me in negotiation and international relations.

Andrea: What about experiences at ICSID?

Meg: ICSID has been a whole other amazing experience, I have to say. It has been "the" experience of my life. This is an aside, but actually Andrea was one of the people who said to me you ought to apply for the Secretary-General job, and I said "Oh, I do not think it will ever happen." At the time, my young son had a motivational hockey poster on his wall saying "you miss 100% of the shots you do not take." I remember thinking that was exactly the point, and decided "alright, I am just going to take a shot at it." And I was fortunate enough to be selected. And ICSID has been an incredible experience. Some of it I expected: obviously I knew about ICSID arbitration, I knew that from doing NAFTA Chapter 11 cases, so I knew that angle of it. In retrospect, I do not think I had a really good sense of what the World Bank was and ICSID's place at the World Bank, or what it meant in terms of the other types of responsibilities you have. You are part of the senior management team at the World Bank where they talk a foreign language called "economics" and you have to add value to that discussion when what you are thinking about is provisional measures and things like that. But you also have this incredible relationship from an institutional perspective with various countries, and really explaining to them what you are all about and why you are of value to them. More generally, your role includes speaking to the profession and the public, explaining why this is a valuable institution and how arbitration works. Sometimes you are speaking with people who don't see the value of investment arbitration, and you need to explain that there is so much good in this system that is important to preserve. One of the things that is a privilege about this job is that you see every day on the ground how it really works and how people are really dedicated to making it work.

Andrea: I think that leads very well into the next question, "Which is which of your professional accomplishments are most important to you and why?"

Meg: Maybe it is because it is the most recent. I think, obviously, becoming Secretary-General has been the honour of my life. But, in particular, the new rules that we have just passed have been a huge achievement, both exhausting and exhilarating. And it was a really incredible process. It was a lot of technical drafting, but it was also a lot of creativity. It was a lot of talking to people, a lot of suggesting ideas. We had a number of in-person consultations with member states that were fantastic. And the ideas were so interesting. And the ideas, 150-some member states, some with very high levels of ISDS experience, some with no ISDS experience, but everybody coming to the table and participating was absolutely incredible. So, I think the net result is both a very good product, but what I am especially proud of, quite frankly, is that it got done. I recognize it is procedural, it is incremental progress, but to me it is concrete, and it got done. And in an era where we hear so many ideas, comments, and critiques, it is good to have something that got done and is now having immediate impact. I am pretty proud of that and so proud of the staff at ICSID who are extraordinary.

Andrea: How has the practice of law changed since you first started? What do you think is the biggest change?

Meg: To me, it is technology. When I started in litigation, we literally had typewriters. We would type up a submission or a pleading, and then when you wanted to edit, you would cut the parts you wanted to keep, tape typed changes on top of the rest, and then photocopy so it did not look like it was cut and paste. That is the original cut and paste!. And I see now what we can do literally with cut and paste and all the other types of computer skills. We can have thousands of cases at our beck and call. It is extraordinary. And obviously it is an incredible tool that has advanced the practice substantially. But I also think we need to use technology mindfully, because there is a huge temptation to cut and paste massive numbers of cites and massive quotations. So you have to be disciplined and always edit, always asking: is this at the core of the argument? Technology advances have been an enabler of some good practices but of some bad practices as well.

Andrea: Shifting back a little bit, compared to some people in the room, you entered the practice of arbitration a little bit late. What was your first arbitration as counsel?

Meg: My first arbitration as counsel ... Well, I did a couple of labour arbitrations and those kinds of domestic proceedings, but my first investment arbitration was a case called *Pope & Talbot v. Canada*. I should tell you that when I first went to Canada's Trade Law Bureau they had traditionally done WTO work and that was their specialty. And I felt like the new girl coming down the hall on my first day, hearing the trade lawyers say, "Here is the new girl, let's make her do NAFTA Chapter 11." And indeed, I did take that on. It was actually an incredible experience and one of the things that I always remark upon—at the time, all of this was brand new. This was late 1990s, early 2000s—that does not sound like a long time ago, and it is not. But frankly, it was not easy to find law, it was not easy to find principles. We were often borrowing WTO-type law, which you rarely see now in an investment case. We were really down to first principles with all of this. It was a fantastic learning experience. And I used to talk monthly with my colleagues in the U.S. State Department and in Mexico's Secretaria de Economía and we would all compare notes on this phenomenon: "Have you ever seen that?" Oh, no, I do not know. What would you do with that? It was really quite extraordinary and having done that, I got to see some of the most interesting pieces of it. We negotiated the NAFTA Notes of Interpretation, which was fascinating, and a number of bilateral investment treaties. It really opened up a whole world for me.

Andrea: You mentioned that this happened because you were new at JLT—at the Trade Law Bureau. What had drawn you to applying for the job at JLT?

Meg: I had spent the three years prior as the Executive Assistant to the Deputy Minister of Justice, which was a really interesting job and gave you a glimpse of the political level and policymaking in a big Department of Justice with diverse responsibilities. It was fascinating from that perspective, but it was not what I would term hardcore law or hardcore litigation, and I was really missing that aspect of my career. The job came up at the Trade Law Bureau and the Deputy Minister I worked for had been one of the original US-Canada Free Trade Agreement negotiators. And he said "you are going to love this stuff. It is really interesting. You ought to do this." That is what drew me there originally.

Andrea: You have been involved in a lot of cases as counsel and from more of a distance as Secretary-General, but do you have a favorite international arbitration case and why would it be your favorite?

Meg: I do have a favorite. A case that I keep coming back to is the Philip Morris v. Uruguay case, for a number of reasons. First, I think the facts are quite interesting. Indeed, one of my Uruguayan colleagues actually brought me five packs of cigarettes with the labels that were in question in the case, and I used to travel with those five packs of cigarettes because we would use them as a demonstrative exhibit when we did presentations. They got pretty dog-eared in my luggage, so I threw them out eventually. But the facts were so interesting, and the media discussion of this was substantial. You will remember that when the Philip Morris case was working its way through, there were a lot of people saying this could be the end of investment arbitration. Imagine if you could not pass anti-smoking legislation. There was a lot of discussion, and it was tied to a view that investor state arbitration is not a good tool for this kind of dispute settlement. I thought it was interesting that it was being held up as a basis not to have investment arbitration. And the other reason I think it is really fascinating is the interesting and strong majority award with Professor Bernardini and Judge Crawford touching on the police power, which of course at the time was still debated. But the dissent by Gary Born is also fascinating, because it approaches the issue from a completely different angle. It is based on procedure in the court system of Uruguay. To me, both the dissent and the majority opinions are compelling, so I think it is really a classic case.

Andrea: My judge used to say that if you read the claimant's brief and you were not convinced that the claimant should win that was a losing case, but if you read the claimant's brief and then the respondent's brief, usually they both have really good cases. I mean, they should be. If you are at the appellate court, the quality should be at that level. But in a sense, in these difficult cases, it is interesting that you can have compelling and thoughtful decisions coming down in different ways. Speaking of arbitral decision-making, there is a lot of debate about whether arbitrators in investment disputes should be more concerned with developing the law or with simply deciding the particular case in front of them. Where do you come down in that debate?

Meg: I have to say that I find the question frustrating, because the process is based on applying facts to law. Sometimes it is more fact-based and sometimes it is more law-based. But the concept that arbitrators should "make law" or "make policy" seems problematic.

Andrea: I have to say my judge Sam Ervin used to say, your primary job is to decide the case in front of you, but then you also do other things as well. You mentioned Gary Born's dissent; what is your opinion about the controversy over dissenting opinions in arbitration? And there is even the situation in Germany, where it might be impossible to have a dissent on the grounds that that is a betrayal of confidentiality in arbitrator deliberations and that therefore in commercial arbitration you cannot have dissents. Where do you come down on the role of dissents or the importance of having them?

Meg: It is situation dependent, and clearly there is a role for dissents, especially where they are outcome determinative or deal with something that is very much an open question in the law. But there is great value in consensus, especially in international arbitration, and sometimes you wonder, for example, if procedural dissents are always necessary. A well-placed dissent obviously is a good thing, but each arbitrator should ask themselves, how much is this going to contribute?

Andrea: What do you think are the most valuable things that arbitrators can do to control what seem to be perennial and maybe perennially growing problems about the costs and time taken by international arbitration and especially investment arbitration?

Meg: It is a huge issue, as we all know. First of all, I do not place this entirely at the foot of arbitrators. I think everybody, including the institution, but also counsel, has a large role in making sure that the time and cost are reasonable, and I worry that sometimes we do not. One of the areas where investor state could do better is with the small and medium sized enterprise and that is largely a function of cost. We have put expedited arbitration rules in our new rules, and I am hoping that will help. But the biggest thing is for arbitrators and counsel to know the case and be in control of the case. For arbitrators, this means knowing where you have questions and letting the parties know your questions. And again, one of the devices we put into our new rules was a case management conference to narrow down what is truly in dispute. Time will tell the extent to which people use this and how they use this. But I think it is extremely useful for tribunals to say to parties, "Here is an area I would really like to hear more about." I have read your submissions on this, and I understand them. If counsel want to continue down that road, obviously that is up to them. But I think counsel sincerely appreciate some guidance and some focus as the case goes on, and arbitrators, if they know the case well, can give exactly that kind of guidance. One of the other things that people talk about is not having what has been termed "annulment paranoia," the fear that everything you do might motivate an annulment application. The statistics show that the rate of annulment is about 3% to 5%. So odds are that a decision that is taken in good faith and knowing what is in front of you is not going to create an annullable situation. So, it is having control of the case and proactively managing the case.

Andrea: You said earlier that you thought technology was the biggest single change that you have seen in the practice of law since you started. How do you think that has affected arbitration in particular?

Meg: Again, as I say, technology is great in terms of giving us all the law at our fingertips, literally. You look at something like Jus Mundi and that kind of tool, and it is extraordinary. Another example is conflict checking. Technology allows us to know what a proposed arbitrator googled last week or stated at a conference a month ago. It is just extraordinary the extent of information we have. But there is a flip side of the coin, which is that sometimes so much information makes it hard to handle a case, and it makes cases balloon in size and cost. And that is the part we need to manage.

Andrea:, I am thinking about when you started, you said there was so little, and now there is the Investor-State Law Guide, Jus Mundi, Investment Arbitration Reporter. So that has made a difference. But what do you think has happened to the actual practice of law, like the length of memorials and the like?

Meg: Memorials and affidavits are huge. To use an anecdote, I remember once we had to open the World Bank's loading dock, where they put huge shipments. And I remember the days where cases arrived in multiple bankers' boxes. This is when we still used boxes. Thank goodness that is gone, but still, we saw boxes and boxes of documents. And I remember one of the arbitrators who was in that case said, partly sarcastically, but partly with a grain of truth, if the World Bank loading dock needs to be opened for these boxes, how am I supposed to read them all and take it all in? Which is not a bad question at the end of the day. And you see it as well with discovery. Discovery can get pretty voluminous.

Andrea: If we think back a little bit, our morning was spent on reform, even on this meta question, reform of reform of arbitration. What do you predict for the future of international investment arbitration?

Meg: This is the million-dollar question for sure. I believe that there is a very strong future for investment arbitration. And we are constantly making it better. So I think there is a very important role for it. It does have its weaknesses, but I think it has many more strengths, and it works really well in 99.9 % of the cases. This is especially so when you compare it to a lot of domestic legal systems. I have often had state representatives or domestic counsel tell me they are so glad to have the ICSID capacity because their own courts take 15 and 16 years for a case. Or people do not feel confident about their domestic courts. You hear that as a justification for investor-state, and it is a very real phenomenon.

Andrea: What advice would you give law students and young professionals today as they contemplate future careers in international arbitration?

Meg: I would say 100 % to go for it. I think it is the most interesting career in terms of litigation challenges, advocacy challenges, and subject matter challenges. When will you ever have to understand the political situation of a certain country or the mining policy of another country? It is really quite an extraordinary context. But as you do that, I would highly suggest finding a way to see different sides of it. Do the claimant side. Do the respondent side. Come and do the institutional side. Every time you flip your perspective, you learn something.

Andrea: You mentioned at lunchtime that you were actually quite risk-averse. Yet, we have just heard that you have really moved from very different types of practice of law to an institution. Do you have any regrets about that?

Meg: No, in fact, my experience has been that every time I contemplated changing jobs, I really worried that I was making a mistake and should stay right where I was. And then when I went to the new job, all of a sudden, I learned new things and decided that this job is the best job in the world. My experience has been that it just gets better. Interestingly, everything you learn in one job makes you a better candidate for the next job, even if you think your new skills are not relevant to the job. For example, when I was at the Deputy Minister's office, they gave us media training. I thought "When are you ever going to need media training? You are not going to be talking to the press." Well, in fact, that occasionally happens at ICSID. Everything you learn just makes you a better, more capable professional. I would say for sure, do not hesitate. Embrace challenges. And risk. And change.

Andrea: Well, thank you very much, Meg. Thank you for your time. Thank you all for your attention. And I am sure that Meg will be delighted to chat with you afterwards if you have any further questions for her. Thank you for being part of our oral history project.

Meg: No, thank you. Thank you.

Tom Sikora: Well, let me thank Meg and Andrea for a fascinating Preserving Perspectives interview.

We are very grateful to you both. But let me say that we are also tremendously grateful to Meg for everything that she has done over so many years now. She has been a good captain who has steered this very precious and valuable institution safely for many years and has saved it and preserved it to continue for future generations.

For the younger practitioners, I should say that there was a time our great friend Antonio Parra was gone for a few years from ICSID. There were a few cases where some would say there were runaway annulment committees. And we were all very worried about the future of ICSID.

Thankfully, Meg appeared and took the reins of the institution and preserved it for many years. We are very grateful to Meg for everything she has done and what she continues to do. I should mention that Meg just arrived from Paris last night, from Paris Arbitration Week. And tonight, she is going to be on a train to New York City because tomorrow and Friday, UNCITRAL Working Group III will take up the Code of Conduct for Adjudicators again. She is truly relentless. Thank you again.

Thanks, Victoria, for another great Preserving Perspectives program. Thank you to the audience for staying with us. I have to say, looking around, there are so many phenomenally talented practitioners and truly distinguished arbitrators.

I hope the younger members of the audience, the younger practitioners, got to visit with some of you. Getting to know each other is one of the great benefits of the Institute for Transnational Arbitration. I encourage you to mingle and get to know each other.

With that, let me say that I hope you join us 14-16 June in Austin, Texas. For those who have been to Austin, they need no encouragement. For those of you who have never been to Austin, you need to come and see it for yourselves.

We invite you to join the ITA for the annual workshop. This year, we will be looking at the scope of remedies open to tribunals, a particularly interesting program also for tribunal members.

And with that, ladies and gentlemen, we are adjourned. Thank you very much.

CHAPTER 19

The Future of International Arbitration: Evolving Values

Victoria Shannon Sahani

The Twentieth Anniversary Joint Conference of the Institute for Transnational Arbitration (ITA), through its Academic Council, and the American Society for International Law (ASIL) provided a prime opportunity for reflection and engagement about the future of international arbitration and how its values will evolve in the twenty-first century through this book.

The conference on 29 March 2023 bore the same title as this book, and the keynote speech and panels addressed wide-ranging, cutting-edge issues. Professor Hélène Ruiz Fabri, Director of the Max Planck Institute Luxembourg for International, European, and Regulatory Procedural Law, delivered a keynote speech titled 'Taking Intersectionality Seriously'. Professor Ruiz Fabri explored the term 'intersectionality', coined by Professor Kimberlé Crenshaw of UCLA Law School and Columbia School of Law, to express the complexities of how multiple identities of individuals influence their experiences and senses of self, particularly those who have identities that have been historically disadvantaged or oppressed.[1] She reminded us to take intersectionality seriously as we calibrate the sliding scale between repetition and reformation in international arbitration and that discrimination can be explicit or subversively hidden inside state regulation. She also reminded us that promoting the sovereignty of

1. For a brief introduction to intersectionality, *see* Kimberlé Crenshaw, *Demarginalizing the Intersection of Race and Sex: A Black Feminist Critique of Antidiscrimination Doctrine,* Feminist Theory and Antiracist Politics, University of Chicago Legal Forum: Vol. 1989: Iss. 1, Art. 8 https://doi.org/10.1093/oso/9780198782063.003.0016.
   Available at http://chicagounbound.uchicago.edu/uclf/vol1989/iss1/8. For a more detailed discussion of intersectionality, *see* Kimberlé Crenshaw, *On Intersectionality: Essential Writings* (The New Press 2017).

Indigenous people around the world includes recognizing them as agents of change and societal progress.

The first panel, moderated by Professor Crina Baltag of Stockholm University and then-Vice Chair and current Chair of the Institute for Transnational Arbitration's (ITA's) Academic Council, examined the emerging set of high-profile and behind-the-scenes stakeholders who are prioritizing increasing inclusion and belonging through task force exploration of gender diversity, regionally focused initiatives, and UN Working Group III. The panellists also discussed elevating the voices of smaller states and Latin American state respondents in the International Centre for Settlement of Investment Disputes (ICSID) and the rise of third-party funding, artificial intelligence (AI) technology, and Big Data as another voice, almost literally, whose impact we are only just beginning to feel and understand.

The second panel, moderated by Interim Dean and Professor of Law Mark Feldman of Peking University, School of Transnational Law in Shenzhen, China, and former Vice Chair of the ITA Academic Council, addressed regionalism as a critical force driving international arbitration reform as regional arbitration institutions begin to move closer to centre stage. The panellists grappled with the tensions between certainty and uncertainty, institutionalization and ad hoc innovation, and convergence and individuation among states. Examples the panellists highlighted of regionalism in rulemaking for international arbitration practice include the significance of the Association of Southeast Asian Nations' (ASEAN's) 'centrality' principle, Mercado Común del Sur (Southern Common Market)'s (MERCOSUR's) 'regionalization' of Brazil's investment treaty practice, the role of the African Union's Pan-African Investment Code in the development of an African Continental Free Trade Area on Investment (AfCFTA) Investment Protocol, and near-term priorities for European Union (EU) investment treaty practice.

Building on the reform ideas explored during the conference, we must examine with a critical eye the world in which arbitration, as we know it today, was forged so that we can better understand how far we have come even as we drive forward arbitration's evolution. Arbitration is among the oldest forms of human dispute resolution, stretching back to the earliest days of human civilization. Modern international arbitration was built to serve merchants and governments in an analogue world in which trade, transportation, and transmissions all moved at a snail's pace compared to today. Forged to build peaceful trade networks informed by the wisdom of expert, elder arbitrators, modern arbitration between merchants began to flourish rapidly in the aftermath of the First World War of the twentieth century. When the International Chamber of Commerce (ICC) was founded in 1919, the phrase 'merchants of peace' was included in the founding documents.[2] The ICC Court of Arbitration was founded soon after that, in 1923, as a means of peaceful, transnational dispute settlement among merchants. In those days, as the literal and proverbial smoke was still clearing from the First World War, the meaning of 'merchants of peace' was clear and visceral.

2. *See* International Chamber of Commerce, *Our Mission, History and Values*, available at https://iccwbo.org/about-icc-2/our-mission-history-and-values/ (accessed 16 Dec. 2024) (explaining the term 'merchants of peace').

The founding of formal means of peaceful dispute settlement by a third-party neutral was in direct opposition to the 'gunboat diplomacy'[3] – or, in the case of the First World War, gunboats without diplomacy – that the world had recently endured. Yet it was not nearly enough, as the Second World War followed shortly after that, a bigger and more gruesome display of violence. In contrast, the long-lasting, multi-decade period of relative global peace that emerged following the Second World War until today is quite precious. Among many global benefits, this peace has allowed international arbitration to flourish and spread worldwide and become the dominant method of cross-border dispute settlement.

With that historical reminder, we will review some of the classical values of international arbitration and how they will evolve as we move through the twenty-first century.

The first and most fundamental of the classical values of international arbitration is nonviolent dispute settlement. Nonviolence in international arbitration is so taken for granted that we almost overlook it and find it too elementary to articulate in arbitration rules. Yet, in today's world, neither nonviolent resolution of disputes nor nonviolent regime change is assured. Sadly, a brief glance at recent global news headlines demonstrates this quite clearly. Against this backdrop, international arbitration is sometimes called an 'alternative' method of dispute resolution. An alternative to what? The Pavlovian reaction is to say that arbitration is an alternative to civil litigation, but both arbitration and civil litigation in court are nonviolent means of dispute settlement.[4] I posit instead that cross-border arbitration is an alternative to violence as a means of dispute settlement; taken to an extreme or mass scale, such violence equals war. This may seem like an exaggeration of arbitration's importance to today's reader in the twenty-first century. However, the 'merchants of peace' in the aftermath of the First World War a century ago had first-hand experience of arbitration as an alternative to war. The world has enjoyed nearly four score years of widespread global peace that has lulled us into forgetting that modern *peaceful* arbitration was forged from the fires of twentieth-century global warfare. Let this history always remind us that nonviolence is timeless and evergreen among the classical values of international arbitration; nonviolence need not evolve because there is no viable alternative.

A second classical value of international arbitration is choice, which can further be broken down into the sub-values of customizability and autonomy. In sum, this involves the freedom to choose without interference. Rather than the one-size-fits-all rules that litigation requires, parties are free to select arbitration rules or design their own arbitration procedure, to directly select their arbitrators or design their own method of arbitrator selection, to select each of the logistical aspects of their arbitration (including the number of arbitrators, the seat of arbitration, the applicable law, the

3. *See* R. Doak Bishop, James. R. Crawford & W. Michael Reisman, *Foreign Investment Disputes: Cases, Materials and Commentary*, Chapter 1 (2nd ed., Wolters Kluwer 2014) (explaining the term 'gunboat diplomacy').
4. This chapter focuses on civil litigation as an analogue to international arbitration because criminal matters cannot be arbitration, and criminal prosecution can lead to violent outcomes in some jurisdictions.

language, confidentiality or publicity, and so forth) or to delegate this selection to the arbitrators or the arbitral institution. Customizability also includes both transnationality (i.e., meeting the needs of parties from all jurisdictions) and transsubstantivity (i.e., applying to all subject matters and categories of arbitrable disputes). In most New York Convention Member States, the parties' choices of how to customize their arbitration experience also enjoy the norm of autonomy, meaning that courts do not interfere in arbitration sua sponte but instead wait for one of the disputing parties to invite court intervention through a motion, application, or other filings.

The classical arbitration value of choice has come under scrutiny because we have all become more aware of our inherent and often subconscious biases. We mistakenly assume that we make choices based solely on conscious information and voluntary thought processes. Yet, social psychologists have proven that we are all subject to unconscious and implicit biases that can hijack our decision-making processes in nonconscious ways.[5] Recently, tensions between choice and inclusion in international arbitration have emerged.[6] Parties want to choose their arbitrators, but their choices may not consider the multiple identities and perspectives needed among arbitrators to ensure inclusion, representation, and trust, all of which are essential for the continued legitimacy of international arbitration in the eyes of parties, courts, and governments. International arbitration must be inclusive to be legitimate in the twenty-first century. To that end, Professor Ruiz Fabri reminded us to consider Professor Crenshaw's intersectionality admonition as we attempt to move international arbitration towards a more inclusive and fair future.

The preceding discussion reminds us that choice is tempered by a third fundamental, classical value of international arbitration: fairness. Fairness is invoked to describe the arbitrator's mind through the complementary values of arbitrator independence (referring to the absence of relationships that may influence the case's outcome) and arbitrator impartiality (referring to the absence of the arbitrator's preconceptions or biases for or against any of the parties).[7] Fairness is also invoked to describe the arbitration procedure.[8] Parties are free to define whichever international arbitration rules they wish as long as they are fair to both sides. This includes due process, reasonable notice, unbiased arbitrators, and an equal opportunity to be heard

5. To read more about how to outsmart your own implicit biases, there are resources on the website here: https://outsmartingimplicitbias.org. If you wish to test your implicit biases, you can do so through the website of the long-running implicit bias study here: https://implicit.harvard.edu/implicit/takeatest.html (accessed 16 Dec. 2024).
6. *See* Harris Institute, *Defining (And Defending) Values in International Arbitration: Sophie Nappert's Keynote Address at the 2018 International Arbitration & Dispute Resolution Symposium* (1 Apr. 2019), available at https://sites.law.wustl.edu/WashULaw/harris-lexlata/defining-and-defending-values-in-international-arbitration-sophie-napperts-keynote-address-at-the-2018-international-arbitration-dispute-resolution-symposium/ (accessed 16 Dec. 2024).
7. *See, e.g.*, Edward Brunet, Richard E. Speidel, Jean E. Sternlight & Stephen J. Ware, *The Core Values of Arbitration* in Edward Brunet, Richard E. Speidel, Jean E. Sternlight & Stephen J. Ware, *Arbitration Law in America: A Critical Assessment* (Cambridge University Press 2009), available at https://www.cambridge.org/core/books/arbitration-law-in-america/core-values-of-arbitration/8D6A9119D247AF271A0CB18EB1056F4E (accessed 16 Dec. 2024).
8. *Ibid.*

and present evidence. Regarding both the arbitrator's mind and the arbitration procedure, fairness also includes freedom from corruption and bribery.[9]

In recent years, international arbitration has begun facing a legitimacy crisis for various reasons beyond the scope of this brief intervention. International arbitration designed in the twentieth century was not fair in an objective sense because capital-exporting states designed a self-serving regime in which capital-importing states had to 'take it or leave it' to compete for global trade partnerships and investment. United Nations Commission on International Trade Law (UNCITRAL) Working Groups II and III and arbitral institutions are leading the reimagining of international arbitration by including the voices and perspectives of those excluded from the conversation when the current regime was negotiated and adopted in the mid-twentieth century. The perspectives and voices from the Global South, Indigenous peoples, racial and ethnic minorities, persons with disabilities, and other historically disadvantaged constituencies are robustly engaged in these impactful discussions and represent decades of progress that we should celebrate, knowing that we still have far to go. Moreover, the default modality of privacy in international arbitration may soon begin to recede in light of recent calls for transparency as a key means to combat corruption and bolster the legitimacy of the international arbitration system in the eyes of the public.[10]

Finally, efficiency has long been a classical value of international arbitration. Parties have often chosen arbitration to obtain a faster, cheaper, nuanced, and more expert resolution of their dispute. However, parties cannot consistently achieve this result, as arbitration can be complex, arbitrators sometimes make mistakes (just like judges), and arbitration is sometimes slower and more expensive than litigation. Nevertheless, efficiency has long been a stated goal of the international arbitration system. As we transition from the information age to the AI age in the twenty-first century, however, efficiency may become an obsolete goal. This is similar to how the goals of memorizing phone numbers or the best routes to drive to work in different traffic conditions have become obsolete in the smartphone age of endless saved contacts lists and turn-by-turn navigation at our fingertips. One consequence of Big Data and AI is that we may feel that arbitration no longer needs to be efficient. With these tools, arbitrators and counsel can consider everything that can be measured, notated, or quantified, and the AI of the future will help arbitrators and counsel understand, organize, and evaluate presently unfathomable amounts of data. In the not-so-distant future, efficiency will likely seem as quaint as the long-gone norm of always carrying an appropriately sized coin for payphone usage. Furthermore, with third-party funding increasing in prevalence, yesterday's cost efficiency may give way to today's risk allocation as the primary mindset for assessing the reasonableness of pursuing or defending against a claim in international arbitration.

In closing, Sophie Nappert of 3VB Barristers in London delivered the opening keynote speech at the 2018 International Arbitration & Dispute Resolution Symposium hosted by the Whitney R. Harris World Law Institute at Washington University in St. Louis School of Law. In her keynote speech titled 'Defining (And Defending) Values in

9. *See supra* n. 6.
10. *See supra* n. 6.

International Arbitration', Ms Nappert described the tensions between classical and modern (which she termed 'Millennial') values in international arbitration and urged the audience members to incorporate Millennial values of dynamism and making a difference into their daily practices.[11] Ms Nappert concluded her 2018 keynote by quoting Nobel Prize Laureate Albert Camus, who said in his 1957 Nobel Prize acceptance speech that the task of his generation was preventing the world from destroying itself.[12] Six tumultuous years after Ms Nappert's speech and sixty-seven years after Mr Camus spoke those lines, we can observe that this burden of preventing the world from destroying itself never fully abates but is passed from generation to generation, albeit morphing, but still fundamentally the same problem. There are dozens of public (and countless nonpublic) examples of situations where arbitration has prevented open warfare.[13] We must continue to evolve and improve arbitration so that it remains one of our timeless and evergreen tools for peaceful dispute resolution across societies, technologies, and generations.

11. *See supra* n. 6.
12. Albert Camus' speech at the Nobel Banquet at the City Hall in Stockholm (English translation), 10 Dec. 1957, available at https://www.nobelprize.org/prizes/literature/1957/camus/speech/ (accessed 16 Dec. 2024) ('Each generation doubtless feels called upon to reform the world. Mine knows that it will not reform it, but its task is perhaps even greater. It consists in preventing the world from destroying itself').
13. *See, e.g.*, Stockholm Chamber of Commerce, *The Quiet Triumph: How Arbitration Changed the World* (2017), available at https://vimeo.com/205567614 (accessed 16 Dec. 2024) (video) (describing examples of arbitrations and arbitrators preventing conflicts and wars).

www.ingramcontent.com/pod-product-compliance
Lightning Source LLC
LaVergne TN
LVHW020643300926
849161LV00004B/785